ISLAY

A
Novel
by
Douglas Bullard

Cover design by Eugene Orr

T.J. PUBLISHERS, INC.
817 Silver Spring Avenue, 206
Silver Spring, Maryland 20910

ISBN #0-932666-27-2 Paper
ISBN #0-932666-28-0 Cloth
Library of Congress Catalog No.: 85-052384

Those who try to interpret mankind through its eyes are in for much strangeness—perplexity.

Saul Bellow

Dedicated to the memory of

Dean Rutherford Bullard

and

Julia Frances Rutherford Bullard

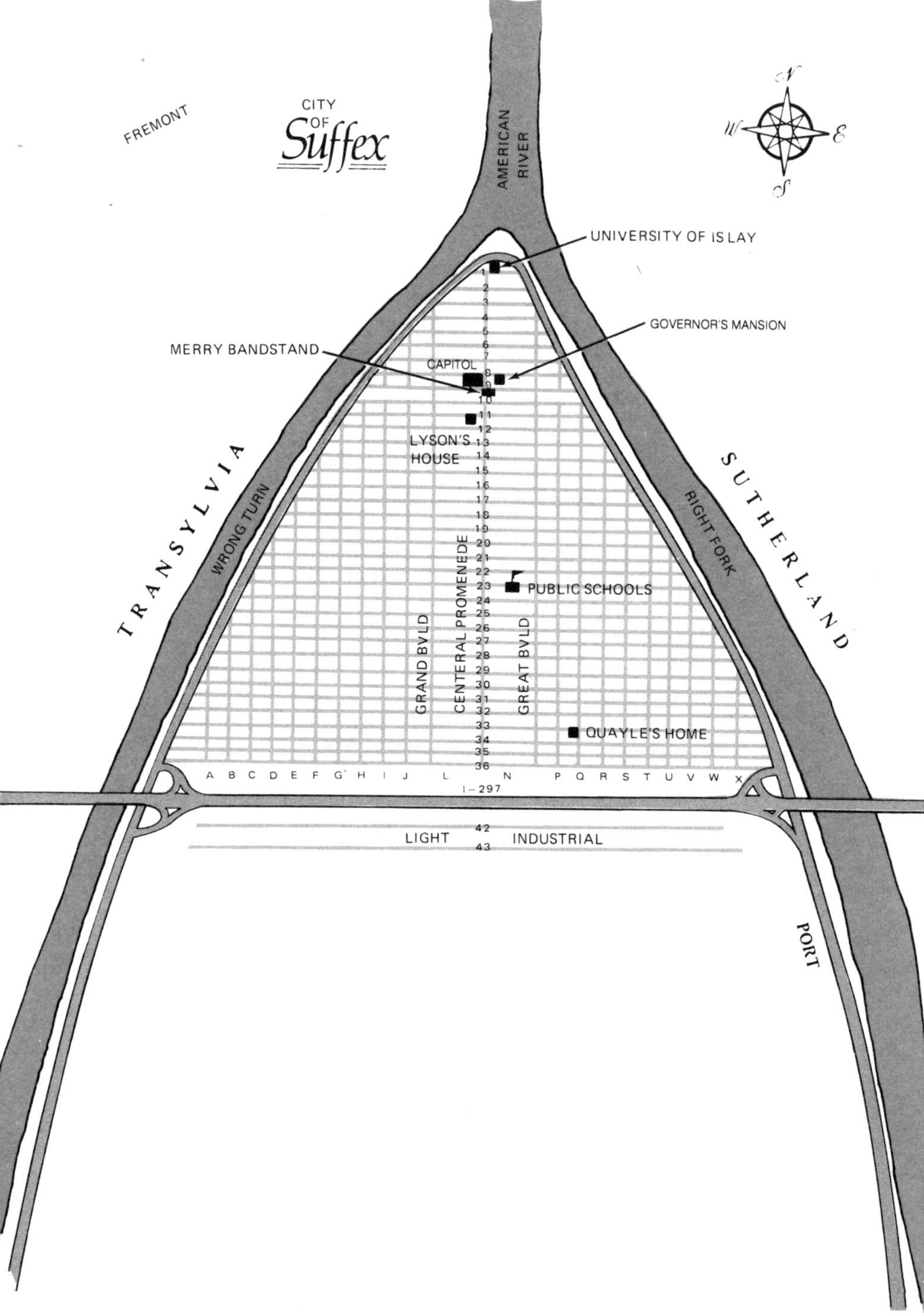
CITY OF Suffex
FREMONT
AMERICAN RIVER
N
W
E
S
UNIVERSITY OF ISLAY
GOVERNOR'S MANSION
MERRY BANDSTAND
CAPITOL
LYSON'S HOUSE
1
2
3
4
5
6
7
8
9
10
11
12
13
14
15
16
17
18
19
20
21
22
23
24
25
26
27
28
29
30
31
32
33
34
35
36
TRANSYLVIA
WRONG TURN
SUTHERLAND
RIGHT FORK
PUBLIC SCHOOLS
GRAND BVLD
CENTERAL PROMENEDE
GREAT BVLD
QUAYLE'S HOME
A B C D E F G H I J L N P Q R S T U V W X
I–297
42
LIGHT INDUSTRIAL
43
PORT

The author wishes to express his thanks to Trent Batson, William and Greta Boland, Terrence J. O'Rourke, Ramon Rodriguez, Frank Portugal, and Barbara Olmert. *Special thanks to Ruth and Darry and Dena for their patience and love. This book was made possible in part through a special grant from the Laurent Clerc Cultural Fund of Gallaudet College.*

FOREWORD

We are all familiar with the saying that "a picture is worth a thousand words." And yet we are also aware that even the most carefully chosen thousand words could not, for example, capture the beauty of the Mona Lisa. Nor could those thousand words instill in the reader the sense of appreciation and wonder that is conveyed by a single glance at the masterpiece. This is, in part, because the written or spoken work is linear—written or spoken one at a time—while the visual bombardment of a single glance is simultaneous. Additionally, the English language (and, for that matter, any spoken language) is not particularly suited to the description of visually perceived material or events.

Imagine, then, the difficulties involved in writing a novel in which the characters interact with one another in Sign Language. Sign Language, which is gesturally produced, must be visually perceived in order to be fully understood. In spoken languages, specific movements of the mouth and tongue combine to produce sounds. These sounds, when combined in certain ways with other sounds, make words. These words, when combined in certain ways with other words, make sentences. In a signed language, specific handshapes are moved in certain ways to specific spatial locations to produce signs. These signs, when combined in certain ways with certain facial movements, make signed sentences.

At the present time there is no standard way of writing Sign Language sentences (nor, for that matter, is there any standard way of writing sentences for the vase majority of the world's spoken languages). As one can imagine, this presents certain difficulties when trying to present a written record of a Sign Language conversation. However, there are three general approaches that have been used in trying to record Sign Language sentences. The first, used by linguists and researchers, is to describe the specific handshapes, movements and locations of signs. Signs can be described by a symbol system (e.g. "GG $^{x-}$") or by using English words (e.g. "index finger of both hands extended; right palm faces left, left palm faces toward the body; tips of index fingers touch"). While such descriptions are useful for researchers, they are quite meaningless to someone who does not know the sign being described or the symbol system being used.

The second approach is to use an English word to represent a sign. The English word is called a gloss. Generally glosses are chosen that reflect the most frequent meanings of the sign. However, since glosses are English words themselves, there is a danger that the reader will assume that all of the meanings of the gloss can be conveyed by the sign or that all of the meanings of the sign are conveyed by the gloss. For example, whereas the

English word "mother" can be a noun or a verb, the sign for mother can only be used as a noun. Unless this is clear, the gloss may be meaningless or misunderstood.

The third approach is to provide an English translation of a signed sentence. A translation can be "literal" (focusing on the grammar and syntax of the original) or it can be "free" (focusing on the meaning and content of the original).

In this unique novel, Doug Bullard has chosen (wisely, I think) to represent Sign Language discourse in an eclectic fashion. Rather than describe signs, he uses glosses written in italics. Bullard has also taken great pains to choose his glosses carefully so that they reflect the range of meanings of the signs they represent. At the same time, they are easily understood by those who do not know Sign Language. In addition, when presenting signed sentences, he is neither totally "literal" or totally "free." Rather, he walks the fine line of trying to present the best of both—signed sentences that are both readable and insightful.

Furthermore, Bullard must also represent communication among the hearing impaired who use TTY's and other devices connected to telephone lines. To do so, he has resorted to the use of full capitals for those words that convey electronic sentences. Thus, the reader is presented with three distinct forms: words used for the novel's narrative, for glosses, and for teletype communications. Each is presented in a slightly different visual way by Bullard to help the reader perceive the intended differences.

It is indeed a difficult and challenging undertaking to present this work in written form. The difficulty stems from the lack of an agreed-upon system for writing signs. Bullard has dealt with this difficulty in a way that enhances, rather than detracts from the novel itself. As a novelist, he has also accepted the challenge. The challenge stems from the dynamic, visual nature of signs. Like the Mona Lisa or fireworks on the Fourth of July, Sign Language must be seen in order to be fully appreciated.

Silver Spring, Maryland
January 1986

Dennis Cokely, Ph.D.

PROLOGUE

I know at last what I want
to be when I grow up.
When I grow up I want
to be a little boy.

—Joseph Heller

There in the den, shut against the world, against Mary as well though he would never admit it, Lyson C. Sulla spent his Saturdays. Mary was uneasy about this. Uncomfortable also with the semantics by which he called the room a den. She knew there was no such thing as a den in an apartment, but Lyson was obstinate on this point. She would have been more comfortable had he called the room, really a spare bedroom if you asked her, an office. A nice, domestic ring to the word office: bright, airy, dustfree bustle; efficient and purposeful as her own kitchen. Everything in its rightful niche where it can immediately be found.

But a den is where bears go in fat, happy, and warm and come out hungry, disheveled, and irascible with a momentous hangover. Not that Lyson was that bad, really. Just that—that something was going on that must never be allowed out, out in the light of day. In other words, she was never quite satisfied just what was his hobby, exactly, but knew enough to keep it a tight secret. She wasn't even sure it was wise to refer to it as a hobby, as Lyson insisted. She'd have preferred something more dignified, more officious like project but Lyson explained that men respect hobbies more than they do projects. Hobby is only fun, see? Project is—you know—can be mad.

If only he could see, she sighed, the mirth in the eyes of her friends as they inquire after the locked door. At first he had thought she could simply say he was out, but that would be a brazen lie. And what if he forgot and opened the door early, before her friends had left? No way! A vexation: he wanted his hobby kept a secret, and she agreed, but she had no way of satisfying her friends' curious glances at the tightly locked door.

She was rather loathe to refer to it as a hobby any longer. The last time she had played the brave wife, explaining that Lyson took his hobby far more seriously than his job, her friends smiled not so secretly at one another: don't all men? All her friends smiled; that is, except Mortima Gooser who saw absolutely no humor in the foibles of men. If only men would take their jobs, and consequently women, seriously, she snapped indignantly, her gestures sharp and jabbing. And she would glare hard, her lip curled, at the locked door behind which Lyson hid, no doubt totally oblivious of them, the society of women, ignoring them as if they did not exist. The nerve!

Mary had every reason to be cautious around Mortima. Not for nothing was the name sign among the deaf for Mortima Gooser synonymous with gossip. Just how such a derogatory name sign got attached to Mortima is not certain but her old classmates claim that Mortima herself was the one who gave herself that sign. What mattered, though, was that Mortima did not at all blush when referred to by such a sign. In fact she introduced herself to strangers by that sign. It was natural with her. She just never thought to be embarrassed by it, not any more than a bull is by the chewed swallowed digested processed and passed remains of hay drying on its rump raising a stink and a whirring cloud of flies.

Once a minister of the gospel dared a bit of Christian sanitization by pointing out to her the impossibility for gossips to ever find happiness in heaven. No sin up there, you see, therefore nothing to gossip about up there, hehehe. But Mortima had returned him a certain stare—blank, unstudious, inscrutable, yet so pregnant. So even a minister of the gospel, as did Mary and everyone else, learned to be circumspect around Mortima.

"I am a card," she also liked to tell hearing people. She never said this to the deaf as she doubted they'd appreciate it the way she thought it deserved to be. They'd only curl a lip while the hearing at least had the courtesy to smile. When she was little, her favorite aunt had once gushed, "You're a card!" Mortima had wondered about it for a long while, until she looked it up in a dictionary. Among other things, it said a card was an attraction and a comical person. She took it to mean she was attractive and funny, and gushed to every new hearing acquaintance, "I am a card."

So Mary was leery of Mortima and never invited her to the apartment. But such was Mortima's craft when she invited herself to the Saturday teas at Mary's that Mary hesitated to shut the door in her face. Furthermore it was with uncanny timing that Mortima always managed to arrive at the same moment as the other, more welcome guests. So an armchair, one of the more comfortable in the apartment, actually Lyson's, where he'd always presided during the teas, was especially reserved for Mortima. This was only because Mary wanted to locate Mortima facing away from the door to the den. That heavy chair just happened to be the one ideally suited for this maneuver; unfortunately it gave Mortima the impression it was the place of honor. That couldn't be helped. Better she should think that than be allowed the awful way she could glare at the door, as if she could look right through it at Lyson and discern his secret. This glare also would only serve to draw all the eyes in the room toward the door, to contemplate, to speculate, to wonder.

* * *

One Saturday Mortima arrived in a strange, incongruous good cheer, with a kind word for all present, and did not protest as was her wont to appear modest when ushered to the chair of honor, the one facing away from Lyson's door. Mary took perverse delight in the way Mortima seemed to wear her girdle: upside down and backwards so that the front was pushed in and down, the rear up and out so that her buttocks worked laboriously to the motion of her little legs as she made her way around to her seat. Yet this new twist disconcerted Mary: Mortima giggled along with everyone around the little gathering. And her gestures seemed softer, more graceful. Obviously today she had something up her bosom, something big, juicy, delicious. Mary could only hope and pray it was not about some poor husband, hers or any of her friends. She bustled busily about, making her guests at home, all the while keeping a secret eye out for any evidence of the hobby Lyson might, just might, have absently left laying about for Mortima to slip into her bosom.

Informal and laid back is the way Mary liked the gatherings at her home, coffee and tea perpetually steaming, ever fresh, and little snacks on trays kept thoughtfully full. Easier said than done, though. Around Mortima you sit straight and watch yourself, and your posture.

Today, many friends came, all of them Mary's. For some reason Lyson's did not. Then Mary recalled that today was the opening day for trout. Lyson had been invited, but he'd begged off; there were some unresolved things he needed to work on for his hobby. Mary ached inside for Lyson: he so needed to go out in the sun, out in a creek and let the little fish nibble away his worries. She glanced over at the locked door and let her shoulders drop.

She wished she'd caught on, really she ought to have caught on much sooner and headed off all this nonsense. She'd known all along her husband was a fool but never could she have dreamt he could be so foolish. Yet, there it was, this enormous enormity, entrenched in her home! *Grotesque!*

It'd happened, somehow, because she'd grown up with a raftful of brothers, and it was a given to her that boys would be boys. She believed, unlike girls raised in homes untroubled by brothers, that foibles of men are better humored than censored. She'd allowed the project to take over the spare bedroom—he'd called it the den—and also his Saturdays: far better to allow the husband to make a fool of himself in the home than out. And people do make allowances for Saturdays, the day of days for boys to be boys. At first this arrangement appeared to be working out well; at least Lyson was so happy in his project that she couldn't but allow herself to be lulled into contentment too. That's the nice thing about happiness: it's so catching.

Now this! Before she'd caught on, his hobby had blossomed into a full flower of scandalous dimensions. She was appalled: it was that monstrous. *Grotesque!* Almost immediately she saw that the circumstances left her no recourse but to secure the den with a new lock and to keep close track of the key, to see it to its hiding place with its own key that needed to be hid too.

Mary was adamant about keeping his dream a secret. Under lock and key. And she guarded the key, even from Lyson. He had to ask to be let into his own den.

Yet, the trouble with locked doors is they attract eyes; in her case, Mary thought ruefully, like a murderess drawn day after day to the tomb to lay a rose. This kind of thing can get your fingers stepped on, Lyson.

I understand! I understand!

Lyson, we must do something about your dreaming dreaming—

I'm thinking! I'm thinking!

Even then, it dogged them everywhere, its shadow as stubborn as the tendrils of a dream whose roots have long been forgotten, yet that continue to grow and grow so that it cannot be let go. Mary sighed at the door.

Mortima saw and wanted to turn for a look at the door. Instead, she merely turned to Ursula on her side. Mary wasn't fooled: Mortima could see out of the tail of her eye almost as good as straightforward.

Ursula was telling her close friend Charity across the circle of friends, *Oh, we're planning divorce*. Her gestures were strong and bold, purposely large in defiance of Mortima who perked up, intensely interested, her eyes fixed on Ursula rather than on Lyson's door.

You see, Ursula went on quite unmindful of Mortima, *recently read new book that proves 99 percent of deaf-hearing marriages fail, divorce.* A shrug. *That's why decided, better divorce now while husband still good friend, still have love.*

Everyone stared, every hand stilled, as Ursula nonchalantly helped herself to a cracker and bit of cheese. Mortima licked her lips.

Ninety-nine percent! Janice finally exclaimed, her hands making the gestures in a flurry of jumps.

Oh yes, Ursula nodded her fist in the exaggerated manner of confirming an indisputable truth. *Deaf-hearing marriages impossible succeed. Fact, the book said those one percent deaf-hearing marriages that don't divorce, that's because hearing suppresses deaf, prevent associating with other deaf—*

Ninety-nine percent! Janice exclaimed again. *Never dreamt! You know that my husband, himself hearing, always good to me, better than some—* glancing secretly at the sister Monica—*husbands, themselves deaf but always selfish, trouble, trouble—*

Mortima looked sharply at Monica, and Mary too, to see if perhaps their masks would drop enough for a secret or two to slip through. But she had looked too sharply: Monica and Mary caught her sharpness and held their faces nonchalant.

I love him regardless, Monica managed to reply, calmly reaching for a mint.

Because himself deaf, agreed Ursula.

I love my husband, notwithstanding himself hearing, insisted Janice.

Thought myself too, Ursula frowned. *But that book said 99 percent, makes me wonder.*

Believe book? cried Janice in astonishment.

Psychologist wrote, protested Undresa. *Himself Ph.D.*

Ph.D! laughed Professor Stumpt heartily. *Wish people read and believe my book about pennies.*

Psychologist himself deaf? Hearing? inquired Monica.

Book says nothing. Probably hearing. But Ph.D.—

Ph.D. nothing! Not impress me! Janice announced hotly. *My husband wonderful, no-matter hearing. I cherish him!*

My husband too, Ursula agreed sadly, *but 99 percent!*

Ninety-nine percent absurd, invented number!

Can't fool statistics—

Psychologists themselves confused, divorce, divorce, suicide, alcoholism—

Mortima eyes suddenly narrowed. She remembered the secret hidden in her bosom, her plan to catch Lyson at some secret she knew he would succumb into her power to keep quiet.

That book itself true science! Research! Serious—Ursula protested.

Myself counsel deaf all day, everyday, Charity cut in. *Noticed myself that most percentage marriage trouble truly between male, female. Women suffer too-much frustration, no-matter deaf, hearing. Men too-much macho!*

Doctor Stumpt laughed and said, his signs alive with irony, *Men truly bigheaded. Won't listen to me, think my book frivolous, not worth reading!*

Lyson agrees with you, Mary said drily. *Kind-of. His own*—She nearly began a cranking motion around an ear but caught herself.

Gene Owles, whispered Janice to Monica, her hands low and out of sight. But Mortima was all seeing and saw all.

Darling, giggled Monica. *See him?*

Janice took a quick look around and met the stare from Mortima. She dropped her hands lower and made a remark out of Mortima's sight that tickled Monica very much.

Gene Owles! That old satyr with the rear half of a horse and the devil's smirk out front. Everyone knew about him. Broken hearts dumped in gutters drowning in rivers of tears. No shame, no wife to amuse, no more morals than a dog and proud of it too. Mortima well knew about him. He never so much as gave her tail a whiff, let alone deign to look at her. Quite beyond the power of her wagging fingers.

Mortima shivered with excitement. At long last a topic teetering on the edge of scandal, grabbing the attention of everyone—how many here have known him?—now, all eyes are upon the one who is speaking of him. The conversation was so hot and riveting, her opportunity finally arrived, the kind that does not arise when conversation is ordinary, dull, and eyes are casting aimlessly about, searching everywhere for something to fix on. And Mary's were always on her whenever possible but just now, finally, were chasing Gene Owles' name flying on fingertips about the room. Lyson's door is where the action is, Mortima knew, just knew, where pay dirt could be found, the ultimate scandal! Silently, unobtrusively she slipped out of her chair and despite her bulk and laboring buttocks, glided on tiny steps behind the chair to the door. Her dark dress melted into the shadows at the edge of the room, masking trembling fingers that drew from her bosom the key, and before anyone noticed the empty chair, she was in the den.

* * *

There! Lyson was at the blackboard, his back to the door, furiously chalking calculations. Mortima silently shut the door, her hands behind pushing in the lock button. She remained in the shadows, not daring to move, her back against the door, her hands out of sight on the knob, her eyes unwavering.

On a strange-looking table in the center of the room, filling half the room, stood an enormous doll house brightly illuminated by a conical lamp hung low from the ceiling. Only the table was in direct light; the window was heavily curtained, so that the dollhouse almost seemed to float in the dim room. It was the fanciest dollhouse Mortima had ever seen, and it was almost absurd that a grown man should have such a toy when so many little girls like Mortima had to grow up with cardboard types, if any at all. Mortima gripped the doorknob tighter. A plaything like this in a den!

Yet, it was no ordinary dollhouse. More like a two-tiered wedding cake, she thought; a silvery conical roof, something like a Chinese coolie's hat, supported on slender white columns arranged on a round platform and topped by a spire resting on a smaller circle of columns over a round opening in its peak, like a church steeple. No, not really. More like the Capitol with its lantern that crowns its dome. Only more conical. And more open. No walls. Just Grecian-like columns. Really a very pretty model, as large as any she'd ever seen.

Before she could complete the thought process leading toward a suspicion that Mary was expecting a new Sulla, Lyson made a quick motion that startled her. He turned without warning to the table and hunched over a large book, staring intently at it, his lips tightly puckered and twitching with silent figurings, sweating profusely, the beads shining like crystals on his face from the light reflected from the pages, their white rectangles reflecting in his eyeglasses. Mortima thought it odd too that he was wearing a business suit, and a tie to boot. The suit was wet under the armpits, and a grimy ring could be seen around the collar of his white shirt. His suits always seemed too tight on him, as if they had been washed all wrong. The sleeves hung short, making his arms appear long. His hair was damp and disheveled; normally it was beautiful shiny black wavy and meticulously brushed. All this sweat reminded Mortima that she had a nose and she started at the pungent male odor at close quarters. It reminded her of musk, but before she could establish an opinion about it, Lyson slapped his head and rushed back to the blackboard, and resumed the figurings, his hands and sleeves now dusty with chalk.

The blackboard covered much of the wall to the left. Writing with his right hand, Lyson's back was turned toward the door as he scribbled, so

Mortima was safe for the moment. On the wall opposite Mortima was a window heavily curtained, no doubt, against prying eyes. A cluttered desk sprawled on the right. Her eyes laughed at the huge mirror above it: it was framed by a bank of bare lamp bulbs, like an actress' dressing room. A vanity mirror in a den! Her mouth opened in a humph but she shut it quickly. The fillings and caps on her teeth might catch the light, and his eye.

Something he had just written on the blackboard thrilled Lyson and he gave a tiny leap, thrusting a fist high in the air. Mortima cringed back against the door, gripping the knob ever tighter. Lyson happily bounded back to the table and pushed little matchbox automobiles, trucks, earth-moving machines, and tanks closer toward the dollhouse over roads painted grey over the green of the table, his eyes feverishly bright, his lips putt-putting little engine noises. Whoa! A sudden roadblock brought everything to a grinding halt and he became visibly distressed and bit his knuckle. He anxiously consulted the big book, frantically turning the pages and gingerly touching the little cars. Finally he slapped his forehead and went back to the blackboard, shaking his head in chagrin at some gaffe, unknown and incomprehensible to Mortima. His damp hand erased some of the figures and chalked in new ones.

His intensity perplexed Mortima as she looked hard at the numbers on the blackboard. Islay—302,074. Pinnacle County—198,862. Suffex—121,483. Sanday County—28,704. Crewe—18,573. Flint County—40,669. Wrexham—22,154. Mortima allowed her mouth to fall open. Islay and Suffex seemed vaguely familiar. Something she thought she'd seen on a green sign somewhere, along a freeway to New York. Ah, Islay, a tiny state she recalled. How come such an interest in such a nothing place? she wondered. A geography freak? Bah! Not much of a scandal.

But then why the locked door and secrecy, she reminded herself. The dollhouse too. And the vanity mirror. And the sweat and the smell and the fever. She looked harder and in the dim light noticed framed portraits arrayed on either side of the mirror. Abraham Lincoln so grave. Tight-lipped George Washington. Napoleon proud as a peacock. Gandhi in a sheet. Einstein with a halo of unruly white hair. Martin Luther King, Jr., his eyes bearing the sufferings of three centuries. Uncle Sam pointing directly at draft dodgers. John F. Kennedy in PT-109. So true. He was a brave man. Lyndon Johnson in a World War II aviator's leather helmet and goggles. Ludicrous! Mortima wasn't impressed in the least with such fancy grandeur.

She stared accusingly at the back of Lyson's head bobbing slightly as he wrote vigorously on the blackboard, the chalk worn down to one tiny fragment difficult to hold so that it slipped often, making a mess that upset Lyson almost to distraction.

On a shelf by the desk were piled book upon book, horizontally for some reason rather than vertically as is the custom of most. That much easier to find a particular title, though, thought Mortima as she strained her eyes to read the titles in the gloom of the room. *The Compleat Candidate. Marketing of the President. Strategy and Your Election. Winning the Female Vote. Care and Maintenance of the Gastro-Respiratory Tract.* Mortima went over them again and again, intent on recalling them for future reference.

Taking a cautious step toward the dollhouse she saw that all the roads led to the apex of an irregular triangle painted green on the table. Tiny plastic trees, columns of tin soldiers, even plastic models of warships! Just like the war rooms she'd seen at the movies! A closet Dr. Strangelove?

Suddenly Lyson was back at the table, full of renewed enthusiasm. The roadblock was broken! He gleefully rolled cars, trucks, bulldozers, tin soldiers, even trees up closer to the edifice, surrounding it in a splendid military procession. The warships sailed majestically up blue ribbons painted on either side of the triangle to the apex, and laid seige to the dollhouse. Two tanks crashed clumsily into each other due to mixed signals between Lyson and his hands. He berated them in the manner of a drill sergeant and set the tanks straight, roaring on their way. With fiercely sputtering lips, he bulldozed down a couple of little bridges, isolating the triangle from the outside world across the blue ribbons of rivers. Thus accomplished, he marched the bulldozers triumphantly back into formation alongside the tanks and other engines of war. The enemy was taken! He thrust a fist in the air and held it there in triumph. A sigh of tremendous satisfaction, and he dropped his fist slowly, surveying his great victory, his eyes bright and dancing, his face flushed with victory and dripping wet with the passion of battle.

For a long moment everything was still in the room; Lyson, with his chin high, proud, gazing with affection at the beautiful dollhouse, eyes shiny, chest heaving, while Mortima retreated against the door, her grip hard around the knob. Again the strong male odor startled her and her heart accelerated, setting off heavy throbbing in the veins in her neck and temples. His happiness over such trivia was absolutely disgusting, even when viewed against all the foibles she knew of the husbands of her friends. He had no right to be so happy while his wife Mary had to contend with the real, oh so real, situations she and her friends were put to everyday just so that their husbands could enjoy silly things like toy soldiers, breaking a 100 at golf, bowling a 200, and God knows what else men get into. Her lips hurt from having been pulled tautly over her teeth. Lyson's fault! she declared to herself. But she restrained herself: after all it was her skill at her vocation that still was her best, most devastating weapon. And it was an actual, living weapon not some little tin car pulled out of a matchbox. And she would use it, when the time was right. When it hurt the most!

Lyson is insane, she nodded to herself vehemently, then quickly stopped herself lest he saw her. But she needn't have worried: Lyson caught sight of something he didn't like of himself in the mirror and hurried over and turned on the lights. He blanched. He seized fistfuls of Kleenex and mopped the sweat off his face and neck. He even tried to dry the armpits of his jacket, but it was futile. He was visibly upset and slammed the ball of Kleenex at a wastebasket. Seizing a can of deodorant, he let loose a spray against his armpits. Sniffing all over himself busily like a bloodhound, he found new areas of further concern and pushed the button again, raising a cloud of spray between his legs. Never before had Mortima been this intimate with a man and her neck began to feel hot. She imagined her neck sweating and she involuntarily wiped it, cursing Lyson for the mess he was creating in her person. She caught herself again. The light from the vanity mirror was so bright she felt exposed and vulnerable; she held herself stock stiff, like a deer caught in headlights.

Finally, his face and neck were wiped dry enough to be presentable, and Lyson calmed down somewhat. Now he examined his ears by employing a small mirror held up at such an angle against the big mirror that he could see deeply into his own ears. Out came the Q-tips from a drawer and he reamed his ears so clean that if wax had been the culprit behind his hearing impairment, he would've heard Mortima's gasping perfectly clearly by the time the little mirror satisfied him that his ears were clean down to the drums. An examination of his nostrils brought out some tiny scissors from the drawer and he snipped around inside until all the offending little hairs were gone. His shoulders brushed clear of dandruff, his tie pulled straight, his hands and sleeves wiped clean of chalk, he nodded sharply to some imaginary flunky beside himself: Ready!

With the slowness of a very important man heavily weighed down with the cares and responsibilities of the world, Lyson pushed himself to his feet, a deep thought furrowing his brow; he moved slowly to a position behind the table where he could face both the dollhouse and himself in the mirror. For a fraction of a moment his brow furrowed ever deeper. His demeanor collapsed and he hurried back to the desk. Out of a drawer he retrieved a matchbox and slid it open. It was no ordinary matchbox, but the kind that formerly held huge wooden matches.

With the tenderness of servant toward master, he brought out a shiny tin soldier. Mortima saw incredulously that it was a knight in shining armor astride a horse with—of all things—wings! Over and through the assembled troops on the table he marched and flew the little knight, his lips pursed to emphasize the seriousness and solemnity of the occasion. Around, round and above the dollhouse, Lyson flew the little knight on the wings of—of—Mortima thought aghast, the Mobile Gasoline Company's winged horse, banking one way, then sharply like a jet zipping the other. Mortima had never heard of Pegasus, the winged horse; nor has she heard of the story of how Pegasus came into Lyson's life, how his grandmother had started it all, how his dream had begun in a matchbox. Had she known the story, she'd have bolted out the door back to the tea party, screaming and wagging her finger. Instead, she gaped at Pegasus and worked her mouth like a fish out of water.

It was his dear grandmother who gave him the matchbox. It was uncanny just how she knew what would please him. For some reason, perhaps because they do not bear any guilt over the child, grandmothers do seem to know their grandchild far better than the parents do.

"Open it," she urged, wiggling a finger in his dimple. Lyson would have torn open the box but she caught his hands and showed how it could be opened without tearing. Out came a Rolls Royce. A Silver Cloud the size of an ordinary matchbox, yet its four doors opened like the real thing to reveal a steering wheel, seats, even a dashboard; and the bonnet opened to a miniature engine. So real that, even though Lyson had to set his ear on the floor to achieve this end, he could imagine himself driving the automobile around, under chairs and tables that transformed themselves into houses, skyscrapers, mountains.

This Silver Cloud began the great matchbox collection. And so the Dream. Everytime she came to visit, his grandmother brought a new automobile. Cadillacs, Lincolns, Mercedes, BMWs, Ferrari's, MGs, Bugs, even jeeps. As Lyson grew, so did the matchbox collection: trucks, semitrailers, tractors, bulldozers, tanks, even warships. As the collection grew larger and more extensive, so did the dream. People thought the collection the finest they had even seen of the matchbox set; Lyson thought his dream the neatest.

Yet, the dream remained formless, like stardust, lacking content and substance, until one day his grandmother, the only one he ever confided his dream—at least until Mary caught on years later and pried it out of him—anyway, this selfsame grandmother returned from a trip to Vienna with a genuine matchbox, a large one that formerly held wooden matches. The kind that, when struck, made fire.

"This is very valuable," she stressed as she held it out of reach of his eager hands. "Be careful!"

"Say thank you," his mother insisted.

"Promise," insisted his grandmother, "you'll be careful."

Gingerly she slid the box open and out flew Pegasus, with Lyson close behind. It was a shiny tin knight on a flying horse, the knight so straight and courageous in the saddle, the wings so proud and jaunty. Lyson ran after it, holding it high aloft, little engine noises sputtering on his lips. Around, above, and under the furniture went Lyson and Pegasus, sweeping around tremendous thunderstorms, soaring above mighty mountains, swooping under great bridges. Grandmother screamed and mother seized him by the sideburn and took away Pegasus.

The shiny knight on his Pegasus was put away, never to be seen again, except on two or three occasions under the watchful eye of Grandmother, until Lyson was a grown man, when it was deemed prudent to allow him to be alone with Pegasus.

Mortima never knew any of this as she gaped at Lyson who, with dramatic aerobatics, deposited the little knight inside the dollhouse. He pranced it about some, allowing the spirited horse to calm down, and turned the little knight to face his troops with a salute. The force of her breathing drew Mortima's attention to her mouth, and the fact it was wide open to the lights, her teeth sparkling. She shut it promptly.

His demeanor firmly in control, Lyson held up his hands, palms outward to silence whatever tumultuous applause he could see that she couldn't. For an unseemly time he held this pose, his head bowed in mock humility, pleasure etched in his face, branded by the obvious adulation of his troops. It took time, inordinately long it seemed to Mortima, for the applause to die down; Lyson took a deep breath, nodding humbly in recognition of the momentousness of the occasion.

My friends, wonderful deaf, his hands came to life slowly, wonderment all over his face, his eyes moving lovingly over the assembled troops, cars, trucks, tanks, bulldozers, warships and trees. *We here, finally successful—* His eye flickered up at the mirror in admiration at himself but he saw his hair. He quickly abandoned his speech and leapt over to the desk and pulled out a comb.

A clicking on the doorknob nearly made Mortima jump. Her heart pounding in her throat, she kept a finger pressed tightly on the lock button. Somebody on the other side of the door, most likely Mary, tried the knob, sending anxious jerks through the knob into Mortima's hands. She held on. Not now! Not now!

Lyson combed his hair real neat—no chance at the blown-dry look under these circumstances—wiped his face again and restraightened his tie and jacket. He admired himself seriously for a moment and turned off the lights around the mirror. By this time the knob had given up and Mortima could feel through the floor steps retreating in defeat. Get going, she urged Lyson. Get on the job!

My friends, wonderful deaf, Lyson resumed his oratory, his hands tracing a florid pattern through the air, as would Pegasus fly. *We here, finally succeed, capture Islay, our own island, our own state; deaf only allowed here from now on. Hearing finally pushed-off* —A giggling arose in Mortima, rising from her stomach up toward her throat, and she tightened her chest to suppress it.

Many, many years ever since hearing repress us deaf, make us slaves, pat our heads and say be good, think us dumb, mock us—his hands roared defiantly, slashing in the light so that they flashed against the darkness behind, as would attack her enemies Pegasus. His fist slammed the table and some of the soldiers toppled over. Hastily he set them back on their feet and regained his composure. The giggle reached Mortima's cheeks so that they puffed in and out as she pressed her mouth tightly to prevent its escape.

My first decision, now me Governor here Islay, our beloved State, myself decide, announce—he paused for the proper dramatic moment. *All hearing must out before time, 12 Midnight!* Again the pause for effect. *Islay for deaf only. Deaf only allowed here. Hearing can't enter. Command: block bridges!* His lips resolute, he marched some tin soldiers toward the bridges.

But the bridges had fallen. His eyes wide with surprise he stared incredulously at the bridges laying on their sides. He had forgotten he'd bulldozed them into the river. He slapped his forehead and stepped back helplessly, biting his knuckles, trying to figure a way to backtrack.

Mortima could no longer hold back and exploded in that wonderful rolling bouncing laughter of the obese.

Lyson nearly died.

PART 1

STRINGS

If we don't meet with what we like
we are sure to meet with something new.

—Voltaire

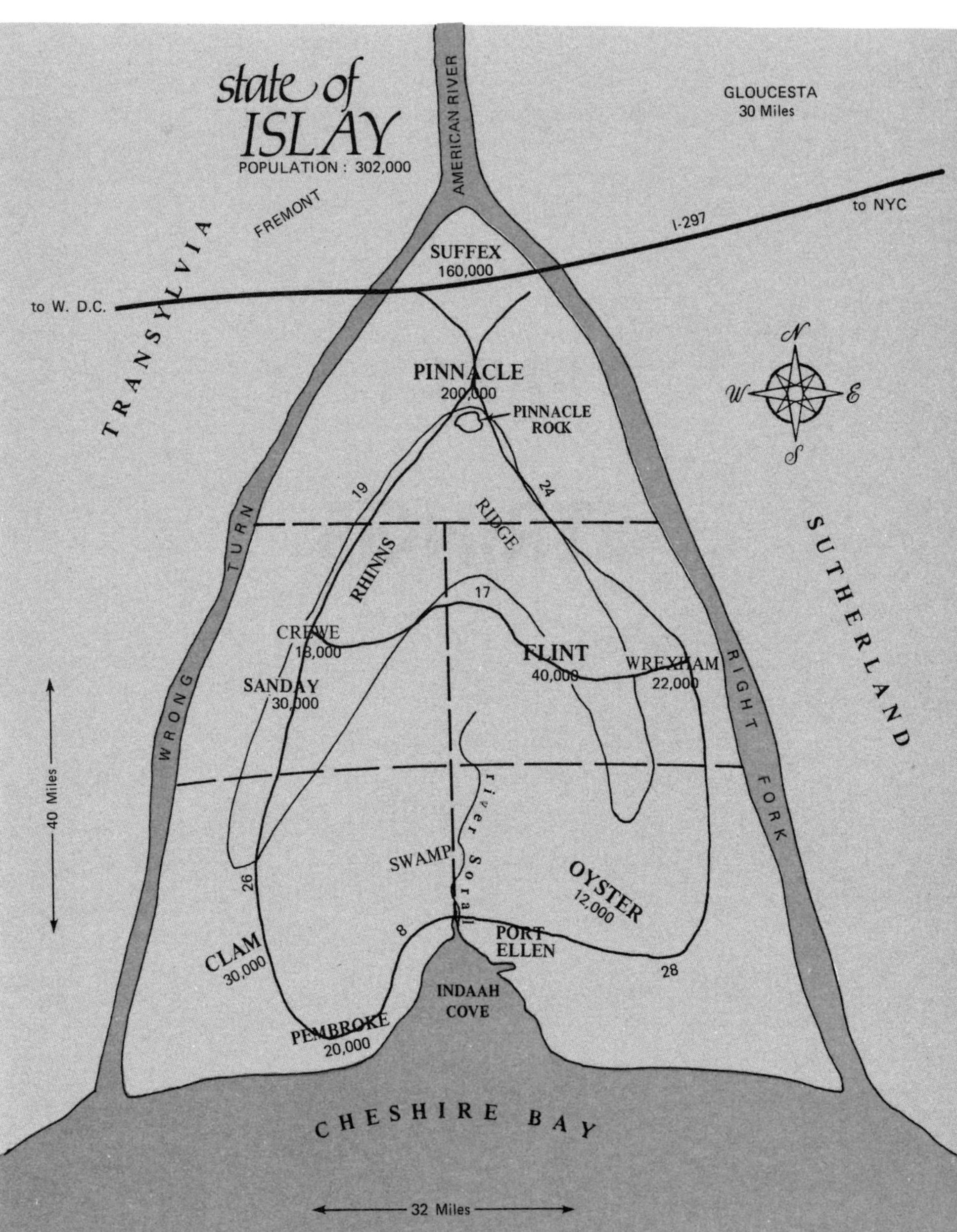

state of ISLAY
POPULATION : 302,000
AMERICAN RIVER
GLOUCESTA
30 Miles
FREMONT
I-297
to NYC
SUFFEX
160,000
to W. D.C.
TRANSYLVIA
PINNACLE
200,000
PINNACLE ROCK
N
W
E
S
19
24
RIDGE
WRONG TURN
SUTHERLAND
RHINNS
17
CREWE
18,000
FLINT
40,000
WREXHAM
22,000
RIGHT FORK
SANDAY
30,000
40 Miles
river Soral
SWAMP
OYSTER
12,000
26
8
PORT ELLEN
CLAM
30,000
28
INDAAH COVE
PEMBROKE
20,000
CHESHIRE BAY
32 Miles

CHAPTER 1

Its peculiar position on the map, hidden away in a recess like a hind tit tucked up under the tenderloin of the great states of the Union, gave the distinct impression that the State of Islay was an afterthought, which indeed it was in fact. At first glance Islay appears to be a river delta where the American River spills into Chesire Bay on the south. On closer look, however, a sharp chevron-shaped ridge of hills called the Rhinns is what splits the river into two forks so that Islay has a nice looking delta shape, with an inviting southern coast where Chesire Bay, encroaching a low area between the ridges, creates a smaller bay—Indaal Cove. Overall, the little island is only 32 miles along its southern coast and some 40 miles from Suffex at the northern apex down to the coast.

Seems very small, commented Mary, her mouth pushed very small, and folded her arms, hiding her hands out of communication.

Exactly! Perfect for my, I mean our plan, Lyson beamed anxiously. *And larger than Rhode Island but fewer people. Look!* He pointed out the legend in the corner. *See? Official Highway map Islay! Altogether only 302,074 people. About half live there, Suffex.*

Mary stared at him bleakly, as at an eccentric, and dropped her shoulders. *Forget lock door, you! Why?*

Tell you! Lyson crossed his heart and stamped his foot. *Did lock!*

She shook her head sadly at the door the way a banker would at a vault that yielded all too easily to a burglar. *How? How?* She tested the knob again. It was locked as locked can be.

Nothing can do! Lyson pleaded with small hops. *Mortima herself promised shut-up—*

Wonderful promise! she wagged her head and plunked away at an imaginary harp.

Lyson bared his teeth like a cringing dog. *Smile and be satisfied that myself upset, very upset, same you—*

Stupid hobby!

Not stupid! Let me explain—He bravely set the bridges back upright. They were the only link between the island and America. In the old days before the Interstate System, there only was a rickety wooden trestle a lane and half wide across the Wrong Turn between Suffex and the great state Transylvia, just below Fremont. This made it easy to overlook Islay. Exactly what the people of Islay wanted. And what Lyson wished was still true, but the Federals thought otherwise.

Insisting that the people of Islay step up into the twentieth century along with the rest of the country, the Federals some years ago relentlessly punched a freeway through Islay, near the top of the delta just below the capital of Suffex. And they ceremoniously burned down the old bridge, ostensibly in observation of the opening of the new freeway bridges but more likely in recognition of the old bridge's notoriety as an attractive nuisance, in particular for Chevy joustin' matches. The bridge had won this game of chicken all too often, robbing the United States military of potential knights and jockeys for its own engines of war. Lyson had read all this, he said, in response to Mary's weary brow, in *THE HISTORY OF ISLAY THE LITTLE STATE THAT COULD*.

Look! He smoothed the map and spread it out on the table, pushing aside little cars and trucks. Her arms still folded impatiently, Mary followed his finger as it traced the great green line of Interstate 297 slashing through the tip of the delta below Suffex, connecting it with Transylvia across Wrong Turn to the west, and Sutherland to the east across Right Fork. The heaviness, the very green of the line brought forth the image of a nation in motion, in a hurry, hurtling inexorably right by the insignificant little state with hardly a glance. Lyson began rumbling his lips like heavy trucks but he checked himself at Mary's sharp glance.

Remember? he said, hastily wiping his mouth. *Ourselves drove through many times going to New York. Remember?*

Maybe, she shrugged skittishly, wary as a horse skeptical of the intelligence of the rider spurring it into a strange, deep river.

See! Most people never notice Islay! That's why perfect for deaf! The force of his gesture lifted his torso in a little hop. *Notice, only two!* He urged her eyes to note the fact that there were only two exits from the freeway into the State of Islay. His eyebrows wiggled significantly but her arms remained folded firmly. *There!* he tapped the map and ran a finger along the one and only highway that wound in a perimeter around the state, first down Right Fork and the coast, then up Wrong Turn back to Suffex. Only a few towns appeared on this map of Islay, and the names appeared as ancient as England itself. Crewe on Wrong Turn about halfway down from Suffex. Wrexham on Right Fork opposite. Pembroke basking on the coast at Indaal Cove, with little Port Ellen in its own little cove on one side of the bay. Lyson clamped his lips tight together so they would not flutter or splutter as his finger traveled up and down the map. He held up five fingers meaningfully. *Imagine!*

Mary allowed a shoulder to do all her communication. *So?*

Can't you see? Lyson gave a little leap on stiff legs. *Perfect for my—I mean our plans. Only five towns, easy for us deaf conquer, control—*

Mary sagged wearily. *Nice dream. That your hobby?*

Not so! Real dream! I mean goal!

Wish never! Mary rolled her eyes in exasperation. Lyson looked so sad, so put down she explained, *Wish you didn't forget lock door.* She double-checked. Still locked as can be locked.

Eagerly Lyson flipped some pages in the book *THE LITTLE STATE THAT COULD* and came up with this anecdote:

"From the time of the colonies through the War for Independence to the War Between the States, Islay was claimed by the great States of Transylvia on the west and Sutherland on the east to be a county belonging to the other. In short, it was an unwanted orphan shifted back and forth across the River American, its parentage and legitimacy denied and its heritage uncertain. It was not until its most illustrious son, Sloppy Wenchell, returned home a full Colonel from the War between the States, his eyes wide from seeing the world, did Islay find its rightful sovereignty among the States of the Union. Colonel Wenchell gathered all the veterans of the War into a mighty army and petitioned Congress for full statehood for Islay.

"Miraculously, it was easier done than thought. The Senators from Transylvia and Sutherland were surprisingly its most vigorous supporters, and the motion passed swiftly through Congress making Islay a state! Only after the fact did it come to light that the Senators of Transylvia and Sutherland had each thought Islay to be a county belonging to the other."

Lyson tapped the book with the back of his hand. *Interesting history!*

Yes, interesting. Mary agreed politely with a twist of the head.

Fascinating! Lyson insisted as he turned the pages of the book. *More, read.*

"Having seen the splendors of the whole wide America, as far west as Nashville and as far south as Savannah, Colonel, now Governor, Wenchell decided in the year 1888 to erect a stupendous, beautiful, and outstanding monument to his Army. For this he chose a bandstand! Governor Wenchell believed that the only ones to appreciate useless monuments such as heroes on horses or obelisks were pigeons, and even then he suspected such appreciation to be less than wholehearted, for witness how spattered such edifices become in time. But, said Wenchell, a bandstand would be a more fitting and appreciated monument to his army, which he noted proudly still assembled every year to whoop it up. A monument to the finer elements of the human spirit: horns, drums, cymbals, and strings rather than to the baser: guns, swords, and cannon. The Governor knew what he was doing and no expense was spared after he commissioned the best architect in Islay for the job. This was the young Sam Phelps, whose forebears had laid out the streets of Suffex in Colonial times and had built the Wenchell Mansion, now the Governor's Mansion, as well as many of the finer homes of Suffex.

"Alas, Governor Sloppy Wenchell never lived to see the completion of his beloved monument. It took many long and arduous years of travel, study, and consultation with world-famed architects and conductors in Paris, Venice, Rome, Athens, Palestine, Egypt, and the Caribbean before Mr. Phelps came across exactly the right design in a little village in Massachusetts. There in Rockport at the head of a little cove by the sea stood the most exquisitely beautiful little bandstand he ever saw. It was almost entirely in stone and its roof was crowned by a magnificent little lantern, so that tears came to his eyes.''

Mary looked up sharply, and Lyson blinked quickly. *Look!* He hastened to draw her attention to the dollhouse. *Thirty-seven feet and four inches, diameter. Sixty-three feet, seven and half inches from ground to peak.* He smiled and bit his lower lip at the same time. *Huge, eh?*

Oh, wiggled her little finger.

Interesting! Tentatively, encouragingly.

Interesting, politely said.

Imagine! he extolled.

Imagine! she bristled. *Mortima saw!*

Beautiful! Hope she like it, he said bravely.

Exactly! she exclaimed. *Exactly! She loved what she saw!*

She promised! he jumped.

Dream dream dream wiggled her index fingers slowly up from her forehead away into never-never, her eyes crossed and her head and hips swaying in the manner of a ballerina dancing out a dream. *Dreams never true!*

Can't help! Lyson burst out with wild hands. *Your parents rich, selfish us deaf! Give money your hearing brothers, sisters, help them become rich, fat cigars. But not us! Think us deaf and dumb. Pat head and say be good. That's why can't do anything about dream! Hearing parents think deaf children their dreams silly, not worth helping!*

Not true! Mary hit the table.

Your brothers own bank, shopping mall, have huge houses, luxury cars, long cigars—

They earned their money!

Not so! You know that, want to become rich, must first have money for start! Your father helped them!

Because their ideas good, real! she pounded the table. *Your's dream—dream—*

Your parents think deaf dumb, pat head Be Good! not worth helping become rich. Only good for government job under hearing boss—He kissed his ring finger obscenely.

Shut-up! she slapped down his hands. *Let me finish. My brothers, their ideas good, true. Explain clearly, reasonably. Father agree right, reasonable, that why he loans money, help establish business. But*—she paused sadly, wearily—*your idea dreamy.*

You know that Laurent Clerc had same dream! Himself greatest deaf in history, started Golden Age for deaf there France. Then brought sign here America; almost started new Golden Age for us deaf, but hearing oralism frustrated him, broke up deaf cooperation and almost destroyed

Sign Language. That why Clerc liked idea for deaf gathering into one state where deaf itself normal!

Impossible dream—Too-many hearing!

You know that since several years myself study, research, analyze, he argued, his signs flying almost too fast for the eye, *Now know for sure can true!*

Did you talk my father, and explain, yet? she asked mildly.

No! No! he shook his head and rolled his eyes as at a silly question. *I know better. Hearing never listen us deaf!*

Why not? she folded her arms and rested back against the table.

Deaf! Because deaf!

Explain, rolled her hand as in summoning a reluctant child.

You know that hearing think deaf means dumb, pat head— Lyson mimed patting his own head.

Afraid ask, right?

Not!

Afraid your dream come true, spoil your fantasy—

Not! he denied, flustered. *Not fantasy! True dream, goal same Clerc!*

Dream easy, cheap, but doing difficult, right? she taunted.

No! Want dream become true! Look! He turned the map over to the city of Suffex and pointed to a red notation in the middle of a long narrow green park: Merry Bandstand. *See! Proves true!*

Mary refolded her arms and twisted her lower lip.

Lyson gave the map a sharp shake, almost as if to prove it wasn't a mere filament, a gossamer, a wispy cobweb, and pointed out the Governor's Mansion, the Capitol, Islay University at the very apex of the delta, the Suffex Public Library, the Courthouse, Islay Hotel, and various symbols denoting schools, churches, fire stations, cemeteries, hospitals, and other points of interest for anyone who might care to be interested in such things. *Real city! Not dream! See wonderful design!*

Indeed it was a neat design. The city occupied the entire northern apex of the delta above the freeway and was entirely surrounded by a greenbelt along the freeway and the rivers. The long narrow park where stood the Bandstand crossed the city all the way from river to river, neatly dividing it into a business district above and residential below. South of the freeway was nothing but farms and forests. "Future factories for the deaf" Lyson had written neatly in purple felt-tip all along the southern margins of the freeway from river to river. Lyson's eyes glittered as he pointed out that hearing people driving by on the freeway would be certain to see huge signs proclaiming deaf proprietorships.

Mary sighed with the exasperated weariness of futility.

Lyson gripped her shoulders and cried aloud, "Look!" The business district of Suffex was very small, only some eight blocks deep, wedged between the rivers on either side with the university on top at the very apex of the state of Islay. Right where Lyson thought it appropriate, above it all, above the baser strivings of commerce and government. A businessman had a problem, he can look up to the university for the solution, can't he?

Mary shut her eyes and nodded irritably, *Of course, of course.*

Now, see the business district sprawls from Second through Ninth Street where now the long narrow park begins. Then the residential area from Tenth down to Thirty-Sixth Street, after which begins the greenbelt along the freeway. That is why when you pass through Islay on the freeway you never notice anything but trees and trees. See?

Mary wanted to scream. To stifle which, she covered her mouth and chin, assuming the proper appearance of active interest. She had to, of course, under these circumstances, what with Lyson being hyper and Mortima's deceit.

To aid the north and south movement of traffic, Lyson enthused, the streets running up and down were named after the letters of the alphabet. Less confusing, see?

Mary lost control over her mouth and it opened crudely in a yawn.

Listen! Lyson beseeched with his fists. *Two and only two streets cross park strip, But look!* His palms came together as in a prayer, and he continued, *See this: the most important street, north-south Central Promenade.* He pointed out its name on the map. *It can't cross park! Why? See Bandstand right-there. It's so—it's so—*

Mary couldn't help but collapse at the idiocy of the whole plan. She huddled over, hugging herself and burying her face in her lap, her shoulders bouncing in little spasms. Lyson was mystified. *Don't cry, Mary!* he begged, caressing her back. But then he realized the spasms were not exactly the crying kind. He turned from the table in a sulk, slapping his head.

He slapped his head again. A prophet had no honor in his own house, he was telling himself, when Mary finally composed herself and tactfully covering her mouth, nodded at the dollhouse.

Lyson glared at the dollhouse. *That's bandstand,* he said testily, *not dollhouse.* His teeth bared, his hands twisted into claws, he lunged for the bandstand with the obvious intent of wrecking it. Mary grabbed him and pushed his head down where she knew he could best be calmed, against her softness, against the softest of the soft comforts of the earth, where men are most at peace. Holding Lyson she thought about male baboons who on a rampage could be instantly pacified by females moving backwards, on all fours toward the males, as to defuse the males' rage quickly before anybody got hurt. After a little while Lyson relaxed enough in her arms to be safely released. *Sorry, didn't mean-to—*

Oh that's all-right, he sighed with the air of a man who knows he's beaten. *After-all, perhaps you're right. From different perspective, from outside looking in, it probably does look like dollhouse.* He gave the bandstand a sidelong look, the kind a man gives something that has badly let him down.

No, no, Lyson. Mary put his head back against her breast for another dose of softness and deep steady breaths so useful for restoring his well-being and self-esteem. Thought she to herself, nothing like breasts to bring a man to a good opinion of himself. She put a finger in his dimple. Lyson writhed like a quivering, trembling little dog and she giggled. Such a man, she said to herself, is docile, domesticated, and in the bag.

After a while, Lyson upped and paced around the State of Islay painted on the table, first one way then the other, all the while eyeing the bandstand. The knight on his Pegasus still reposed proudly, resolutely under the roof. Mary stared at it: she had never seen it before and could never have dreamt he'd have such a toy. She was about to comment on it but caught herself. Instead, she thought it better to be circumspect and ventured: *That's nice bandstand,* nodding pointedly at the shiny tin knight on its winged horse.

Yes! That's it! he reverently held his hands cupped above and around the bandstand, as if that would make it all that more significant. He was happy again and this showed in his gestures as he explained, *That's true very exact scale model of that one, I mean the real one over there Suffex, that one this map.* He pointed again at the red notation, Merry Bandstand, and opened *THE HISTORY OF ISLAY THE LITTLE STATE THAT COULD* where it had been opened many times, to a full page photograph of the bandstand. Mary compared the picture with Lyson's model, detail by detail but with some distraction as in the back of her mind she was still marveling how little it took to make Lyson so happy. After all, they're only blobs of fat, really that's all they are.

Marvelous, she nodded, *Make yourself?*

Lyson was happy now. *Oh no, myself not skilled making things you know that. My friend, you know Emil, himself carpenter, expert—*

Expensive? she began but quickly subdued herself.

Let me tell you interesting story, he stubbornly went on. *Know how happened, called Merry Bandstand? Governor Wenchell, himself Governor more than fifty years. Imagine! Lived nearly 100 years, apparently! Anyway, himself Governor, wanted name it bandstand, but Mr. Phelps thought pavilion better, more appropriate name. Governor's wife agreed with Mr. Phelps, said pavilion itself prettier name, means can-be used many purposes like parties, dances, theatre, rallies. But Governor Wenchell himself very stubborn, said better bandstand because if named bandstand would be largest in world. Pavilion can't be largest because many huge pavilions in South—*

Lyson stopped abruptly. He could see that Mary wasn't giving him her undivided attention: her eyes flickered ever so slightly to her left, uneasily sensing somebody but not quite certain who was there. They both turned and looked.

It was Mortima, her back pressing the door closed, her eyes wide and bright, her mouth moist. *Kept my promise one hour!* She signed the hour as if it had been the longest in her life. As soon as her finger returned to the noon position, she slipped her hands quickly out of sight behind her back, on the knob. Her expression was the sort, eyes shiny with anticipation, smile open but without showing the teeth, that gave the impression she expected, or more likely hoped for, some sort of reward, perhaps congratulations for keeping the secret so long, as promised.

Maybe Lyson was fooled but Mary saw the flush in Mortima's face.

CHAPTER 2

Down the freeway to Islay, Lyson drove along with what his eyes saw as hundreds of vehicles but what his mind perceived as millions bound for New York, all bypassing Suffex. He stayed in the slow lane on the right. If his new car was to be damaged, let it be minimized to one side, he anxiously thought. Besides, it is the king of beasts that moves slowly, deliberately, while the lesser, more nervous animals proclaim their inferiority by their frantic speed. And his Lincoln was a truly splendid automobile, with tremendous length and breadth, enhancing in his mind the space he allotted himself on the surface of the planet earth. He still marveled at how readily Mary's folks had come forth with the money. All he had to do was, at Mary's prodding, tell his dream, and the vault fell open. *That easy,* he shook his head.

At first Mary had resisted trading in their Datsun for the Lincoln but as she sank in those rich velvet seats and saw how they could be adjusted to various positions with a little switch, even being able to lower the back of the seat all the way down for a nap; and marveled at the sliding skylight, napkin dispenser, adjustable steering wheel, padded seat belts, map lights, cassette player—for Mary had a bit of hearing, enough to enjoy loud music. There was even stereo; outside mirrors adjustable with little levers inside the car; a battery of switches on the drivers side that controlled all the windows, door locks, even the trunk and hood; and also the amenities offered in the backseat: vanities, cosmetics, toiletries, and other goodies that overwhelmed the middle-class prudence instilled in her psyche by so many years of budgets. Even the ashtrays were roomy enough to serve as auxiliary glove compartments, but she exacted a concession from Lyson to never, ever smoke cigars, a practice certain to occur once his head swelled with the idea that he was an important man. He certainly could flourish a cigar all he wanted to but if he ever lit it. . . Mary did not need to spell out the consequences: the look in her eye said it all.

Yes, it would be a costly smoke, Lyson thought, as he rolled a cold cigar in his mouth, keeping his hands firmly on the glove-leather steering wheel and away from the lighters concealed in the ashtrays. There was relief though in the aroma of hot coffee, dispensed in the car, that somewhat helped alleviate the craving for the satisfaction that Lyson's firing up the cigar would give his new status. Another button unknown to Mary opened a secret compartment out of which slid a bottle of whiskey to spike the coffee for further gratification. He sat back and luxuriated in his new status as the great automobile smoothed the maddening, chaotic journey toward his destiny. He really believed, now that Mary's folks finally came through with the grubstake, that his dream was within reach, that he really could take over the State of Islay. So easy! He sucked happily on the cigar. Buy it all up, and—and—

A slight hitch on that journey: just a few miles before Fremont the Lincoln did what the Datsun never did—it ran out of gas.

What could be wrong? Lyson panicked as he pulled over on the shoulder. He surveyed the dashboard glowing with red warning lights: G-E-N, O-I-L, and G-A-S. Lyson slapped his forehead as he remembered the salesman warning that instead of a gas gauge, the car had an audible speaker that, upon pressing a button, called out the quantity of gasoline left in the tank. The speaker also shouted a warning whenever the tank was running low. Lyson recalled feeling some kind of noise on the back of his head a while back but thought it was from the roar of passing traffic. It never occurred to him, seriously, that the Lincoln could talk.

The automobile rocked from the passing traffic that seemed to burst out of his left and shoot down the freeway like tracer bullets. It was as if the world were passing him by, despite the fact he was right in the epitome of success as measured by his Lincoln. Lyson collapsed into laughter upon the steering wheel, rocking his head in his hands.

A little while later the giggles subsided enough for him to feel a strange, persistent buzzing. The horn! He was leaning on it! He sat upright immediately and was startled by a shadow close by his shoulder. A state trooper was peering through his window. The trooper was standing in a stance trained to perfection in anticipation of a fast draw. Bewildered, Lyson meekly raised his hands.

A stern look came over the trooper's features as he made almost imperceptible movements with his lips, movements impossible to read. Lyson sat up even straighter and made a helpless gesture, pointing to his ear and shaking his head. The trooper nodded in recognition and made a cranking motion, pointing to the window. Lyson groped for the crank, frantic that any delay in opening the window might strain the trooper's patience. The array of switches on the armrest reminded him that this was a Lincoln, not a Datsun. He fretted that his obvious unfamiliarity with the automobile would arouse unfounded suspicions in the trooper. With shaking hands, he fuddled with the switches. The hood startled both Lyson and the trooper by springing open. Finally Lyson hit the right switch and the window slid down in front of the trooper whose fists were now on his hips.

Lyson beamed and, with a finger in an ear, said, "Sorry but I'm deaf. I can't hear, understand?" He was careful and mindful how he pronounced his words. He had no way of knowing how the words came out, other than other people's reaction to them.

"I know," the trooper's head acknowledged while his fingers formed a square: "License."

In his haste to pull his wallet out of his hip pocket Lyson dropped it under his seat. "Excuse me!" He grinned sheepishly as he bent down, groping for the wallet among the machinery and wires that ran the adjusting mechanism under the seat. The thought that the trooper might misunderstand all this as an attempt to pull out a gun rattled him into a sweat. "Ah!" His fingers strained as they closed around the wallet. With a shaking hand, he surrendcred his license.

Satisfied that the resolute man in the picture on the license was indeed the same person as the one with the helpless grin in the Lincoln, the trooper held up an open hand: "Wait!" and went over to his cruiser behind Lyson.

In his rearview mirror, Lyson watched the trooper get into the cruiser, pick up a mike, and call out the details on the license and also the Lincoln's numbers. The blue lights above the cruiser flashed out a big lie about his predicament. Lyson adjusted the mirror lower to block them out. The stares from passing traffic, some accusing, others blank, but most of them mocking, brought down the sunvisor against the side window and kept up the hood. If I'm going to look like a man on his way up, I'm going to have to clean up my image, Lyson thought, as he felt the sweat on his face. A Swipe N' Dry towellete from the glove compartment helped freshen up his image, using it again to remove greasy fingerprints from the leather covering on the steering wheel. Don't be silly, Lyson grumbled at himself, hey, that suit on you is perfectly respectable. Why, it's practically government issue.

Yet, Lyson was worried. Why was the trooper taking so much time in handling this minor crisis? Lyson studied the trooper in the rearview mirror. But the trooper was just drumming his fingers on the steering wheel, while staring vacantly at passing traffic. He seemed to be just whistling away the day. What is taking so long? Lyson asked himself as he avoided watching the seconds flashing away on the clock. He almost thought he could actually see the shadows from the trees slipping along the grass as the earth rotated away the day, carrying Lyson toward the coming night and the day after, which would then leave him one day less than the number allotted to his days upon the earth.

An official-looking car with flashing red lights suddenly pulled in front of the Lincoln. Peering from under the hood, Lyson saw a man get out, wearing what looked incongruously to be a blue waitress smock, and walk up to the Lincoln, announcing by signs that he was an official interpreter of the deaf for the State of Transylvia, his job specifically to help the deaf communicate with the police. Lyson stared blankly at the interpreter.

Did you understand me? the interpreter asked, signing even more slowly. Lyson stared blankly at the signs so strange to the eye, because they were in the form of signed English, a form much easier for hearing people to learn since the signs follow the word order of English. However, to the deaf they are as confusing as a juxtaposition of Chinese characters and the Roman alphabet. Nevertheless, most hearing people choose to impose their language on that of the deaf rather than learn the mysterious and intricate grammar of the true Sign Language. So when the deaf are confronted with such weird signing, so jarring to the rhythm of the eye, they cannot help but be taken aback. Which explains why Lyson's mouth fell open and his eyes lost their focus.

The trooper came up beside the interpreter, jolting Lyson out of his daze. *Oh yes, I understand you,* he quickly signed. *I'm just surprised.*

The interpreter laughed. *That's O.K. Transylvia is the first state in the USA to have full-time interpreters on 24-hour call anytime the deaf need help with the police, ambulances, hospitals, psychiatrists—*

The trooper interrupted by saying something to the interpreter whose hands relayed the message, *"What are you doing?"*

I'm going to Islay, Lyson signed for the interpreter to relay to the trooper.

That's not what he meant, the interpreter signed the trooper's words. *Why are you parked here?*

Oh, I'm out-of gas, Lyson explained.

The trooper and the interpreter stared at Lyson and slowly exchanged embarrassed words with each other. The interpreter shrugged apologetically and signed, *We're so sorry at all this trouble. Please understand that we have to follow the state rules that the police have to call us whenever they meet the deaf—*

Oh, that's all right, Lyson signed grandly, *Just tell me where I can get some gas—*

Disappointment came over the interpreter as he said something to the trooper who immediately restored Lyson's license with apologies.

Fine, fine, Lyson signed diplomatically, *I'm glad that your state Transylvia has this wonderful service for the deaf.*

Good, I'm glad you understand, the interpreter signed, while talking simultaneously to the trooper who went to the trunk of the cruiser and came back with a can of gasoline. *He says he will give you one gallon. Should be enough to get you to the gas station at the next exit.*

The trooper called, and the interpreter requested of Lyson, *Please open the gas door.*

Oh! Lyson searched among the switches and pressed the lever marked GAS. *Thank you very much!* Lyson used both his hands to emphasize his gratitude. *By the way, what's your name? I'm Lyson C. Sulla from Washington, D.C.*

I'm Fred Wyler. Do you mind if I ask you why you are going to Islay? Nothing for the deaf there but Transylvia has everything—

Oh I'm just curious—looking around for fun, Lyson answered blandly.

That's funny, nothing there—rundown, population decreasing, really sleepy place—

Excellent! Better than I expected, Lyson chuckled to himself.

The trooper appeared beside Fred and said something, holding up a finger. Fred interpreted: *You now have one gallon of gasoline. Should be enough to get you to the next exit about 7 miles down the road.*

Thank you! Lyson exulted with both hands, *I'm real grateful.* He proceeded to start the Lincoln, which responded after a few cranks.

Fred and the trooper burst out laughing and noted Lyson's puzzlement. Fred said, *We can hear something in the car yelling One gallon! One gallon! Can you feel it?*

Now that you tell me, I feel something. Lyson patted the dashboard, searching for the source of the noise. *Can you tell me where it's coming from?*

Still laughing, Fred pointed at the radio speaker on top of the dashboard.

Yeah, I can feel it, Lyson said, putting his hand on the speaker. His hand studied the rhythmic pattern the sound made: three distinct syllables, with emphasis on the middle. *So that's how one gallon feels.*

Right! Fred signed, *So long!*

Lyson pulled back on the freeway gratefully and sped away with one hand on the speaker anxiously feeling its incessant warning. He glanced at the instrument panel and noted that the red light was indeed shining GAS.

"He's speeding, isn't he?" Fred said to the trooper as they stood watching the Lincoln zooming into the distance.

"Sure is," the trooper agreed.

"Well?"

"Well."

When the green exit sign appeared in the distance ahead, Lyson felt the rhythmic pattern on the speaker changing to four syllables. Must be saying one half gallon, he insisted to himself. He stepped harder on the pedal, urging the Lincoln on even while trying to hush the speaker with soft pats.

"Ah! We made it! Now you be quiet," he slapped the speaker as the Lincoln followed the ramp away from the freeway toward soaring oil company signs atop slender posts.

The speaker responded by changing its tune to two screeching syllables as he felt the power of the Lincoln collapsing. Shut up! Lyson beat on the speaker with his fist as the car coasted down the ramp. But the demon continued chortling "Empty! Empty!" No mistaking the nasty screeches.

His lip curling at the stop sign, Lyson urged the Lincoln off the ramp and onto the road toward the nearest service station, feeling the massive car losing momentum all too rapidly. They just made the driveway when the Lincoln finally gave out with its rear end still way out in the road.

Out of the service station came running the attendant yelling, "Shut up! I know you're empty! No need to tell me!"

Lyson stared at the man until he quickly realized that the infernal speaker was still on. He firmly turned the key off and noticed the attendant looking up at something behind the Lincoln. Lyson turned for a look too. There behind him were the flashing blue lights of a patrol car.

Another thirty minutes shot! Lyson sighed to himself and dropped his head on the steering wheel.

CHAPTER 3

Up a tremendous bridge the Lincoln soared high in a dizzying arc above Wrong Turn rippling far down. Far ahead and below, the forests of Islay suddenly unfolded before him. All that could be seen were trees and trees but Lyson was on the lookout for where Islay lay; and so saw it immediately, and whooped. There it is! He thrust a fist in the air but it knocked the rearview mirror silly. A glimpse of the Rhinns away to the south and, in an instant so quick he nearly missed it busy as he was trying to realign his rearview mirror, the Lincoln hurtled off the freeway down and around a loop, and he found himself on Wrong Road. Abrupt was this transformation: one moment borne along as in a school of sardines in the bustle, hustle, and rustle of an American freeway. The next, here he was all by himself on a rather derelict road in an overgrown forest. This road was barren and empty, and cracked all to pieces as mud drying in the sun—triangles and polygons ringed with weeds defiant against herbicides and bludgeoning rubber for the right to life in the cracks, however untenable may be such life. High grass unmowed, unbowed along the verges. Insects zipping across, some splattering the windshield.

Making a conscious effort at deliberate thinking, Lyson took note of business opportunities in the lack of businesses: not one service station to catch any car coming or going. Visions of the future suggested this thought: Hasn't anyone ever thought of a McDonald's? A long shot certainly, but plenty room for new ideas in my head, he congratulated himself. Good job, Lyson. He wished Mary were here to observe at first hand the sharpness of his mind.

A pothole struck suddenly and an awful clank jolted the Lincoln. He hit the brakes, but too hard, way too hard. He was used to the Datsun with its tin brakes. But the Lincoln was different, stopping and nosing over like a bronco that threw him forward into the steering wheel. Yet a few moments later, the badly bent steering wheel seemed to come to life, as it was literally designed to do, and it slowly straightened itself back in position under Lyson's astonished eyes and bruised chest.

"Thank God Mary isn't here," Lyson yelped to himself and was immediately ashamed to have taken the time and trouble to say aloud the obvious.

He got out of the car. There sat the pothole in the road, a faded black void in the shade of trees so that it was invisible to the unwary eye. It was deep, though, and a pile of gravel lay on its downside so that it was as nasty as any speed bump. No official markings or warnings marked it, though, for the motorist, and the asphalt on its upside sported heavy scratches and grooves. Lyson wagged a finger at the hole and uttered expletives entirely appropriate for the circumstance, and anxiously looked the Lincoln over for damage. The gas tank was all right, no dents or leaks. It was the bumper, though, the underside that suffered a depreciation of another thousand on top of the two or three Lyson himself only yesterday unwittingly inflicted on the new Lincoln by simply driving the new automobile off the lot and out among the vulgar.

His first day in Islay and here he was, no denying it, down on all fours looking under an automobile. He was visibly upset at this scenario.

Quickly before anybody saw, Lyson was back in the Lincoln, and in the space of a few short blocks the Lincoln sped out of the forest and into town. Another pothole and the Lincoln, bloated with gasoline and heavy on soft springs, very soft to accomodate the class of people for whom it was precisely designed, rose high in the air before slamming down again on the road. Detroit has had sixty, seventy, or is it eighty years of experience in automobiles, Lyson cried to himself, and yet they've not got it all—Another bump and banging steel. So much for experience: the more you have the less—Another pothole, this one worse than the others so that the automobile struck the road with such force his glasses nearly fell off. He slowed down, way down, and switched his concentration from Detroit to the reality ahead. And helped himself to a little bottle.

No more potholes now that he was in Suffex proper, although the road was still a mosaic of cracks, except that instead of weeds, grass—good and proper town grass—now filled the cracks. There was no traffic to speak of as the Lincoln went northeast up Wrong Road toward Suffex, following the bank of Wrong Turn. Along the left, a long narrow park fronted on the river, with tall unkempt grass and fine trees. Plenty of recreational opportunities along the greenbelt, Lyson grunted sagely to himself. On the right marched little homes, modest but a few rather nice. They looked to Lyson like real, heartwarming Tudor bungalows of the thirties: brick walls, steep roofs, asymmetrical gambles and oddly shaped porches. He thrilled at the profusion of For Sale signs, and noted the condition of the finely crafted woodwork around the doors and windows: they needed scraping, sanding, and painting. In other words, they needed people, namely deaf people, to fall in love with this town and stay forever. Almost a ghost town, he exulted, and again bumped the rearview mirror.

Soon a change in the road announced a different neighborhood: the cracks were now filled in with tar. Homes in Colonial and Georgian styles stood behind iron picket fences, among towering trees but marred by sentimental ornamental statues of angels, cherubs, virgins, and even satyrs playing fifes, artfully installed no doubt by interior decorators at studied locations on cultured lawns that had the appearance of Astroturf. He suddenly noticed: hardly any children at play and no people yet.

Then he recognized it. The park strip that marked the boundary between the residential and the commercial areas of Suffex. That park where the

Merry Bandstand lay so prominently in red on the map, the spot now rubbed pale by his finger! This fading of the bandstand on the map was disconcerting, almost as if his dream were fading away into the mists, right under his eyes. Anxiously, he followed Tenth Street down the park. Trees marched on and on, one by one: green foliage above and green grass beneath connected by dark trunks in a sea of pale emerald light so that the very air seemed different, cooler and heavier under fluffy green clouds of leaves. Still no people anywhere. Not a soul so far. The sun emerged at Grand Boulevard cutting to the north across the park, where Lyson could glimpse rows of buildings with canopies and awnings over storefronts, before the Lincoln entered the sweet green shade again. Another stretch of trees and the light changed again, this time lighter, more airy, a softer emerald.

There it is! Right there! White columns rising from an elevated platform up into the leafy overcast. Lyson stepped on the brakes and the Lincoln bucked in an abrupt stop. He waited for the steering wheel to realign itself as he looked furtively about; fortunately no audience had witnessed it. He was stopped right in the middle of where Central Promenade would have crossed the park but did not because of the Bandstand. To the south, opposite, he saw that Central Promenade was indeed by far the handsomest street in town—wide and elegant, divided by a long row of fine trees as far as the eye could see down the middle, with parallel rows on either side of the street so that a tree canopy met overhead in great arches. Quite reverent, almost cathedral. Homes along this street, what he could discern of them behind foliage, seemed grand too. No grass or weeds grew in this street, and no cars were parked along it either. Strange!

The steering wheel finally worked itself back in driving position and he pulled off and parked, his foot ginger on the brake. Tenth Street, said the signpost. Just as on the map! He consulted the map again and saw it was all for real. It was so easy to make Lyson happy again.

What happened next is the kind of thing that might someday be a source of debate, perhaps controversy, though maybe not so vociferous as the ancient one over the number of angels that could dance on the head of a pin. At any rate, biographers who admire Lyson no doubt would say he strode purposefully, resolutely up to the Bandstand in the teeth of a hurricane and bounded up the stairs two at a time and stood tall, fist on hip, fearless of the lightning zapping the lantern above, sending down showers of sparks. Historians who for some reason refuse to properly admire him would claim he actually danced, or more likely pranced about, rose in mouth, slow motion at that, something in the manner of chasing butterflies. Others with axes to grind would snidely report that he tripped over the curb and fell flat on his face, so euphoric was he. Gossips will whisper, he had to take a pee; the only possible spot was behind the Bandstand of all places. The only known potential witness that day was an old man in baggy black on a bench tossing nuts to squirrels and pigeons. However, he's not saying. Could be, he wouldn't want to admit having missed such a momentous event.

Never mind how Lyson got from the Lincoln to the Bandstand. What counted though was the atmosphere, the magical quality of the air, the light filtering through giant elms, a pale green, glowing translucence. His spirit so buoyant he had to watch his balance, he stared up, mouth open, hands on hip, at the interior of the lantern high above. Claims that a golden shaft of sunlight beamed down upon him from the lantern at that moment have been proven impossible given the angle of the sun. Lyson had to remove his spectacles and wipe his eyes for they had become misty. It was hot, he will tell you. Anyway, as he was cleaning his spectacles, he noticed through the blur a quivering all about, very much like a great mass of people waving and cheering. It was only a breeze coming up and stirring the leaves in the low green overcast, only slightly above eye level from where he stood high in the Bandstand. But Lyson liked the illusion better, and wanted to enjoy it so banished the glasses to his jacket.

There high in the Bandstand he stood, with his grin silly, revelling in the lovely blur made all the more delightful by the exquisite emerald light, thousands upon thousands of hands cheering him on, urging *Speech! Speech!* The grin spread ear to ear and his hands went up, even while his head bowed, calming the crowd. Leaves fluttering side to side just like the sign Speech! Speech!

Now here we begin new era for us deaf, his hands flew toward the leaves. *We ourselves deaf, now ourselves in charge!* An insect flashed by in front of his nose and he suddenly saw himself, what he was doing, and hastily put on his glasses, and glanced sheepishly about, his ears burning. Only the old man—his very first Islayer!—sitting on the bench tossing nuts to squirrels and pigeons was there, oblivious, it seemed to Lyson, to the beginning of such an important new era. Lyson studied him casually out of the tail of his eye and satisfied himself that the old man had never noticed a thing.

He now turned to the ceiling where the rafters swept up rising, curving to join together at the lantern high above, bright with sunlight from above the trees. Lovely! he thought. Golden light descending upon Lyson to merge so exquisitely with the emerald. Insects darting about led his eyes to the maze of spider webs and wasp nests infesting theceiling. A wasp dropped from a nest toward him, it seemed, and he beat a hasty retreat, stumbling down the stairs.

The steps of the Bandstand, because they faced north, also pointed toward the other end of Central Promenade that ran from the park through the middle of the business district of Suffex to its far end where the university stood. Rows of trees stood stiffly at attention along either side of Central Promenade as Lyson caught sight of some gothic-style building in the distance, barely visible beneath the trees. The university, he mused to himself.

Almost hidden by trees, on the left across Ninth Street, was the Capitol. Rather small it seemed, and insignificant, almost seedy with its dark red-brick walls and wooden window frames decorated with leaky, rusty rear units of air conditioners in the style so favored by maintenance men, the sort that favors gray khaki uniforms. Surprised, Lyson looked quickly to the right for the Governor's Mansion, but because of the trees could only see that the lower windows were similiarly decorated.

Lyson forgot to watch out for traffic as he crossed Ninth Street toward the Mansion but only one car came along. Just one car; even then it only narrowly avoided him. He never heard the nagging of the driver. She got furious and raised her voice but he was deaf. The shouts didn't go to waste, though: they caught the attention of a man rocking on the porch of the Mansion. A handsome mane of long wavy, silvery white hair blending grandly with his soft white cotton drill suit. Black string tie and alligator hide boots gave him a touch of wildness, enhanced by his craggy face and remarkable blue eyes.

The wicker rocker stopped as the man watched Lyson walking slowly, pausing now and then, mouth agape, head thrown back in awe, up the walkway toward the mansion. He noted the shiny dark-blue suit and the baby-blue necktie on the starched white shirt. A flash betrayed a diamond tie pin. Such an outfit meant one and only one thing: such a man could not possibly be up to any good whatsoever. As Lyson came to stop, his head still thrown back, directly under the porch, the man's hand slipped under the chair arm and pressed a button.

The mansion, Lyson noted, was a blend of French Provincial on the upper story and Colonial on the lower. Easier to remodel the Colonial part into the French than vice versa, Lyson was musing to himself, his hands clasped behind his back, when the door to the mansion opened and two men in business suits, in police blue, came out in that wary shuffle peculiar to lawmen and stationed themselves by the man in the rocker. All three stared hard at Lyson who almost whirled around and ran off but caught himself. He wiped his mouth with the back of his hand and was quick to spread his face in an innocent smile and show his empty hands. Pure instinct moved his feet forward in casual, almost carefree steps toward the three men on the porch. The officers patted the bulge of guns under their suits and visibly, though not quite entirely, relaxed. The old man lifted a finger in polite greeting as Lyson with slow, measured steps came up the stone stairs whereupon he was shown a wicker chair so located across a tiny round table from the old man that the message was clear: that chair was for supplicants. As Lyson sat down, he noticed all six eyes staring at his flashing diamond tie pin. He managed to suppress a reflex to cover the diamond. Instead, speaking very carefully, very precisely, he said, "Excuse me, but I'm deaf. Can you understand me?"

Blue eyes bored into the blank black eyes of Lyson as if dissecting Lyson's very soul, which at this moment was withdrawing, cringing within itself. The blue eyes saw all this and frowned. They turned their attention toward Lyson's ears. The man tilted his head for a better look, a more thorough examination of the supposedly deformed ears in question. Lyson could feel his ears getting warm and red, so he quickly diverted the man's attention by holding up a finger and pleading, "I'll write!" He reached in his coat for the pad and pencil he always kept for such emergencies. The other two men quickly reacted, reaching into their coats too but pulled their hands out empty when they noticed that the pen Lyson drew was indeed a pen. Just an ordinary pen.

"Excuse me! I'm not sure you understood my speech, but I'm deaf," Lyson wrote on the pad and handed it over to the man who, his blue eyes still fixed on Lyson, passed it on to one of the bodyguards with hardly a glance at it.

The bodyguard read aloud the note as the blue eyes reexamined Lyson's ears. The thin lips moved almost imperceptibly and the bodyguard took the pen and wrote on the pad in front of Lyson's eyes: "If you are deaf, why did you come to the Governor's Mansion? What is your business?"

"Oh!" Lyson said eagerly as he reached for the pad. But before giving back the pad, the bodyguard carefully tore out and kept the page already written upon. "I'm Lyson C. Sulla from Washington, D.C.," Lyson wrote hastily, shakily, "I wish to see the Governor."

The white haired man frowned as he listened to the bodyguard. They looked oddly at Lyson as they talked with each other, apparently trying to figure him out. Lyson struggled to keep himself from thrusting his hands between his thighs.

Finally, the bodyguard wrote, after tearing out the page with Lyson's name on it and pocketing it: "This is the Governor, His Honor Slappy Wenchell. Are you with the government?"

Yes! Lyson nodded eagerly but the exchange of guarded looks between the Governor and his bodyguards prompted him into writing: "I'm on vacation and here on my own time. Just visiting."

Oh! could be seen in their eyes as he watched the Governor say something for the bodyguard to write: "Pleased to meet you, Mr. Sulla. Would you care for a drink?"

Lyson nearly wrote that he had no time but thought better: "Yes, please. I'm much honored to meet you."

As they waited for the bodyguard to bring the drinks, the Governor stared rather speculatively at him, so Lyson wrote: "I realize we had a rather awkward beginning, and I must have given you some wrong impressions. While I'm really on vacation, I'm here to investigate—" the Governor's eyebrows shot up as the other bodyguard read over Lyson's shoulder, "—business opportunities—" the eyebrows relaxed a bit, "—in your fine state."

The first bodyguard soon returned with drinks and set them on the little table between Slappy and Lyson. The glasses were frost covered, and the lemon slices and mint leaves floating in the frothy pale-green liquid told Lyson the drinks were mint juleps. Didn't know the South came this far north, thought Lyson nodding to himself as he sipped the intoxicating brew. He bared his teeth, shook his head and shuddered. Delicious!

Rolling the liquor pleasantly around his tongue, he let the sensation trickle down his throat and spread slowly, gently throughout his body, just as an honest drink is supposed to. The Governor, his eyes closed, had his bodyguard write: "We are very pleased that you are considering our fine state as a place of opportunity—" He opened one eye to make sure the bodyguard was keeping apace, "—but we like it slow and quiet here." The eye opened again and fixed itself on Lyson. "We don't want no McDonalds, ya know." Aside to his aide he mused, "Won't mind a Dairy Bar though. Damn great shakes, don't ya tink?"

"Exactly! That's what attracts me here!" Lyson wrote slowly in response to the note, while his mind feverishly sought to think ahead. "I'm interested in the kinds of businesses that would fit in with this kind of state, make this a—" He almost wrote "better" but caught himself, "—state that continues its splendid tradition." He handed over the paper with shaking hands and hoped the men did not notice.

The Governor looked dreamily at Lyson while taking another leisurely sip—but the very calmness of his manner made Lyson gulp down his drink—and instructed the bodyguard to write, "The Bureau of Commerce is in the State Building right next door, down Central Promenade. They can do much more for you than I can."

Lyson jumped and thanked Governor Wenchell profusely, scribbling in parting, "I'm glad I stopped by. I really appreciate the delicious drink and your hospitality."

The Governor reflected, his brow crinkled vaguely, for a moment, then stood up with the tired ponderous dignity of an old man weighed down with the burden of state, and said through the bodyguard's pen: "You are most welcome. Come by whenever you have call for." And, for some unfathomable reason, he frowned uncertainly, looking intently into Lyson's eyes, then at his ears, while the bodyguard wrote his parting advice: "Maybe the Asylum for the Deaf and Dumb down at Crewe can help you learn to speak and read lips."

"Thank you! Thank you!" Lyson cried as he retreated down the steps and hurried down to Central Promenade and out of sight around the front of the State Building.

He stopped abruptly and slapped his head. My 14K gold pen! Still with the bodyguard! He rolled his eyes as his lips vibrated with a huge sigh. That was an expensive pen! But he decided to chalk it up as a business investment. Suddenly, he wondered if the Governor could read and write. Impossible! An illiterate in such an august position!

The Bureau of Commerce occupied a typical economy model government building, just plain brick with casement windows, without even rusting air conditioners to relieve the sweat of labor within. Thermometers, instead, hung at every window.

Cumulus clouds flying high overhead gave the illusion that the building was slowly leaning over him, threatening to fall down upon him. He shook his head and slapped his cheeks. That julep must be getting to me. He looked up again. A head was sticking out a window on the third story; the glare from the sky made the face indistinguishable but its attitude was inquisitive enough that Lyson quickly decided not to enter but instead hurried northward down the sidewalk, toward the center of the city.

As he reached the end of the block he couldn't resist peeking back. The head was no longer at the window. He blew and took off his glasses, and rubbed his face. It was beginning to feel numb from the mint julep. A look at his wristwatch advised him to call it a day. It was nearly four o'clock and already about time to be looking for a place for the night. Besides, he had forgotten to eat lunch. No wonder the julep acted so quickly and forcefully today, Lyson convinced himself.

There on a strange intersection in a strange city stood Lyson Cornelius Sulla trying not to take a misstep. He looked for and found the signpost. His inability to read the sign reminded him to put his glasses back on. In spite of the smears his nose left on the lenses in his effort at the correct placement of the glasses upon his nose, he was relieved to see the name Central Promenade on one of the signs. Holding on to the metal post, he steadied himself and leaned over to see that the other sign identified the cross street as Eighth Street. His brow knitted, he groped amid the mists of his memory to recall just where he had parked the Lincoln.

Ah, Tenth Street! he exclaimed to himself. Looking back down Central Promenade he recognized the Bandstand hidden among trees. But this direction led back under that face leaning down upon all who passed under. And just beyond was the Governor's Mansion. No way was Lyson going back up that street!

Holding on to the signpost, he searched through his memory for the layout of the city on the map still in the Lincoln. Lyson could only come up with one fact: to avoid retracing his path under that face and past the Governor, he had to go east on Eighth and he would find a safe detour to the Lincoln.

Bravely releasing his grip on the signpost, he staggered resolutely down Eighth Street. This new sense of purpose helped Lyson down the sidewalk, past a haberdashery, a shoe store that featured vinyl shoes, a greeting card shop, and a very narrow magazine dispenser. He came across Mick's Cafe. Gathering his breath as he felt the liquor vaporizing from his body he paused to notice that the door latch was genuine brass, smooth and shiny where hands naturally gripped it, but dark and dull otherwise. The door frame was of handcrafted wood whose grain rose in long, swirling ridges beneath fresh forest-green paint. The bevelled glass panel authenticated itself by its wavy, distorting surface. This solid but exquisite touch of reality made him feel better, and as he slowly opened the door, admiring its design, he sensed eyes upon himself.

The cashier, waitresses, patrons, even the cook all watched as he entered with a sheepish grin and looked around for a table. One waitress, with hair rolled in a bun but with enough strays escaping to soften her features, stared a moment but recovered herself and presented a menu on a table by the wall and pulled out a chair. Lyson managed to maneuver between tables, chairs, and other patrons without mishap and he gratefully lowered himself into the chair.

The nameplate on the waitress' smock identified her as Dottie. Amber and soft was her skin and her hazel eyes mirrored a kind soul. I came to the right place, Lyson congratulated himself as he could clearly read "Coffee?" on her lips so gentle and supple.

He nodded, "And water, please."

Lyson liked the lightness with which Dottie carried her soft figure as she retreated toward the kitchen. The menu said that today's special was breaded veal, boiled carrots, potatoes, and salad or soup of the day. And apple pie. A la mode of course. Mary would never allow such a dinner, but then he had not eaten lunch, he reasoned. Besides, he needed to dilute that julep.

The coffee tasted greasy but rather than complain and offend such a nice person, he drank the water instead. He was surprised at how clean it tasted, not like the heavily disinfected water of Washington, D.C. Dottie saw all this—indeed all the people in the cafe were fascinated by the spectacle of a foreigner so outlandishly out of his element—and brought tea in exchange.

"I'm sorry but something's wrong with the coffee—" she began, but Lyson did not seem to hear and busied himself with the tea. She tried once again; yet he didn't respond. Her hand flew to her mouth.

She inquired, as soon as he raised his head and looked full in her face, "Are you deaf?"

Lyson blushed, so much that she hastened to apologize, "Just wondering. It's just that—just that—" She threw up her hand then dropped it.

Lyson studied her eyes and saw they were honest, that they were in pain too. His shoulders rolled in a large shrug and he remarked, "I suppose my ears do look funny—"

"No, no," protested Dottie. "I was just saying something and you didn't reply, look up or anything—"

"No wonder."

"What?"

"I'm deaf, of course."

Dottie broke out laughing, Lyson laughed too. A good laugh makes a lot of things right, and Dottie exclaimed, "I think your food's ready!"

Lyson tore into his dinner, heedless of his mother-in-law's admonishment that people of consequence are known by their leftovers. Such was his pleasure in eating that Dottie forgot she was a waitress and sat with him and rested her chin on her fists.

Lyson pretended not to notice. Instead, he cleaned his plate with a piece of bread and gave out a belch. Heads turned and he giggled and ducked, holding up the glass of water as a toast.

Dottie smiled and he opened his mouth. But the Dr. Pepper clock on the wall reminded Lyson that he was to call his wife within the hour. It was time to find a hotel room and then make the call. Dottie brought the check and he asked, "Is there a hotel nearby?"

Dottie's eyes widened but the innocence in Lyson's huge eyes said: it was an honest question. "There's one around the block on Ninth Street in front of the park, right by the Governor's Mansion," she replied with an almost imperceptible tilt of her head.

"Oh thank you! I'm much obliged!" He put a twenty on the check and seized her hands. "Your service has been magnificent! You can be sure I'll be here again."

All eyes in the cafe followed his springy steps out the door. Once outside he headed back in the direction he had come from. Now that his body and mind were clear, the State Building with its face no longer held any terror for him as he sauntered by. He kept his head and eyes straight ahead as he passed the Governor's Mansion. When he reached Ninth Street he wanted to look for the hotel but decided to wait until he crossed the park strip and reached safety in the Lincoln. The Bandstand looked as magnificent as ever except that now the old man desecrated it somewhat by lying down in the center for a nap; his position, stillness and paleness, his hands folded over his heart, gave the impression of lying in state, and Lyson felt the hair on the back of his neck rise as he hurried toward the Lincoln.

The automobile was stuffy and hot as he got in; his face sweated and his neck chafed against his collar while he waited for the air conditioner to pump fresh cool air into the car. From the Lincoln he could see the ground level of the hotel across the park, standing out beneath the trees beside the Governor's Mansion. What a juxtaposition! He found it hard to imagine himself sleeping within a dream's breadth of the Governor's very bed; the awesome proximity. Snores echoing together.

* * *

Over in the mansion, in his office, Governor Wenchell watched through binoculars as the Lincoln pulled out and drove down Tenth Street toward the east. "Wonder what he's up to, now?" he said to the bodyguards breathing on his neck, jockeying for a peek through the binoculars.

"Want a tail on him?" one asked, his hand on a telephone.

"Wait. He's turning left on Great. Now he's coming this way. Oh-oh, he's parking in front of the hotel. Yeah, he wants a tail."

* * *

As he pulled up, Lyson had the distinct sensation of having arrived in a different era. The hotel facade was of light sand-colored brick and the central part of the building was recessed away from the street, creating a small courtyard over which arched a blue and white striped canvas canopy with the name Islay Hotel. At the sixth story, a balcony with concrete columns and guardrail ran entirely across the central indentation between the two wings. Must be the Presidential Suite, Lyson thought. The place looked like something out of a movie set in the Roaring Twenties as he carried his luggage through the brass-framed revolving door into the lobby, and he half-expected to encounter some flappers.

The rich pile carpeting yielded pleasantly beneath his feet. Habit instilled in him by his wife caused him to wipe his shoes as on a doormat. The light was soft and dim from the high bare ceiling, reflecting light thrown up from lamps hidden behind fern-leaf brass shades hung high on the walls all around the lobby, so that the light came down soft and not in the eyes. Rich dark panelling glowing softly with an oil polish that also gave off a pleasant scent, filling the room with an aura that reminded him of leather.

A hand tugged at the suitcase Lyson was holding and he tugged back angrily. It was only the bellhop trying to help. "Oh, excuse me!" he apologized sheepishly and relinquished his grip, offering also the smaller case in his other hand. "Careful, this one is fragile."

The stooped, old bellhop maintained his proud dignity as he bowed slightly, took the baggage, and nodded in the direction of the desk. The bellhop's face was pale, his skin thin and translucent, and his demeanor—through long experience—maintained the correct intimacy between guest and servant. Years of resentment at being treated as a mere pair of extra hands were buried deep in his joints, producing a permanent stiffness not only in motion but also in manner.

The clerk, of the same vintage, came out of the office, folded his frail hands upon the desk, and waited with patient, disinterested eyes, quite prepared to indefinitely maintain that position with the same calmness, stoicality as the potted palms in the lobby. The timeless dignity, the preponderance of polished brass in the ashtrays, spittoons, lamps, elevator doors, light switches, even the buttons on the uniforms, called for a certain dignity on the part of the guests as well.

Carefully and meticulously, the clerk studied Lyson's AmeriCard, even the reverse side as if he had never before seen such funny money. He was frowning to the point it almost seemed he was going to reject the card but he simply turned and went into the office. By shifting his weight from one elbow to the other Lyson moved to a position where he could observe the clerk at a desk pulling a telephone closer. That telephone must be an original fixture with this hotel! It was a pedestal type, with ivory base, earpiece, and speaker with shining brass trim. How exquisite!

Time passed but the clerk did not return and Lyson became uneasy. He shifted weight from one foot to the other, scrupulously for he could sense, out of the tail of his eye, the bellhop examining him from head to toe. The telephone reminded him that Mary was undoubtedly sitting by their telephone at home, awaiting the light on their teletyping machine to signal his faithfulness. Finally, the clerk put the earpiece on its hook, reexamined the card, scratched an ear, picked his nose, and returned to the counter. Only when he slid the registry toward Lyson and put out a pen, after first testing it on a scrap of paper, was it apparent that the card had passed muster.

While filling out the registry, Lyson sensed that the clerk was speaking to him. "Just a minute," he cried and, pulling out his pad, wrote: "Excuse me, but I'm deaf."

The clerk read the note very cautiously, looked up at Lyson's ears, and said something to the bellhop who also seemed to look at his ears, which by their expression they thought to be queer. Lyson sighed, suddenly very tired, bone weary, and took the pad back and wrote: "Kindly get me a room on the top floor, in the front, on the west side." A good view of the Bandstand! The Governor's Mansion too!

Reading the note, the clerk said something but his lips were unreadable, so stiff they hardly moved. So Lyson rolled his eyes and urged him to write on the pad. The clerk frowned, took the pen, stretched and positioned his writing arm, and wrote with the deliberate care of a traditional clerk, fidgeting his wrist between each stroke: "Bath?"

The elevator, probably because it too was old, took its own good time in lifting Lyson and the bellhop up to the sixth floor. He scanned the man's face as his mind silently yelled at the bellhop to hurry. Then in the room it seemed the man was too meticulous in setting his luggage in the dressing hall between the room and the bathroom, drawing apart the curtains, checking that all was in order with the room. Only after he was satisfied that all the ashtrays had matchbooks and that all the switches turned on lights and the television did he go to the door and hand Lyson the key.

A dollar bill shooed him away and Lyson could feel through the floor the rumbling of the elevator, as he eased himself into an ornate chair upholstered in pink flowery silk, allowing his mind to drift back in time, to a more leisurely and simple-minded era. The pleasant cream color and uneven stucco of the walls fitted in well with the florid furnishings and with the many panelled French windows on both sides of the far corner. Shedding his shoes, his feet luxuriated in the caress of the rich deep carpet. Yet he had never learned to simply relax, and jumped over to the windows to see if the view was as good as his guess.

From his vantage point on the 6th floor, Lyson could look down on the Governor's Mansion so far down below his feet that it was almost like a dollhouse he could tip over with a toe. The Capitol, dwarfed by trees lining the streets, seemed no more significant than the stores next to it. He opened the window for a better look to the north and saw that the walls of the State Building extended three or four feet above its black, flat roof. Newspapers, paper cups, candy wrappings, bottles, crumpled paper sacks, and other trash littered the roof. Perhaps the employee lunch room, he mused to himself, recalling the sterile cafeteria under a neon sky where he worked.

Trees seemed to be the principal feature of the city, as he leaned out the window and looked further to the north. Not that much of the city could actually be seen, so green and vibrant grew the trees. Chalk-green copper sheathed roofs of the university floated above the forest, marking the northern boundary of the state of Islay. Beyond in the haze loomed the great towers of Fremont, so soft in the waning light of the setting sun that they seemed to be in another world, another time, in the clouds. That's a fact, Lyson nodded emphatically to himself.

His gaze turned toward the south and it struck him funny that the Bandstand surrounded by its audience of rich elms, resembled a fur-ringed Mongolian war helmet. He compared the Bandstand with the Capitol, and smiled at his own opinion over which was the more appropriate seat of government. The great orange and red sun was melting liquidly into the horizon when he ended his reconnaissance of the city with a final look at the roof of the Governor's Mansion. A man was on the flat roof! By his stance he was obviously watching him through binoculars, his arms up at his face, elbows out. Lyson restrained himself long enough from ducking back into the room to pretend not to notice. A flock of starlings flew en masse like a cloud across the last of the sun's rays as Lyson craned his neck, pretending to search the dark blue sky tinged with pink for the first star of the evening. Only then did he feel it was all right to step away from the window.

How did they know my plot—I mean, plan? Lyson admonished himself as he paced the room. What did I do to tip them off? Was I so obvious? As ear plugs? How'd they even know my room?

He stared at the mirror over the dresser, sternly dressing himself down. His features slowly relaxed as it came to him that he was way too overdressed. Too many diamonds. Too shiny a suit. Too white a shirt. Too pretty a face, such cute chubby cheeks with darling dimples, almost cherubic, he chuckled at himself. That's right, mustn't scout too far ahead of the troops. He clicked his heels, saluted the way his President on television salutes the Marines when he gets off the helicopter shrugged, and went over to the bathroom.

Fortunately he had to pause to turn on the light before entering the bathroom because only then did he notice that the tiled floor was one step higher than the room proper. The bathtub on four leonine paws was huge and old-fashioned and stood apart from the walls. The toilet matched the general decor, with its tank hung high on the wall with an ivory handle dangling on a brass chain attached to the flushing lever. How quaint! Beside the toilet was a contrivance strange to Lyson but familiar to world travelers: a bidet. Must be an old fashioned urinal, he decided as he acted to get his money's worth out of this extra piece of plumbing.

Now how to flush this thing? A pair of enamel faucets at the rear of the bidet seemed the answer. Why two? Probably a convenience for left-handed customers, guessed Lyson as he leaned over and turned one on. A jet of water shot up in his face.

I've got to learn the ways of high class, he cried to himself as he dried his face, glaring at the bidet. The front of his clothes were soaked and a pool of water on the floor squished under his socks. A disheveled self grumped back at him from the mirror: So you thought you knew your way around. The Great Cosmopolitan Lyson C. Sulla of Washington, D.C., Center of the World!

A satisfying bath requires adequate prior strategy so after starting the water running in the tub, Lyson went to his suitcase for the whiskey. He filled a glass and, for want of a flat surface on the rim of the tub, set it in the soap dish recessed into the wall. Cheating a bit, he realized but nevertheless deciding that the circumstances justified it, he took a long swig from the bottle before tucking it away for the night. A capful of bath bubbles dashed into the rising water soon frothed into an airy white foam. But he hadn't noticed that while he was leaning over the tub, some more, quite a bit more, of the bubble liquid spilled from the bottle into the tub. He propped up *The Wall Street Journal* within easy reach on the floor by the bath mat.

He remembered the shampoo and went to the small suitcase. He opened it and found the teletypewriter. It glared back in the mocking way only a machine can muster. Forgot to call Mary! Lyson slapped his head, lifted the teletypewriter out quickly, and rushed into the bedroom, searching frantically for the telephone. The telephone was also a period piece, similar to the one downstairs in the office. He set the teletypewriter carefully on the table, and after a bit of searching found the outlet and plugged in. Then he recognized a problem: the teletypewriter was designed for the modern cradle telephone. He tried fitting the pedestal telephone on it and was relieved that it could be done though he would have to hold the speaker on the sending part of the machine while typing with his free hand. The earpiece of the phone could balance itself just fine on the teletypewriter receiver.

The teletypewriter is a marvelous machine, he thought to himself, that makes it possible for the deaf to use the telephone, though only if there also is a teletypewriter on the other end. Lyson's model had an additional feature: a small lamp originally designed to signal only sounds coming over the telephone but further developed to catch any sound reaching it such as knocks on the door, the crying of a wet baby, the sound of a smoke alarm and other supposedly useful signals. The only complication was that it also signalled the noises of passing traffic, airplanes, coughing, and other superfluous noises.

When Lyson turned on the teletypewriter, the light immediately flickered, announcing the presence of sound in the room though he had yet to dial the telephone. The big problem with this feature, he thought, was that it is sometimes too helpful in catching any and all sounds, making it difficult to interpret the signals over the telephone: perhaps a busy signal, a ringing, or people answering by voice. Maybe someone was at the door, he thought, and went to check. But there was no one, and the hallway stood empty throughout its entire length. Inside his room the light was still flickering irregularly. Ah! It's the traffic outside, he reasoned. He shut the windows and drew the curtains close. But the machine still blinked. He removed the ear piece from the receiver on the machine. The light winked, almost wickedly, maniacally mocking him. Lyson looked around the room, vexed.

A scent of soap bubbles brought a slap to his forehead and a rush for the bathroom. Soap bubbles frothing out of the bathroom floor onto the dressing hallway covered the step; he tripped over it and disappeared into the bubbles. He slid on his stomach beneath the bubbles over a pool of water and slid to a stop against the tub. His glasses slipped off into the foam. His eyes burning from the bubbles, he groped along the rim and found the faucets, shutting them off. For a long moment he remained kneeling in the bubbles, his head on hands still gripping the faucets, sobbing and giggling. Because his sense of balance was as nonexistent as his hearing, he kept a firm grip on the tub rim as he struggled to his feet on the slippery floor, his eyes shut tightly, his head swathed in bubbles. He tried to remember exactly where the lavatory was but could only remember the bidet. Don't step on the glasses! he reminded himself. He gingerly moved his toes along the floor, groping for the glasses, one hand steady on the tub, the other thrashing in the bubbles for the bidet. Ah! He grasped the bidet firmly and kneeled over, bracing his face, and turned the faucet.

The water was cool, refreshing, wonderful as he turned and twisted his head in the geyser, wallowing in the same luxury the French enjoy while using bidets the French way.

Drying his eyes, he noticed that the bubble foam was thigh high, higher over the tub. How to get rid of them? The problem irked him as he felt for his glasses in the bubbles. He just simply couldn't find them and had to content himself with the hope that at least they weren't where he could step on them. His clothes were soaking wet and he struggled out of their wet grasp, thanking Mary for having insisted on drip-dry material. He wanted to call her but decided to get the bath over and done with before something else happened and he ended up in the soap all night. He lowered himself into the tub, unmindful of the water pouring over the rim unto the floor. The hot, caressing water soothed his battered ego as he played with the floating foam, blowing grooves in it, carving his name and drawing pictures. He remembered the glass of whiskey. It seared away the soapy taste from his mouth and gave a satisfying palatable aroma as he exhaled through his nose. He held the glass up to the light, admiring the ethereal amber color of the liquor and then in one swoop drained it, wincing deliciously, shivering, baring his teeth, reveling in the sensation of a flaming fireball sizzling, sinking down his throat. He lay in a happy stupor in the tub, senseless but quite luxuriant in the weightless comfort of the warm water and the tingling of the whiskey through his bloodstream.

As the whiskey reached his nose and toes, setting them atingling, he opened his eyes and remembered Mary. The water was cooling, losing its zest so he reluctantly heaved his sluggish body out of the tub. Having already soaked the two bath towels, he was dismayed to find only the washcloths and face towels still on the rack still dry. He dried himself the best he could with these tiny pieces of cloth and threaded his way through the condensing, sticky foam to the dressing room. The carpet was wet there too but fortunately not in the room proper. He moved his luggage beside the bed and slipped into pajamas, robe, and slippers. Now I'm ready to call Mary, he decided.

He sat down on the chair and prepared to dial the telephone. But he could barely make out the numbers without his glasses. Squinting and looking closer, he could just make out their forms, so he went ahead and dialed the number. The lamp flickered with just one ring before Mary started typing. Lyson never failed to marvel at the green letters streaming across the display board of the teletypewriter.

MARY HERE GA.

HI. LYSON HERE ISLAY HOTEL ROOM 628. HOW ARE YOU Q GA.

LYSON WHY YOU LATE CALL ME Q GA

STOP MAD AT ME PLEASE—

I'M SORRY CANT HELP IT WORRY AND WAIT AND WAIT FOR FOUR HOURS GA.

FORGIVE ME BUT CANT HELP VERY BUSY DAY. VISITED THE GOVERNOR AND THEN HAD IMPORTANT DINNER AND THEN CRAZY BATH—

Mary interrupted again: CRAZY BATH WHERE Q GA.

MY HOTEL ROOM. HAD A LONG BATH. THOUGHT ABOUT YOU ALL DAY GA.

The teletypewriter was silent for an unconsciounably long time before Mary typed: STILL CANT UNDERSTAND WHAT YOU MEAN, CRAZY BATH. GA.

WILL EXPLAIN WHEN I GET HOME —

YOUR FAMOUS ALWAYS EXPLAIN EXPLAIN. AND WHY NOT YOU CALL BEFORE DINNER Q GA.

I DID TRY TO CALL BEFORE DINNER BUT GOT LOST —

WHAT YOU MEAN —

Lyson cut in: WILL TELL YOU WHEN I GET HOME GA.

OK SURPRISED YOU FOUND HOTEL OK. AND SURPRISED YOU ALREADY VISIT GOVERNOR. GOOD Q OR BAD Q GA.

REALLY JUST HAPPENED. ACCIDENT. HARD TO SAY IF IT WAS GOOD BUT DONT THINK ANYTHING BAD HAPPENED —

LYSON YOUR WAY FAMOUS ALWAYS ACCIDENT. WATCH YOURSELF GA.

I KNOW, CANT HELP —

WHY CANT YOU KNOW —

SORRY—he butted in, exasperated at the inquisitive way of women.

MAYBE I SHOULD GO UP AND TAKE CARE OF YOU BEFORE SOMETHING HAPPENS GA.

SWEET OF YOU. I WOULD LIKE THAT BUT I AM OK AND LETS WAIT A FEW DAYS UNTIL—Lyson paused, trying to think of a good stall.

YOU DONT WANT ME WITH YOU, IS THAT WHAT YOU MEAN Q GA.

NO NO NO I MEAN UNTIL I FIND OUT IF THIS STATE IS A GOOD IDEA. ABOUT TWO DAYS THEN DECIDE IF I GO HOME OR IF YOU COME HERE. MISS YOU GA.

OK BUT PLEASE BE CAREFUL, THINK TWICE. MISS YOU TOO GA.

YES LOVE GA OR SK.

LOVE YOU, BE GOOD, SK.

SKSK. He hung up, and an awful shame came over him how he handled the call with his wife. Poor Mary. To shunt aside the shame, he assigned himself the task, before turning off the teletypewriter, of studying its little lamp. It flickered very dimly, barely perceptible. Must be people next door. Could be, he shrugged as he crawled into bed and found the whiskey under the pillow. He couldn't remember ever putting it there but decided to seize this fine opportunity to take a long, lingering sip. Almost immediately he dropped off into the deep sweet sleep of the innocent, hugging the bottle.

* * *

In the next room the second bodyguard pulled out the ear molds, rubbed his ears, turned off the tape recorder, and pursed his lips grimly while dialing the telephone.

"Hello this is Agent P-51."

"B-52. Bombs away."

"Bet this Sulla is a Fed."

"No doubt. Caught him plain as day spying on the Mansion. Any blips?"

"Yeah, taped the whole thing. Uses a coding machine over the phone."

"Indeed?"

"Indeed. Want to hear it? All funny little clicks. Weird. Kinda spooky."

"Take it to the lab. See if they can't decode it."

"Will do. Another thing: the clerk said the call was to Washington."

"That's it! Anything else?"

"Oh yes, I'm sure he knows I'm here —"

"Idiot! What makes you think —"

"He left the water running a long time. Many strange sounds, kinda crazy. Also he checked the door —"

"You imbecile! You'll have to pull out."

"I'm sorry, B-52, I can —"

"Shh! Not so loud! He might be listening!"

"But he's deaf —"

"Bull!"

CHAPTER 4

Usually Lyson rose with the sun, but this morning he was startled that the light behind the drawn curtains glared with the intensity of full daylight. Impossible! He threw back the bed covers and looked around for his wristwatch. He found it on the suitcase and saw that it was 8:33 A.M. Tuesday the 8th. Can't be! He pulled open the curtains and had to admit to himself that two hours and thirty three minutes were forever, irrevocably lost to his life.

On the double! Grabbing his electric razor and toothbrush, he hurried to the bathroom. The soggy *Wall Street Journal,* the sticky floor under his feet, and towels heavy with water reminded him of the great bath fiasco of the night before. A quick search uncovered his glasses under the tub, covered with sticky, drying residue of the bubbles. He washed the glasses and his face too. He had to use his pajama top to dry them. A toothbrush could be rushed, but not the electric razor and he fretted over the ticking minutes as he mowed his jaw with the old grinder.

Mary had insisted on packing his suitcase for him, imperiously contending that she knew best. The suit she'd packed for him was exactly the same as the other one, to avoid clouding any impression that Lyson was a solid stable predictable respectable reputable republican citizen that could be absolutely trusted with an investment or, at worst, a vote. "Dear Mary, this is Suffex, Islay, not Washington, D.C.," he cried aloud as he rummaged through the luggage for a shirt that was not so glaring white and stiff. But Mary had seen to it that he had no choice in the matter so he reluctantly arrayed himself in the best Washington, D.C. style. Even the tie was an indistinguishable twin of the other one now drying over the lamp. An uneasy thought intruded that people would think he never bathed, never changed clothes. The diamond tiepin and cuff links were now drab and sticky, and quickly relegated to their little velvet box. He picked out gold-plated ones shaped artfully in the form of the letter S. Before leaving the room, he hesitated whether or not to take the attache case Mary had insisted on packing along with the underwear. Too Washington, D.C., he decided, and opened the door, remembering just before the door closed that the keys were in the other pants.

Sighing over his own absentness, he went back to the dressing hallway. From the soggy suit, he retrieved the keys, small change, comb, penknife, nail clippers, and nail file all sticky from the bubbles, and rinsed them out in the sink. The note pad, cigars, Vick's inhalant tube, matches, rabbit foot, Q-tips, and other assorted pieces of papers, important or not, would have to be dumped in the trash. He absently tossed them into the bidet. Fortunately, his billfold wasn't too badly off and was easily wiped clean with dampened toilet paper. What a night! Satisfied that he had overlooked nothing in the pockets of the old suit, he impulsively rolled it into a ball, tying the old tie around it. Guilt so well ingrained in his psyche by his mother and Mary over the mess of his own doing was relieved by a twenty dollar tip on the bed for the maid.

By the elevator he found a trash chute. Down went the suit and he nodded sharply to himself, dusting his hands. While waiting for the elevator, he examined his image in the polished brass doors and realized he'd forgotten the belt on the old pants. He quickly opened the trash chute and stuck his head inside to see if maybe the bundle could be retrieved. But the chute disappeared into the black depths of the hotel. Before an idea had a chance to occur to him that he could go down to the basement, a clanking noise jerked his head out and he found himself face to face with the bellhop already holding open the elevator doors, waiting with a ponderous frown, pretending not to have noticed.

"Oh, hello!" Lyson smiled lamely as he ducked into the elevator. "Nice hotel, eh?" As the elevator creaked slowly down, he stood, his hands clasped behind his back, rocking nervously on the ball of his feet, silently urging the elevator down faster. The bellboy, one hand on the lever, the other remaining on the cage handle, kept his demeanor correct and proper, closely watching the descent as if he had to constantly keep cognizant of their exact position like an airline pilot on instrument approach in a fog.

At the desk Lyson greeted the clerk with the straightest face he could muster and wrote a note: "I shall be staying at least two more nights and am very sorry about the mess in my room. Please have it cleaned. If there is any damage I will gladly pay for it."

Handing the note to the clerk he decided it would look better if he did not wait for a reply but left with purposeful strides. The clerk looked up from the note and watched over his glasses as Lyson escaped through the revolving door. Then he shuffled to the office and picked up the telephone: "Go ahead and clean out Number 628."

* * *

Agent P-51 took a quick glance down the hallway and, with the help of a master key, slipped quickly into Lyson's room. The first thing to catch his eye was the teletypewriter on the dressing table. It had a look of high tech about it, like something out of a James Bond movie. Warily, his heart pounding, he studied it from one angle, then another, taking care not to leave any evidence of his fingerprints. The name on the machine "SILCOM" was eagerly recorded in his notebook as were the various numbers on the reverse side. He noted that the keyboard was just like a regular typewriter, though smaller. He carefully measured its dimensions with a cloth tape, drawing the machine to scale in the notebook, with drafting skills of which he was very proud. He was tempted to try out the thing but was restrained by the idea it was Federal property. It might even sound an alarm and bring in the Feds. A few pictures at various angles with his Minox, and he figured he got the machine down good. A spy gadget if he ever saw one, he professionally concluded.

The suitcase proved disappointing and inconclusive except for the whiskey. It was very good whiskey. He couldn't fault Sulla his taste in whiskey. But the Sears/Roebuck underwear proved, he sneered, that Sulla was all appearance without substance. However, the attache case offered proof of the treacherous sort needed to satisfy the Governor's hunch. Kneeling on the floor in the light from the windows, P-51 pulled out incriminating evidence: application forms from the Small Business Administration, Departments of Health and Human Services, and Commerce; and the clincher: Geopolitical Administration for the States. "GAS!" he roared in triumph but then immediately hushed up. No knowing if there's a bug in that machine. He glanced apprehensively at the teletypewriter but it just sat there mutely, almost as if pretending to ignore him. His hands trembled as he arranged the incriminating documents in the sunbeam on the floor for picture taking.

His hands were shaking, so anxious was he that the pictures turn out clear and sharp for the Governor's perusal. He had to steady the Minox on the back of a chair. After the last picture, he realized he couldn't remember the order the papers had been in the attache case. Too late now, he grimaced as he reshuffled them the best he could back into the case and wiped off possible fingerprints with his sleeve.

Gotta scram, he urged himself as he hurried his eyes around the room. The twenty dollar bill on the bed caught his hand just as the door opened.

"Evidence!" he blurted out as his eyes met the startled eyes of the maid.

"Excuse me!" she apologized as she started to back out of the room.

"No, don't go!" P-51 quickly reassured her, waving his hand, afraid she might think it unnecessary to come back and clean the room, which surely would arouse Sulla's suspicions.

The maid stared indignantly at his waving hand. He followed her stare and his neck turned red when he realized he was waving the twenty.

"Ah-uh, this is your tip." He thrust the bill in her hand as he bolted out of the room. "Sorry 'bout the mess!"

She held the twenty away from her person like a worm and looked around. The mess in the bathroom was absolutely appalling. "No wonder!" she hissed as she reexamined the twenty and shoved it into her blouse. "Pig!"

* * *

Lyson was happy to find Dottie on the job when he reached Mick's

Cafe. The manner by which she greeted and seated him at the same table gave him a feeling of being an accepted, regular patron. It felt nice.

"You shouldn't tip so much," she scolded him as she opened the menu on the table. "This breakfast is on me," she insisted, her eyes round.

"I—uh," he blushed, "I didn't mean—I mean—I just wanted to express my—"

"That's all right." She patted his shoulder. "Just don't do such a naughty thing again. Coffee? It's good this morning, I cleaned the pot myself."

"Yes, please." Lyson had yet to get over his amazement at the clarity of her lips, and her grace.

"May I recommend Number One, there?" She pointed at the menu where Mick's #1 was displayed in an appetizing picture of fried eggs, bacon, toast, hash browns, orange juice, and steaming coffee.

"Great! Over easy, please!" Then he added, "And apple pie! A la mode of course."

"Good! Now don't run off on me," she teased him and went to the kitchen. Lyson noticed that, aside from a couple of men deep in discussion over cups of coffee at the counter, he was the only customer. Dottie returned with two cups of coffee and took a seat across from him. This informality surprised but very much pleased him.

"What's your name? she asked. I'm Dottie Smida."

Lyson was captivated by her eyes as she sipped her coffee with both hands, looking up at him in that strange and unfathomable inquisitive way of women. But then he remembered Mary and groaned aloud to himself, "Mary!" Dottie's eyes widened. "Oops! I mean, I'm Lyson Sulla," he chuckled weakly, "Mary's my wife."

"Oh," her eyes rounded again. "Pleased to meet you. What brings you to Suffex?"

"Thinking of moving here," he said carelessly, and immediately regretted it.

"Really!" Her eyes were so warm he felt much better, less of an indiscreet fool. She cocked her head, "Why?"

Before he could get his brain and mouth together, he blurted out, "I guess it's because I'm deaf." Her wrinkled brow was touching, he thought, and he hastened to add, "It's a long story."

"Your coffee is getting cold," she urged with that amused look that he liked so much.

"That's right!" He sipped the coffee, frowning pensively, wondering how to best get his brain and mouth together.

Dottie rested her cheek on her hand. "Is it bad?"

"Oh no, no," he apologized, quite unnecessarily, "just thinking, I mean I'm thinking."

"So you're deaf. What about it?" She softened her gaze as if to say it would be safe to open up, to tell all. "Is that what brings you here?"

Lyson studied the rich brownish-black depths in his cup and looked into her eyes. "Well, let's face it. When us deaf are among our kind, we don't of course forget we're deaf—We just don't think about it, dwell on it—it's just that we feel normal among ourselves. Nobody is around to remind us—" he blushed at how easily the warmth of a woman's eyes could elicit a confession out of him, out of his secret self. "Nobody to make us feel—feel—" He made a rolling gesture. "I think you know what I mean."

Her eyes seemed on the verge of melting: "I think I do."

"Is it my voice—" Lyson smiled wryly, "—or the words you understand?"

"That's all right," she patted his hand. "I understand you both ways. The cook is calling."

Dottie returned with the breakfast on a tray, setting it with a flourish in front of Lyson. He hugged his hands between his thighs, sniffing in the aroma of freshly cooked breakfast. "Mmmmmm—"

Suddenly, out of the bright blue she fingered his dimple. "Actually, I can understand your voice just fine."

Lyson tried to chew and grin at the same time and held up a finger as he washed down his cud with coffee. "That's nice, Dottie, but the trouble is, we deaf never know for sure: you see, to most hearing people, our speech—quality, pronunciation and all—can be very foreign—very strange indeed—" He whirled a finger around an ear, "You see, we can't hear our own voices so we can never really know what people—the hearing—think."

"Lyson, your speech is good enough for me—"

"Thank you, Dottie. Thank you, but there're only a few people like you who are open—who keep their ears open and clear of wax—"

Dottie laughed, "I can believe that!"

"Yeah." They both laughed.

She sat back and reflected for a moment, studying him, and said, "You must be a busy man. What do you do?"

"Officially," Lyson finally said, "I work at the Bureau of Statistics, button pushing, counting pencils and paper clips;" he threw up his hands. "Now it all seems unreal, just numbers." Now that he'd said it aloud, it indeed seemed all unreal, as if he'd never ever worked there at all, as if all these years had never occurred, never existed. Such a waste!

Dottie sympathized: "You look tired of it all."

"Indeed I am," he nodded. "All those millions passing under my fingers, none sticking." He brightened: "That's why I'm here during my little government-issue vacation."

"You hope to make your million here?" she asked dubiously.

Deftly changing the subject, he inquired, "What about you?"

Leaning back in her chair and cradling her cup as if warming her hands, Dottie looked out the window at the leisurely pace of Suffex, and said with a bemused smile, "I came here to find my fortune." They both had a nice, warm laugh. "Not really. I just wanted time out from the mainstream, to think, to enjoy myself and my son, to—" she sighed, "find myself."

Lyson sipped his coffee thoughtfully, and said, "That's more than I can say about myself, always too busy to look for myself, let alone try to find myself." He paused reflectively, and continued, "I must congratulate you. I think you've found yourself."

Dottie searched his face for signs of deceit, and saw none. "What makes you think so?" She smiled shyly.

He could not conceal the smile in his eyes under his solemn outer expression. "You're not afraid to be nice, to please people," he said simply.

"Oh!" Dottie giggled. "Bosh!" She refilled their cups and they sat back, sipping coffee, basking in the wonder of how enjoyable their little chat had been, the sudden marvel of it all.

"This name of yours, Smida," Lyson finally asked in all innocence, "is it Italian for Smith?"

Dottie burst out laughing, burying her face in her hands, rocking in her chair, shaking her shoulders so hard Lyson feared she was sobbing her heart out. The other people in the cafe turned and stared, laughing at Dottie. Lyson glared back: Not funny!

"Dottie!" he cried, "Please don't cry. I didn't mean to hurt your feelings. It was not a joke. Believe me please."

Still laughing helplessly, Dottie raised her eyes above her hands and saw Lyson's confusion and chagrin. Keeping one hand over her mouth she gripped his hand with the other. He realized she was laughing, not crying, and he sighed with enormous relief. "You're too much!" she exclaimed, squeezing his hand as she arose. "Excuse me." She disappeared into the ladies room.

Lyson, left alone with his thoughts, stared at his coffee before sipping it. He looked up and caught the stares of the others in the cafe and bowed his head with great dignity. Embarrassed, the other people nodded in acknowledgement and turned away.

When Dottie returned, he stood up. "You've been wonderful to me, so wonderful I could stay all day, but I must get going. I'll return this evening. Will you be here?" he asked nervously.

Dottie blushed, yet she couldn't resist fingering his dimple. "Of course I'll be here. I enjoyed talking to you so much." Quickly she restrained his hand as he tried to pick up the tab. "Not this time, please!"

"Oh, thank you very much! See you!"

"Take care! Tonight!"

Lyson went out through the door, and as he jaunted toward the Central Promenade he waved at Dottie through the window. Her wave was so tiny, so fragile, his throat caught as he turned the corner. Suddenly he stopped to look at his watch. He slapped his head and hurried away.

* * *

Governor Slappy Wenchell's nap out on the porch was disturbed when Agents B-52 and P-51 brought in the freshly developed pictures. He grumbled, "You disturbed my mediation for this?" and picked up the pictures with an impatient jerk. He examined the pictures but sneered, "They look fuzzy to me. Some photographer you are."

"Your Honor," Agent P-51 blanched. "I'll get the magnifying glass." It was an unspoken secret that Slappy Wenchell needed reading glasses but would never admit so. He thought the magnifying glass was a magnifying glass but Agent B-52 discreetly had the lens exchanged for a reading lens, optically corrected for Wenchell through much trial and error.

"Here it is." Agent P-51 returned with the lens. "The pictures are clearer up close."

"Indeed they are," Slappy Wenchell frowned, examining the pictures closely. "These are incriminating evidence as any I ever saw. A Fed for sure."

"Here," P-51 pointed eagerly, "See this, Geopolitical Administration—"

"GAS," the Governor said tersely, as if it explained everything.

B-52 elbowed P-51 aside and put another picture under the lens. "See this coding machine for secret messages he uses over the telephone."

"What's this?" the Governor asked, trying to read the trademark on the front of the machine.

"SIL-COM," Agent B-52 read aloud.

"What could that be?"

"Most likely Silent Communications," volunteered Agent P-51.

"That does it!" the governor roared. "Arrest him immediately!"

The bodyguards traded glances and Agent B-52 said gently, "I'd like to, but there's no law against Federal Agents."

"Oughta be!" Slappy snapped, and reclined in his rocker, thinking. "We can't let him snoop around."

"Don't worry," Agent B-52 soothed him. "We'll get him one way or the other."

The Governor nodded. "Be sure you do. But first give him enough rope to hang himself."

"Certainly!" Agent P-51 eagerly promised. "We'll make tapes of all his phone calls and I can replay them on his own machine—"

"Good idea!" Wenchell brightened. "Just like dear old Richard Nixon."

"But first we gotta play him, then net him," cautioned B-52.

Governor Wenchell put his feet up on the table and declared, "That's what's meant by, Use Your Smarts."

* * *

On entering the State Building, Lyson confronted a dim hallway running straight through the building to the very rear, where a door with a frosted glass window glowed as at the end of a tunnel. Hardly enough light for Sign Language, he mused, as he noted that the bulbs in the ceiling were either broken or turned off in compliance with some Federal energy measure. The musty odor, the rows of doors with little signs above them, beyond the reach of aspiring graffiti artists, the linoleum floor, the pale green paint work all reminded him of his old school. He searched near the entrance for the building directory, but there was none. Going down the hall, he examined the little signs. State Treasury. Education Bureau. Roads and Sidewalks. Vehicle Registration. Bureau of Control. Investigation. Then he saw the Tourism and Public Relations Office. Ah, maybe this one will help.

Lyson gingerly opened the old wooden door, its squeaking loud and grating to his hand. Inside was a balding middle-aged man in the process of stuffing a magazine hurriedly into a drawer in his desk. The office was narrow and long. Only one desk, a pair of filing cabinets, and a brass spittoon. The lone window faced a brick wall—the Governor's Mansion! All around on the walls were pinned travel posters. The Washington Monument. Florida. Bahamas. New York City. The French Quarter in New Orleans. The Golden Gate. Anything but Islay. On a nail hung the man's suit jacket. It looked like it had been hanging there since the fifties. By the desk rested an old ponderous wooden chair, its varnish fading and splotchy.

"Excuse me!" Lyson apologized as he sat down.

The man said something but Lyson again said, "Excuse me, but I'm deaf," and fumbled in his pockets for the pad and pen, right then remembering the pen was still with the Governor. The man stared at him, following the course of the hands under the jacket. "Lost my pen," Lyson smiled hesitantly.

"Oh!" The man opened a drawer and after a bit of rummaging found a wooden pencil and a piece of stationery.

"My name is Lyson C. Sulla from Washington, D.C." Lyson wrote. "I'm interested in Islay. Do you have any information on your fine state?"

The man held the note, adjusting it up and down so that it could be focused through the correct lens in his trifocals. He looked up at Lyson, shot up his eyebrows inquiringly, and pointed to his ear.

"That's right, I can't hear," Lyson acknowledged, pointing at his own ear.

Taking the pencil from Lyson, the man wrote, "What specifics are you after?"

"Whatever attractions your fine state may have, then maybe you can give me some specifics," Lyson wrote, his tongue flicking over his lips.

After reading the note, the man pondered for a moment with his knuckle on his lip. The skin hung loose on his face as if his skull were shrinking from within. He closed his eyes, pulled up his brow, and reopened his eyes. He rolled his swivel chair over to the filing cabinets. Tapping his nose with a finger, he studied the labels on the drawers, craning his neck to get the labels framed within the middle lens of his trifocals, squinting and baring his upper dentures. Lyson watched, hands between his knees, shoes snug together, like under a bed.

"Ah!" The man gave a finger a shake, "There!" and pulled open a drawer. Pursing his lips, he walked his fingers through the folders, picking out some papers that he offered Lyson.

Fading mimeographs featured the attractions Islay had to offer tourists and other visitors. Islay Hotel. Indaal Cove Resort. Wrong Turn Camp for the Old, Tired, and Broken. Pembroke Clams and Oysters. Wrexham Mills. Islay State Park. Rhinns Ridge Farms. Suffex Bandstand. "Thank you! Thank you!" mumbled Lyson as he folded the papers and put them in his pocket. He picked up the pencil and wrote, "Can you tell me what kinds of business do best here?"

"The Bureau of Commerce," wrote the man, "is the proper authority to consult for that kind of information."

"Thank you very much," Lyson wrote and shook the man's hand. Before getting up to leave, he paused to write: "Where would that be?"

The man pointed up, holding up three fingers. Exactly where the inquisitive head had looked down upon him the day before.

Lyson found the stairway, behind the last door at the far end of the hallway. An odor of garbage and a few flies followed him as he bounded up the first flight taking two steps at a time. At the first landing was an open window. He stopped to catch his breath and wipe the sweat off his face and neck. The window faced a brick wall only a few feet away and he poked his head out and saw that the wall was part of his own hotel. He looked up to the sixth floor and saw, in a window in the far corner, a pair of hands angrily shaking a blanket. Why that's my room! He withdrew from the window and blushed at the opinion the maid must harbor of him.

To avoid any further sweating he walked slowly up to the third landing. A quick peek out the window there showed only an open window at his room and he slipped through the door into the dark hallway. To give the sweat time to dry out he studied the little signs over the rows of closed doors behind which lurked state offices: Vocational Redemptional Department. Employee Parking Permits. Housing and Building Authority. Driver's Licenses. Bureau for Pest Control. Department of Agriculture. Boundary and Fencing Authority. At the very end of the hallway, at the front of the building, was the Bureau of Commerce.

Lyson patted his face to catch any traces of sweat, pulled up his pants, restuffed his shirttail, and smoothed his hair. Opening the door revealed a shocking bright, airy office with windows on two walls painted a cheery soft sunny yellow, with a large picture of the Tetons stretching across one wall. Potted palms and ferns and flowers lent a fresh smell to an atmosphere that, by the very nature of the very function of this kind of office, should have been sober, solemn, smelling of electronics.

His eyes finally met those of the two women in the office who were smiling at him. At the front desk sat a rosy, cheery woman who could have been called grandmotherly except that something about her was rather disconcertingly irreverent, dressed as was she in a soft and billowly dress, with luminous white hair, sparkling teeth that had to be false, and wire-rimmed round glasses framing bright irises of various colors in a mosaic of tiny diamonds—brown, blue, green, even yellow. In the back by the window, enjoying some sun, was her partner, much younger and startling in peasant shirt and gypsy skirt, Indian necklace, silver earrings with colored beads, silver rings on several fingers, even a few toes—and barefooted! Lyson gulped at the tiny, thin ring on the side of her nostril. Her American Indian heritage held strong calm and proud in her long shiny black hair and pitch black eyes.

Lyson thought he must be in the wrong office. "Excuse me!" he stammered, backing out the door for another look at the sign. Bureau of Commerce it said. Across the hallway was another door that announced Bureau of Mental Disorders. Lyson looked up again. Bureau of Commerce was where it said he was.

"Is this the Bureau of Commerce?" he asked the women.

Quite amused, yet surprised at Lyson, not just by his funny accent but by his manner, and evident confusion, the white haired lady laughed and motioned him in.

As he was shutting the door, Lyson took a quick glance again at the sign across the hall. Bureau of Mental Disorders, it said. That must be where the face was peering at me yesterday, he shuddered.

"Coffee?" the woman brightly suggested, holding up a Styrofoam cup.

"Uh-oh yes!" Lyson gratefully sat by her desk. "Black, please."

Normally, one would expect the woman, whose name Lyson noted on a little name plate on her desk to be Beatrice Quayle, would then take up her proper station at the desk. Instead she sat on the desk, pulling out a drawer for a footrest. Lyson was dumbfounded: all his years at the Bureau of Statistics had imbued in him a sense of what was proper and appropriate in a government office. But this! Yet, he felt confused: something inside him liked this gay informality; he wanted to put his feet on the desk too.

"That suit," said Beatrice, pointing, "is rather loud for Islay. It's gonna make people hide their money."

Lyson's hands sped to their safe harbor between his thighs. Beatrice's lips were so clear, so easy to read it was almost as if he weren't deaf at all. So few hearing people are so clear, and Lyson's mouth fell slack.

"I'm sorry!" Beatrice giggled. "Guess I'm way too forward for you!"

"Oh that's all right," Lyson said, trying to keep his ears from turning red. "It's just that I'm from Washington—"

"Washington!" Beatrice said as if it were something very remarkable. "Washington," she said again to the other woman who winked at Lyson.

The wink reassured Lyson that no malice was intended and he explained, "I'm Lyson C. Sulla, but excuse me—"

"You need an excuse?" Beatrice deadpanned.

Lyson couldn't help but giggle. "Not really. It's just that I'm deaf and—"

"Deaf?" Beatrice was impressed. "You speak so well! I thought it was just an accent." She turned to the other woman and remarked, "Imagine that!"

"Isn't that something? Where'd you learn that trick?" Her lips were as clear as Beatrice's, although the way she formed the words was quite different. Just how different he wasn't sure, but different.

Lyson hugged his hands tightly between his thighs. "Uh—"

"Oh, that's all right! Are our noses big!" The younger woman let Lyson off the hook. "By the way my name is Crystal." She giggled in an effort to put him at ease.

"Pleased to meet you," Lyson dipped his head. He knew that he ought to get on with business, but he liked the women. Besides, they didn't seem to expect, let alone want, him to start talking business. At least not yet. Suddenly, inexplicably to himself, he teased Beatrice, "You forgot the coffee."

Startled, Beatrice looked at the cup. "Oh!" She jumped off the desk and flew to the percolator. Crystal half giggled. In the sun, her flesh—shoulders and toes—looked so soft, so delicious, that he had to avert his eyes lest they get too round.

"So sorry!" Beatrice apologized, shaking her head in amazement at her own forgetfulness. "You're so irresistible," she teased as she set the coffee before Lyson, "that I just can't help myself."

"Can't help my good looks," he cried in mock defense and was startled at himself, his newfound wit. "My nose stopped growing when—"

"When you started telling the truth," Beatrice finished for him, and immediately held her head in mock shame. "Aren't I awful this morning?" she exclaimed to Crystal.

"Not really," Crystal chipped in, puckering her nose, "just terrible."

"Not as terrible as the coffee!" Beatrice shot back, and turned to Lyson, "You mustn't mind us." She sighed and rolled her eyes. "You see, if we took our jobs seriously, we'd go crazy, wouldn't be able to work at all, and we'd jump out the window—"

"Now you know why I'm here," he chuckled.

Beatrice looked in mock amazement at Lyson, and at Crystal. "Then what are WE doing here?"

Crystal pulled up her eyebrows in a crooked line as she sighed, "Waiting for the right man, must be."

They burst out laughing, and saw Lyson's ears reddening. Beatrice gave his hand a squeeze. "Get it? Waiting for the right man!" She guffawed.

"That would be nice," Lyson held up a finger in mock solemnity, "except that I'm not so sure my wife would agree."

"You naughty boy!" Beatrice poked his dimple.

"The coffee must be terrible," Crystal pouted. "You've not touched it."

"Oh!" He took a sip and winced. "It's gone cold on me."

"Tsk! Tsk! We've wasted your day!" Beatrice exclaimed, grabbing the cup out of Lyson's hand. She went to the open window at the rear of the office, looked down, and dumped the coffee. Refilling the cup she said, "Might as well get me one too. You?"

"Yes, please." Crystal then turned to Lyson. "I hope we've not been wasting your time. You see—"

"Oh no, no," Lyson protested, "I've enjoyed—"

"Still—" Beatrice set the cups on the desk, "you must be a terribly busy man."

"That's all right," he demurred. "I'm—"

"And you came on business, I presume?"

"Ah, yes I did, but—but—"

"And got sidetracked, like me." Beatrice nodded at Crystal. "I used to be a terribly busy woman until Crystal came along and—" she nodded again at Crystal affectionately, "liberated me."

"You should've seen her when I first came here," Crystal said to Lyson, her eyes full of wonder, "she was a real bureaucrat, and her lips were so tight—"

"And she was a real hippie," countered Beatrice. "Why, she even smelled—" She paused, giving Crystal a wink, "—of flowers."

"And she smelled," Crystal rolled her eyes in horror, "of perfume!"

They both turned to Lyson with a nod, but he was sipping his coffee, his brow wrinkled in thought. "My! What's the matter!" Beatrice cried, solicitous, patting his hand.

"Oh no, no," he apologized and suddenly became disgusted with himself, this dumb habit of being apologetic when there was no need. "I'm just—just glad I came here. Your lips are so clear, so easy to read that—that—''

''You forget you're deaf!'' Beatrice exulted, clapping her thigh.

Lyson smiled softly. ''That, but all these years in Washington, those government offices—why, it's all one color, colorless really.''

''Oatmeal!''

''Yes, and—and'' his hand waved in a circle.

''And it tastes like cardboard—''

Lyson sighed loudly. ''Yeah, all that, and all those numbers, numbers—''

Beatrice clapped, and held his face firmly in her hands and kissed his forehead. ''Same here!'' She could feel his cheeks growing hot under her hands as she patted them. ''Aren't they cute!''

Crystal nodded in agreement and came over and put a soft tender kiss on his forehead too. ''Not only that. But we like you too.''

''Oh! I smeared your glasses!'' Beatrice removed them and cleaned them on her skirt. While blowing on them she looked quickly at the window. ''The bell! It's noon.'' She put the glasses back on Lyson who was hugging his hands tightly in his thighs. ''My, does time fly! We hadn't realized we were—''

''That's all right! I enjoyed it very much.'' Beatrice's perfume still clouded his senses.

''You're too sweet!'' Beatrice patted his cheeks. ''Let me tell you, I have to go home to my husband. We always lunch together. Old habit,'' she sighed. ''Crystal has to meet her friends.'' Brightening, she promised, ''You be here at one, and we'll take care of your business. OK?''

''Fine, fine! I'll be here.'' Lyson agreed.

''Great!'' Beatrice saw him to the door. ''And we'll be regular bureaucrats for however long it takes to take care of you.''

''Thank you! Thank you!'' Lyson went out into the hall and down the stairs while other people, the employees, were coming up those same stairs, carrying little brown sacks and cans of pop, bumping into him and staring at his suit with such interest they almost seemed on the verge of touching, fingering it.

* * *

Lyson returned to his room, having got past the Governor's Mansion without being seen, he thought, and also the hotel desk. The bellhop couldn't be helped as he was virtually a fixture of the elevator itself. But the bellhop never let on that he ever recognized Lyson, although he did acknowledge Lyson's presence by closing the doors, pulling the lever, and slowly elevating him to the sixth floor without asking. When Lyson arrived at his door, it was open, and he had to push the cleaning cart out of his way to get in. The maid was still working in the bathroom, and looked up from her position on her knees on the tile floor, her eyes blazing at him.

"Excuse me!" he apologized, his hands out where they could protect him. "Don't mind me at all."

She continued staring at him and said something he could not comprehend, so distorted were her agitated lips.

"Excuse me!" Lyson now felt even more on the defensive, and had he had on a hat, he would have raised it apologetically. "I'm deaf! Can't hear!"

The maid stared incomprehendingly at him and said something; the force by which she said it warned Lyson that she had raised her voice, and that she could be heard all over the hotel, maybe even by the Governor next door.

"Excuse me! Wait!" Lyson was frantic as he rushed to the smaller suitcase and found a pencil in the attache case. The maid made no secret of her incredulity and disapproval. As Lyson scurried about, she rose to her feet, holding the bucket full of soapy water in a threatening manner, quite prepared to defend the security of the room.

Quickly Lyson wrote: "I'm sorry about this mess. Believe me I feel as bad about it as you do. And I'm deaf and have difficulty reading your lips. Please don't mind me. I won't be long."

The maid recoiled in horror as he held the note out to her, beseeching her to please at least read it. The helplessness in his eyes compelled her to accept the proffered note, though she still held the bucket ready to splash him. Reading the note quickly, she looked up at him: his eyes were round with pleading. She grabbed the pencil out of his hand and furiously scribbled "What are you doing here?"

"Oh!" Lyson retrieved the pencil and wrote: "I can imagine you're mad at me for making this awful mess. I'm really, truly sorry and promise not to do it again."

Mystification and confusion clouded her eyes as she read the note, and she looked at Lyson, who, because he was standing, couldn't hug his hands between his thighs but could only wring them. "I don't understand," she said slowly, clearly enough for Lyson to read.

He couldn't bear the impasse and took the pad back and, sighing, added, "It's a long long story. Please bear with me. I have to get a few things, then I'll be gone, and you can finish your work." He thrust the pad back in her hand and went to the suitcase. He checked out the attache case and found all in order, and on impulse seized the bottle of whiskey and jammed it into the case. The teletypewriter was a bit off center on the table, but he knew he wasn't in exactly a good position to berate the maid about it. He pushed it back carefully so that it would be right where it could be used immediately should he receive a call later today. A quick look around the room, and an easy wave to the maid who still held the pad in one hand and the bucket in the other, her mouth open, and he slipped out of the room.

He made anxious steps to the elevator, and realizing the timeless way the elevator operated, fretted until the doors finally slid open, erasing his bronze image upon them, and he darted into the cage. On the way down he and the bellhop studiously ignored each other, and were careful to preserve the atmosphere so necessary to maintain between each other, lest its rendering expose each self to the horror, not just of the other, but also of oneself.

* * *

Lyson fled across the street to the park, ignoring the traffic, toward the Bandstand. The attache case felt uncommonly heavy and bulky, and he remembered the bottle: he hugged the case ever closer as out of the tail of his eye he scanned the Governor's Mansion. The porch was empty. Lunch, he guessed.

A streak of wildness overtook him as he bounded up the stairs of the Bandstand. He stood in the shade of the great roof, forgetting the wasps and spiders, wavering on his feet, sorting out the events of the morning, strange and unreal. He reached in the case for the bottle, and held it up to the light. He admired the rich amber liquid swirling within, power to be had with each sip. He threw his head back and took a swig.

The fiery liquor blasted through his very being, causing him to rub his now numb lips and demand to himself, "What's going on?" He shut his eyes, keeping in mind the majesty of the Bandstand, as he allowed the hot ball to sink deeper into his consciousness and make it abundantly clear that he was completely out of his element. The floor felt unsteady, as on a ship at sea, and he grabbed the rail.

Faces flashed before him: the maid and the moustache on her lip. The old man and his mimeographs. The bellhop and his brass elevator. Dottie and her wonderful eyes. Beatrice and her lips as readable as a book. Crystal and her toes.

Lyson opened his eyes and saw the bottle, the wonderful amber color, in front of his face. Ah! He took another swig, but before the fierce power of the liquor could lay him low, he recapped the bottle and put it out of harm's reach in the case.

Pale emerald light suffusing into the Bandstand lifted his spirit, despite the unsteadiness of his feet. Holding on to the railing he staggered around the perimeter, watching his shoes, taking satisfaction in the honest solid thumps when he stamped his feet on what he took to be the white clay of the floor, to shake the numbness out of them. Feeling a bit more steady, he let go of the railing, put his fists on his hips, and studied the ceiling. A row of light bulbs hung all around the perimeter; a wasp shot across his view, and braking, flew up in a graceful arc toward its nest. But an unseen web entangled it. Its struggles signaled a spider out of its dark recess in a rafter and sent it scurrying after the prey. Before Lyson's very eyes, the spider quickly rolled the wasp into a cocoon. How like people, chuckled Lyson, thinking of the boss at the Bureau.

A sudden movement in the tail of his eye startled him. A fat, gray squirrel was busily investigating his attache case on the clay against the railing and tipped it over. Lyson froze, paralyzed at the animal's audacity. Finding nothing edible, the squirrel stood on its haunches on the attache case, saw Lyson, and bounded toward him. Rabies! His grandmother had often warned of the horrors of those terrible shots, even worse than the disease itself. Lyson whirled and sped down the stairs and around the Bandstand. He reached through the railing for the case and backed away, clutching the case as a shield. The squirrel sat up on its haunches, confused, watching the man retreat backwards towards the hotel. The squirrel shrugged and bounded away to the old man and his nuts. The old man, he's not saying. Could be, he doesn't want to get involved.

* * *

Governor Wenchell lowered his binoculars and remarked, "Imagine a little squirrel frightening a Fed Agent!"

"A disgrace!" agreed Agent B-52 indignantly.

"If Hoover could see this," Agent P-51 said, scandalized, "He'd crack his coffin."

"What's the great FBI come to?" Agent B-52 was thoroughly disgusted. "They send a spy that a darling little Islay squirrel can handle."

"Can you?" the Governor put the binoculars on his desk thoughtfully.

"Of course!" Agent B-52 was taken aback. "But think of the honor—"

"Honor, my eye!" Wenchell scoffed. "Since when did the FBI have any?"

Agents B-52 and P-51 stared at Wenchell and at each other and back at the smug Governor. B-52 finally got his mouth working, "Honor or no, we'll keep an eye on him."

"Maybe it's all a ploy," P-51 snapped his fingers. "A clever trick."

"Gotta be!" Agent B-52 was quick to agree. "The FBI knows what it's doing. It must!"

"I hope not," said Wenchell, shooting a withering look that weakened their knees. "Bring me a julep," he smiled sweetly and went out on the porch to his rocker. "A squirrel!" he chuckled, shaking his head as he eased himself down to a good afternoon's work.

* * *

Loathe to reencounter the maid or the bellhop, Lyson decided to lock the attache case in his Lincoln rather than his room. His watch read twenty past noon, so he walked away from the mansion, toward Great Boulevard along Ninth Street. Most of the buildings he passed were brownstone apartments of a decidedly thirties flavor, with concrete flower pots and urns carved into the brick stoops. No flowers though, and many for-rent signs behind glass in the doors. At the corner of Ninth and Great he found a drugstore, and he was pleased it still retained an old-fashioned soda fountain. As American as the Fifties! A bacon lettuce and tomato sandwich on toast, a hot fudge sundae and apple pie, a la mode of course, restored his confidence in the prospects for the rest of the day, despite the slow start and the rabid squirrel.

Armed with a pocketful of BreathSavers, TicTac, Band-Aid, Swipe-N'Dry, and a new pen and pad, he sauntered down Great Boulevard to Eighth Street and turned west. Doctors, lawyers, dentists, even accountants, he smiled to himself, prefer home-like offices clustered in the shade of towering trees along Great, whereas Eighth Street lay open to the heat of the day with a variety of ventures behind glass facades: clothing and fabric shops, taverns, cafes, dime stores, pawn shops, grocers, liquor stores, sporting goods, a tobacco and magazine shop, even a soup mission that attempted to evangelize the poor through the stomach. As he passed Mick's he saw Dottie, her back to the window, wiping a table. He liked very much her elbow, so small and frail yet so industrious. See you tonight, he said to himself and rounded the corner at Central Promenade. But he stopped abruptly. That head was again at the window on the third floor of the State Building. Though the glare from the sun made the face indistinguishable Lyson suspected it was staring straight at him, and he pretended to consult his watch. Still a few minutes till one.

A hand tugged at his sleeve and he nearly jumped. It was Beatrice, laughing and clearly glad to see him. "We're early."

"Beatrice! Pretend you asked for the time!" He held up his wrist. She went along with the ruse, though puzzled. "Somebody is watching us!" Lyson warned under his breath. "Don't look!"

"Oh!" she laughed, "that's the state shrink. He's going crazy trying to figure you out." She covered her mouth, enjoying a good laugh, her eyes dancing at Lyson.

He looked up at the window in time to catch sight of the head disappearing inside. "I thought he was a spy or an agent or something."

"That's what he thinks he is," she clapped her hands and clasped them on her chest, rocking in mirth.

Lyson stared, his mouth open, at the window as if expecting something extraordinary, perhaps the spectacle of a state psychiatrist throwing himself out a window, and Beatrice had to tug at his sleeve. "Lyson, don't mind him at all. Let's go up to the office. I've something for you."

At the door of the Bureau of Commerce, while Beatrice fuddled with the lock, Lyson sneaked a wary glance across the hall. But the door to the Bureau of Mental Disorders remained shut, closed to them as they went into the safety of Beatrice's office. "Don't mind that nutcracker," she reassured him again.

Suddenly, as she sat down behind the desk, she broke down in tears, burying her head in her hands, her back rising and falling in sobs. Lyson stared at her, dumbfounded and helpless, feeling guilty and shamed. With a shaking hand he tried clumsily to comfort her, patting her back gently.

"I'm sorry! Please!" his voice quivered.

Keeping one hand over her eyes, she covered his hand with her other, squeezing it, nodding that it was all right.

Just then the door opened and Crystal entered. She seemed to understand immediately as she went to Lyson and put her arm around his shoulders. "Don't worry. She'll be all right. She needed this."

Beatrice stood up. "Excuse me a min," she said, going over to a pitcher of water by the window. Crystal continued to comfort Lyson, "She'll be all right. She'll tell you herself. Coffee?"

"Please!" He slumped in his chair, hugging his hands between his thighs, trying his best not to break out in a sweat.

"Relax!" Crystal said brightly as she set three steaming cups on the desk. "It wasn't your fault. Don't be so befuddled."

Lyson wanted to reach for the cup, but he knew his hand would shake and maybe spill the coffee on the desk, so he nodded with a weak smile as he held his hands even more firmly in his lap. Crystal sat on the desk, her bare toes wiggling enticingly before him, her finger softly touching his dimple. "Such a chubby cheek," she teased. Her delicate feminine scent, unspoiled by perfume, rich in a pleasant way by the lunchtime sun, lulled him nearly into a stupor. The aroma of the coffee broke the spell. Crystal was holding the cup under his nose, urging him to drink. His hand was surprisingly calm and steady as he took a sip. He sighed so loudly that Crystal giggled.

Beatrice returned to her seat, refreshed and composed, quite lovely. "Forgive me! I was overwhelmed." She apologized as she sipped her coffee. "I couldn't help it. I'll show you." She turned a picture frame around on her desk so that he could see a solidly shouldered, swarthy young man glaring at the camera. "My son. You kinda remind me of him." She held the picture in her hands, looking softly at it and up at Lyson. "His name is Sean." She looked fondly again at the picture and her eyes brimmed.

"What happened?" Lyson asked, his sympathy very real.

"He's deaf, like you," she said hesitantly. "He split, couldn't stand it here. My fault, our fault, we didn't realize—didn't understand that deaf was okay by him—"

"I'm so sorry! Must be hard on you." He shook his head sadly. "Us deafies. Us deafies—"

Beatrice nodded slowly, closing her eyes, and confessed as she reopened them, "You see, when you first opened your mouth, I knew immediately you were deaf but thought maybe you didn't want it known—"

Lyson half smiled.

She chuckled too and continued, "That was the way we were with Sean but—but—" She shook her head regretfully. "We should've used our own heads, our own hearts, our own vibes. They told us if we'd treat Sean like he weren't deaf—oh my, they said never to use the word deaf—they said it was an horrid word, an insult to the deaf! Anyway they said we oughta always refer to him, Sean, as hearing impaired—because we had to encourage him to use whatever hearing, however little he might have—My God he had—I mean he still has none whatsoever—he's stone deaf! Yet they insisted he wear a hearing aid all the time. Unfortunately, we believed and agreed, we were that dumb. We even went along with the so-called experts and insisted he wear a bra—"

Lyson chuckled loudly. "The one cupped variety for freaks—"

"You too!" exclaimed Beatrice.

"Yeah," Lyson laughed ruefully. "On the outside of my shirt for all the world to see."

"Bra? What's that?" facetiously asked Crystal who never wore one. Anyone could see that. Lyson firmly, resolutely kept his eyes on the level.

Lyson was about to enlighten her that bras were harnesses for hearing aids when Beatrice cried, "My God! We really should've known! We love him so much we really should've realized, empathized—It's amazing how we didn't—"

"Not your fault!" Lyson began, but Beatrice declared, "Really we should've! We didn't know until one day Sean—the day we explained why we couldn't—or wouldn't, really—call him deaf, he upped and said I'm DEAF!"

Lyson thrust a fist high up.

She could not help but smile at this. Then seriously: "That was the day, that night he went away." Fighting back tears, she went on, "We understand now, finally. No reason to be ashamed he's deaf. Finally, but the bad part is he went away before we could tell him—oh it's awful! We want to tell him but we just don't know where he is, and—and—" She gave up and shook her head sadly, slowly. "And the government doesn't care."

"What do you mean the government doesn't care?" asked Lyson. After all, he worked for the government, didn't he?

She nodded. "Why should they? They didn't help him find a living here on Islay. And—and what's so awful, they're so official, so professional, so—so awful! They wouldn't help us find him. Don't even want him here in Islay."

Lyson stood up abruptly. "That's terrible!" He paced the office with angry steps, stomping, fuming. He stopped in front of the women and, holding a fist in the air, his face flushed, bacon bits on his suit, he declared dramatically, "When I become Governor, I'll find him! I promise!"

His fist stopped in the mid-air, petrified in the stance of an orator surprised at his own words; they all stared at one another, in the shock of his declaration. He couldn't believe that he'd actually done it, that he had blurted out his dream—a dream fit only to be laughed at, mocked, sneered at. His ears turned bright red as his fist slowly dropped to his side and he hung his head, tears welling in his eyes. Crystal and Beatrice quickly embraced him, rubbing his back, poking his dimple.

"Crystal! Get the washcloth!"

Beatrice helped Lyson to a chair. "There, there." Crystal handed him a cold, wet washcloth. He tried to wipe his eyes but forgot to take off his glasses. He smiled weakly as he removed them and wiped his eyes. Crystal cleaned them for him while Beatrice comforted him with pats and smoothed his hair.

"Now you know." sighed Lyson, searching for the safe place between his thighs. "Why I'm here, what I'm after." He blew and confessed, "And my delusion—"

Beatrice, her hands on his shoulders, looked up at Crystal with wonder in her eyes. "That's great! Isn't it?"

"Wonderful!" Crystal agreed enthusiastically and grasped his hand.

"Do tell!" Beatrice urged as she and Crystal sat on the desk in front of him. "We'd like to help!"

"Right on!" Crystal held up a fist. "You've got my vote!"

"Two! No! Three!" Beatrice held up three fingers. "My husband too!" She added imperiously, "he'd better!"

"Five! My wife too!" Lyson grinned impishly.

CHAPTER 5

At the corner of Tenth and Great as prearranged for two o'clock, Beatrice picked up Lyson in her Volkswagen. Quickly she drove eastward toward Right Road. "Did Dottie get the message?" Lyson asked anxiously.

"Yes," Beatrice replied cheerily. "In fact she's all for this."

"You told her!" Lyson moaned.

"Of course. She's your sixth voter."

Lyson squirmed in his seat for a more comfortable position. "Six down and 99,994 to go."

"Halfway there already!" Beatrice teased. Her spirit and grit were infectious as the Volkswagen peppily negotiated the right turn into Right Road running alongside the much wider and smoother right fork of American River. The homes along the right side seemed replicas of those he had seen yesterday coming down Wrong Road from the freeway, except that the trees seemed larger, grander, and the road more freshly coated.

"I see many houses are for sale?"

"Yes, we could never really figure out the reason." Beatrice nodded, frowning at the houses. "Guess the new generation likes the bright lights."

"Splendid, splendid," Lyson muttered to himself, forgetting Beatrice can hear.

She heard and chuckled. "Looks like you've come to the right place."

"And the right people," Lyson added with an impish grin.

"Is this going to be fun!" They sped up the ramp to the freeway west toward Fremont. The ramp carried them above the trees and a view opened to the river rushing under the bridge to Sutherland. A freighter was moving in slow motion upstream from the sea, and though huge, was passing under the bridge with room to spare. "Didn't know there was ocean traffic—" Lyson said to no one in particular.

"Oh yes," said Beatrice "They go to Fremont, and even further up, Philadelphia. For years we've been trying to rebuild a seaport—there used to be one right here under the freeway, a small one called—Port Askins—but seems they decided not enough reason to—excuse me!" She accelerated down the ramp to merge into the bustling, hurtling traffic flowing like a multicolored steel and glass river toward the west, Fremont, Washington and beyond.

"Maybe we can," Lyson mused. "Just maybe."

"No reason why not," Beatrice said on the upbeat. "Besides, the property south of the freeway, along Right Fork, is already zoned for a seaport. Look!" Her finger indicated the trees along the other side of the freeway, "All that is zoned for light industry."

Ground floor! The north side of the freeway was also wooded, though he could glimpse the city of Suffex between fleeting trees. "What about this side?"

"Residential. But the town stopped growing a few blocks away, even before the freeway was built. Aren't even any streets laid yet in that zone. All woods."

To Lyson, the forest looked wild, primeval. "Since coming here it seems I'm seeing trees for the first time."

"Like 'em?"

"This city boy will have to admit they're not bad-looking."

"You men!" Beatrice laughed.

"Funny, Washington is a forest too, but I never noticed! Too busy, I guess—"

Already they were on the bridge over Wrong Turn and Lyson studied the river with fresh eyes. Even he could tell it was shallow, with ripples sloshing over rocks. Looking upstream, he could see the immense American River from whence Wrong Turn split, glittering at the apex of Suffex. Above the trees to the right he could glimpse his hotel, the lantern of the Bandstand, and the towers of the university. Further to the west, the trees along the far bank, though grand, were dwarfed in the distant mist by the immense skyscrapers of Fremont.

Beatrice followed the line of flashing right taillights onto a ramp and entered the local freeway into Fremont. Bricks concrete asphalt and glass, absorbing storing and reflecting the heat from the sun, unfiltered undiffused and unsoftened by trees, created a virtual oven into which they were driving. Lyson opened his window but a traffic light halted them in a cloud of exhaust fumes percolating from countless overheated engines, further bending the sun's rays.

On either side, among factories of crude brick and rows upon rows of blank windows, refineries of rusting and artless steel, smokestacks mute as monuments to the dollar—now long gone to Palm Beach, Palm Springs, Paris—stood clusters of houses, red brick with peaked roofs end-to-end like the teeth of a saw; some rentals, some homes: the rentals being rundown and dejected, though some flowers stood in a few windows with an eye to something better in the future, sometime somewhere later on, assuming all hope is never lost; by contrast, the owned homes were neat and prim in the hope of the immediate, right now, though they be under innumerable power lines. Lyson was awestruck. What could be the outlook on life from such a vantage?

"I never thought trees made so much difference!" Lyson panted, as he offered Beatrice a Swipe N'Dry and wiped his own face.

"You're an Islayer already!" She laughed at his squirming in that suit of his so unsuitable to Islay, let alone an automobile crawling along a broiling street in the sun. "We'll get you to look like one soon. The works!"

She'd succeeded in convincing Lyson that conservative dark suits and white shirts were the mark of achievers, graspers, climbers, brown noses, sycophants. What he needed, she declared, was to change spots. Why, look at Johnny Carson! Isn't he a most splendid man, looking every inch like he owns the world. And couldn't care less! Take it or leave it!

Lyson was becoming nauseous from the heat and fumes, and dizzy when Beatrice cut off a prestigious-looking Mercedes and whipped in front into a parking place, ignoring the righteous indignation of the obscenely well-heeled man at the wheel. "In Fremont you do have to grasp for your rights," she declared, putting a soft hand on Lyson's knee. She pointedly ignored the man glaring at her as he pulled even with them. She urged Lyson out the right door and followed him out. "Ignore him," she calmly wrinkled her nose as she led him into a luxuriously decorated store called the Rake. But Lyson kept glancing back to see if he was being followed and nearly stumbled on the thick pile carpeting but Beatrice caught him. The air conditioning and agreeable odor of new fabric and oiled paneling was so welcome after the muggy exhaust fumes outside. In the soft diffused lighting, the racks of men's clothing of various subtle hues gave Lyson the comforting feeling that they had come to a discreet, caring place. They came to a semicircular cubicle of high wainscotted walls with a little sign that read "Appearance Counselor."

The counselor was with them in a flash, having appeared unobtrusively, seemingly out of nowhere, perhaps from behind one of the heavy curtains they use in lieu of doors within such shops. He bowed slightly and mumbled something Lyson couldn't catch. But the words mattered not at all, for his appearance said it all: he was splendidly, even exquisitely apparelled in a two-toned suit of soft camel, cream-colored shirt with a contrasting green tie, and suede oxfords. The perfect tan, blow-dried cultivated sandy hair and blue eyes rounded out the image of landed gentry, out somewhere beyond the suburbs, beyond the country club, out where the mist was gold and soft in a faraway sun. Fox hunts. Clay trap shooting. Horse shows. Parties in gardens around fountains. Frail darling southern belles demure, sweet as lemon custard pies, floating gaily about in clouds of inflated hooped gowns among birdbaths and trellises built at great expense to support vines and roses.

"First of all," Beatrice said in the assured manner of knowing what she wants, "we want to run Lyson here through your program."

The man looked solicitously, gravely at Lyson, taking note of his color build features shape ancestry status and, Lyson thought, destiny. The man also looked into his eyes.

"Excuse me!" Lyson blurted out, "but I'm deaf—"

Beatrice laid a gentle hand on his arm. "Don't worry. I told him. He says he's never met a deaf person, but I said don't think deaf, just think same as anyone else, and we'll get along just fine, won't we?"

Lyson nodded gratefully and said, "Tell him—"

She tugged at his sleeve firmly: "Go ahead and tell him yourself."

He stared at the counselor who was uneasily staring back. "Well! I'm Lyson Sulla!" Lyson boldly said, offering his hand. The man smiled broadly, somewhat relieved, and shook his hand. He said something but his lips were unreadable.

"Excuse me! But I can't read your lips."

Beatrice tugged: "Of course you can! You read mine, don't you?"

"That's different!" Lyson explained, pointing to his mouth, "You form your words at the front of the mouth where I can see them. Some people, mostly men, even myself too, form their words in the back of their mouths where they can't be seen." Turning to the man he said, "I hope you understand this, and that it's not your fault, nor mine."

The counselor smiled and led them behind the cubicle to a luxuriant, deep red-velvet sofa. He said something that Beatrice relayed: "Drink?"

"Please! Black, no sugar."

The man looked apologetically at Lyson, his lips moving. "He says he's so sorry they don't have coffee," Beatrice told Lyson. "They only have cocktails."

"Indeed!" His eyebrows went up in delight.

Pushing a bell on the desk, the counselor sat down and drew Lyson's attention to the diploma on the wall testifying that F. Addison Walish IV had completed a program in Men's Personal Appearance and Image Formation and was thereby certified in the practice of Appearance Counseling.

"You may rest assured," he said through Beatrice, "that our program is the best, and, may I add, the only established method of bringing out the best man in you. It is the highest state of the art, designed to make you look the very prettiest you possibly can."

"And I notice you're very uncomfortable in that suit of yours," Beatrice added, fingering the lapel of Lyson's suit. "No wonder. It is harsh to the touch, isn't it?" Lyson squirmed and tucked his hands between his thighs.

"The reason you're uncomfortable and self-conscious," Addison said suavely, "is that, first, the fabric is unnatural. Second, the fit is not right, which not only makes you uncomfortable but also compounds the problem to spoil your appearance." He paused to allow this point to sink in and continued, pointing to a third finger, "Third, the colors themselves do not occur in nature, and the clash of unnatural and unattractive colors produces a negative impact upon your appearance. Come to the mirror."

Lyson stood in front of the wall-length mirror and cringed. His suit, though new, looked garish, baggy and wrinkled already. But what startled him the most were his eyeglasses that now looked huge and ludicrous, dwarfing his nose. He turned quickly away from that awful image of himself and declared, "Why you're right! I never noticed before! Too busy dreami—

I mean planning! Let's get started!'' And to Beatrice: ''I'm forever in your debt—''

''Shh!'' said Beatrice. ''This is fun for me.'' And to Addison, ''Can you help him?''

''Certainly,'' he said expansively. ''First, the questionnaire.'' He drew back some curtains to a small booth. Inside were a swivel chair, heavily padded and covered with velvet, and a walnut desk in which a computer had been built. As Lyson sat down, a beautiful woman in a deep emerald lowcut evening gown arrived with the cocktails on a silver tray. Her soft green eyes framed by long wavy auburn hair, delicate tan, and fire-engine red lips mesmerized Lyson so that she had to raise her eyebrows inquiringly and glance down to get him to notice the glass she was holding out to him.

''Oh! Thank you!'' he jumped. ''Excuse me but—''

She smiled demurely and rested her finger softly on his mouth and in his dimple before disappearing with the deliberate strides of a woman perfectly aware of her attraction for men, her gown trailing. It suddenly felt hot and stuffy in the little booth, but Lyson dared not remove his jacket, conscious of the way he must smell after such a long hot day, hoping that the jacket could successfully contain the inevitable odor. The sweat breaking out on his forehead and neck disconcerted him and he thrust his hand in his hip pocket for a handkerchief that wasn't there. The woman, however, had placed a napkin on the desk so he used it, dabbing his forehead and neck.

Addison observed all this, a finger curved across his mouth, and suggested through Beatrice, ''You seem a little too uncomfortable to be in the desirable frame of mind for this vital questionnaire. Would you like to refresh yourself?''

''That would be nice. Please.'' He picked up his drink and followed Addison through another curtain into a fully equipped bathroom. Rich carpeting, gold foil and grass-green velvet walls, the large deep tub, the oak seat on the toilet, and luxuriant towels astonished Lyson. ''Never knew a bathroom could be so nice!''

Suave Addison said something indistinguishable to Lyson, and seeing the futility, called out to Beatrice. She too was surprised at the splendor of the bathroom and exclaimed, ''You're lucky! I just think I'll be next! Isn't this something!'' She took a closer look at the tub. ''Why, a whirlpool! If I didn't like you so much, I'd shove you out and be first myself!''

Addison smoothly intruded for Beatrice to remind Lyson, ''You are welcome to refresh yourself in any manner you may wish. When you are done, may I suggest you use this—'' behind the door hung a silk bathrobe in cherry red and soft terry slippers. As they were leaving Beatrice happily shot back, ''He says there is another one like this, so I don't have to wait.''

Unfortunately Lyson couldn't get rid of the thought that others were impatiently waiting for him, so he hurried out of his clothes into the tub for a quick rinse. Rather than simply savoring his bath, he was careful to scrupulously lather those parts offensive to the nose. Yet, despite the haste, the cool water succeeded in refreshing Lyson, whose grandmother told him that a clean body belonged with a clean mind. Drying himself, he noticed his cocktail on the lavatory but disdainfully poured it into the drain. A clean and happy man don't need it, he cheerily proclaimed to himself. He put on the bathrobe and slippers and strode out into the store.

Addison, alone in the cubicle, looked up from his paperwork on the desk and his eyes widened, aghast. He rose quickly and led the dumbfounded Lyson back to the bathroom. Picking up Lyson's pants from the floor, he said slowly but forcefully, "Put on!"

"Oh! Excuse me! I thought—" Lyson blushed, and when the door shut, put on the pants, careful to pull the zipper up fully. His face burnt hot and red; he had to rinse it again before he could face Addison again. "Dumb Dumb!" He knocked his head, berated his image in the mirror, and cursed himself for having discarded the cocktail. Taking a deep breath, he went back out to Addison, suppressing an urge to explain, saying to himself that the time has arrived for the deaf to cease forever explaining themselves, as if explanations were the only way the hearing could ever understand the deaf. He managed a sheepish grin as he rushed to sit in the booth before Addison could again get the better of him.

Without Beatrice who was already bubbling in her own whirlpool, the counselor felt helpless, a bit panic-stricken, over how to explain the computer to Lyson. As he hovered over his client, wringing his hands and trying to think, Lyson was already studying the buttons and keys. "Ah! I think I know how this thing works." Lyson exclaimed, turning the machine on. The screen lit up with the command: "Please type your name and credit card number." No wonder Addison was so upset about my pants, Lyson snickered to himself as he pulled the wallet out for the card. He typed the long number carefully, honestly, accurately and conscientiously: Addison was looking over his shoulder. The screen blinked on the first question: "What do you want?"

"Another drink!" Lyson said decisively to Addison and turned to the keyboard and typed: "Governship of a State for the Deaf only."

Addison was still hovering over him, and Lyson looked up, politely demanding, "Didn't I tell you I wanted another drink?" Holding up his hands anxiously: Wait! Addison went to his desk, pressed a button, and returned with a pencil and sheet of paper. Kneeling on the floor by Lyson, he wrote: "This computer understands only specific answers such as fame, money, power, love, etc. Your answer is too vague. Please start over and answer with one word only. OK?"

"I see." Lyson pushed the repeat button, and when the question again appeared on the screen, typed: "Respect."

"Good," Addison wrote. "Now I'll leave you alone. Your drink will be here shortly." He left, drawing the curtain, and exhaled.

The next question appeared for Lyson: "Who are you?"

* * *

Two hours later, Lyson finally stood in front of a mirror, resplendent in exactly the clothes the computer had prescribed. Sport jacket, plaid with thin stripes of brown and orange against a pleasant buff-yellow background. Burnt-umber slacks. Canary-yellow shirt with orange stitching. Orange tie. Reddish-brown oxfords. Woven fabric belt with gold buckle engraved "LCS." And gold-rimmed aviator's glasses.

Lyson stretched his arms; yet the jacket did not pull, bind, or distort. "Perfect! Isn't it amazing what a computer can do!" he exclaimed, and to Addison, "Did you say the computer actually cut and sewed these clothes?"

Addison nodded modestly. "Even the shoes. And the glasses."

"Remarkable!" Lyson inspected the soft leather flight bag designed to accomodate the rest of his wardrobe. In one compartment rested his camel jacket, folded gently to avoid creasing. In another were the two other pairs of slacks, one pale yellow, the other sombre maroon. Another compartment held two shirts of shimmering canary yellow, stitched with brown and maroon. Also a wool sweater intricately weaved in yellow and maroon yarn so that it looked soft and casual yet not too informal. And a tweed Tyrolean hat in the same colors folded neatly with the sweater. The ties, umber and ocher, were in a smaller side compartment together with socks of the same color scheme and handkerchiefs to complement their companion shirts. On the opposite side were the underwear, cream-colored but with different colored stitching as well. Lyson was not in the habit of taking his underwear seriously, but these would have to be considered each morning. There was still room for his personal effects, business and personal papers, tickets and magazines, and a special instruction booklet—imprinted with Lyson's name—on how to combine the various articles of clothing and colors for the best effect on a wide variety of occasions restricted to the great and near-great. It also listed a telephone number through which personalized emergency advice on appearances could be obtained.

"Perfect! Perfect!" Lyson exulted. "Just think how this little bag contains everything I need for every occasion!" He turned to the beaming Beatrice and hugged her. "Why, I have two large bags in the hotel," he said, "each bigger than this little one; yet they together contain no more than this!" He held up the new bag for admiration.

The lovely hostess reappeared, bearing a silver tray on which stood a golden hip flask surrounded by four glasses of wine. "This flask is our personal gift to you,'' she announced, mesmerizing Lyson with her soft, deep eyes as she slipped the flask into an underwear compartment of the new bag. Then they each raised a glass and drank to each other's health. Addison shook Lyson's hand warmly, saying, ''It's been a pleasure serving you. Anytime you need anything, feel free to come back or call my number in the booklet.''

''Thank you, thank you!'' Lyson pumped his hand effusively. ''You've made a new man of me! You broke the old mold, thank you!'' And turning to the woman in emerald, he took her hand and kissed it. He was surprised at the tingling on his lips and stared up at the woman, so much so that Beatrice had to tug at him.

It was dusk already when they got outside; the Mercedes was still double-parked beside the Volkswagen, its driver still fuming, glaring at them. Beatrice strode resolutely to a pay-phone at the corner, Lyson stumbling to keep up with her. Winking, she pretended to dial the police, motioning with her hand vigorously, pointing to the Mercedes, all the while mouthing words into the telephone. She hung up with a smug nod when the Mercedes disappeared in a cloud of exhaust down the street. ''A little pluck is all it takes,'' she said sweetly, and led Lyson by the arm to her car.

* * *

They picked up Dottie in front of Mick's Cafe. As Lyson got out to allow her into the backseat she exclaimed, ''You look gorgeous! Super!'' She fingered the material of the jacket, the tie, even the trousers. ''Excellent!'' She turned and brought forth a grave young man. ''My son, Darcy.''

''How do you do!'' Lyson shook his hand. The boy looked very mature for his age. Couldn't be more than twelve but his bearing, his demeanor was that of a young man. ''Pleased to meet you.''

They headed north where Great Boulevard merged with Right Road. A freighter was sailing downstream on the Right Fork, headed out to sea, its white superstructure glowing, floating above its dark hull visible only against the lights across the river. Lyson was charmed and could almost smell the sea. Beatrice found a spot to park and they all got out. Lyson stood for a moment, watching the ship approaching the freeway bridge visible in the distance by lights along its roadway. He turned and saw that Darcy was beside him, watching the ship too. The ship drifted slowly, ponderously, with great majesty under the bridge, white froth bubbling fluorescently in its wake, kicked up by its propellers. The fact that the bridge lay at the south edge of the city, and yet was so close, gave Lyson a sense of the smallness, the snugness of Suffex, a place where everything, everyone was within easy reach, close to each other.

They crossed Right Road and promenaded in the pleasant night air down Second Street. "Lyson, you look so good!" Dottie whispered, touching his arm. "Now I'm not ashamed to be seen with you," she teased.

Lyson stopped, looking at Dottie, at her rough-woven peasant cotton shirt with large sleeves and skirt of denim. "Don't tell me!" she hushed him as she saw him struggle to return the compliment. Darcy raced ahead of the others, urging them to hurry on. Lyson finally thought of the right thing to say. "That boy of yours is a fine one."

"Sure is," Beatrice agreed. "A nice sight too."

Darcy found the restaurant and waited impatiently for them. It was Italian, with red and white checkered tables lit by candles in wine bottles. As they entered, the rich aroma of garlic and dough and pasta made Lyson lightheaded with hunger. Crystal was waving at a large table with two men Lyson had never seen. Both rose to greet him. He could see from Crystal's eyes that his new outfit was already working. Smiling with delight, she enthused, "Wonderful! So handsome!"

"Thank you, thank you!" He blushed. "We have Beatrice to thank, really."

He looked down at her toes. The rings on her toes were still visible through the openings on her sandals. Crystal laughed and hugged him, and then introduced him to the two men at the table. "My man Trent," she said to Lyson coming face-to-face with a huge, powerful man with curly dark hair and bushy mustache who crunched his hand. His lavender silk shirt opened to the navel, revealing a heavy mat of tightly curled hair on a massive chest. A rough bronze chain hung around his neck, glittering in the candlelight. Lyson's mouth fell open. He managed to stammer, "Pleased to meet you! Your wife is a wonderful woman."

"Woman is the word. Wife is for wimps," Trent replied tightening his grip.

"Trent was a linebacker for the Outlaws!" Crystal gushed in awe. "The baddies, you know," she added with a thrill in her eye. Trent grinned wickedly, revealing heavy carnivorous teeth, undamaged, fully capable of tearing out a chunk of quarterback, and released Lyson's hand. He grunted, "Welcome to the team!"

"Captain John Quayle," Beatrice beamed, hugging her husband by the upper arm. Captain Quayle was a grand old man, with red hair speckled with white stuffed under a Greek fisherman-style leather cap. He had long white sideburns, deeply weathered features, and intense pale blue eyes that without the habitual twinkle could be said to be piercing. Trim and fit, the Captain was clothed in the manner of a distinguished perpetual traveler of tropical paradises: white cotton jacket with thin vertical blue stripes, sky-blue pants, cream-colored shirt with denim tie, and white buck shoes. So Addison had a go here too. His hand was slender and cool as

Lyson took it, and felt calm and sincere. The Captain said something Lyson couldn't catch.

"Excuse me!" Lyson said apologetically. "But I'm—"

"He knows," Beatrice assured him with pats on the arm. "He said he's honored to meet the future Governor of Islay."

Lyson blushed. "Ah—uh, I'm pleased to meet you." Then aside to Beatrice, "You sure it's a good idea to let people know our plans?"

"Can't help! I talk in my sleep!" Beatrice laughed, and said sweetly, "Only those who can help us."

"Let's sit down," the Captain said, more careful this time to form the words where Lyson could read them. "And let's get something to eat. I imagine you're hungry."

"Ravenous!" Lyson gratefully agreed, rolling his eyes.

Already a large pitcher of frothy beer was on the table and Trent poured Lyson a mugful. They all looked on in admiration as Lyson noisily gulped down the brew. Trent refilled the glass but Dottie touched his hand, cautioning him, "Easy does it." Lyson sighed expansively, took a sip, but then put the mug down. Trent filled everyone's glasses, including Darcy's, and they all toasted each other and sat back, enjoying the satisfaction of good fellowship and the glow of a shared secret.

The waiters came, bringing a huge pizza that they set in the center of the table, with bowls of steaming spaghetti for everyone and more pitchers of beer. Captain Quayle leaned forward toward Beatrice who was sitting beside Lyson and said something, nodding at Lyson. "He wants me to tell you," she relayed to Lyson, her hand on his forearm, "that he is impressed with you—"

"Aw, it's only clothes—" Lyson blushed modestly.

"—and that he wants to help in any way he can."

"Thank you! Thank you!" Lyson said, trying to think of something appropriate to say. "Beatrice, really, so many good things have happened today that I'm overwhelmed. Everyone has been so good to me—"

"That's because you're—you're—" Dottie began but noticed Lyson's blushing. She giggled and poked his dimple. "Cute."

"And we think your plans are so—a lot of fun," Crystal interjected. "Why, it's so dreadfully dull here."

The Captain leaned closer to Lyson. "When Beatrice first told me about you, at first I thought she was in love—" They all laughed, even Lyson. "But," the Captain held up a dramatic finger, "I said to myself that it was about time!"

"Lyson!" Dottie touched his hand. "You haven't eaten!"

"Oh! That's right!" Lyson jumped and twirled the spaghetti around on his fork and shoved the mess in his mouth.

"He can't lipread and eat too," Dottie explained to the others.

"And I can't talk and eat too," the Captain joked and helped himself to a slice of pizza. "An old man likes to talk but has to eat too."

"That's how he kept his figure," Beatrice boasted, patting his stomach. "He knows how to eat. Say, John, remember Sean—how he had to use his eyes to eat? Dottie is right—can't lipread and eat too."

"Shame on you Trent!" Crystal scolded. "You've already eaten half the pizza!"

"No sweat," Trent mumbled through a mouthful of pizza. he held up two fingers to the waiter. "More pizza! Beer too." He drank from the pitcher as would a true Outlaw.

"Wait!" Lyson cried. "We can't keep up with you!"

"Aren't quarterbacks enough for you?" Captain Quayle asked with mock horror.

"They're just all skin and bones," Trent grunted with disgust. "Besides, they taste of pain killers."

"Trent!" Crystal covered her mouth with surprisingly long and slender fingers.

Lyson drained his beer and pulled two slices of pizza to his plate, enjoying himself and his new friends thoroughly. He was still confused at the events of the day, and his great good fortune, but it was the kind of confusion a man cannot but enjoy, and it made the beer and pizza all the tastier. Trent poured him another mugful and then finished the pitcher himself. "Better hurry before I clean out the table."

Everyone but Lyson sat back from their plates, satisfied, and watched him rushing to finish. "Relax. Enjoy yourself," the Captain admonished. "Trent's only foolin'." Red wine arrived, and yet another toast to future success was made.

Lyson burped. The force of the burp shook him so that he was quick to cry, "Excuse me! Didn't mean to—"

"Oh Lyson," laughed Beatrice. "Don't be silly. Perfectly natural!"

"Natural as farting," chimed in Crystal. "Everybody does it."

Lyson blushed and felt himself getting hot under the collar. Never before had any woman in his life used such a word, not his grandmother, not even his wife. They were more polite. They used terms such as pass gas, or Phew! Terms used by polite folk that keep a tight reign on themselves.

"Lyson, cool it!" giggled Crystal.

The Captain burped hugely in an effort to help Lyson off the hook. Trent made a fanning motion behind his seat.

"Trent!" remonstrated Crystal, shaking her head, face in hands.

Lyson finally finished his pizza and tried to wipe his hands clean on his napkin. But an alert waiter brought forth steaming towels for everyone. Refreshed, they again toasted each other around the table and allowed the spirits to drift through their souls as they sat back at ease, meditating on the flickering candle. Lyson relaxed happily in his chair, intoxicated by his new friends, who looked back affectionately; even Trent grunted. The Captain nodded sleepily and leaned forward to Lyson and commented, "Ain't Beatrice pretty?" In the candelight Beatrice looked young and vibrant, quite lovely. Crystal shone, very feminine and mysterious beside her huge strong Trent. Dottie soft and warm, her eyes luminous as she admired Lyson. Lyson giggled. Darcy frowned, mature beyond his years, as he carefully sipped his wine and bravely swallowed it without screwing his face. Lyson's head felt pleasantly soft in the restaurant's atmosphere, made intimate and secret by the candles, dark furnishings, rough brick walls, discreet waiters, and small private groups of diners speaking softly with each other. There must be music also, he was thinking when his eye in the course of its survey of the restaurant noticed the pay telephone in a dark corner.

Telephone! Lyson suddenly slapped his forehead startling his friends. "Forgot to call my wife!" he groaned and checked his watch. A quarter till eleven!

They all stared at him, amazed. Dottie asked, "You mean you can use the telephone?"

"Of course. That's not the problem," Lyson said remorsefully, nervous and anxious. "The problem is I'm supposed to call her at six every evening."

Beatrice leaned forward. "But how? I thought—"

"Oh I see," Lyson broke out laughing. "You see, we deaf use a teletypewriter—"

"Teletypewriter?" his friends, asked, glancing at each other.

"Confucius say, a pichah is woath a thousand woads," Lyson suggested brightly. "Why don't we all go to my room and you can see how it works?"

"Great!" The Captain declared. "Let's go see it!"

"We'd better get moving," Dottie urged. "Your poor wife—"

"Righto!" Lyson reached for his wallet but Beatrice squeezed his hand. The Captain had already taken care of the check. They picked up two extra bottles of wine on the way out.

* * *

As they entered the hotel the clerk rose expectantly, startled to see Lyson at the head of the procession. "Excuse me," Lyson said apologetically, "these are my friends and—" He stopped, embarassed by the clerk's incomprehending stare.

Beatrice came to the rescue, explaining to the clerk, "We're his friends. We're just visiting him for a little while." The clerk stared, still incomprehending, at Lyson so she said gaily, "Let's go up!"

The bellhop operated the elevator in his usual manner, very gravely, seriously intent on his job of transporting them to the correct floor, so rigidly oblivious of his passengers that Darcy was drawn, fascinated, into a better look up at his face. Dottie with a firm grip on his shoulders drew him back and held him in the correct posture of elevator passengers, eyes up at the pointer showing their progress.

As they entered his room, the teletypewriter was flashing its signal light. Lyson rushed over and cradled the telephone on the machine and quickly typed:

LYSON HERE GA.

Over his shoulder, he explained to his friends that GA means Go Ahead.

MARY HERE. WHERE HAVE YOU BEEN Q. I WAITED SINCE SIX. DISGUSTED GA.

SORRY! LONG DAY—

EXCUSES. EXCUSES. I AM FED UP—

MET NEW FRIENDS! Lyson interrupted quickly. THEY ARE HERE WITH ME WATCHING HOW THIS WORKS—

NEW FRIENDS Q GA.

He turned to his friends and explained, "Q stands for Question Mark."

YES. DOTTIE BEATRICE CRYSTAL—

WONDERFUL WONDERFUL GA.

YES. WONDERFUL—

HA HA! BEAUTIFUL Q GA.

SILLY—

SILLY YOU TOO! WOMEN IN YOUR ROOM Q GA.

FINISH! THEY ARE WATCHING—

DO THEY KNOW YOU ARE MARRIED Q GA.

YES! THEIR HUSBANDS ARE HERE TOO—

I'M SORRY! CANT HELP WORRY. LONESOME, MISS YOU VERY MUCH GA.

THATS ALRIGHT. I MISS YOU TOO BUT—A long pause.

BUT WHAT GA.

BUT I WISH YOU STOP BELIEVING HOLLYWOOD MOVIES ABOUT TRAVELING MEN. THOSE MEN ARE TALL GOOD-LOOKING SLENDER. YOU KNOW THAT I AM SHORT FAXXXXX PLUMXXXXX HUSKY AND NOT VERY PRETTY—

I DID SAY I'M SORRY! GA.

OK. OK. ANYWAY MANY THINGS HAPPEN TODAY. HOW THINGS FOR YOU Q GA.

NOTHING MUCH BUT YOUR BOSS CALLED. WANT TO KNOW WHEN YOU GO BACK WORK GA.

TELL HIM SHOVE IT. THINGS LOOK GOOD HERE. FRIENDS WANT TO HELP US—

DEAF Q GA.

NO, HEARING—

THOUGHT WERE WERE LOOKING FOR DEAF HELP GA.

RIGHT! BUT JUST HAPPEN MEET HEARING WHO WANT TO HELP. VERY NICE PARENTS OF DEAF SON. EASY TO LIPREAD, UNDERSTAND DEAF FEELINGS. YOU WILL LIKE THEM VERY MUCH, NOT LIKE MOST HEARING GA.

GOOD BUT BE CAREFUL HEARING THEIR FAMOUS DECEIVE DEAF—

DONT WORRY! THEY ARE DIFFERENT, NOT LIKE OUR PARENTS AT ALL, WANT TO HELP DEAF—

YOU KNOW MANY HEARING THEIR FAMOUS SAY WANT HELP BUT—

TRUE! BUT—Lyson said quickly over his shoulders to his friends even while typing, "Hope you understand how she feels. She doesn't mean—" Dottie reassured him with pats on the shoulder. THESE ARE FRIENDS NOT LIKE MOST HEARING. REAL PEOPLE. THEY ARE SINCERE, WILL ACTUALLY HELP GA.

FORGIVE ME FOR BEING SUSPICIOUS. I MUST TRUST YOU AND HOPE YOU KNOW WHAT YOU ARE DOING. WHEN CAN I COME Q GA.

TOMORROW I WILL KNOW BETTER—

YOU BETTER GA.

OKAY. WHEN I CALL YOU TOMORROW WE WILL KNOW WHAT TO DO—

IF YOU DONT KNOW WHAT YOU ARE DOING MAYBE YOU BETTER COME HOME NOW GA.

STOP INTERRUPTING! I MEAN WE WILL FIND OUT IF OUR PLANS WILL WORK GOOD HERE IN ISLAY GA.

SORRY. OF COURSE I UNDERSTAND. ANYWAY PLEASE BE VERY CAREFUL GA.

DONT WORRY, THINGS ARE BETTER THAN I EXPECTED. TOMORROW IS THE DAY WE KNOW FOR SURE. GA.

OKAY. PLEASE DO NOT FORGET TO CALL ME TOMORROW GA.

I WONT FORGET BUT MIGHT BE LATE GA.

MISS YOU! CAREFUL GA.

MISS YOU TOO GA OR SK.

LOVE YOU SK.

LOVE SKSK.

Sighing, Lyson lifted the telephone from the machine and apologized to his friends, "I'm sorry—"

"Don't!" Dottie brushed her finger over in his dimple. "This is amazing!'

"Never knew science has come this far!"

"What'll they think of next?"

"Marvelous!"

"I assume," the Captain said, "that SK means you're finished—"

"Right," Lyson said. "Actually it stands for Stop Keying."

"Can I try it?" Darcy asked, making an effort not to appear too eager.

"Darcy!" scolded his mother.

"That's okay," Lyson interjected. "There's a number he can ring up and get a newsbrief. Let me look it up." He found the National TTY directory in his old suitcase and gave the number to Darcy.

In a moment the teletypewriter came to life and spelled out: TODAY IS TUESDAY JUNE 5. THE PRESIDENT ANNOUNCED NEW CUTS IN PUBLIC TELEVISION. NO MORE FUNDS FOR TELECAPTIONING FOR THE HEARING IMPAIRED. AMERICAN ASSOCIATION OF THE DEAF PROTESTS THAT MOST DEAF PEOPLE HAD ALREADY BOUGHT TELECAPTIONERS AT $350 APIECE BUT THE PRESIDENT SAYS NEED TO CUT TAXES SO INVESTORS CAN INVEST IN TELECAPTIONER MANUFACTURERS. SENATOR UMBRIDGE COUNTERS THAT THIS WOULD ONLY RAISE THE PRICES OF TELECAPTIONERS WITHOUT ANY PROGRAM ON TELEVISION FOR THEM. TEMPERATURE 84° FAHRENHEIT. CHANCE OF MORNING FOG AND AFTERNOON THUNDERSTORMS. SORRY FOR THE NEWS. GOOD NIGHT.

Lyson slumped, looking sadly at the teletypewriter. Dottie knelt beside him, patting his back. Beatrice rubbed his neck. "Isn't this awful! You get this wonderful machine and now them mean reactionaries—"

"Here!" The Captain handed Lyson a glass of wine. "Now we know why you're here, what you're trying to—"

"Yes! We're with you!" Crystal declared, and they all drank to Lyson and his dream. He grinned slowly, gratefully, almost shyly, and held up his glass and drained it.

"What's this?" Darcy startled them with a cry from the bathroom. But before Dottie could reach him, his curiosity had already gotten the best of him.

CHAPTER 6

A grand morning it was as Lyson drove down Great Boulevard for breakfast with the Quayles. The sun gave forth delicate rays in that hour before it became hot, so that the air had a light pleasant glow to it and the trees soared weightless and vibrant. The homes along the boulevard sat comfortably the way well-built structures do. Various creative styles—mainly Tudor—but also Spanish, Floridian and Cape Cod. Crab grass either had won or had been accepted on many of the lawns. Likely some of the people rationalized that crab grass required less mowing, Lyson thought as he drove slowly, contentedly down the boulevard, already feeling at home though the sights be fresh and new to his eyes. He liked the many colored awnings in front of the bungalows, although the colors had faded on most of them. He particularly noted the ones for sale.

At Thirty-fourth Street he turned to the east and, with the sun now shining directly into his eyes, the neighborhood appeared very different. The backlighting heightened the scruffy appearance of the lawns, the cracks in the street, the curling of the shingles on roofs, and the weathering on the homes. Backlit, the trees floated grander, lighter, more vibrantly alive. Majestic trees make the soul so glad to be on this earth.

The Captain heard Lyson's Lincoln screeching against the curb and came out to greet him, clearly glad to see him and looking forward to a fine day with such a special person. "How are you this morning?"

"Fine! Just fine!" Lyson grabbed his hands as they stood in the sun admiring one another. "Slept like a baby! You?"

The Captain laughed. "Like an old man. Let's go eat."

His house lay at the southwest intersection of Thirty-fourth and Q Streets and and was designed with two faces so that a different look fronted on each street. The one on Thirty-fourth presented a Tudor facade with an asymmetrical archway: on the left the little roof ended at a normal height while on the right it sloped in an outward parabolic curve directly to the ground. Leading Lyson aside to the Q Street side, Captain Quayle with a wry smile pointed out the Georgian features: steep gabled dormers on the roof, two bay windows in rough brick walls and a columned porch providing an alternate entrance. "Beatrice has a great sense of humor, she does," he chuckled. "She entertains socially on this side and," leading Lyson back to the true front on Thirty-fourth, "welcomes friends here."

Beatrice appeared in the archway in a fancy apron with "Beware the cook!" stitched on it. She hugged Lyson and kissed his nose; she looked into his eyes and said, "You look great this morning."

"You too! John was just showing me the house—"

"Weren't we crazy! When we were young—" Beatrice laughed, and asked, "Is that your car?"

"Oh, yes! Want to see it?"

"Lyson," she sighed, "I hate to throw cold water on you, but that car—" She frowned and bit her lip.

The Captain cut in. "Son, Beatrice can be rather blunt, but I must say her tastes are—" he glanced fondly at her, "—are quite exotic—"

"We don't want to hurt your feelings, but—" Beatrice spoke so earnestly that Lyson couldn't help but appreciate her openess; "that style belongs to fat snotty smug achievers—not you!"

Lyson looked with new eyes at the Lincoln, in its present setting in Suffex, Islay, against the backdrop of his new surroundings in which trees played a prominent role among houses designed more for living than profit, in the company of people so different than the environs the Lincoln was designed for. "Why! You're right! That—that is—is—" he pointed at the Lincoln as at some monstrosity.

"Obscene!" Beatrice finished for him triumphantly, not over him but Detroit. "Let's get our breakfast," she suddenly suggested and the Quayles took his arms and welcomed him into their private life.

A huge painting of a flying schooner, bravely cresting storm waves whipped by a fierce gale, dominated the panelled wall behind the sofa which was covered in denim, the thin variety favored by sailors. Behind an oak roll-up desk hung smaller watercolors of small working sailcraft in pleasant settings of calm seas, soft sun, hazy clouds, sea gulls, with sailors placidly at work on sails, nets, and brass. Over the fireplace reposed a rusty anchor that looked so heavy as to have required a crane to lift it into place: huge bolts held it up against the masonry. A deep navy-blue carpet fringed with real rope with a white spoked ship's wheel woven into the center covered the polished wood floor. In a little semi-hexagonal bay facing Q Street stood a tremendous ship's wheel riding on a brass pedestal with a hooded compass. Lyson saw that the compass pointed slightly south of east. Magnetic declination, no doubt, he thought to himself, proud of this bit of nautical knowledge. "Turn it," urged the Captain. Lyson turned the wheel to the north. "More! Spin it!" Out of the ceiling blinds descended, covering the windows in the bay. On them was painted a mosaic of a ship's prow crashing into a heavy sea.

"Fantastic!" Lyson mumbled appreciatively as he turned the wheel back to the south, sending the blinds back up so the sun again filled the bay.

"Sean used to play with it all the time," Beatrice said quietly.

"Down at Port Ellen we have a nice old Herreshoff sloop," the Captain said slowly. "We've not sailed her since—since—"

"We'll take you down sometime," Beatrice promised. "Let's get our breakfast."

The dining nook was in a bay also, and the sunny yellow walls cheered them as the men took their seats around the round heavy wood table covered with grass-green cotton cloth. Already coffee steamed in cups, sending up vapors bright in the sunbeam. On the walls hung black and white photographs: summers of family fun aboard their sailboat over the years. The largest picture showed a small boy proudly, resolutely standing upright on the afterdeck, his legs spread wide for balance on the steeply heeling deck as his little hands bore on the spokes of the wheel. A John Quayle at the prime of life sat on the gunwale, leaning out over the water, hair flying as he looked affectionately at his son. The tumult of the sea, the billowing clouds, clothes and sails whipping in the wind and the intensity on the boy's face told of a splendid day. The kind that did not need a photograph to be memorable. . .

"Sean was only seven years old," Beatrice proudly informed Lyson. "There was nothing he couldn't do."

"He even drove the car," the Captain said with a shake of the head, "when he was only ten. He'd have done it sooner, too, except he couldn't see over the wheel or reach the pedals." He pointed out a picture of Sean in a shiny Chevrolet of the early fifties. The boy was craning his neck as he struggled for a clearer view over the hood.

"Seems like only yesterday," mused Beatrice slowly.

"We had such good times it's hard to believe he'd go—"

"Islay is such a nice place—the seas, the fields and forests, the beaches—"

"Hard to, but we try to understand where we went wrong—"

"We tried too hard—too hard to make him talk—"

"That's it, we went about it in the wrong way, the way the professionals—you know how it is with them—they're so so—"

"Authoritative," the Captain shook his head. "That boy had so much spirit—like us, that—that—"

"He had to go."

"Yes. If we had only—"

Beatrice noticed Lyson blinking back tears and brightly suggested, "Let's get some breakfast," and whisked into the kitchen.

"Lyson," the Captain laid a hand on Lyson's, "Beatrice and I have been most fortunate that you—" He squeezed his hand as Beatrice brought in their dishes.

The omelet smelt of cheese, peppers, onions, and bacon. Lyson smacked his lips as he allowed the aroma to prime his taste buds before the first juicy mouthful. Slices of crisp bacon, orange, and buttered toast surrounded the heap of omelet topped by a tree of parsley. "Beautiful!"

"A work of art," agreed the Captain.

A leisurely breakfast makes it more of an event, a happening, and Lyson felt right at home. Breakfast all his life had been a rush, something to hurry through, a necessary refueling stop in the grim race of life so that he would not falter in the coming day's competition. Each day a stop on the way to something better, sometime in the future, maybe. Here, now, in the Quayle nook, there was no maybe: the breakfast was delicious; a celebration in its own right. Lyson rolled each mouthful and noted its own identity and delight. Already the day was a success though it was only morning, so nice was the breakfast at the Quayle's. Lyson was very happy.

Beatrice smiled at the way he was eating and remarked to her husband, "It's fun to watch him eating, isn't it, dear?"

"Ahh, eating a breakfast like this is fun," replied Lyson with his mouth full. "I never before realized this."

"Let me tell you," the Captain said to Lyson conspiratorially, "You're quite a man. You've brought out the best in Beatrice."

"Bosh!"

He responded with a squeeze on her hand.

"This is a dream," Lyson mumbled with food in his mouth, "People like you—I've never known, never experienced such—such—" He shook his head in wonder as he crunched a slice of bacon in his jaws. For a while they were all quiet, lost in their own thoughts as they shared the moment together.

"I'm so corrupted by Washington," Lyson said suddenly, "I need your help—"

The Captain smiled. "That's one reason we asked you here—to be with us—and—and—"

"And we just happen to believe—" Beatrice added with an aimless, groping wave of the hand.

"Not just that—" the Captain declared with a searching frown, his hands clawing the air as if trying to grasp a morsel of truth out of thin air. "There's something, something somewhere that makes us—" He finished with a sigh.

"Of course some shrink can come up with the answer—" Beatrice announced dramatically with her arms folded, "but—"

"But he'll spoil the fun," finished the Captain, reaching for more bacon.

Lyson crunched another slice of bacon and said, musing, "Funny, I came to conquer, only—"

They all laughed over this, and Beatrice said mischievously, "Only to find a pair of old folks—"

"Aw! You're not old," Lyson protested, "Why, because of Washington, I'm an ancient fogy."

"Welcome to the fountain of youth!" the Captain declared in the manner of a promoter.

Beatrice seized both men's hands as they reached for still more bacon. "What you two need to do is go sailing!" she said as their hands slipped away from hers.

To admire the sea and to actually brave it are two very different matters and Lyson hastened to say, "That would be fun! But first let's—let's let me relearn how to swim—"

"Swim?" the Captain asked, trying not to be so incredulous.

"Right, it's been years and years since I was the eleventh best deaf swimmer in my class—"

"You're in luck!" Betrice slapped her hands, "Why there's a darling house with a pool on Central Promenade—"

"Yes! That's a great house!" The Captain whipped his finger. "It's really something too. You'll love it. I daresay it's one of the nicest in Suffex."

"Lyson," Beatrice held his hands, "It's not the biggest house; it's just very unusual, sort of like a castle. You'll love it!"

Lyson thoughtfully wiped his plate with toast. "It's a gamble, getting a house before checking out the—"

"Oh! The plumbing is fine!" Beatrice cried, "No gamble there, no leaks."

"Young man," the Captain advised, "with a house like that, the other things will come just fine."

"Imagine the swimming, the sailing, oh, the parties," Beatrice dreamily said.

Lyson could not help but break out in a wide grin. Why I do believe those people know what they're doing!

"There!" Beatrice smiled slyly, tapping a finger on his dimple. "You're getting into the right mood."

Captain Quayle leaned toward Lyson: "Let's go conquer that house! Confucius say thousand mile journey start with—"

"House!" Beatrice triumphantly finished for him.

* * *

As Lyson rode with Captain Quayle in the old Volkswagen, he fretted over having given Beatrice the keys to the Lincoln. Why, we've only known each other one day! But she was so charming, so motherly that he'd yielded the keys without a thought. Even the hotel key. Yes, some people could do that to him. He looked at his watch. Less than 24 hours! He felt as if they had known each other for years. He nodded to himself, making a deliberate determination to cast off the old Washington caution and plunge into the new style.

Central Promenade south of the park strip was really broad, with a wide divider running its entire length. Ancient elms marched in straight lines down the divider and on both sides of the street so that they formed a green canopy above, blocking out the sky. Lyson revelled in the cool shade as the Captain drove slowly, smoothly down the roadway. The homes were mostly hidden by foliage of all types: black beech, willow, maple, locust, honeysuckle, and various flowering bushes—but enough could be seen to reveal Central Promenade as neo-Victorian in character. One house was even painted lavender with violet trim; yet strangely enough, because of its multifaceted shape, the colors appeared entirely appropriate to its character.

At Eleventh Street the Captain made a U-turn, parking the car at the corner. "The agent will be here soon," he assured Lyson as they got out and stood on the sidewalk in front of the walkway leading straight to the house.

What a house! It was vaguely Victorian but done in smooth brown brick, with rounded corners and deeply recessed arched windows so that it gave the appearance of a medieval castle. Two cylindrical turrets like beacons rose up from the sides. The one on the left reached the main roof and was two stories high; the one on the right rose a full three stories high, towering above the house, nestling among the trees. Both turrets were topped by conical roofs of slate. Windows in the turrets were narrow and deeply recessed; and they faced three of the four points of the compass.

The agent drove up, and the Captain took Lyson's elbow and said, "Andy's an old friend. He'll help us get a good deal." As Lyson went to shake hands, Andy produced his calling card. Andy Tuper, Tuper Homes Realty, "Where Realtors go there goes America." Andy was a ruddy, brawny man in short sleeves and western style pants and Wellingtons. His greying hair showed shedding. Granny spectacles gave him a warm, grandfatherly look. Lyson found it easy to trust such a man. After exchanging pleasantries with the Captain, he said something to Lyson.

"Excuse me!" Lyson apologized, "but I'm—"

The Captain stopped him with a squeeze on the shoulder, and explained to Andy, "You just have to speak in the front of your mouth where he can see the words."

"Oh I see!" Andy said widely, contorting his jaw and lips, displaying excellent teeth.

"Relax!" Captain Quayle laughed. "Talk normally, but just move the words to the front, the way I do."

"Okay!" Andy laughed too and turned back to Lyson, "Bear with me! I'm just an ole country boy with a fat tongue. Let's go look at the house." As he led the way up the walkway a bulge in his hip pocket revealed the shape of a flask.

The entry was in the left turret: an open archway out of view of the street admitted them onto the black slate floor of something like a porch on the first floor of the turret; it was open to the air, with two open windows so that Andy half-joked, "If you want, you can put in windows and door, and call it something fancy, like vestibule. Haha." The inside of the porch was bare brick, and the entrance was where the true corner of the house would be were there no turret. It was arch shaped too and had convex double doors of heavy oak painted red, with black iron hinges and bands. From the center of the off-white stucco ceiling hung a black wrought-iron chandelier with flame shaped lamps, further graced with webs intricately spun by spiders comfortable and secure in such a fine environment for their occupation.

Andy finally found the right key and the doors swung open. They went through a large foyer with varnished louvre doors on either side into the main living room. Heavy oak beams gleaming in the ceiling. Rough white-plastered walls with oak posts serving as corners. Vines and leaves carved into the beams and posts. Brass carriage lamps on the walls from the days of gas. The wide-planked oak floor, highly waxed and polished, gleamed beneath Lyson's new shoes. An enormous stone fireplace dominated the room, almost large enough to roast a cow. High arched windows recessed deeply enough into the walls to curl up on the oak sills with a book. The windows contained wavy, old-fashioned glass, clear on the lower half but stained on the upper in colors of red, yellow, green, blue, and lavender, all arranged in floral shapes. A slight pleasant smell of danish oil in the woodwork filled the room.

The Captain and Andy stood respectfully at attention while Lyson wandered slowly around the room, his mouth agape. He stopped under the huge ship's wheel hung on iron chains from the ceiling, sporting brass ship's lamps all along its rim. "Lyson, watch!" Andy leaped and grabbed the spokes and swung wildly like Tarzan, sending Lyson shrinking back out of danger. Andy let go and dropped to the floor. "See! Solidly built. Look!" He jumped up and down on the floor. Lyson looked down and noted he could hardly feel any vibrations. A solid house indeed. The chandelier was still swinging like a pendulum and Lyson, concerned, reached up on his toes and stopped it. Andy caught this evidence of growing proprietorship and smiled broadly and asked, "Want to see the ballroom?"

"Please." Lyson glanced up for a last look and satisfied himself that the chandelier no longer required his attention. He followed Andy through another archway and into an immense room two stories high. It was a ballroom, the size of which he had only seen in hotels. The room seemed the size of an entire house. Lyson felt his mouth going dry. He promptly shut it and sucked up some saliva. The turret across in the corner was open to the room; a wrought-iron stairway spiralled up inside the turret to a round landing protected by an iron railing at the second story, and on up again through the ceiling to the third floor. Like a child, Lyson bounded up the stairs two at a time to the landing, large enough to serve as an open alcove in the turret, with a view of the entire ballroom below.

On the far wall of the ballroom stood an even larger fireplace. On either side of the fireplace at the second story level were two iron balconies with arched doors filled with stained glass panels. They were open and Lyson could see the hallway beyond. Fittings and two chandeliers each in the form of ship's wheel hung by long chains from the high ceiling. The ceiling, supported by even more massive oak beams, appeared to slant ever so slightly. Lyson asked Andy if it was the roof.

"Let's go see!" Andy urged. He and the Captain followed Lyson up through the staircase to the upper turret. The heavy plaster walls, the arched windows all around, and the beams rising to the center of the white conical ceiling gave the room the feel, the air, of a private little chapel. "What an office!" Andy prompted Lyson.

The Captain nodded solemnly at Lyson in agreement.

Andy opened a narrow door and Lyson stepped out into the sunlight and found himself on the roof. The copper sheathing had weathered into a pleasant pale green. He noted that the outer brick walls of the house rose higher than the roof, forming a parapet all around. Walking up the gentle slope to the huge double chimney sprouting a lightning rod and a television antenna, Lyson gloried in the tremendous exhilarating view all around of tree tops, leaves fluttering in the breeze. They obscured his view of the city, but, walking up and down the peak, he found a notch in the forest through which the sight of the lantern of the Bandstand sent his heart thumping. The pleasure on his face drew Andy and the Captain behind his shoulder for a look too.

"That's the Bandstand!" he cried.

"So it is," the Captain agreed.

"The person that built this house," Andy explained very helpfully, clasping his hands lovingly, "also built that Bandstand."

Andy took them back to the ballroom and tap danced his way to the kitchen in the rear. It was big and well-equipped enough for a small restaurant, with a walk-in refrigerator and an oven large enough to roast a pig biting down on an apple. In the dining room stood a long, heavy oak table with twelve chairs, and a glass chandelier twinkled in the light from the window. The breakfast nook covered in yellow wallpaper with falling leaf imprints lent a feeling of being out in the forest on a fine morning, so that every day, rain or shine, would be certain to get off to a good start. A broad, grand stairway carried them up to the mezzanine Lyson had seen from the ballroom turret. On the left the two doors opened out to the balconies overlooking the ballroom. Along the right were three bedrooms and bath. Why, the bathroom is as large as our living room, cried Lyson to himself. It was tiled entirely in white; on some of the tiles were baked colorful leaf patterns. The arched window displayed a life-sized Venus de Milo made entirely of stained glass, and because it was deeply recessed into the wall, gave the appearance of a living statue in a niche in some temple. Lyson approached the window for a closer look but Andy grabbed him before he could fall into the sunken bathtub, its rim nearly level with the floor. Stainless steel jets all around the middle level of the tub were poised, ready to spray on command. On one side of the room squatted the toilet. On the other was a bidet which drew together the eyes of Lyson and the Captain. They broke out laughing, and recalled to Andy Darcy's accident the previous night.

The master bedroom astonished Lyson with its full mirrored ceiling. He stared up at himself, his image staring back down. The Captain and Andy appeared in the view and they stared at each other and then broke out laughing. The Captain put his arm around Lyson and managed between fits of laughter to remind him: "I told you this house's really something, didn't I?"

"This is crazy! If Mary saw this—" Lyson couldn't finish so overwhelmed by mirth was he. He was laughing so hard he had to sink to his knees to keep from toppling over. This only served to bring Andy and the Captain down, too, in helpless guffaws. They all lay on the floor but the ludicrous sight of themselves in the ceiling mirror sent them ever deeper into laughter. Exhausted and keeping their eyes shut, they calmed down enough for Andy to get up, panting, on an elbow and fish out his flask. The whiskey numbed the laughter, although it must have taken at least another quarter of an hour of deep breaths before they could follow Andy to the sewing room in the turret off the master bedroom. It was done in feminine style, with filmy drapes and pink sheepskin carpeting. The men were warm and sweaty and weak from their bout on the floor. Andy slapped his thigh. "The swimming pool!"

Down a secret stairway, they came out in a huge glass-domed patio where lay a large kidney-shaped swimming pool. The one single door was the only opening to the pool, which was surrounded by brick walls. The floor was carpeted in green and around the pool stood white wrought-iron furniture.

"Ain't this super!" The Captain quickly stripped and dove in before the others knew it. The avid pleasure on his face as he swam around induced the clothes off Andy and Lyson and they dove in. Cavorting around like little boys, gleefully splashing one another, racing across the pool, floating on their backs squirting water up toward the dome, showing off diving tricks off the spring board, they had a grand time. Andy proved to be a most skillful diver, capable of a spin and half. Captain Quayle could manage a single flip but Lyson kept landing on his behind that soon became cherry red.

"Lyson, you're not kicking back hard enough," Andy advised. "Watch!" He ran down the board and sprang up into the air. He was just beginning his spin when Beatrice barged in cheerily calling out, "Hi Boys!" Lyson quickly jumped into the water. Startled, Andy began flailing his arms and legs, breaking the spin, and smacked flat on his back.

"Bravo!" Beatrice roared, clapping merrily.

"Beeetrice!" Andy admonished, swimming toward her.

"Don't pay me no mind, boys!" she held up her hands. "Go ahead and enjoy yourselves. I'll just sit and relax." She sat in one of the deck chairs at poolside, pretending to admire the dome above. Lyson helplessly treaded water as a means of covering himself. The Captain was laughing so hard he had to dog paddle to the shallow end lest he sink and drown. Andy splashed some water on the deck near her feet, suggesting with a gleam in his eye that he just might splash her dress. Beatrice grabbed his pants and covered her lap and legs with them. "My feet are cold," she said facetiously, and called out to Lyson, "Isn't this a darling house?"

"Can't see!" Lyson yelped, desperately roiling the water in front of himself. "My glasses!"

"Oh, that's right!" She got up, keeping Andy's pants between herself and the pool, and found the glasses. She set them on the rim of the pool and sat down, carefully smoothing the pants on her lap. "Nice pants aren't they, Andy?"

Andy sank moaning under the water, sending up bubbles. Lyson swam to the edge and put on his glasses. "What did you say?"

"I said, isn't this a splendid house," she said expansively.

"Fantastic!" Lyson agreed. "But it must cost half a mil—"

"Hush! I think we can get a good deal." She turned to Andy and said in her sweetest voice. "Isn't that right?"

Andy sank again, sending up ever greater bubbles. Beatrice seized the moment to cue Lyson: "We've got him right where we want him—" Andy rose to the surface and she quickly said to Lyson, "Would you like this house?"

Clinging to the pool's rim, Lyson nodded. "If the price is right."

Beatrice brightened and suggested to Andy, "A hundred would be about right, wouldn't it, dear?"

Andy moaned loudly as he sank down for the third time, holding up his hands in surrender. "It's done, Lyson!" She jumped up and dropped to her knees and kissed Lyson on the forehead. "Let's celebrate!" She pulled the flask out of Andy's pants and they all pulled from it.

Even Andy, ever the good fellow, had to admit it was an occasion worth celebrating and held up the flask, toasting Beatrice, "Let's all become partners!"

"Great!" She clapped. "With your inside knowledge, John's good looks, Lyson's money, and my charm, we've got Islay boxed in!" They laughed and passed the flask for another round.

* * *

The telephone roused Agent P-51 from his nap on the dressing table in Room 626. He quickly pressed the receiver to his ear but a stab of pain reminded him he was still wearing the ear phone. Cursing, he jerked out the ear phone and turned off the recorder.

"P-51 here," he finally said.

"Anything on 628?" asked B-52.

"Oh! I wouldn't know," P-51 apologized. "You see, I was—"

"You were what?"

"Ah, I was, I mean I was working—"

"I see."

"Some strange going-ons last night, very late," P-51 quickly explained. "And a message was sent to Washington on the coding machine."

"And—" B-52 prompted.

"And—" P-51 desperately tried to think of something, anything.

"And you fell asleep!" roared B-52, blasting P-51's ear.

"Look here," pleaded P-51. "I was up all night—"

"Okay, okay," said B-52 wearily. "So what's the score now?"

"Oh, ah—let me take a look." P-51 hurried over to 628 and after a quick look out for the maid, slipped in. He came out quickly, aghast and rushed to the telephone and cried out, "He's gone!"

"Not so loud!" yelled B-52.

Rubbing his ear, P-51 transferred the receiver to his other ear and said, "Sorry! I said he's gone!"

"Gone? What'd you mean?"

"There's nothing in the room. He's split."

"You mean he's checked out?"

"Apparently, unless he smelt us and—"

"Bitch! You clumsy lout!"

"I was careful! No way he could know—"

"Of course he knew!" roared B-52.

"But—but how?" cried P-51.

B-52 gave out a great sigh. "You and I are little league. Them Feds are big league."

P-51 became frightened. "Could he be tracking us?"

"Of course! Why else would he play deaf?"

CHAPTER 7

Refreshed from the swim though a bit sheepish the boys arrived at the Quayles for lunch. Bacon lettuce and tomato, the all-American favorite. But the pineapple sandwich was new to Lyson and delicious. The boys happily munched away while Beatrice propped her elbows on the table and rested her chin on folded hands, watching with a faraway look and, for once, quiet. Finally Lyson noticed, and asked lightly, "The cat caught your tongue?"

"Not exactly," she smiled wryly, "just kind of feel funny, a little awful—"

Captain Quayle leaned over toward Lyson, mischief bubbling in his eyes, and joked, "Well she might!"

"Andy is such a dear friend, a darling," she sighed.

"Aw, that's all right," Andy threw up his hands good naturedly. "It's only money—"

"But you're a friend and I—I—"

"You outsmarted me," Andy laughed, "before I could hoodwink Lyson."

"And every man of consequence," the Captain held up a finger, "needs a paper loss. To tangle up the taxes, you know."

"And besides," Andy said cheerfully, determined to be the good sport, "I'm glad to help Lyson get that fantastic house! Believe me, I really am!"

"Thank you! Thank you!" Lyson blushed.

"Lyson! You really don't mind, do you?" Beatrice suddenly asked, the kind of asking that comes in spite of oneself, when one ranges so far ahead of others that awkward waiting is necessary to allow the others to catch up. "I've been too pushy?"

"Oh no! No! You've been such a tremendous help. I'm ever grateful!" Lyson said quickly. He was about to gush some more but Captain Quayle urged a sandwich on him with a suggestion of enough said.

"Has it occured to you that I might be hungry?" Beatrice asked, pouting.

"Good!" The Captain passed her the sandwiches and declared for all to hear, "She and I have been married for thirty-two or is it three?"

"Thirty-four!" Beatrice reminded him through a mouthful.

"Right, thirty-four years, and let me tell you, there's not been a single one day, not one, that's been dull."

"John!" Beatrice giggled, very pleased.

"That woman still fascinates me," the Captain declared shaking his head.

"Let me tell you a secret," she said to Lyson and Andy, hiding her mouth from her husband, "John swept me off my feet when I first met him, and I've never, ever regained my footing—"

"Can't let her!" the Captain cried in mock fright. "She's too smart!"

Beatrice laughed, dropping the sandwich from her hands to cover her mouth.

"I can believe that!" Andy exclaimed. "I learnt that today. The hard way."

Beatrice was so pleased she decided to serve them ice cream and brownies before seeing them off in Andy's old McNamara Falcon. She watched them drive away toward the south. After a suitable period of timc to be sure they were good and gone, she jumped in Lyson's Lincoln and drove toward the west, toward Fremont.

* * *

Beyond the bridge Andy pulled off Right Road down a bumpy muddy forest lane to a small clearing on the river bank, twigs scrapping and slapping the underside of the car. In the center was a stone-ringed pile of ashes from numerous bonfires and all around in the trampled grass and weeds were litter from picnics: bottles, cans, paper, plates, sacks, plastic ware. "At night the place belongs to kids," Andy joked, "but on paper it is the Quayles. The Port of Islay." He spread his hands expansively. The clearing was on a shelf some ten or twenty feet above the river. They looked down the steep bare bank to the brown swirling water drifting massively on toward the sea. Above them on the left soared the bridge toward the east, the forests of Sutherland on the far bank. "We cleared this piece of ground years ago," the Captain waved his hand around, "hoping to build a wharf, but so far the only timber raised is in those trees."

"Yeah, amazing how fast the forest is growing back," agreed Andy. "It's only the kids that are keeping this little spot clear."

Lyson watched carefully where he trod his feet, to keep mud off his new oxfords. He stopped frequently to brush sticky seeds and dandelion puffs off his pants. Andy saw this and joked, "No worry, ain't but a few little snakes—"

"Snakes?" Lyson cried.

"Let me find one." Andy searched among clumps of weeds and suddenly lunged. He held up a writhing snake. "See! Just a garter snake." He brought the protesting snake over to the cringing Lyson. "Look, no teeth." He allowed the snake to clamp its jaws on his finger.

Lyson was about to draw out his new handkerchief but thought better and wiped his forehead and neck instead with a Swipe N' Dry. "No snakes in Washington, D.C., you know. Never get used to 'em."

"No snakes! You sure?" the Captain asked with a laugh.

"There's plenty. I know!" Andy agreed. "Congress, IRS, the Fed—lots!" He let the little snake go and it slipped away into the briars.

"Let's show him the industrial zone," the Captain suggested wryly and they drove back, slithering up the mud, on to Right Road and crossed onto another dirt road into a forest bordering the Freeway. "See, the Industrial zone. Not exactly the way it was planned but you could call it the lumber industry."

"Beatrice told me about this area," Lyson remembered. "She said it's zoned for light industry."

"Right," Andy said as they bumped along avoiding mud holes. "And it belongs to the Quayles, too." Lyson turned to the Captain who smiled back a Cheshire.

The oaks, hickorys, sassafras, poplars, and maples grew great and thick over the little road, with impervious underbrush slapping the sides of the car. They saw nothing but twigs, leaves and startled insects until they reached Wrong Road, a distance of some four long rough miles. Andy stopped on the shoulder of Wrong Road and pointed out the rapids on Wrong Turn under the great bridge to Transylvia. Andy asked Lyson, "What do you think?"

"Any Indians?" Lyson asked facetiously with wide eyes, jerking his head back toward the forest.

Andy laughed. "You're looking at one now!"

"Hold on to your wig," the Captain cautioned Lyson, "He's never really left the reservation."

Andy bumped Lyson. "No sweat. I've better, more agreeable ways of scalping you."

"Whew!" Lyson blew with relief, patting his head. "Just so you leave enough on my head to—"

"Pluck," finished the Captain with a wink.

Andy looked up and down the road and asked Lyson, "Seen the houses in town?"

"Oh yes! Must be hundreds for sale."

Nodding with a conspiratorial look in his eye, Andy said, "We'll sell 'em all, won't we?"

"Hope so," Lyson held up crossed fingers.

"For sure!" Captain Quayle declared. "With Beatrice on our side we can't lose."

"Plenty of time for Suffex," Andy was musing. "Lyson, why don't we drive around Islay? It's not too far."

"Ah, I'd like that!" Lyson agreed. "In fact I was going to suggest it myself."

"Let's go!" The Captain urged. "I'd like to check on my boat in Port Ellen."

Through wonderful, cool forests the highway ran to the southeast from Wrong Turn. Two lanes paved with asphalt meandered until they met the one running southwest from Right Road, and together they merged into an ancient concrete highway going south through farms and field up toward the apex of the Rhinns. There the road split into two routes, one running to the southeast and the other southwest, both following the ridges of the two arms of the wishbone shaped Rhinns.

At the top of the ridge, right at the apex of the wishbone, was an outcropping of white rock soaring some hundred feet in a rounded pinnacle above the fields and woods. Andy parked the car and urged them under the barbed wire into the field. He joked about an old bull thereabouts and Lyson worried about his new clothes. But Andy found a dusty old blanket in the trunk, shook it, and spread it beneath the fence. The Captain and Lyson removed their jackets and rolled under the fence and walked up the slight slope to the base of the pinnacle. "Look!" Andy pointed back toward the north. The city of Suffex ten miles away could be seen where the American River split into two forks. The bridges on either side of Suffex, and the towers of Fremont beyond rose softly in the haze.

"This is the highest point in Islay, 973 feet," Andy remarked in the way of realtors, patting the sheer rockwall. The rock loomed above them, resolute against the blue sky as Lyson stared up at its magnificence, and the thought of Mount Rushmore came to him. He briefly toyed with the idea of his visage carved on this solid rock and smiled.

"Splendid, isn't it?" Andy bumped him.

The rock was too steep to climb and Andy led them around its base to the south. The entire Sorn Valley spread out below their feet to the south, open all the way to Chesire Bay glimmering some thirty miles away in the haze. Lyson noted that the valley floor was flat until it climbed steeply up to the crest of the Rhinns. From there the slopes dropped normally to the rivers on either side. The nearly crater-like appearance prompted Lyson to ask Andy: "Could this be an old volcano?"

Andy laughed, "No, all this is sandstone and flint."

"Sandstone, sandstone," Lyson muttered to himself.

"Right, sandstone." Andy said in the agreeable manner of a working realtor.

Though the steep walls around the valley were forested, here and there some bare rock walls showed. Well-kept green fields with farmhouses and barns checkered the nearly flat valley floor. Dust rose from some of the roads behind moving dots that occasionally flashed in the sun. Sorn Creek could be seen meandering down toward a large squarish thatch of woods just beyond the center of the valley. Beyond the woods a pale-green patch stretched toward Indaal Cove barely visible in the distance. "What are those woods?" Lyson asked, pointing.

"Where? Oh, that's a big swamp," Andy answered.

"When we were kids we used to go in there," chuckled the Captain. "Scary. Lots moccasins."

"Moccasins?"

"Snakes. Poisonous, huge!" Andy held up his hands in a ball the size of a coffee can.

Captain Quayle hung two fingers from his mouth. "Big fangs. Bad snake!" He slithered a hand low toward Lyson who jumped back. "Real aggressive snakes."

Andy laughed. "When we were kids we hunted dinosaurs in there. With frog gigs." He took up the stance of a caveman with a spear. "I lost a gig to a big moccasin once. I aimed for his head but he moved and the gig stuck in his middle and—" He wound his finger up and around an imaginary spear toward his other hand. "Boy did we run out of there."

"Those were the days," the Captain agreed mirthfully. "When we got bigger we went in with 22's. Bang! Bang! But them snakes still kept after us. Tough!" He shook his head in wonder.

Lyson couldn't help but recall educational films on the oil industry that always seemed to begin in swamps. True, true, swamps are supposed to be the beginning, not the end product of oil fields. But he remembered seeing funny shaped hills—just like this one! "I want to buy that swamp!" he suddenly popped.

Andy and the Captain stared incredulously at Lyson and at each other. "That swamp!"

"Can't let them snakes stop us." Lyson put a foot on a rock, one hand on his raised knee, the other fist on the back of his hip and struck a purposeful stance as he gazed upon the swamp. "Hobby farm. Yes, a hobby farm to foul up them taxes," he said, nodding sagaciously, mysteriously.

"That swamp," Andy mumbled dubiously.

"If I remember correctly," the Captain said to Andy, though careful to speak clearly for Lyson, "That swamp has been bought and sold many times through tax delinquency."

Lyson pulled up his eyebrows. "Maybe it's delinquent now."

Andy shook his head, still doubtful. "It's never earned a penny for anybody but swamp rats."

"We could sell the snakes to some zoo," joked the Captain.

"Just the same," Lyson folded his arms, his foot still perched on the rock, "We'd better get it on our side."

"And raise moccasins," Andy weakly cracked, but promised, "We'll check the tax records."

"I believe it's in two counties," remarked the Captain.

"Right. We'll check when we get down there. This afternoon."

On their way across the field back to the car they encountered a herd of dairy cows that had suddenly appeared from the woods nearby. Lyson was judicious to keep the other two men between the cows and himself. "Can you tell which are the bulls?"

"Oh, the ones that are black with white spots are the boys. The girls are white with—look out!" But Andy was too late to stop Lyson from stepping on a pile of fresh manure.

They drove along the ridge top around toward Crewe. The road mostly went through heavy forest but occasional farms opened up the view so that they could see into the valley and across to the eastern ridge. The sight of cows reminded Lyson of milk, cheese, ice cream, and, most important, his new shoe. Once Andy stopped beside an impressive looking large, black animal, raw power rippling under its skin. "That's a bull," Andy explained helpfully, then burst out laughing. Lyson studied the eyes and shuddered at the malevolence burning at him. "That's no bull, for sure," he remarked to himself in respectful acknowledgement of its indomitable defiance, its masculinity.

Suddenly a little boy appeared running after the bull with a stick, yelling and whooping. His bare feet, caked with dried green matter now all too familiar to Lyson, flew over the sod as he ran the bull, now docile, toward the barn. Lyson stared in awe at the back of the boy's head, the wild hair flying and whipping, so heedless of the great danger rolling ahead of him.

"That's insane!" Lyson cried as the boy casually prodded the bull into the barn with his stick. "He could get hurt."

"It don't hurt the bull," reassured the Captain jovially. "The electric jolt ain't all that bad."

As they approached Crewe, the road gradually left the ridge top and slipped down its flank to a broad, treeless plain. The town of Crewe had roughly the plan of medieval towns: the institution for the handicapped dominated the center townscape, looming above the cottages surrounding it. The little houses looked exactly alike. White stucco walls, and black roofs without any eaves or overhangs. Red white and blue striped awnings over the front doors. Draperies drawn over all the windows. Neat lawns with hedges marking the lots. Flags limp on poles in the still heat. Were the institute not so omnipotent, serving as a beacon, they would have gotten lost on the streets, so alike did the houses and blocks look.

"How do they find their way home?" asked Lyson.

"This is where wife-swapping got its start," joked the Captain. "By accident."

"That's one of the attractive features of a company town," cracked Andy. "Fringe benefit."

"A company town?"

"Practically," nodded Andy. "The institute owns all this."

They arrived at the square in the center of Crewe. A sign announced: Islay Rectification Institute Square. The locals likely have shortened it to IRIS, the Captain said wryly. Little shops, cinemas, pharmacies, insurance agencies, cafes, haberdasheries, shoe repair, and other stores surrounded the square. As they drove around it, Lyson noted flat, heavily built, gray-brick buildings arranged so that their fronts faced the streets, with a huge playing field behind them, the very center of Crewe. Lawns perfect, bright green under the sun, unhindered by trees of any kind. The identity of the buildings were engraved into tomb-like concrete slabs standing in front of each building: Institute for the Blind. Institute for the Retarded. Dangerous Diseases. The Insane. Ambulatory Disorders. Corrections. Lyson was wondering where the school for the deaf was until they drove by the slab marking the Institute for Communicative Disorders.

"Let's stop here," he cried. "Let's visit this place."

"I'm not so sure you can buy this building," Andy said with mock dubiosity.

"No profit in it," agreed the Captain with distaste at the architecture of the building, the bricks painted a heavy gray. "Sean's stupid school."

"Just a quick look, then we can have a soda," Lyson nodded at the pharmacy on the corner across the street.

Andy drooled at the poster of a hot fudge sundae on the store's window. "You go on. I'll be there."

"I'll go with you," the Captain told Lyson, "Beatrice will never forgive me if they lock you up in there." Up the walk, through a gate apparently open for the summer, they went toward the institute. Its windows stood tall and very narrow in perfect rows, and as they got closer, chicken wire could be seen in the glass. Inside, the first thing they noticed was the strong odor of disinfectant, which brought forth memories for Lyson of his own school days and stung his eyes. The floor gleamed freshly waxed, reflecting the long straight rows of fluorescent lights through all the halls. Clay-grey walls. Battleship-grey doors. White ceilings. Sterile. Lyson and the Captain wandered down what seemed to be the main hall, wondering where they hid the office, checking the numbers on the doors, trying to figure out the system, hoping it would lead them in the right direction toward the office.

A door at the end of the hall opened and out came a woman with a pile of mimeographs in her arm. She was attired in a dark-green pants suit with lacey blouse and blue and white striped neck tie. Her hair was cut page boy style and, as she marched past them, her black shiny oxfords stomping on the floor, evidently in a big hurry, she responded to Lyson's raised finger with a sidelong glance, the kind people give when suspicious of disorders in others. A piece of paper fell out of her arms. He picked it up and cried after her but she stepped up her pace.

RULES FOR THE DEAF announced the title of the paper as Lyson and the Captain read it. "The behavior of hearing impaired and speechless children at the Islay Institute for Communicative Disorders has required the formation of new, more appropriate rules. September's rules are to be attached to your conduct notebook between pages 83 and 84."

1. The children must be respectful of their betters.

2. No gesture of the hands nor the face is tolerated.
3. The children must not speak first but are to wait until spoken to.
4. When speaking the children must mind their speech.
5. The children must sit on their hands in the dining room except when necessary for eating, drinking, or passing food.
6. Hands must be kept under the desk except when writing, turning pages, or adjusting hearing aids.
7. No note passing is allowed in class.
8. Hearing aids must be worn at all times except when swimming, washing, or sleeping. They are to be left ON at all times.
9. The children must keep their ears clean and free of wax.
10. The children must not speak with their mouths full.
11. No pointing is allowed. This is a gesture and as such is forbidden.

"Hopefully it will not be necessary to add any more rules next—" The paper was snatched out of Lyson's hands. The woman fixed him with those fish eyes of hers, then whirled around and went marching back down the hall.

"Hey, where's the office?" Lyson pleaded after her but she continued down to her door and shut it after herself. He and the Captain shrugged and continued down the hall. One door was different from all others: it had a typed note taped on it. "Problems with hearing aids are to be taken to the audiologist."

"Are hearing aids that much trouble?" asked the Captain curiously. "Sean would never wear his. Hated it here, cried everytime he had to come."

"Well, sticking a hearing aid on the deaf is like sticking big arrows in their ears," shrugged Lyson. "Galls them, reminds them of their disability."

"Did you wear one?"

"Of course. That was the rule," Lyson said rolling his eyes. "They make you look like a nerd."

The Captain scratched his head. "Do they actually work?"

"For a few, yes. The hearing impaired."

"Not the deaf?"

"The deaf know they're deaf," Lyson said with a slow shrug.

A few moments of silence, of pondering, of mulling, and the Captain turned to Lyson: "Did they ever ask your opinion—"

"Oh, no," laughed Lyson. "They never ask us. When we do volunteer an opinion they'd just smile and whisper among each other."

"Wouldn't it be nice if they listened for once—" mused the Captain.

"That would help," sighed Lyson.

They strolled down the hall, silent for a moment, and Captain Quayle brightened, "Maybe the Japanese come up with a honest hearing aid. Someday."

Lyson struck his palm. "And we'll sell 'em!"

"That's the spirit!" The Captain slapped his back.

"Only if they really work! Remember that!"

Captain Quayle lamented, "That's why I couldn't get rich! Couldn't even sell our old cars. Had to let Beatrice handle that."

"A splendid woman, that's for sure," agreed Lyson, admiration on his face.

"Fantastic! Lucky me." They reached an intersection of hallways and noticed a small sign pointing toward the office. There!

A woman was typing with her back to them as they entered. Grey hair rolled up in a bun and her necklace of pearls juggled as she typed. Navy-blue silken dress printed with pink roses. Plastic nameplate on her desk said she was Gladys. No windows, and the gray walls stood bare under harsh fluorescent lights. "Excuse me," Lyson called out as they rested their elbows on the counter, "but is this the superintendent's office?"

Gladys jerked around, startled, and studied them through cat's eye glasses with blue frames and jewels sparkling on the upper rims. "Excuse me," Lyson said with a quavering voice, apologetically. "I'm deaf and would like to meet the superintendent."

She stared strangely at him for a moment, and at John Quayle, and then back at Lyson, her eyes magnified by the lenses. Her eyebrows shot up signaling the appearance of an idea and she swiveled back to her typewriter. Out of a drawer came a fresh piece of paper that she rolled into the typewriter. As she began typing, Lyson whispered to the aghast Captain, "Let me handle this; play deaf but keep your ears wide open." The Captain winked and dropped his face into a blank look.

Gladys pulled the paper out and rolled her swivel chair across to the counter, shoving the paper and pencil in front of them. She had typed: "Are you hearing impaired and speechless?"

"No, I'm deaf," Lyson said in his best voice. "And I'd like to meet the superintendent."

She frowned, took the paper and slid back to the typewriter. She typed: "We only accept patients of school age. You should go to the Vocational Redemption Department in Suffex for help."

"Oh!" Lyson and the Captain exchanged indignant glances. Lyson said as carefully and clearly as he could, "We did not come for help. We would like to meet the superintendent."

With the same officious frown Gladys slid back to the typewriter. Lyson whispered anxiously, "Is my speech that bad?" The Captain shook his head in amazement. Perfect! She came back: "He is too busy serving patients with communicative disorders to see everyone that comes here. You should write a letter and make an appointment."

"Thank you, thank you," Lyson hastened to say and made for the door.

Gladys held up a finger and typed: "Your speech is very good. So this puts you in this category: hearing impaired but not speechless—"

"Thank you!" Lyson and the Captain fled the office and the building. Andy was already in the car, waiting.

"Let's go!" he urged. "The sundae is terrible. The ice cream tastes like powdered milk and the soda is flat. Here's some pop. Sorry, no beer. Here's the whiskey," he held up the flask.

"Keep it out of sight!" cried the Captain. "This is a dry town."

"Oh that's right. I keep forgetting."

A skinny old man in a baggy suit of fading grey with his obese wife in starched white, so white her bandy legs were clearly backlit by the sun, glared at them open-mouthed, angry and scandalized from across the street, the woman doing the talking and the man nodding indignantly. "Let's scram!" gasped the Captain and Andy accelerated the car down the street.

"Hope we find the road to Pembroke." Panic crackled in his voice and eyes.

"Mind the sun," advised the old navigator, "that's south."

"I've driven to Pembroke all my life and still have trouble finding my way through Crewe," confided Andy to Lyson.

"That's because your eye is always on the rearview mirror," laughed the Captain.

When I'm Governor—Lyson was thinking to himself when he spotted a fading sign: Pembroke. "There!"

The car lurched as Andy pulled quickly toward the Pembroke road. "Whew! Those are good eyes you got there."

"Right! We deafies can see," Lyson chortled as he held up his cola for the whiskey the Captain was doling out. "Why, my wife Mary can see germs with her naked eye."

"Come to think of it, so can mine." Andy shook his head.

"Indeed, Beatrice too." Captain Quayle held up his can. "Here's to our women!"

They clicked cans and drank to their women as the car left the city limits and raced down the pastures of Sanday County toward the south, and the waiting coast. Again the road climbed back on the Rhinns and followed the ridge top. A checkerboard of forest and field flashed by, and glimpses of the valley floor showed the coast drawing nearer. Already Lyson could smell the sea and could see that the pale green patch between the swamp and the coast was a marsh, with the creek meandering widely, leisurely, broadening into the River Sorn at the coast. The village of Port Ellen could be seen way across the river, surrounding a little harbor off Indaal Cove. "That's where the sloop is," Captain Quayle pointed toward Port Ellen. "We'll stop by and check her out."

"And sail it?" Lyson asked anxiously, eyeing his new shoes, one still neat, the other needing a good buffing.

"Not today," the Captain shook his head regretfully. "We have to let it soak in the water for a while, to seal its seams."

Lyson did not quite understand so Andy helped. "Just like soaking an axe in a pail. Lets the wood swell."

Lyson was confused even more. "I'm just a city boy. Won't that rust the steel?"

"If it rusts, it's good steel."

"Oh, I see," Lyson frowned and the Captain laughed, patting his back. "We'll learn you, my boy!"

A sign announced they were entering Clam County and the road started dropping down along the ridge toward the sea. "Hurrah! In a few minutes we'll have our beer!" declared Andy.

"Delicious!" cried Lyson as he drained the cola can and made a move to toss it out the window.

"Here!" The Captain grabbed the can. "Five-hundred dollar fine for littering. Besides, this is our state, isn't it?"

"Used to toss beer cans out in Sanday County," reminisced Andy. "Scandalize them preachers."

"Him and me used to dump beer cans in the garbage cans behind the churches," laughed the Captain. "We'd save 'em up just for that."

"We were only helping 'em." declared Andy with exaggerated innocence, "in their litter campaign."

"What happened?" Lyson asked eagerly.

"We didn't stick around to find out."

The car left the ridge behind and entered Pembroke. Immediately Lyson liked the town very much; the most unpretentious and charming town he thought he had ever seen. Practically all the houses had a widow's walk on their gabled roofs, and weathered cypress shingles for siding. Tall beach grass and driftwood for lawns. Small-paned windows heavily caulked against the salt-laden air. Overhanging porches supported by driftwood and enclosed with fishnet screens. Some windows even had fish net in lieu of draperies. Windblown sand drifts piled in gutters. Abandoned boats here and there lay in the sand, now serving as playhouses for children. Scruffy barefoot children were everywhere, racing down the middle of streets.

The road now followed the beach. Though a wind was blowing inland there wasn't much of a surf but the water was blue and flecked with whitecaps. Sea gulls soared and pelicans glided in the wind. "Perfect sailing day!" moaned the Captain.

Andy halted by a small old weather-battered building, its boards and battens silvery gray and smoothed by blowing sand. A fading sign swang over the dull red door: TAVERN. Before entering, though, they went around to the beach behind. On the sand thrown about quite haphazardly were some picnic tables. Andy and Lyson sat and stared out at the bay while the Captain went in the open back door for the beer. The sun felt good in the sea breeze. "I doubt very much that, outside of Florida, you can find a nicer place than Islay," declared Andy the Realtor.

"There is something to this place," agreed Lyson, enjoying himself, his companions and the setting very much. "Better than Florida, I think. Too commercial down there."

"It was a nice place," the Captain teased, bringing out three frothing mugs, "until you showed up."

"And will be even better," Lyson retorted as he reached for his beer, "When I—I mean we buy the swamp."

"We?" the Captain cried in feigned surprise. "The swamp?"

Lyson chuckled, holding up his mug with a sly nod, and they drank to their new enterprise. "Let's think of a new name for us," he finally suggested after a moment's reflection.

"Tuper Homes," Andy mused aloud. "Say, now that I can see the possibilities, it's too—too—"

"Corny," joked the Captain.

"Too near-sighted," nodded Andy.

"Islay Investment," Lyson piped up. "How's that sound?"

"Would impress bankers," agreed the Captain. "But people?"

"Islay Investment, Development, and Opportunity Corporation," laughed Andy. "That would wow 'em."

"Islay Success Incorporated," winced the Captain.

"We're barking up the wrong tree," announced Andy with a straight face. "It oughta be Islay Land Works."

"Crystal would love that," nodded Lyson gleefully.

"So would Beatrice," agreed the Captain. "Bless 'em."

"Swamps, real estate, filling stations, apartments, restaurants, malls, electronics, publishing, shoes, recreation, education, government, shipping, nursing homes, medicine—" Lyson counted aloud on his fingers the possibilities. "Why not just Islay Company?"

The Captain and Andy stared at Lyson in awe, and Andy snapped his fingers, "This calls for another round."

* * *

Clam County Courthouse was a frame building on a sandy lot between two houses, one converted to a medical clinic and the other to a secondhand marine shop. The county clerk was watering her plants when the boys came in. She wore blue jeans and a man's shirt, her long hair was streaked with gray, and her handsomely tanned skin gave her a wilderness seascape flavor. Lyson noted that her toenails, peeking through leather mesh sandals, were painted bright red though her fingernails were not. A little sign on the counter identified her only as Terri.

"Hi Andy and John!" she greeted them, obviously old friends. "Going fishing?"

"Kinda," grinned Andy. "Here's Lyson Sulla, our hottest new friend. He'd like to raise moccasins for the malice market."

A slow soft smile appeared in her brown eyes as she winked at Lyson. "You gotta watch Andy—" she teased Andy with a scolding frown and confided to Lyson, "That place is an awful swamp."

"Exactly!" Lyson cried enthusiastically. "It's perfect for—for—" He giggled and clamped his mouth shut.

Terri frowned with puzzlement, giving an accusing wink to Andy. "That'll cost you all of three dollars and eighteen cents."

Lyson stared at her and blurted out, "Excuse me! But I'm deaf! Here, let me—" He reached in his coat and pulled out his pen and pad but Captain Quayle patted his hand.

"She understands you very well."

"I do understand you perfectly," she assured Lyson. "I just am not so sure what Andy is up to."

"It wasn't my doing," Andy protested. "In fact—"

She stopped him short. "I love you! You're so innocent!"

"Fact is, Beatrice is the crafty one," the Captain said proudly.

"And how!" Andy rolled his eyes. "But that wasn't what I was going to say. Something tells me Lyson is the crafty one."

Lyson blushed and his voice cracked, "But it's for the good of—"

"Come on, Lyson!" The Captain grabbed the back of his neck and shook it affectionately. "We know you're guilty as hell."

"Lyson, if you could hear their voices," Terri soothed him, "you'd know they're only playing. They're like that all the time."

"Oh thank you! Thank you!" Lyson effused. "It's just that I've been in Washington, D.C. so long—"

"No need to apologize!" Terri patted his cheek sweetly. "Anyone needs to apologize, it's Andy for trying to sell you that swamp—"

"Don't blame Andy—" Lyson began but she put a finger on his lips and went to the filing cabinet. She found the papers for that part of the parcel within Clam County.

"This part is 320 acres," she pointed at the sketch. "The rest is over in Oyster County. Hey, let me call my friend at the Oyster office and see what's going on there."

Before going to the telephone she first pulled some cokes for them out of a battered refrigerator in the back. The boys had drained their bottles by the time she finished the call. "You're in luck! It's in arrears there, too. Eight bucks thirty one cents."

"Great!" Lyson pulled out his wad and peeled out three singles. He hunted in his pocket and came up with a dime and two pennies.

"Wait!" Andy cried. "I want in too!"

"Same here." The Captain slipped Lyson a dollar and six cents. "The Islay Company, remember?"

Terri put her elbows on the counter and rested her chin on her hands, watching with amusement as the fellows made sure they all contributed equally to the fund. She counted the money dumped on the counter and declared, "There's a ten dollar filing fee and a two dollar title-transfer fee."

As she typed up the forms, she asked for the address of Islay Company. The hesitation with which they came up with the address, finally deciding upon the old Tuper Homes address in Suffex, prompted Terri to remind them to register the new company with the Islay Commerce Department.

"Oh that's right!" Captain Quayle knocked his forehead. "Remind me to tell Beatrice."

* * *

Around Indaal Cove the road took them toward the village of Port Ellen, only four or so miles across the bay from Pembroke but thirteen by road. Across the distance from the west side, Port Ellen looked like a toy village, cottages built against each other in tiny rows, with a profusion of masts and white hulls tied to docks. Steep-roofed houses painted a variety of cheery colors, soft and muted though by the weather: yellow orange green blue and purple. Already Lyson liked the town.

"The channel from the creek runs close by there," explained the Captain, "that's why boats are there. This side the water is too shallow. When the tide's out it's all sandbars. Lots clams. Pembroke's a beach town."

"Splendid!" Lyson said, slowly nodding his upper torso so that his head, though itself held firm, nodded along with his torso. "Beaches, fishing, sailing, mountains, meadows, swamps, everything! Something for everyone!"

The Captain and Andy laughed at the entrepreneur's spirit in Lyson. Instead of just spending money on hobbies, he was scheming ways to make money out of them. "Softball, basketball, football, golf, swimming, tennis," Lyson counted aloud on his fingers, "bowling—hey! Is there an alley in Suffex?"

"Bowling alley?" Andy thought for a moment, and said, "No, I don't think. Over in Fremont."

"Ah! We'll build one!" Lyson declared. "I know a deaf manager of an alley in Washington, D.C. A good one, too. We'll make Islay the Deaf Bowling Capital of the USA."

"Bowling?" the Captain frowned, puzzled.

"Oh," Lyson turned to better face the Captain in the back seat. "That's a game where you roll a heavy ball—"

"I know that!" the Captain sighed, still frowning. "But—"

"Oh! I see what you mean. You see, bowling is a very important social function among us deaf in the U.S.A. Tournaments all the time. Local, state, and national. Big business! Attract deaf to Islay!" He thrust his fist in the air and struck the rearview mirror. "Ow!"

The Captain examined Lyson's fist and noted a skinned knuckle. "We'll have to get Beatrice to kiss it well."

"Now you know why I'm not much at sports," Lyson chuckled, rubbing his knuckle. "Ole Ten Thumbs, that's me."

The car rattled on the bridge over the creek and Lyson saw that it was a ancient wooden trestle. A peeling sign said River Sorn, Welcome to Oyster County. Andy stopped right above the creek and they all got out. The silvery timbers of the bridge were splattered white by many generations of sea gulls: even now the present generation was flapping, soaring, screaming, and defecating around them so that Lyson was much concerned for his fine clothing. Keeping clear of the snowy white tops of the guardrails by putting his fingers stiffly, carefully against their sides, he leaned out and peered down. The creek flowed deep and coffee dark and gentle. He looked up and followed its course up through the green wavy grass of the marsh to its source in the tall trees of the swamp simmering in the heat waves.

Andy rested his elbows on the railing, quite unmindful of what the sea gulls were doing to his elbows, and studied the marsh grass. "Look!" he bumped Lyson, "There's one." A vee wake was treading its way along the edge of the marsh grass. "A moccasin." Andy pointed so Lyson could find it. "Right there."

"Ah! I see it." His eyes were wide at the sight of his very first moccasin. "Let's get out of here!"

"Aw, not just yet," Andy chuckled, holding Lyson by the elbow. "They can't climb bridges."

The vee wake stopped as the snake raised his head out of the water, staring coldly at them. Like a periscope the moccasin's head drifted with the flow of the creek toward one of the pilings under them. Its eyes baleful, fixed on the boys, it started up toward the bridge deck, right where they were standing.

Andy and the Captain grabbed Lyson by the elbows and jumped into the car. Fumbling with the key, Andy said out of the edge of his mouth, "Maybe they can open doors!" Finally the car started and as they rattled down the bridge Lyson looked back and saw the snake's head rise above the timbers of the bridge deck.

Captain Quayle saw this too and declared to Andy, "Betcha that one remembers you and your gig."

"This calls for another beer," Andy panted, steering the car straight as they sped down between the frail guardrails.

"The day's getting late," commented the Captain. "Maybe we'd better stop first at the county and claim possession of all the moccasins of Islay."

"Smart thinking!" Lyson enthused. "Then we can really enjoy our beer."

The country clerk already had the papers waiting for them when they came into his office in the back of his tackle and bait shop. Harold Simpson had been a sportsman all his life and smelt faintly of fish. The only reason he agreed to the clerking work was that it brought more people into his store. He was tanned and weathered so deeply it was not easy to take seriously his function as county clerk, so that county business never became very governmental in Oyster County.

"Terri already gave my wife the particulars," he announced as he brushed aside the fishing lures on the counter and arranged the papers so that they all faced the boys for their signatures. "The property is all yours for $8.31 plus the usual fees, of course."

"How's fishin'?" asked Andy grandly, glad to take possession of his boyhood haunts, finally, though it be swamp.

"Pickin' up," grunted Harold. "The blues startin' comin' in. Trout too."

Lyson was studying the papers very carefully, to make sure all was in order. Harold frowned and the Captain quickly told Lyson, "Go ahead and sign. They're O.K."

"Oh! Sorry!" Lyson apologized, his face turning red. "Old habit—Washington—"

"That's O.K., we know," the Captain reassured him. Then to Howard, "Care to join us for beer at the boat?"

"Mabel!" Harold cried out. "Mind the store!" He pulled two six-packs out of the cooler in which was also stored bait.

They went over the cowpath behind the store to the boat. Indeed it was a real trawler, its timbers too long gone for floating anymore so that it had been hauled and parked on this lot. Now it served as a summer home for the Quayles. Beside it, propped up clear of the sand, was *Seajay,* the Quayles' sloop. Though the paint was peeling, the lines were fine and graceful so that even Lyson could appreciate them. Captain Quayle walked around *Seajay,* knocking on the hull, inserting a fingernail into its joints and seams, snapping the stays and shrouds, pulling the rudder to and fro, and proclaimed, "Why, she's as stout and tight as ever! All she needs is a bit of sanding and painting."

Harold laughed, and confessed. "I was afraid she'd dry and crack up. So I filled her with water." He reached under and pulled a wooden plug out of a sea cock; water gushed out.

The Captain opened his mouth and put his hands on Harold's shoulders. "That's a friend!"

"She leaks!" Lyson cried, crestfallen. "Can't you see?"

The other three men laughed, and the Captain ruffled Lyson's hair. "She's all right! Let's go in."

When they climbed aboard and entered the pilot house, Lyson saw that a U-shaped sofa had been built around the great spoked wheel. He marveled at the view all around through its little windows, like a tugboat, and at the brass bell, lanterns, compass, gauges, barometer, iron wood-burning stove. And the sea odor. A most excellent hobby, he congratulated Captain Quayle with his eyes.

"Like it!" the Captain laughed and put his arm around Lyson. "She's yours anytime you come to Port Ellen, hear?"

As the sun sank, the power of its rays waned and the sea breeze gave out. It was that sort of time when people, people attuned to the forces of nature about them, pause and take stock of their day as do sea gulls musing on their perches on pilings. That is how we so well remember our days at sea, the mountains, anywhere the sun holds sway over us. Lyson was humming all this to himself, swilling his beer. And the summers as a result are what we remember best, most enjoy recalling. Only seventy some summers do we experience and we remember them all so well, so fondly.

The beer was so good it took a few moments for the thoughts to sink in. The wind died down and the bay went glassy; and the realization came rushing of the dwindling number of summers left in his life—he panicked and sat up. "Time's wasting! Let's go see the town!"

The beer and fellowship was so good among the hearing, it took a few moments for the idea to hit them. "Sorry, we didn't mean to leave you out—" The Captain began an apology as he arose from his stupor on the sofa.

"No, not at all," Lyson quickly said. "The sun is setting—"

"Mabel!" Harold slapped his head and he went back to the store.

"A little nap, if you don't mind," Andy excused himself and stretched out on the sofa. "I'm who's gotta drive tonight—"

"Let's go see the house where I was born," suggested the Captain. Lyson was a bit dizzy and experienced difficulty in climbing down the iron rung ladder embedded in the side of the boat. The hull curved away from his feet, was why. The Captain had to leap to the ground and help Lyson down.

Ah terra firma, Lyson signed, and they promenaded into the village proper. There was something about this village that delighted Lyson very much. Just like a toy village it was, the houses so small and neatly joined together, broken only by side streets, and alleys too narrow for the passage of anything more than people. This village, Lyson thought to himself headily, is built for people, by, for, and of people. Mystical, timeless. He and the Captain walked slowly, bumping into one another and stopping often, taking the bumping to be a summons from the other. Rather than confess the bumping to their giddiness, they would point out features that impressed them, and comment on the goodness of the people encountered, their openness, freedom, lack of restraints so necessary to survival in, say, Washington, D.C. Lyson remarked on the willingness of the people to use gestures upon discovering he was deaf. More Irish than Scot appeared the people and the village, declared Lyson, and agreed the Captain.

When they got deep into the village, around a curve in the street so that they were entirely surrounded by houses, nothing to see but houses and endless houses, they noticed the little details that made the whole so unique. Each and every house was built up of individual stones, each stone was cut to fit its own niche. No one niche like any other. Lyson looked closer at the stones and was surprised to discover no mortar. The stones fit, just fit together somehow. To wreck a house, Lyson and the Captain marveled to each other, you'd have to take it apart stone by stone, starting from the top. Nobody wants to do that kind of work anymore, so will the houses, the village, remain a good long time. Yes, timeless is the village of Port Ellen. Lyson was very charmed.

The house where John Quayle was born stood where the curve straightened, so that a grassy knoll could be seen rising at the far end of the street. Pink stucco over stone was the house, and the Captain remarked with some humor, "My ma wanted a girl."

Lyson stared at the house, his mouth open, and the Captain added, "Not really. It was white when I was little. Otherwise it's just the same." It was a solid house, with walls at least three feet thick. The many paned windows along the ground floor were recessed maybe a foot, enough for flower boxes on the outside sills, and all manner of bric-a-brac inside. The people of Port Ellen were a practical sort, so most of what Lyson could see were what he would have to call useful: lamps for the most part but also books, vases of all kinds filled with this spring's flowers and last autumn's foliage, cattails and ferns mostly. Fireplace pokers and shovels, pillows for pets and children, even a wicker crib with an actual baby sleeping in it. Through one window could be seen a family watching television. Lyson backed away embarrassed but the Captain waved.

The woman opened the door inquisitively, and the Captain sheepishly admitted, "I was born here in this house."

"Oh!" she said and pointed to her ear and mouth, shaking her head ever so gently.

Lyson fell back very surprised. *Deaf?*

The woman's eyes widened as she nodded. *Deaf?*

Yes! My name first Lyson, last Sulla. Formerly Washington D.C., now live there Suffex. He was so astonished he signed awkwardly.

Really! Surprise, first time ever meet deaf here, she signed wonderously, in a charming, old-fashioned manner.

Never dreamt!

She took them in and served tea. She was plain in a very pleasing way, attired simply in a cotton-print house dress and loafers and probably older than Lyson himself, yet somehow she appeared ageless. Her name was Susan Donaldson, formerly Ross, she said, and her husband Randy was hearing, a carpenter by winter, fisherman summers. He's gone fishing, where she didn't know. Maybe Maine, she shrugged. Her two children were too busy watching television to mind them. She sighed and said they were hearing too.

Thrill, come here you? she finally inquired of Lyson.

Visiting, he hastened to say. *See, my friend here Captain Quayle, himself born here, same house, that why popped-up here—*

Susan explained she was born here too, same house, and grew up in Port Ellen. No she did not go to Crewe, but went to school with hearing right here in Port Ellen. No problem, most of the people here were related to each other one way or the other. In fact, her great-grandmother was a Quayle. Her husband, though, came from Sutherland, across Right Fork. He was a good man and understood, so they lived in Port Ellen where everyone knew and accepted her, same as hearing, no problem.

You mean, hearing here treat you same hearing, no-matter deaf? Lyson asked incredulously.

Of course, we grew-up together.

Wonderful, wonderful, he mused as he sat back far enough to notice the chair was deeply padded.

Again, Susan inquired of him, *Thrill you here?*

Lyson bit his lip and thought of the peace of the good people of Port Ellen, and Pembroke too, and how that peace had been achieved. He bit his lip again and shivered.

Captain Quayle, unable to keep up with the conversation between the two deaf people, beyond the fact Lyson just now had hesitated and shivered, stood up apologetically and said, "We gotta go to the harbor before dark, and get back to Suffex tonight."

Come back, will you? she cried to Lyson at the door. *Never see deaf here.*

Certainly! Lyson promised and followed the Captain out.

"Captain, we didn't mean to leave you out—"

"Oh, that's okay, just thought we better get going—"

They hurried down a very narrow alley and came out on the harbor soft and fluorescent in the dusk. On the right, on the lawn circling the harbor, was a little bandstand, a toy, a miniature of the big one in Suffex.

CHAPTER 8

Night was well established when they arrived back at the Quayle's in Suffex. A note on the table read: "We're over at Lyson's new house. Come on over. Love, Beatrice."

"We?" puzzled the Captain. "Let's go."

More cars than the people had ever seen in Islay were parked in the street around the house and Andy had to park near the Bandstand. As they walked back to the house, Lyson wondered aloud: "Somebody must be having a party."

"If I know Beatrice, I'm afraid it's us," commented the Captain.

"It's us," agreed Andy, indicating the lights in all the windows of Lyson's new house. Lyson could feel his knees weakening, his feet and hands growing numb, his heart racing, and his brain reeling. The Captain and Andy gripped him under the arms and helped him up into the house.

At the door stood Mary, resplendent in fire-engine red satin evening gown, a necklace sparkling around her neck, a teasing scold in her eyes. Lyson stopped abruptly, staring at his wife as at a vaguely familiar stranger. Mary also had a new hairstyle, so exotic as to be stunning.

Remember me? Mary signed with laughing eyes.

Lyson crossed himself as her signing style dawned on him he was facing his own wife. They fell into each other's arms, laughing, their eyes wet. As they gazed at each other, wondering how all this had come about, she suddenly looked up at Lyson's head and narrowed her eyes. *Comb!* She whisked him into one of the closets in the foyer with the familiarity of a woman who knows every corner of her house. To Lyson's surprise, a light turned on, and there in the side of the huge closet was a wash room. *Andy never showed—*

Sunburn your face! She ran her fingers solicitously over his forehead and cheek and pale dimple. *Out all day?*

Yes! Bought land very cheap!

Smell beer! She scolded him, brushing his new jacket. *Beautiful.*

That land, I feel sure have oil! Secret you! Mum you!

How know? She lowered her eyelashes sceptically.

With a few smooth gestures he described the crescent of hills with the swamp in the middle.

Swamp! You bought swamp! Oh no! She dropped her shoulders in exasperation.

I saw oil movies show swamp! He protested defensively.

She searched his eyes, wonderingly. *I always thought oil found where area sandy.*

Lyson brightened as he recalled the sandy expanses of Pembroke, Indaal Cove, and Port Ellen, and the clear coffee-colored water of the creek. His hands described the picture with enthusiasm, *Sand there! Under! I saw!*

Mary smiled fondly at his irrepressible optimism. *I trust you.* Then her face changed to an awe: *You adept buy this house cheap, how?*

Thank Beatrice help me.

Yes! Wonderful woman. She help me come-here.

They looked at each other, overwhelmed by the wonder of it all. *How? How?*

Mary smiled. *She borrow your TTY. Call me this morning. Told me meet her there Fremont train.*

Wonderful! Then he half-smiled. *Did she take you there store buy new clothes?*

Yes! Her hand laughed along with her body. *She take you, too?*

They hugged, laughing happily.

You lucky meet many many wonderful people.

Yes! He sighed gratefully. *Thank Beatrice and Captain. Magnificent help help me. Their help mean we sure success!*

Sweet! Her eyes softened with admiration for Lyson. *Warm heart.*

She finish tell you about her son?

Yes! They hugged and rocked together. His nose noticed a new aroma, delicious and dizzying. *New perfume?*

Yes! Like?

Very!

*You smell like sun beer grass and—and—*She frowned, sniffing at a strange and unfamiliar odor. Startled, Lyson looked down quickly at his offending shoe.

Cow—he explained lamely.

Give me! she commanded. *Comb! Wash! Brush teeth!*

Before opening the door and going out into the party, Mary whirled and bewailed, *Before forget: parents can't come tonight.*

Lyson stared at her, incomprehending.

You see, Beatrice called my mother, and yours, invite them come here house celebration. But my mother said couldn't come, because have to-go to big benefit dance, important thrill there Boston.

Oh.

Yours cannot come because your mother has-to chaperone tonight meeting their oral deaf club. Herself patron oral, you know that. Your father himself has-to stay home, take-care-of cats, can't leave them alone.

Oh.

Yes.

* * *

From where he reclined in his rocker out on his porch, Governor

Wenchell noticed, across the park strip at the other end of Central Promenade, an inordinate number of automobiles parked on both sides of the street. Never before during his years of governing Islay from his porch had he ever seen so many cars except perhaps when the Bandstand featured some orchestra or oratory. The night was pleasant and cool as he sipped his mint julep and studied the glint on the cars under the street lights. Soon he spotted a form running across the park strip and up to the porch.

"Most of the licenses are from out of state!" panted Agent B-52. "D.C. Maryland. Virginia."

"Around Washington," nodded the Governor.

"Yeah, but no Lincoln." Agent B-52 threw up his hands.

"I see," the Governor frowned. "What's up?"

"Some kind of party at the old Durham Castle." He wiped his forehead with a handkerchief.

"Party?"

"Yeah. P-51 is crashing it."

Governor Wenchell winced. "Crashing?"

"Oh, I mean investigating," B-52 assured him.

"I know, I know." He sank deeper into the rocker, draining his glass. "Keep hunting for the Lincoln!"

"Right!" Agent B-52 darted down the stairs and made for the park strip.

"Cool it!" yelled Slappy Wenchell. "Not so obvious!"

A car passing by on Ninth Street had to brake hard to avoid the running figure bright in its headlights. The driver stopped in the middle of the street, staring at the man fleeing across the park strip. He turned to look in the direction from which the runner had come and saw the Governor, his suit bright in the light from the porch lamp, sinking deeper into the rocker.

"Hey Guv!" the driver cried out, "You okay?"

"Oh yes! I am!" the Governor groaned. "Thanks!"

* * *

He and Mary had entered the Great Ballroom so quietly, unobtrusively that Lyson had time enough to survey the guests before being overwhelmed by friends. Why, nearly all his friends from Washington had come. Graceful flying hands flitted about the perimeter of his vision. Welcome hands! Teachers from the college in Washington. Government workers. Printers. Businessmen and professionals. Executives from various deaf organizations. People he had known for years since college days. The very people he hoped to bring to Islay! Please! Stage fright caught hold of him and he stood rock still.

In the ballroom as yet was no furniture other than a couple of card tables, likely borrowed from the Quayles. Sparkling glass punch bowls filled with ice-chilled champagne, platters of little sandwiches Lyson believed were called hors de vers. Silver bowls of nuts and cherries stood alongside mountains of dark olives and deviled eggs. Crystal appeared, as out of a mist, at his side and poured him a cup of coffee.

"Things have been going real swell for you, I hear," she remarked, her eyes wide at the wonder of it all. "And fast."

"You look great," he complimented her, noticing her soft, yellow sari wrapped gracefully around her body, over one shoulder, leaving the other bare, covered only by attractive freckles, lissome in the warm, soft light from the chandeliers overhead. In his honor no doubt, she had removed her nostril ring, leaving a pin mark barely discernable only by those who knew it was there. On her toes, however, those little rings remained, and her sandals were of the simplest sort, held on only by a knotted leather thong between the two bigger toes. "You are beautiful," Lyson said softly as she touched his dimple with warm lips.

"Have you met my wife Mary?" He quickly said, looking around. There she was, beside him, looking on him in amusement.

"Yes! Isn't she a darling," Mary said and signed at the same time. "Beatrice introduced everyone already."

"Drink your coffee," Crystal suggested solicitously to Lyson. "And have a sandwich, You look done in!"

"Ah, you're right! Thank you." He gulped down an entire hors d'oeuvre and another and another.

Stop! Save for others. Mary grabbed his arm and led him to the deviled eggs. *Two enough!*

Lyson needed three though, and he sighed and sipped his coffee, signing with his free hand, *We forgot lunch, but stopped, eat clam chowder there Port Ellen. True delicious. You, me must go-there. Like that area you will. Nice people, friendly to deaf. Met deaf woman, grow-up there—*

Yes, we must go, Mary agreed. *When settle-down.*

"I must learn how to sign," cried Crystal, watching the two of them signing so effortlessly and swiftly to each other that to her eyes it seemed ethereal, fluid. "Beautiful."

"Good idea," declared Lyson, gratified at her interest. "Why, Mary here is a certified teacher of signs!"

"I'd be very happy to teach you, Beatrice, and the others," Mary agreed. "It'll be fun!"

Beatrice joined in. "But at my age—"

Dottie chimed in, "Why you'll be the life of the class!"

Lyson stood a bit aside, his hands behind his back, rocking happily on his heels as he watched the women banter among each other. A hand on his shoulder turned him face-to-face with the very person he'd hoped to see: Wally Ballinger, deaf bowling champion for many years, now manager of the Capitol Lanes in Washington, still attired even now in bright-green bowling shirt and shoes.

Wally! Glad see you! Lyson's hand jumped. *Must talk!*

Surprise you bought swell house! They embraced.

That reason why you, me must talk. Lyson signed so fast and small that only Wally could see and understand.

Mary came out and circled her arm around Lyson's waist. *Hi Wally!*

Sorry late, Wally signed apologetically. *Had-to wait until bowling closed, then drove-fast here. Splendid house!*

Yes, like-it! The wonder and surprise was still with her. *Never dreamt would find house like this.*

A distinguished looking man, in tweeds despite the summer, naturally tanned the year round, with a well-formed face made strong and square by the jaw and nose, his black hair grey at the temples, appeared at Mary's side.

Donald! Lyson cried, gripping his hand. *How's Gally?*

Fine! Still growing, the old teacher grinned with the assurance of a secure man. *Thrill move here?*

Long story, Lyson replied mysteriously, and looked around conspiratorially. *Will tell you private later.*

Ah, secret? Really? Doctor Donald Vought laughed skeptically.

Yep! went Lyson's fist nodding vigorously.

Donald's wife Annette leaned past her husband and her hand reflected her surprise. *Never before Lyson secret! Secret! Now change?*

Will tell you when time. O.K.? he teased them.

Curious! Tell me now!

Will! Patience.

Give us hint, insisted Annette.

Lyson took in a deep breath, raising his eyebrows as high as they could go. *Well! How would Donald like chance prove his idea about Ameslan—*

Donald was intrigued. *You mean my old idea that deaf children can learn English better if start with Ameslan at school?*

Yes! And you know I agree—Lyson paused for effect—and support that idea. Why, it's natural! Common sense!

We deaf know that, but hearing people— sighed Donald *even Gallaudet College itself supposedly for us deaf but becoming more more hearing than deaf.* He shrugged at the futility.

Lyson raised a finger to make an announcement, but Mary interrupted, *Right time, now?*

Silently Beatrice, having satisfied herself that the Captain and Andy were settled and comfortable, appeared beside Lyson and hugged his arm, her eyes bright with delight at the way hands flew around, so spirited, graceful and florid, so expressive. She wished Sean could be here now. He would then feel right at home!

"Beatrice!" cried Lyson, "I want you to meet my old friends. Wally Ballinger the great bowler. Doctor Donald Vought, my old professor at Gallaudet College and his wife Annette."

"We've already met." She squeezed Lyson's arm affectionately. "You have such fine friends."

"But I always thought a man is known by his enemies," joked Lyson.

"And the company he keeps," added Donald with a wink.

"Doctor Vought was one of my favorite professors—"

"And Lyson was one of my worst students," laughed Donald. "A regular rabble-rouser!"

"Really?" brightened Beatrice. "That's my kind of boy!"

"Gallaudet was never the same since he became President of the Trumpet," reminisced the professor. "Lots of fun. Nonsense but fun."

"And Islay will never be the same!" trumpeted Beatrice, her fist thrust up in the air.

Donald rolled his eyes. "With Lyson you never know! Sometimes he's shy, other times wild."

Doctor James Shooner, who liked to call himself the village shrink, though his practice was in Washington, appeared in the circle and offered: "Anyone want to know the answer?"

Lyson blushed, quite shy at having his soul dissected, but Mary interceded, *No shop talk here! Party!*

Actually, I want talk with you, Lyson very carefully signed to the good doctor. *Private.*

Doctor Schonner teased him by raising his eyebrows and peering closely at Lyson's forehead: *Emergency?*

Oh no! Lyson hastened. *Business.*

Other friends came forward to greet Lyson and Mary, and to congratulate them on their unique new home. They were all curious about Lyson's move to Islay, a two hour commute from their jobs, so that Lyson had to promise them an annoucement.

He and Mary slipped back into the closet and he lamented, *This happening too fast, faster than I expected.*

Too fast? asked Mary.

Don't-know. Maybe good but you know me, prefer plans.

Flexiblity! urged Mary. *Remember you always told me about tree with deep roots but flexible branches, can stand any storm.*

Yes! But we not-yet grow roots! Tree growing fast,roots not-yet deep enough—

Okay. Mary calmed him. *Tell me what your first plan.*

Lyson sighed and thought for a moment. *I suppose, bowling alley—*

Good. Now I go get Wally. Wait here. She slipped out before he could protest.

Is this the time? If we go too slow, will other smarter deaf barge ahead of me? Lyson was fretting to himself when Wally came in, quietly, tentatively, bearing two glasses of champagne. For many years Wally had attempted to teach Lyson how to bowl, but soon realized that Lyson would never take the game seriously enough to learn it. Lyson had too many distracting thoughts bubbling in his mind to concentrate on a heavy ball or distant bowling pins. Now Wally sensed something significant in this meeting. His eyebrows arched in anticipation as Lyson stopped pacing and faced him, quite gravely. A deep sip of champagne and Lyson began signing. *You want become partner in bowling alley for deaf?*

Wally smiled. *You know that my dream ever-since.*

Lyson returned the smile. *I know perfect place for establishing bowling center for deaf. Not only bowling but other things for deaf, sports, recreation—*

That my dream too, Wally agreed. *But where good place?*

Looking around for a place to set down his glass so he could use both hands to greater effect, Lyson found a hat shelf, and before putting the glass there, drained it. He breathed deeply and plunged into his plans. *You know where freeway off-ramp coming from Fremont?*

Yes, Wally nodded. *That's how I arrived here.*

Near that, where now forest, can get plenty land. First want establish bowling. Then movies captioned for deaf. Pool, ping pong, arcade games. Possible health spa, tennis—Maybe can invite Red Skelton—

Wow! Deaf will love that! agreed Wally.

Sure! Myself thinking about something like mall kind-of buildings for different recreational things. Restaurant, too.

Wonderful! I want you know that myself very interested. Wally paused and signed more thoughtfully: *But where deaf?*

Lyson grinned impishly and took down his wine glass. *Wait. You think for few minutes. Want more champagne?*

Sure. Wally drained his glass and handed it over.

Back soon. Lyson went out and Wally mused over the image of the recreational mall. Beautiful! Beautiful! Instead of the families of deaf bowlers either being passive spectators or staying at home, they could come and play other games. Or watch captioned films. And have dinner together afterwards. Excellent! But feasible?

Lyson returned with two full glasses and they toasted each other silently. *Okay, you ask where deaf?* Lyson began. *That's exactly whole purpose our idea.*

Wally frowned, not quite getting the idea, and urged Lyson on.

Okay, let me tell you whole idea. He placed the wine glass on the shelf and rubbed his hands. *You see, Islay itself very small state. Only 300,000 people, last census. Maybe less because many vacant houses for sale now. My aim, bring deaf people here. More, more deaf move here, grow, grow, become deaf state.*

For a few moments Wally stared numbly at Lyson and then burst out laughing, so uproariously that he spilled his champagne all over his pants. Lyson was crestfallen as he watched his friend leaning against the wall for support until his convulsions subsided. Wiping his tears and pants, Wally shook his head, overwhelmed, and managed to sign, *Good idea! Never thought!*

Greatly relieved, Lyson went into the bathroom and got a towel for Wally. Wiping his pants, Wally looked on Lyson with admiration. *I should've known you would adept think something like this!*

Just happened, notice map and idea grew and grew, Lyson shrugged modestly and raised his eyebrows cautiously, *You still interested?*

Of course!

Lyson was still cautious. *True big gamble. Don't-know if will succeed.*

Worth trying! Wally was the confident one now. *Myself know that many deaf there Fremont and Glouchest, very popular bowling. Not far from here.*

Right, Lyson said happily, his enthusiasm returning. *Fremont only 10 maybe 15 miles from here. Glouchest I think about 30 miles. Myself hope many deaf move here but still keep jobs there. Easy commute.*

Can sponsor tournaments. Washington, New York, Philadelphia, Wilmington, Baltimore. Thousands deaf.

Lyson seized Wally's hand and pumped it hard. Just then a loud booming noise reverberated, resounding through their chests and the back of their heads. *Music! Let's go face music!* Lyson cracked and they went out patting each other on the back.

* * *

Trent had set up his drums in one corner of the ballroom and amplifiers at the other corners. He banged away while Crystal played her electric guitar, swaying and jerking her body, snapping her head to the beat, her splendid black hair whipping and flying. Her eyes had such a faraway look that at first Lyson thought she was in a trance. But then her eyes met his; she flashed a smile and threw up her heels. The bangs, booms, buzzes, screeches of the drums and guitar filled the ballroom like the inside of a drum, while Crystal's dancing mesmerized the crowd of deaf people overwhelmed by the sound and sight. Suddenly, the Captain whirled Beatrice around and they began a rousing, kicking dance. Soon everyone got into the mood and began whirling around, except Mary and Lyson, whose feet seemed hopelessly impaled to the floor.

Mary smiled sweetly, her eyes wide in anticipation, her hand out to him. *Mary!* he pleaded. *You know I can't dance!*

Come-on! She grabbed his hand and began swaying and kicking, jerking his hand so that he too started shuffling his feet. She continued urging him with pulls on his hand until his feet started getting the feel of the music. Soon his shyness melted and they were whirling around at one with the crowd and the thundering beat.

This really dancing? his free hand exclaimed as Mary artfully manipulated him around the floor.

Yes! Good! Her face glowed with pride and joy.

Their other friends noticed Lyson dancing, for the first time in their memory, and urged him on with nods and smiles. He noticed their stares at his feet and looked down too. Even he was amazed at the life in them, the way they flew about quite independent of him. He was still watching his own feet dancing when a hush fell over the ballroom and everyone else including Mary stopped dancing. Only when she squeezed his hand very tightly did he look up and notice a man in the doorway from the kitchen, his hands high in the air, his face ashen.

Though Lyson was himself surprised and agape at this spectacle, his feet continued dancing. Only when the man met his eyes and they recognized each other did his feet come to a stop. One of the Governor's bodyguards!

Through clenched teeth the man declared with all the defiant dignity he could muster: "Name: Bruce Morrison. Rank: P-51. Social Security Number: 527-60-8348. That's all you'll get outa me!"

The deaf people stared incomprehendingly at the strange man and at each other. *Thrill?* their hands asked of each other. Crystal was the first to recover and she announced with clear, easy to read lips what P-51 had said. Everyone was even more confused.

Then P-51 arched his back, wincing at something poking in his back, and stepped forward into the ballroom. From behind his back Darcy poked his head, grinning hugely at his coup, poking his finger into P-51's back, prodding him further into the room. "Caught him!" he gloated triumphantly, one fist in the air.

Darcy!" cried Dottie rushing to his side, wringing her hands.

"He was spying on us!" hissed Darcy through thin, accusing lips.

P-51's face turned a deep red when he saw how small Darcy was, and the finger that was no gun. He dropped his hands to cover his face and groaned loudly, "No! No!" and knocked his head with a fist. "Dumb me!"

Swiftly, sweetly, Beatrice came up, put her hand on his shoulder and rescued him. "Welcome to the party! We don't mind crashers."

"I—I—ah," P-51 groped, his eyes thanking Beatrice. "I was just—just—"

"That's all right," Beatrice reassured him. "Party-crashing is one of the finest compliments a party can have. You're welcome!"

"He was spying!" hollered Darcy indignantly.

Dottie whisked Darcy off to the side, hugging him firmly, her head jerking as she exhorted him into silence.

"He's only a young boy, hehehe," giggled P-51 lamely, frantic for understanding.

"He may be young," Dottie flashed at him. "But he caught you!"

"That's one of the risks of party-crashing," Beatrice quipped as she gripped P-51 by the elbow and led him to Lyson and Mary. "Meet the hosts, Lyson and Mary Sulla. This is Bruce, our very first party crasher."

As their hands grasped, Bruce and Lyson stared dumbly at one another in recognition and their hands shook slowly, haltingly, uncertainly. Bruce blurted out, "Are you a Fed?"

Their hands stopped shaking, though still gripped. "Afeared? What do you mean?" Lyson asked increduously.

Bruce stared back, his eyes wide. "You're a professional, for sure! You know how to play the game!"

The hearing people broke out in gales of loud laughter. Lyson a Fed! Hahaha! Their laughter was so infectious that the deaf, though not yet understanding the cause, could not help but join in. Andy and Wally fell to the floor as waves of laughter washed over them. Their eyes meeting, and seeing each other in such a ludicrous position, pushed them into powerful seizures of laughter again.

The only two people who had yet to see the humor of it all were P-51 and Lyson, their hands still slowly shaking as they looked at the bedlam around them. Their eyes locked together in mutual incomprehension. Slowly, their faces began to crack, each crack in one face leading to a crack in the other, back and forth, until they collapsed in each other's arms in fits of laughter.

Trent managed to stagger back to the little stool behind his drums and finally broke the spell with powerful, overpowering booms on his drums, pouring himself into the music with the wild frenzy of a native pounding tom-toms in the jungle. The amplifiers turned the ballroom into a resounding booming beat that even the deafest of the deaf could feel, and they all began swaying with the rhythm.

Lyson and P-51 released one another as Lyson closed his eyes the better to get in tune with the beat, and his feet began dancing to the powerful rhythms bombarding his body through the air and the floor. He snapped his fingers and swayed his head side to side. He moaned and grunted.

His frenzy calming, his energy spent, Trent wound down slowly, gradually into soft long booms and that howled into a long roaring stop. Lyson opened his eyes and saw a circle of clapping hands and wide eyes all around. His ears blushed as he sheepishly stifled his feet. "Bravo!" they cried.

A round of applause went up, with much clapping and handkerchief waving. Lyson blushed as he took his bows, thinking the adulation was for the performance of his feet. Trent held up his palms and hung his head modestly as was his custom at curtain calls after a performance. Darcy held his fist high, revelling in the recognition he believed his due for capturing the spy. Beatrice hugged Mary and the Captain in ecstasy over the course of the party. Soon the applause subsided into hugs, handshakes, congratulations, mutual admirations, and wiping of sweaty brows and necks. And a consensus arose among the deaf that it was time for Lyson to make good his promise for an announcement about the move to Islay.

But Lyson had difficulty wiping off his sweat, as more poured out in the warmth of the ballroom, and he tried to hold off the clamor. His friends kept up their cajoling and needling and held him to his promise. Suddenly an inspiration came to him: *Let's go-there Bandstand! Cooler there!*

Lyson! Mary admonished. *Dark outside!*

Have lights! he declared. *Let's go! Hot here!*

Bandstand? Where? asked his friends.

Two blocks, north. In park.

Park? Robbers! Doctor Stumpt held up his hands in alarm. *Slit throat!*

No, no, don't worry! Lyson assured his friends. *Islay very safe, not like Washington.*

All-of-us together, should O.K., safe, reasoned Wally.

Mary vigorously pulled Lyson aside: *You think you know what you doing?*

Oh yes, perfect place finish party!

I hope!

Arm in arm they all marched in a stream down Central Promenade in the cool night air, swaying and swinging under the trees lit up from beneath by street lamps so that the sensation was of going through a pleasant, cool green tunnel. Lyson led them across Tenth Street, under the great trees of the park to the clearing around the Bandstand. He stopped, standing reverently in front of the steps, while his friends streamed out around the Bandstand. Silently they all looked up at the old structure, quaint in the soft light, that could not but stir poetic, even musical feelings. Had Lyson worn a hat, he would have placed it over his heart, so huge was the lump in his throat over such a momentous event.

Thinking feverishly to himself to impress the Governor, P-51 fumbled under the stairway and found the light switch. Suddenly the lights exploded all around the eave of the roof. Blinded, Lyson nearly lost his balance and Mary put her arm around his waist and squeezed as if to say *This is it!* But Lyson remained frozen in stage fright, his eyes so wide with terror that Beatrice came up and put a soft, reassuring kiss on his dimple. Friends behind patted his back kindly and Wally massaged away the tension from his shoulders. Doctor Vought came up in front, put a hand on his shoulder and urged, *Courage! We all your friends!*

His eyes filled with gratitude, Lyson asked him, *Can you translate speech for me, please? Doubt I can talk and sign same time.*

Doctor Vought nodded encouragement. *Sure!*

Taking a deep breath, Lyson took slow, halting steps up to the platform, like a condemned man going up to the gallows. Mary bowed her head in silent prayer and clasped her hands until they hurt and Beatrice took them in her own. When Lyson turned to face them, he had on a sheepish grin. *Silly me nervous. You all my friends. Me should not nervous.*

Waving handkerchiefs gave him courage and he began: *Remember you that drama National Theatre of the Deaf titled My Third Eye?*

The handkerchiefs waved wildly.

Well, that gave me idea for move here. He paused to let his friends digest this bit of information and continued, *That's why Wally there—* Wally bounded up a few steps and waved, nodding to the crowd.*—and myself made agreement build huge recreation place for deaf. Bowling. Captioned movies. Pool, ping-pong, electronic games. Attract deaf here!*

The handkerchiefs waved slowly, politely, as he knew they had yet to realize the full implication of his plan. *I plan attract other various industries for deaf. For example: TTY factory, publisher for deaf books, movies for deaf, TV. Attract more more deaf here—*

Wildly waving handkerchiefs heartened him and he pointed dramatically toward the capitol. *There legislature! Will have deaf legislators!*

But this time the handkerchiefs did not wave as he had expected. Instead the crowd seemed to be staring at him in horror. Frantic that he might be losing his audience he pointed toward the Governor's Mansion and declared, *Will deaf Governor!*

Many people in the crowd shrank away backwards, waving and pointing frantically at him. Disheartened, he dropped his arms and searched for Mary among the confusion of the crowd. She finally caught his attention and pointed above his head. He looked up. Hundreds of wasps were swarming furiously in the cone of the ceiling, just above his head. He stared, petrified, unable to move. Swiftly Wally bounded up and jerked Lyson back down the stairs and they dashed after the fleeing crowd back toward the house.

* * *

P-51 sped instead to the Governor's Mansion and burst into the office. The Governor was at the window watching the bedlam through binoculars, with B-52 at his side. They turned and stared at him. "What's going on?" demanded Governor Wenchell.

"Party!" panted P-51.

"Party?"

"Yes, they're planning to take over the state!"

"They?"

"The deaf! They're moving here!"

"Deaf?" Slappy Wenchell was incredulous. "What do you mean, deaf?"

"There, there," sweetly said B-52, pinching P-51 on the cheek. "Let's let you take your vacation early this year."

* * *

All the guests had departed with assurances that his speech was entirely successful, notwithstanding the wasps, and that his plans for Islay were most excellent and wonderful, although they would have to first check their own situations and resources before they too could give more than verbal, moral, heartfelt and enthusiastic support. Besides, isn't it a wonderful house? Well worth whatever happens. And the party! The best in a long time! We'll never forget this fantastic evening! So happy to meet you and your friends. Good Luck! Take care, you need any help, call me, O.K.? See ya! Thumbs up! Love ya!

Wally left with Andy for the night, so that in the morning they could look for a house after breakfast at the Quayles. *Lyson,* he exhorted, *We'll succeed! I know!*

Lyson gripped his shoulders gratefully. *See you, morning.*

The Quayles hugged Lyson and Mary. "Lyson, we're off and running! We're so excited!"

"Hope we can sleep."

"See ya in the morning."

After she shut the door and leaned back against it, finally alone together for the first time in their new house, Mary searched Lyson's eyes with contrary emotions filling her own, mostly awe and wonder. Lyson stared lovingly back, but the questions he could detect in her eyes worried him. The power of a good woman!

Lyson, she finally cried out with her hands, *one thing bothers me.*

His eyes widened innocently, though he felt he must be guilty of something. *What?*

Spend! Spend money!

But this house good buy! he protested. *Good price!*

She nodded agreement though her eyes betrayed uncertainty. *Will we stay here?*

Stay? He was confused. *Why ask?*

Will we trade house trade house trade house?

Lyson stared incredulously at her. *What makes you think that?*

She looked firmly at him, as at a little boy, and reminded him, *We bought Lincoln last weekend, right?*

Yeah right. So?

You drive-car few days, that's-all, right?

The accusing look in her eyes set him reeling. Did Beatrice bend a fender? Did she smoke a cigarette? *Few days, right, but 'smatter?*

Few days she made the signs tiny to emphasize the brevity of the days, and then exasperatedly, *And then trade other car!*

Lyson stared, dumbfounded, his mouth pulled open by the dead weight of his jaw. *Other car?*

Her eyes widened, astonishment coming over her that he didn't really know, or was a better liar than she ever suspected. *Lyson! Come!* She grabbed his hand and dragged him stumbling through the house into the garage.

A new Mercedes 280 gleamed in the center of the huge garage. Its color of sun-ripened wheat and dark leather-like vinyl top, together with the rich deep-brown leather of the upholstery and brass trim, evoked scenes of horses, hunting dogs, gold whiskey flasks, engraved shotguns, clay pigeons, leather elbow and seat patches on tweed. Slowly, haltingly, Lyson walked around the Mercedes, staring at it as if he'd never ever before seen an automobile. His surprise, amazement, and confusion were real enough, so obvious that Mary was convinced he wasn't lying or playing dumb. She felt a twinge of regret that such a doubt had ever crossed her mind. Still, she became very concerned that he had let their state of affairs get so he can't even remember trading cars that very morning! Such careless disregard for money!

How-much money, this car? she asked when he had completed his circuit of the Mercedes.

Money? He looked at her like he had never heard of such a thing.

My money! she snapped. *Can't you remember trading this car?*

He gawked stupidly at her. *You mean this really our car?*

Mary became very concerned. *You okay? Sick?*

I'm fine! he protested. *Didn't-know this car!*

They stared at the car and at each other and back at the car. Again they searched each other's eyes, trying to fathom the depths of the secret the other must be hiding.

Then it came to him: *Beatrice!*

Mary's eyes widened. *Right!*

Loaned Lincoln key this morning, he explained, the picture clearing.

She nodded with growing understanding. *This afternoon one o'clock she met me train there Fremont. Drove this car. Said had-to trade. I though you did.*

I never—he started to protest.

Know that now! She said Lincoln for snob people. Mercedes makes you look intelligent, good taste, good conscience about oil.

They looked at each other affectionately, their smiles growing wider and wider until they burst out laughing, falling into each other's arms.

Beatrice funny woman! he cried.

Yes! Real crazy! she giggled.

They clung to each other for a long time, swaying and swinging, marveling at the coup Beatrice pulled on them and no doubt on the salesman as well. His arm around her waist, he led her into the Mercedes. Luxuriant seats, soft leather-covered steering wheel and dashboard, airplane-style gauges—an actual gas gauge! An altimeter, shiny brass trim and knobs, tweed ceiling lining, and fully reclining seats. A most delightful automobile. She pulled his head to her chest as they lay in the car. And laid a finger on his dimple. The rhythm of her breathing, heaving soft chest soon had him fast asleep. She saw this and brushed his cowlick tenderly with her lips and sighed happily into a sweet sleep. Cozy and snug as gophers huddled cheek to tail in their burrow.

PART II

DRUMS

If the musician could say it in words, he wouldn't bother writing the music, would he?

—Stanley Kramer

CHAPTER 9

Lyson could not believe his eyes, the spectacle he found himself in, the likes of which he had never before seen. All along both sides of the street, in the block right where the National Insurance of the Deaf ought to be, were taverns and bookstores with painted out windows and loud signs warning away minors. Also, dark, dank theatres for lonely men. Inappropriately friendly women dancing on little stages behind shop windows framed with flashing lights, in what he assumed to be lingerie shops. Some of them even attempted to entice him in as he passed by, but his wife Mary does her own shopping, he decided, for such intimate apparel. He found it difficult to believe that any woman would dare to display nighties in broad daylight but rationalized that some might have to, considering Reaganomics. He stopped, though, in front of a brightly lit display of such strange medical equipment that he marvelled at the tremendous advances in the science of healing: tiny spoons, scalpels, decorated clips, colorful metal pill boxes, syringes, although the exquisitely carved little pipes confused him as to their medical purpose. Must be classy inhalants, he guessed, possibly using some exotic healing herbs, and wondered if his wife would like one for the frequent sinusitis she seemed to suffer every month.

Surveying the block again, he was even more confused. Homeless men with red noses sitting on curbs. Young men with wild eyes and red ears prowling in mad dashes up and down the block, fists thrust in pockets. Well-dressed, prosperous, upstanding, respectable businessmen and professionals marching sternly down the sidewalk, tight in the face as if disgusted at what they had to go through to achieve happiness. Then, with a quick furtive look around, darting into one of the lingerie shops. Such courage at getting surprises for their wives, Lyson marvelled, and castigated himself that he never surprised his wife anymore—No! Not true! I got her that splendid castle, didn't I? What greater surprise can there be for a wife, he was congratulating himself when he felt, or rather smelt, a strong presence.

The most unusual woman he had ever seen was beside him, obviously trying to speak to him without moving her lips, without even looking at him, so that he thought she must be awfully ashamed of a problem she needed help for. Her hair was bleached a rather metallic blonde, and her face so heavily made up with green eye shadow, black-penciled eyebrows, startling red lips, heavy rouge, and a gold star over her cheek, that he guessed she might be a player, even a lady clown. Her red beret, red miniskirt, pink cotton turtleneck, black mesh stockings, and shiny fire-engine-red high heels reinforced his impression that she was in the entertainment business. Lyson firmly believed that he was a cultured person, and as such desired to be as helpful as possible to an artist in need.

"Need any help?" he inquired solicitously, tipping his hat and bowing theatrically. "Madame?"

She turned abruptly, her eyes boring into him so hard he burst out apologetically, hugging his hat, "Excuse me! But I'm deaf—" Her eyes darted to his ears and back to his eyes, and before he could continue, she turned her back on him and huffed away, twitching her miniskirt in indignation.

He scratched his head with his hat, watching her disappear into the milling crowd, and sighed with a shrug as he opened his briefcase for the copy of DEAF Magazine that had in the first place led him here. Not only did the advertisement for the American Insurance of the Deaf show the same address as confirmed by the street signs and numbers on doors, but the article about the founder Lester Lieseke also gave the same address. Yet he puzzled at the description of the locale given by the writer of the article: A fascinating, charming block containing cute little specialty shops devoted to every sort of delicacies and pleasures. He checked the writer's name and it was Gene Owles. That no good Owles! That son of a—ah—a woman who does not prescribe to—I mean walk the, I mean straight and—and—never mind. Maybe I should try to call him through the National TDD operator, he mused to himself, as heagain surveyed the buildings, most of which were two stories high. Hey! Maybe the office is on the second story. But he could see no signs on any of the upper windows.

Most of the windows were open and gave the appearance of being walk-up apartments, as in many windows curtains swayed in the breeze. A dejected looking man in a soiled T-shirt sat at one, his elbows resting on the sill as he watched the people beneath him with the same weary eyes that watched television. A wine bottle appeared to be holding open the window, but he took it and drank directly from it. As he replaced it on the sill, his eyes caught Lyson staring at him, and he broke into an obscene wide grin, displaying bare gums and a few stray teeth. Blushing, Lyson looked quickly away and found two patrolmen approaching him, their eyes on the crowd as they twirled their billy clubs.

"Hello!" he cried and caught their attention. "Excuse me, but I'm deaf—"

They stopped and stared at him, in askance as if surprised by his presence in such a neighborhood, so that his voice wilted. "My name is Lyson C. Sulla—here is my billfold. See!"

But the older of the two patrolmen waved it away and said something Lyson couldn't catch. Pointing to his ear, Lyson apologized, "I'm sorry but I'm deaf."

Looking quickly at the ear as if to satisfy himself that it indeed was deaf, the patrolman held up a finger and pulled out a pad and a pen.

Gratefully, Lyson wrote quickly, "Thank you! I'm trying to find this address." He showed them the advertisement in the magazine.

Nodding, the officers led him back toward the middle of the block to a door almost hidden between a bookstore and a lingerie shop just now suddenly empty of models. On the doorstep sat a derelict trying to hide something in a paper sack crumbled into the shape of a bottle. The policemen spoke sharply and the poor man shuffled quickly, unsteadily away.

"Is this the right place?" asked Lyson incredulously.

With a billy club the older officer pointed at the numbers over the door and grunted. The numbers had been painted over in the same color as the rest of the door frame, a kind of beige, so were easy to miss unless one knew just where to look.

"Thank you! Thank you!" Lyson stared at the window of the door where traces of painted lettering had been scraped away. The name American Insurance of the Deaf could barely be discerned, and he fretted that they might have moved away. He hesitated at the darkness of the stairway visible through the window, but the officer opened the door for him, and Lyson saw the way was clear up the stairs to another door on the upper floor. "Go up," the officer assured him. A musty odor greeted him as he took a deep breath and climbed the stairs, feeling them creaking under his shoes. The finely shaped wooden bannister and waist-high, varnished paneling on the walls were decaying representations of the belief of the builders that the area would always remain grand, fashionable, chic, unchanging. But the present tenants had given up trying to paint over the graffiti on the plaster walls so that if you didn't look too closely, the scribblings gave the appearance of printed wallpaper, though now soiled by numerous authors trying to fill in more up-to-date histories on the moods of the community. A treasure for future archaeologists! Rage over Viet Nam. Vulgar jokes about Johnson. Spittle over Nixon. Jest over Agnew. Enthusiasm over pot and sex. Uncomplimentary comments over Carter, less humorous than those for the first three Presidents. Now it was Reagan's turn, and Lyson's ears burned at the thought that someday in Islay it might be his turn too. Some gratitude for our leaders, he fumed as he reached the landing and faced the lone door. Instantly he understood the reason for there being no sign on the door at the street. Just below the bold black letters "American Insurance of the Deaf" painted on the frosted glass someone had so skillfully printed "And Dumb" with a felt tip marker, matching the original lettering so perfectly as to blend naturally with the original and to have been overlooked by the employees arriving for work.

And above the doorknob were no less than three, Lyson counted, deadbolt locks. As his hand touched the knob, he was startled by a bright light that lit up the room behind the glass panel, backlighting sharply the chicken wire mesh in the glass. A shadow appeared on the glass, worked the locks, and slowly opened the door a crack. An eye peered out at him and he was struck at its astonishingly blue iris.

Excuse! Myself deaf! Lyson quickly signed, pointing at his ear and mouth.

Oh! the eye seemed to say as the door closed. He could see from the motions of the shadow that several chains were being unlatched, and the door opened again.

Deaf? a young woman asked, slightly suspicious. There was something about her that Lyson liked immediately, the way she stood, the way she held herself, almost on her toes, like a deer poised to bound away. Her long sandy hair adorned by a single flower at the temple. Her spare, modest figure made more endearing by a simple unpretentious summer print dress. Her eyes, extremely intelligent, slightly out of focus so like near-sighted people without their glasses, her eyebrows light and frail looking. Her face so close to being beautiful but just missing that it was very appealing to Lyson and his eyes brimmed with sentiment.

Deaf? she asked again, her nostrils flaring with impatience, which he liked very much too.

Oh, excuse me! Lyson's hands jumped. *Yes! And I came—*

Quick! She jerked him in. *Afraid people there.* She pointed down the stairs. *Crazy!*

But before she closed the door, Lyson pointed out the "And Dumb."

Know that! She rolled her eyes in exasperation, shaking her head as she slammed the door, turning the deadbolts firmly and relatching the chains. She faced him furiously as if berating him and signed with so much vigor she hopped, *Someone crazy write there everyday. We erase. He write. Erase. Write. Erase. Write, since two years. Every night!* She threw up her hands. *Give-up, decide leave, forget. Let him happy!*

She brushed swiftly past him out of the foyer into the office. Lyson remained standing, stunned, staring at where she had just been, and at the lettering on the door, just barely visible and reversed through the frosted glass. Sighing, softening, she went back to him and tugged at his sleeve. *Sorry. Not mean insult-you.*

Oh! All-right! his hands cried out, grabbing her hand and patting it reassuringly. Her hand felt so small, so defenseless in his that he couldn't resist bringing it up to his face for a closer look.

She slipped it away quickly and laughed. *Not married. Come, have-to lock.* She pulled him out of the foyer into the office and locked a second door, though this one only had two deadbolts. He was still staring, obviously fascinated, at her, when she turned to face him. She saw his confusion and her face sweetened in a smile. *My name—Heather Braley,* she signed slowly, decorously, putting him at ease. *But they call-me Beanpole.*

Oblivious to the stares of the other office workers, Lyson stamped his foot indignantly. *Not right! Not nice!*

Immensely pleased, she blushed and gently got him off the subject by introducing him to the others. There were about a dozen women—Lyson quickly calculated the probable number of husbands, friends, children destined to follow them to Islay. *Happy meet! My name first Lyson. Last, Sulla. Myself very impressed here wonderful for place help deaf get insurance—*

Oh, you need insurance? asked Marlene, whose grey hair and matronly features marked her as the probable office manager.

No! No! Lyson held up denying hands. *I come want meet Lieseke for discuss important secret.*

At the sign secret a dozen pairs of eyes widened and looked at each other, mouths dropping open. Lyson berated his careless hands and tried again. *I mean—uh—I mean to say private—uh, private business*—He hesitated when he saw Marlene's eyes narrowing, and he dropped his hands in defeat.

Very slowly, very carefully so that he had the uncomfortable feeling of being scrutinized, uncovered, Marlene asked, *Ask you, my husband know about this secret? Finish make-appointment, you?*

Lyson stared at her, his mouth dry, for a long moment. She raised her eyebrows: *Well?*

Recovering quickly, he exclaimed, *You his wife? Wonderful! Happy meet!* He grabbed her hand with both of his so clumsily he scratched his thumb on her diamond ring. Ow! He seized his thumb and sucked it, much to the merriment of the women in the room.

While sucking his thumb he sensed the bedlam around him and held very still, his eyes darting about, appalled at the scene of laughter, giggles, hands held over mouths under laughing eyes, huge mirthful signs *Funny!* slipping off noses. Fingers pointing at something under his nose directed his attention down at the fist in front of own his own face. He saw the thumb in his mouth and burst out laughing with such force the thumb appeared to pop out of his mouth.

They had a good laugh together, even Marlene.

You funny!

Should TV you.

Never before FUNNY here.

That dimple, cute!

You should work here!

Lyson giggled and wiggled, loving them all. A tender hand picked up his injured hand. It was Heather, solicitous over his thumb. There was a little scratch in the sensitive area at the base of the thumbnail. He almost thought she was going to kiss it and make it well when one of the others came up with a band-aid, a redhead so freckled that without his spectacles he would have thought she was deeply tanned. Heather took his hand and towed him to the washroom. He tried to resist, but the others urged him on with compelling hands on his back and hips. They crowded around him at the lavatory, giggling as Heather washed, dried, and nursed the thumb. He looked up at the mirror and giggled back at them.

Suddenly, a bald head appeared behind them in the open door and, at the startle in Lyson's face, the women turned away to face the surprise. Lyson remained staring at the mirror and the bald man was equally surprised, his mouth open in a question as their eyes met through the mirror. The man turned to Marlene, and demanded with a single forceful idomic sign *Thrill?*

He came for meet you, discuss important secret, quickly explained Marlene, blushing.

The man stared at Lyson, still at the mirror so that he had to tilt his head for a full view of the strange, reddening face. Deftly Heather turned Lyson around to face the man, shaking him to his senses. *This Lester Lieseke, boss here. And Marlene her husband.* Turning to Lester, she apologized, *Him Lyson Sulla, here want see you about something important secret.*

Lester looked at Heather, Lyson, Marlene, and the others, probing their eyes. *What doing here restroom?* he finally asked.

Oh! Heather giggled and pulled up Lyson's hand, pointing at the band-aid. *Hurt himself there.* She pointed at Marlene's ring. Marlene meekly displayed the diamond. Lester glared at the ring and at the band-aid, back and forth, and gave up with a shake of his head.

Well, that ring have theft insurance, he said, quickly recovering his demeanor and sense of humor. *What about that?* pointing to the band-aid, *Have medical insurance?*

Relieved, Lyson offered his hand, and Lester accepted, shaking it in such a wary, probing way that Lyson felt he was being felt out, tested. Can't afford another gaffe, he reminded himself anxiously.

In the diplomatic way of women, Marlene put her hand on the grasped shaking hands and suggested, *You-two go-there office, private talk. I bring coffee, OK?*

What?! Lester stared at his wife in mock horror. *Me alone with him?*

Silly you finish! Marlene marched them to the rear of the room, where a door opened to the richly panelled office of the founder of American Insurance of the Deaf. All around on the walls were numerous pictures, diplomas, certificates, and plaques. Much like my own den, mused Lyson, except that all the pictures were of Lester himself, mostly in company with other luminaries of the deaf world, at national conventions. His eye stopped at a certain plaque, in honor of Lester Lieseke, presented by American Insurance of the Deaf in recognition for his services to the deaf. Lester saw this and hastened to explain that it wasn't his own idea but the staff's.

Wonderful! Lyson's slow sidewise twist of the head said.

Yes, wonderful. Thankful have fine people work for me, agreed Lieseke who was beginning to like Lyson and his tact.

Lyson looked deeply, meditatively at Lester and said, *Yes, myself lucky too. Have fine people, too.*

Really? Lester brightened. *Sit, let's talk about your secret.*

Marlene entered with two cups and a steaming glass pot rich brown with coffee. *Sugar? Cream?* she asked Lyson.

No, no. Prefer black, thanks.

Welcome. Marlene made the sign with a gracious sweep,and started closing the door, but checked herself, and with pleading eyes and an apologetic cast to her shoulders begged Lyson, *Please don't-look-down-on us because we live here bad area. Can't help because we establish here 1958 when that time here very nice, good stores, restaurants, nice movies, apartments for old people—*

Lester jumped out of his chair, his hands agitated. *Can you imagine? Two-years-ago, short-time-ago, everything nice here until establish one, just one, can you imagine? just one small, tiny, dirty book store. Boom!* His hands shot out, his fingers wiggling, like a fire storm, his tongue out and vibrating in loathing. *Thumbs down!* He bent over to bring his thumbs down even lower. *Funny, all hearing know about what will happen, that why sell, move-away fast. We deaf always last find-out, too-late. Now stuck here.*

Take-it-easy, Marlene cautioned her husband anxiously. *Your heart!* And to Lyson: *Imagine, two years, everything change fast. Restaurant change tavern. Nice movie change dirty. Stores change pot, drug, whore.* She shuddered.

And crazy people flock here, Lester interjected.

Afraid go-out. Used-to go-down for lunch. Now have-to stay all-day, eat here.

People write walls! Lester's eyes burned furiously.

And mock us through window, she sighed sadly. *That why have-to shut curtain. No sun.*

Come! Lester demanded and stormed through the main office, startling the staff, and pulled open the curtains facing the street. Across the street, in the very same window Lyson had earlier seen that seemed to be propped open by the same wine bottle, was the same toothless old man who was already staring at them. As if to say hello, long time no see! a slow leer spread across his face, and he held up his hands, wiggling his fingers in a crude imitation of Sign Language, rather obscene, enormously enjoying his little joke.

See! Told you! Lester snapped and started to jerk closed the curtains but Lyson stopped him and, burning with indignation, thrust his jaw out at the mocking face across the street and decorously thumbed his nose, wiggling his fingers in magnificent defiance.

The leer froze sickly as the old man recoiled, aghast. Triumphantly the women thumped Lyson's back, profusely congratulating him. The redhead hugged him so enthusiastically she tickled him and popped a button on his jacket. But Lester was mortified, and the more so when the old man became angry and thrust a fist at them, threatening reprisals. His elbow bumped the bottle and it fell off the sill down toward the street.

The man grabbed at it and missed, and lunged half out the window, his eyes tearfully following the tumbling bottle. In about the time it takes an object to fall two stories, his dismay turned to horror, and he ducked back into the window in a scrabble so wild he tripped over something, disappearing into the room.

Lester was mortified too and whipped the curtains shut and peeked out through the gap, his shoulders hunched in dread. The women and Lyson crowded around him, clamoring for a peep too but he held up a warning hand as he withdrew slowly, taking care not to move the curtains. *Police,* he said bleakly, and mimed: *Bottle splatter in-front-of their feet. Jump-back, look-up, saw man, run-upstairs.* With trembling hands he commanded the women back to work and to pretend nothing had happened. And Marlene was to keep a watch out and to be careful not to move the curtains.

Come! Have-to hide! He seized Lyson and marched him back to the private office. As he closed the door firmly a graph tacked on the backside caught Lyson's curiosity. It looked like a seismograph of a tremendous earthquake, so nervously did the wiggles, zigs, and zags move in the line carefully drawn across it. Lyson followed the line hypnotically up and down, so transfixed that Lester had to wave a hand in front of his face to catch his eye. *That shows stock market since 1958 when establish here company.* He tried to continue, but anxiety tightened his hands and he wrung them. As if in a spasm he jerked open the door a crack. Marlene was still at the window, peeking through the curtains, spelling out *O.K.* behind her back to the office. She turned to face the room and, seeing his face at the crack in the door, beamed. *Everything O.K. Police handcuff, take jail.* She came toward them, and he opened the door wide, his torso relaxing in relief. She hugged him and brightened, *Think coffee now cold. You-two sit, relax.* She took away the cold pot.

Lester sat down slowly, suddenly looking very old, careworn, so much so that for the first time Lyson noticed his clothes looked too large for his frame. Even his skin looked too large, so that his face hung down loosely, pulling his scalp taut. God, he's shrinking! Lyson thought and apologized, *Myself very sorry, cause trouble for you. Feel lousy!*

Lester waved his hand in denial, *No, not your fault,* and leaned wearily back in his chair, rubbing his eyes behind rimless glasses. He sighed and a tiny smile crinkled one side of his face. *Anyway, insurance very boring—*

Marlene returned with a steaming pot and, with a splendid look on her face, commented to Lyson, *Don't let him fool you. Himself very fascinated with insurance. Just bored with gossip here women.*

Chuckling softly, he said to Lyson, almost in an aside, *She jealous. Many beautiful here want steal me—*

The redhead appeared in the door, holding up a button to Lyson with an expression of mock guilt. *Sorry! Broke from your coat. Give-me.*

Lyson looked down and saw that indeed a button was missing. *Oh no,* he reassured her magnanimously. *Don't worry. Just give-me. Wife can sew.*

Her eyes turned even more round. *Oh, didn't-know have wife.*

Shame you! Lester slapped his hands in mirth.

Wife will mad you, Marlene scolded him with a twinkle in her eyes as Lyson blushed and worried over his jacket, trying to think up a good explanation for Mary about the button.

Give-me jacket, the redhead commanded. *Will sew myself.*

Meekly he removed his jacket and as he handed it over, his eyes fretted, and she with a hint of indignation assured him, *Myself know how sew!*

Just as she shut the door on them, Marlene soothed them. *Leave you-two alone, talk private, O.K.?*

For a long awkward moment the two men sat silently, sipping coffee, lost in private thought. Finally Lyson asked, *Insurance difficult business?*

Well! Lester's eyebrows raised. *Insurance true complicated business. Not just sell insurance. Must take-care-of money that people give-us. You see that chart?* His hands moved with a grace and power that impressed Lyson that Lester was a man who loved his work. *People buy insurance. We must invest their money. Most invest there stock and bond. Have-to watch everyday. When low, buy. When high, sell. Everyday, everyday have-to watch carefully. Can't relax! Makes me very nervous.* He shook his head wearily. *Dumb me, should first place buy land. Long-ago, 1950's—1960's, land very cheap. Now zoom high price, huge profit! Wish think me before!*

Lyson perked up. *Land? You want buy?*

Lester shook his head regretfully. *Too-late now, too-high.*

No! Not too-late. Lyson stood up, excited. *Have land! Know where splendid swamp.*

Swamp? Lester was incredulous. *You mean underwater?*

The enormity of his gaffe struck Lyson and he sank slowly back into his chair, breaking into a sobbing chuckle, shaking his head in a daze. *Dumb me, start with swamp! Lousy salesman, me!*

Tipping his chair back and putting his feet on the desk, Lester commented thoughtfully, *Well, maybe better you lousy salesman. Myself always resist slick salesman. Never trust.* He clasped his hand behind his head in a posture to show that he was all eyes, open to whatever spiel Lyson might come up with. *Come-on, shoot! Feel free!*

Swamp! Lyson chuckled at himself, slapping his forehead, still amazed at himself.

So? Lester shrugged. *There Florida some people buy swamp, drain, become very rich.*

Lyson stared back, nodding thoughtfully. *Good idea. Never thought before.*

Suddenly putting his feet on the floor and sitting up, Lester demanded, *For-for buy swamp first place? What your first purpose for buy swamp?*

With downcast eyes Lyson tried to evade: *That secret.*

You mean that secret Marlene said you came want tell me about?

You-see, Lyson admitted, *Have several secrets—*

Hold! Lester cautioned and went to the door in a roundabout way and opened it suddenly. Marlene was on her knees, her eye still squinting where the keyhole had been just a split second ago. The eye rolled slowly up at him and she blushed. Graciously he helped her to her feet, saying, *More coffee, please.*

Lyson sat still, his hands clasped in his lap, his eyes turned inward, mirroring the storm raging within his brain, trying to unscramble his sales pitch now in shambles. Fortunately, as the redhead returned his jacket, a road map of Islay fell out in full view of everyone.

CHAPTER 10

Absurdly crazy! Here I am, Lyson C. Sulla, formerly of Washington, D.C., ex-government clerk, but now of Suffex there Islay. True, I was officially a statistican but in reality a mere clerk, a pencil pusher, paper shuffler, a lick ass—Lyson shook his head—now here I am, certifiably an entrepreneur, an officer, President of Islay Company, but in reality a common, fawning, sycophantic salesman hustling, drumming on the road!

Rows and rows of corn stretched as far as he could see; so swift was his passage that the rows almost seemed to stand still, as if he weren't moving at all, particularly when his eyes were cast at a certain, almost cockeyed angle. But the dashed centerline hurtled past his vision so that another part of his brain thought the rows were speeding along with him. The corn stood tall and even, obscuring the land, the fences and boundaries, broken only by occasional side roads, powerlines, isolated islands of woods sheltering farm homes in the midst of a lonely sea under an immense, immeasurable sky. Appalling how people could survive, let alone make a living under such wild conditions, exposed to the fury of nature!

The Captain had said to keep an eye out for Indians but Beatrice reckoned cowboys were more dangerous. Mary almost called off the trip but they said they were just joking. Joke or no joke, Mary had said, no stopping anywhere you see Indians or cowboys. Be sure there are no taverns near the motels. Andy thought motels had more of a reputation as thieves than any Indian ever did. "Oh no, no, the oil companies!" said Beatrice. *Listen! Remember! Count every penny! Save all receipts, tax deductions,* Mary reminded him, even though now he was a thousand miles from home, in the middle of nowhere.

A flashing blue light! The speedometer was over 58. He eased back on the cruise control and the light went out. That clever Walt Sisk had installed that light after rewiring their home. Mary had wanted the light to turn on at 55 but Walt said the car's true speed was 55 when the speedometer said 57. And when the tires wore away a bit, the car would be going slower than the needle showed. So 58 was a good compromise, he said. Mary was upset that the speedometer wasn't accurate. Why have them if they can't be accurate? *Listen, Lyson! Don't dream! Pay attention to your driving!*

The dashed line was zipping right under his feet. He quickly tucked up his feet off the floor. Oh no! Dreaming again! He pulled the car back in the right lane. Thank goodness! If not for that dashed line, if it were a solid line, all illusion of speed would be blurred, a fluid. Dream and reality blended into surrealism. Even the road map beside him was no help in all that corn. Tracing his finger across Iowa, so small on the map, he figured he ought be in Nebraska by now. Driving in the corn all day. Two days, really! Nothing but corn since Ohio. Must be going in circles. *Insane!* He twirled his finger around his ear. *Crazy.*

A car appeared beside him, passing so slowly it seemed to float by. An ancient black Chevrolet. A very fat matron glaring at him, her eyes wide with indignation, her mouth scandalized. Surprised, Lyson's finger slowed in its orbit around his ear, its spring winding down gradually. Hissing, the woman bared her teeth and turned snapping to the driver beside her, a small, spare, mousy man under a felt hat as ancient as the Chevrolet. Quickly, he stepped on the gas and they roared away ahead. Fascinated, Lyson watched them get smaller and smaller in the distance, the man still nodding meekly, patiently while the woman vented her rage on him. Soon they diminished into a dot flickering on the mirage, and suddenly disappeared.

Crazy. Lyson shook his head but firmly restrained his finger from his ear, though there was no other car in the rearview mirror, and he allowed his hand, out of sight beneath the dashboard, to express itself, spelling out *C-R-A-Z-Y. Hearing people funny mind! Always misunderstanding us deaf. Yes, hearing very sensitive,* he let his hand rant on to itself. Though he knew what it was doing, and what it was saying, he was afraid it would be misunderstood and so kept it out of sight. *Disgusting that us deaf have-to hide our hands!* His hand protested, *unfair!*

Oh, oh, a blue light. Not on the dashboard, but ahead in the distance. The needle said 57 and he turned the cruise control until it said 55, Walt's calculations notwithstanding. It was a state patrol car, IOWA marked in bold letters on its trunk. Iowa! cried Lyson to himself, still in Iowa!

The fat matron stood beside the Chevrolet, fists on hip, confronting, berating the patrolman who, his foot on the rear bumper, seemed determined to ignore her as he took down their license number. The little man remained in his seat, both hands gripping the steering wheel, his shoulders hunched, staring straight ahead, nodding meekly as if the woman were still beside him screaming. As Lyson passed by, the woman saw him, yelled and pointed at him, pulling on the cop's arm. But it was to no avail, as Lyson could see in the rearview mirror that the cop didn't even look up, still intent on the paperwork.

His eyes anxious on the mirror, watching the blue flashes diminishing way behind, Lyson at first did not notice that he at last had departed the Great Corn Belt. Now forests, pastures, majestic lone trees, cattle, and soon the outskirts of Council Bluffs. Finally! Lyson sighed, allowing his anxiety to exit through his nostrils. The monotony, the tedium of corn forever behind. The trees looked so good he now knew he could not live where there were none. Houses, people, children, even cars. Signs! Information, direction, dimension, guidance. Somebody cares!

* * *

Were it not for his old friend, DEAF Magazine, he would have had a very lonely night near the stockyards of Obeke, in the motel. Without a telecaptioner for the television, too.

True, Robert Altman the publisher of DEAF Magazine had nearly crushed his feelings when Lyson stopped by their offices in Washington, giving a bad start to his trip by refusing—no, not quite refusing, but kind of declining—Lyson's most excellent offer to help the magazine relocate in Islay. Why, the building in Islay costs only a third of what their building in Washington costs. Surely, they couldn't afford to turn down such a deal! Didn't they need that extra working capital?

Lyson, that is a most fantastic deal, beautiful from a dollars and cents standpoint, he had explained, but we have to remain in Washington, near the action, the source. Why, ALL the news about the deaf around the United States ends up in Washington! Here's Gallaudet College, still the one and only college for the deaf in the world. True, true it's becoming more and more hearing, but it's not lost quite yet. Serves all 50 states plus many foreign countries. World Council of the Deaf. National Association of the Deaf with its ties to all state organizations. The very nerve center of the deaf in the United States. The world. Our life blood!

Listen, young man, the worldly publisher had advised, cheap investments don't necessarily yield the best returns. Invest where the returns are. People live where they can get the most return. For DEAF Magazine that means Washington, D.C. After a long pause he went on: Lyson, everybody here has heard the rumors of your moving to Islay and your dream of a deaf state. Well! Well! The publisher reclined in his chair, putting his feet on the windowsill, looking out at the dome of the Capitol, and continued: It's nothing new, really. Actually, back in the 1850's, there was talk of setting up a state of the deaf out in the Midwest, Kansas and thereabouts. Deaf man name of Flournoy tried for years and years to interest enough deaf to move out there but nothing came of it but arguments. The publisher saw Lyson's face lengthening and relented. Maybe you can succeed where Flournoy couldn't. Flournoy himself didn't move to the new state, but you did. A long, long shot, but not impossible, Lyson. Probably worth a try. For sure, you'll need contacts, addresses. Want some?

Alone in the Obeke motel room, Lyson tired of watching people moving their lips on television and opened his briefcase instead. Yes, there was a club in Obeke, and it was open every Wednesday night. Now what day is today? Let's see, two days in the cornfields. One day before that in the Appalachians. That makes three days since Monday morning. Wednesday!

Thanks to the motel manager the club wasn't hard to find. It was in an attic above a beauty parlor at the mall. Why, the beautician could even sign! She explained that she had a deaf child at the school and that the shop wasn't really open for business that evening, just for the club.

Wonderful, Lyson exulted. *Many people here tonight?*

Later. Most there bowling now. Come afterwards. Some upstairs now, prefer cards.

Mind if I go-up? My name Lyson Sulla, from Islay. Traveling, stay tonight there motel.

Pleased meet you! My name Sandy Sand. Funny name, she chuckled. Her hair indeed was sandy.

Happy meet! Lyson shook her hand warmly. *You go-up?*

Oh no, have-to watch door until after bowling finish, she said regretfully, and urged, *You go-up.*

Lyson saw the cast in her eye and caught her yearning. *Old your child?*

Thirteen now. Soon fourteen, she brightened. *Now bowling with friends. Here one, maybe two hours.*

Boy? Girl?

Boy. Love sports. Hope play football next fall.

Big, husky?

Oh bigger than me! She rolled her eyes.

Lyson smiled. She was a small, petite woman, the kind that produces giants. *Good school?*

Oh yes! Doing very good, she said proudly. *Superintendent say think can go-there Gallaudet College.*

Great! Myself imagine yourself very proud.

Very, she smiled softly, and asked, *What about you? Islay, where that?*

Lyson looked around for a seat and she was glad. *Here!* she pointed out a chair under an immense hairdryer. *Comfort yourself.* She pulled up a stool and they sat facing each other for a long moment. Lyson detected a faint odor of coconut oil which pleased him very much. It explained the healthy glow of Sandy's skin, golden amber.

Well, Lyson finally said, *Islay very small, near Washington, D.C., between New York.*

Sandy threw up a hand. *Long-ago my school, my geography teacher very boring, most interested in names, names. That probably why I forget where Islay.*

Me too! Lyson laughed. *And I think very few people know—*

Three women came in, two quite old, grandmotherly in print dresses, the other middle-aged, going on grandmotherly. They stopped signing and stared at Lyson with such astonishment he blushed. Must be my fancy clothes, the aura of the cultured fox-and-hound pastures of the East, he thought to himself, and grandiosely signed, *My name Lyson Sulla, formerly Washington, D.C., now live there Islay. Happy meet!*

The women continued staring at Lyson, and the younger turned to Sandy. *Didn't-know here have men haircut.* The women again looked at Lyson, and then up at something over his head. He followed their eyes and saw the dryer just above his head.

Oh! Sandy quickly rolled the dryer away and they all enjoyed a good laugh.

Thrill here you? the younger woman asked Lyson in the idiom that in this instance means, What brings you here?

Oh, traveling, going California, business.

One of the very old women stepped forward for a closer look, eyeing Lyson's clothes up and down with such intensity he began to squirm. Turning to the others, she exclaimed, *Surprise me! Formerly deaf peddlers always dress poor, hope hearing sympathize, give money, but—* pointing at his jacket,—*nowdays peddlers dress fancy.* She imparted great flourish to the sign *fancy* to give the additional flavor of luxury, splendor, high class.

Apparently! interjected the other old woman. *Heard rumors that nowdays peddlers earn lots money, rich!*

All the women, Sandy included, frowned suspiciously at Lyson in his chair, his face very red, his seat feeling very hot. *Deny peddler!* he protested. *Businessman!*

Business what? the first old woman demanded, her eyes still narrow.

He held up a finger and pulled out his wallet. *Have card.*

A B C card! the woman triumphed.

No! no! Not A B C! Business! Look. He held the card out to her, turning it over so that she could see it was printed on only one side, the other blank, there being no alphabet of fingerspelling customarily hawked by deaf peddlers. She picked it out of his hand gingerly, with the very tips of her finger and thumb, the other fingers recoiling as far away as they could from such an unsavory object. She held it up to the light, turning, testing it for something fishy, and began reading, her other hand spelling out its message:

ISLAY COMPANY
603 Grand Boulevard
Suffex, Islay

ISLAY—THE GARDEN OF THE EAST

An opportunistic Company for, of, and by the Deaf
Residential, Commercial, and Agricultural Properties
Employment, Investment, and Financial Opportunities
Recreational, Social, and Athletic Activities for the Deaf.

Lyson C. Sulla

President and Chief Executive
Chairman of the Board
Himself Deaf

She looked up dubiously at Lyson, and at the others, mystified. *Hard believe.*

Yes, hard believe, agreed the other old woman. *Peddler too-much money. Do-do with money? Invest, establish big company, deceive deaf—*

Lyson waved his hands in chagrin, trying to get in a sign.

The younger woman stamped her foot, confronting him. *We deaf live here Obeke resent peddlers come-here, make us deaf look bad, lazy,stupid—*

*We deaf live here many years, build-up many friendships with hearing,*added the first old woman. *Want keep respect, don't-want peddlers spoil everything, make hearing look-down us deaf.*

Sandy observed Lyson sinking deeper into his chair, defeated, his eyes brimming, and felt for him. With touches of her hand she calmed the other women and asked him, *Really, how establish Islay Company?*

He looked at her with gratitude; the dam holding back his tears burst, and he sobbed, *Sorry, can't help! First time my life someone accuse-me peddler.*

The women stared at him, their mouths open, and then at each other. The younger, somewhat taken aback, remarked, *Doubt himself peddler. Never before see peddler cry.*

Right! Peddlers never cry. Feelings none. The first old woman agreed, grabbing Lyson by the hand. *Sorry! Hurt your feelings. Not intentional.* She pulled out a scented handkerchief from her bosom. The wonderful old-fashioned grandmotherly odor overpowered him as she wiped his cheeks like he were a grandchild. Her finger found the dimple and poked it. *Cute!*

Sorry! Forgive us, apologized the younger one. *Hope you understand that we very sensitive about peddlers come-here, embarrass us, then flee, leave debt there motel for us deaf have-to pay—*

He squeezed their hands, *Alright, alright. Not your fault! My fault, give-you wrong idea!*

The women crooned over him, patting, wiping, comforting, forgiving, poking the dimple. Lyson cringed. He wished little old ladies wouldn't find his dimple so attractive. Then the door opened and three men entered. Two old, grandfatherly, and the third, middle-aged, going on grandfatherly. For a very long, electric moment the two groups stared at each other, and one of the very old men turned to the younger and signed vehemently, *Told you! If you dress better, beautiful women jump on you, will!*

On the stairs up to the attic, the club room, the old man suddenly stopped and confronted Lyson, forebodingly: *Careful yourself! King here Obeke Deaf upstairs.* He nodded sharply the way old men do to embellish their warnings and continued on up. Lyson stood still, staring after the climbing figure, and the women behind had to prod him on.

Don't worry, they urged, *Go-on-up.*

King? Lyson asked, befuddled.

Not necessary worry, we know that yourself not peddler, the youngest woman assured him, and pinched his calf. *Stop silly! Go!*

Up the stairs they went, Lyson scurrying ahead out of reach of pinches. The club was indeed in an attic, right under the peaked roof, covered with sheetrock painted a creamy yellow to brighten the room under a pair of light bulbs, naked so that the shadows were sharp, unsoftened. Scattered about were a number of card tables at which players huddled. Cigarette smoke hung warm and heavy, stinging Lyson's eyes and lungs.

The old man motioned Lyson over to one of the tables and cautioned, *Quiet. Wait.* They stood silently at a respectful distance from the table but close enough to announce their intention. The four men at the table played on, studiously ignoring them. Lyson noted anxiously that two were cowboys, from their jeans and shirts and their sideburns, and that the third man appeared to be a printer, black ink under his fingernails. But Lyson was frightened more by the dried blood on the otherwise white T-shirt on the fourth. That fourth man, though quite small in stature, had huge hairy arms, the hair matted with blood. There was even blood on his brow where he had wiped his arms during the course of his grisly work. Because of his pearly bald head it was impossible to guess his age beyond 40. Lyson almost thought he could smell raw blood through the smoke, and glanced at the old man standing beside him, rigidly at attention. One of the cowboys won the hand and chortled as he greedily raked in the pot, thus ruling himself out as the King in Lyson's mind. The way the other cowboy shuffled the deck had a touch of deference to it, Lyson thought, and he studied the two remaining candidates. The printer, probably, he decided. Yes, must be. Printers are often the leaders in deaf communities, in the smaller towns, and privy to the latest secrets. He congratulated himself for his own acumen and waited patiently.

The smoke made his eyes water, and the blood against the white of the T-shirt seemed to glisten, freshly, wickedly, treacherously. He blinked and thought he saw the blood flowing. He shut his eyes tightly, wanting to rub them but daring not to move. When he opened them the King was staring right at him, balefully, probing, measuring. Without any unnecessary motion, he pulled a cigar, severely bent, from his hip pocket and inserted it in his mouth, his eyes hard on Lyson. The printer was the first with a flame under the cigar, to the chagrin of the cowboys, but the King took no recognition other than a long, slow inhalation.

The old man allowed his elbow to bump Lyson as he raised his hands to announce: *Him that's King here Obeke Deaf. Himself King here since many years. His name secret! Only himself allowed tell who his name.* He curtsied with his head and addressed the King, *His name first Lyson, last Sulla, from Washington, D.C. formerly but now move other state name Islay. Now traveling, on-way there California. Sleep there near motel overnight, morning will gone.*

The King looked slowly down at Lyson's clothes, down to the shoes that Lyson wished he could tuck out of sight under his pants. The cigar glowed, sending up a thin column of blue smoke as the King moved his eyes back up, still slowly, expressionless, almost stonily, until he met Lyson's anxious stare. And keeping his hand otherwise motionless on the table he asked, *Peddler?*

No! No! Lyson quickly denied, too quickly in the King's evident opinion. *Travel, business. Show you!* With shaking hands he tried to pull a card out of his wallet. But the old man patted his arm and put on the table the other card his wife had given him. Lyson was still fumbling with his wallet, so the old man took it and pulled out the driver's license and put that on the table too.

After examining it the King flicked the driver's license back across the table contemptuously, like a deuce, and reclined holding up close to his face the Islay Company card. Yawning decorously, like a lion, and scratching his underarm, the King pointed at the card saying, *Thrill?* in that versatile idiomic sign which in this situation literally meant What's this? but under the circumstances intimated, What's Islay Company trying to do in Obeke?

Well, Lyson began, intensely feeling every eye in the room upon himself, *This company has wonderful idea for help deaf move-there, buy home, get job, have fun bowling*—The awkward stillness in the room and the King's contracting pupils, so rapidly Lyson could actually observe them narrowing in the pale grey irises down to pin points, shamed him into putting his hands meekly down.

The King allowed him to roast in the glare for an appropriate moment, and shifted his glance to the printer who quickly, eagerly went to the defense of Obeke. He stood up and asked all the people in the room, *You have house?*

Oh yes, of-course! Thirty fists nodded around them.

Need job?

No! snapped 30 hands.

Have job?

Yes!

Here Obeke have bowling?

Of-course!

Satisfied here Obeke? asked the printer with mock humility.

Naturally! Silly ask!

Triumphantly the printer sat down to general applause. All eyes were now on the King, who took his own sweet time to direct his own eyes again over Lyson's body in a pattern that chilled him with the feeling of being drawn and quartered like a steer. Sweat running under his armpits tickled him into action, and Lyson explained lamely, *See, I said myself on-way-to California, looking for deaf there—*

One of the cowboys leaned forward toward Lyson, and demanded, *Stop here, for-for?*

A drop of sweat tickled his nose and Lyson absentmindedly flicked it off with a snap of his forefinger and the drop landed on the table. The cowboy glared ominously. *What sign that? Meaning?*

Excuse! Not intentional! Lyson apologized, exasperated with himself. *Itchy!* He rubbed his nose vigorously to convince the cowboy it really itched.

Immensely satisfied with himself for besting a smart-aleck Easterner, the cowboy tipped back on his chair, reclining with manure encrusted boots on the table and expertly rolled a cigarette. In honor of the victory, the printer lit the cigarette for him, and remarked to the King, offhandedly, casually as if it were beside the point, *Doubt himself peddler.*

The King raised one eyebrow: *How-so?*

Too dumb. Peddlers famous glib tongue.

Right! The old man interjected. *Downstairs, first time talk with him, himself talk careless, mistake, mistake, Impossible, can't succeed peddling, and most important, himself finish pay for motel. Already saw paper prove finish pay.*

His features softening to announce that he was satisfied that the matter had been settled, the King allowed his eyes to smile at Lyson, and with a nod directed him to look behind. A huge grinning man with pasted down black hair, in black vinyl jacket, greeted Lyson: *My name Tin. King command me follow-you, help watch protect. Similar bodyguard.* Putting a strong grip on Lyson's shoulder, Tin pulled out the handkerchief from the front pocket of Lyson's jacket and proceeded to solicitously wipe Lyson's face. There, there, said the tender expression on his face as he stuffed the damp handkerchief back into Lyson's pocket while tightening his grip on his shoulder: Don't try to lose me!

Thank-you! Thank-you! Lyson forced himself to say. *Myself very impressed here wonderful club. Friendly people. Good cooperation. Myself think magnificent honor meet you-all but especially you, King!*

But the King and his friends had already returned to the game as if nothing had ever happened; the only reminder of what had transpired being in the dry manure being brushed off the table by the cowboy's sleeve. Lyson didn't know whether to laugh or to cry. Is this a deliberate humiliation? Or is it being forgotten already? Before he could decide, though, the old woman tugged at him. *Want play poker?*

Oh, no, no. Thank-you. he demurred politely. *Always lose.*

Gin rummy? They were undaunted. *Mere pennies. Can't cry.*

No, no. Myself very hungry, he pleaded. *Know where good resturant?*

Oh yes, there across street. Good food, cheap, the younger woman replied.

Thank-you! Now me go eat. He shook hands on his way toward the stairs.

Halt! Tin demanded. *Supposed tell King bye!*

Oh, that's right! Lyson cringed and retreated to the the King's table and stood at attention. He had to wait until the hand was played, won by the King himself this time, before he was granted an audience by the simple expedition of the King's acknowledgement of his presence by looking up patiently at him.

Excuse me! Me go now eat, Lyson said very politely. *Thank-you for everything. Nice club here, enjoy myself very much. Happy, proud meet you King.*

A slight smile flickered in the King's eyes, the quality of which Lyson could not be certain—mocking? friendly? or what?—as the King released him with a curt nod and a twitching of the nose and lips as in a grunt.

With quick waves at his new friends, he hastened towards the stairway but a rush of a crowd on its way up forced him aside. The crowd was mostly young and jubilant over its victory at bowling, taking no note of Lyson, which suited him just fine. In a few seconds they would hear about his ignominious defeat at the hands of a cowboy! Best they never get a clear look at him, he decided. He bounded down the stairs and through the parlor toward the door, when a heavy hand clamped on his shoulder.

It was Tin. *Thrill, hurry?*

Myself very hungry, not-yet eat tonight—

Sandy appeared from behind a curtain in the back of the shop. *Oh! Leaving already?*

*Yes! Hungry, go eat there—*he pointed across the street, his eyes pleading with her to help get rid of Tin. *Want eat with me?*

She brightened at this invitation and signed softly, gracefully yet commanding, *Tin, you guard door, watch shop for me please.* Grabbing her purse she led Lyson outside, assuring Tin that she'd be right back. Tin tried to protest but she towed a stumbling Lyson away, across the street to the restaurant.

Sandy insisted that, considering his face was so pale, he have some red burgundy to restore his good spirits before ordering dinner. Then he would be more sure of ordering something that would be fitting to the occasion. Indeed, he could feel the wine coursing through his body, warming his torso, loosening his limbs, flushing his face, tingling his nose, softening his head. Delicious! He poured himself another glassful.

We need people like you there Islay! Lyson gushed in a sudden fit of exuberancy and, catching himself, put his hands down with a sheepish grin.

Please, she inquired, *What's Islay like?*

Ahh! he exhaled luxuriantly, his eyes bright. *Myself live there only few weeks, already feel MY home.*

Sandy nodded appreciatively. *Sounds good.*

Lyson rolled his eyes. *G-0-0-D, that's not good enough! Need better word.*

That good? She encouraged him on.

Hard believe, he mused, *but really like Eden, oasis, or Three Bears' House midst Dark Forest.*

Three Bears' House? Sandy couldn't conceal her amusement. *Cute.*

Lyson blushed, not in humiliation at her giggles, which were friendly as he could see, not so much directed at him as with him. But it's just that it's rather disconcerting, this admission of his fondness for children's stories. Why, it's, it's like confessing you still like Disney!

She patted his hand warmly: *Tell me more.*

Well, me there only few weeks, already made many friends, wonderful friends help me—

That's because, she interrupted, *yourself good*—She stopped, concerned. His face had turned pale, and he was looking with dread at something over her shoulder.

Tin was slumped at a table halfway across the restaurant behind her, visibly upset, distraught, glaring darkly at them. *Your fault!* his hands slashed. *King mad me!*

Sandy smiled wearily at Lyson, squeezing his hand, and went over to Tin's table and stood over him. *Naughty you! You supposed guard my shop!*

Blanching, Tin protested, *But King told me have-to watch*—he directed two watching fingers at Lyson and sank deeper into his chair.

For a long moment Sandy, arms folded, frowned down at Tin with an intimidating pout on her lips. When his eyes started avoiding hers, she asked firmly, *Why not you go-there shop, let myself watch him for you?*

But King there! Tin pleaded, on verge of tears, hysteria.

She sighed heavily, looking down at him with severe pity, as a nurse might on a drunk brought in, yet again, with a case of delirium tremens, and folded her arms with great finality. Tin turned away from her for a frontal look at Lyson, daring him to slip away, and implored Sandy, *Watch him for me, promise?*

She winked her left eye, the one away from Lyson, and tipped her head. Promise!

With that assurance Tin departed, but before opening the door he fixed a warning glare at Lyson who stiffly kept his hands firmly between his thighs, resisting a powerful urge to blow a bye-bye kiss. Sandy took her seat again and, sighing, remarked to Lyson, *You boys! Never outgrow your old clubhouse in tree!*

He looked bleakly at her and confessed, *Myself never had club house—*

She crinkled her brow sympathetically, tilting her head. *How-come?*

Grew-up in institution, he said sadly. *Live in dormitory. Always school, school, study, study. And always have-to wear hearing-aid. Mother afraid me fall, hurt ear. Not allowed play with boys in clubhouse. Not even climb trees.*

Sandy wanted so much to finger his dimple, but by then the waitress was putting their dinner on the table. *Lyson,* she signed softly, *After dinner, can you come with me? Know where splendid tree for climbing.*

CHAPTER 11

Lyson was on the teletypewriter to Mary when Sandy came in the motel room, bringing what she said was her son's jogging outfit and sneakers. She insisted he needed these for the night she'd planned for the two of them. She herself had on a baby-blue jogging suit that blended very well with her complexion. *Hi! Excuse me, TTY!* Lyson motioned her to a chair.

The machine was rapidly spelling out what Mary was typing back there in Suffex, and he had to keep his eyes on it to keep up. EVERYTHING DOING VERY GOOD HERE. NEW MALL WALLS NOW UP. WILL ROOF NEXT WEEK. WALLY SAYS HI! ANDY SOLD BUILDING ON 6TH TO LESTER. ALSO SOLD THAT HOUSE ON 12TH TO HIM. WOMEN WORK WITH LESTER WANT HOUSES. SURPRISE! LESTER TALK HIS FRIEND LAWYER NAME JACK NELSON, INFLUENCE HIM MOVE HERE TOO. VERY NICE AND SMART. YOU WILL LIKE HIM. SAYS ANXIOUS MEET YOU. BOUGHT HOUSE ON GRAND AND 10TH. WILL OFFICE THERE. OTHER DEAF COMPANY NAME WILSON SHOES BOUGHT LAND NEXT WINDECKER. FRIEND WINDECKER. MORE TO TELL BUT HOW YOU Q GA.

Staring at the fleeting words almost hypnotized Lyson so that he was slow in responding. LYSON YOU STILL THERE Q GA the machine demanded.

OH YES! I AM FINE! JUST DIZZY—

DIZZY Q. SOMETHING WRONG Q GA.

MARY YOU TYPE TOO FAST. MAKE ME DIZZY—

SORRY! MUST FAST. PHONE COST! GA.

DONT CARE COST. HAPPY TALK WITH YOU ALL NIGHT. GA.

The machine was quiet for a long pause, and continued, LYSON HOW COME YOU NOT YET SAY WHERE YOU ARE Q GA.

OH! HERE OBEKE. STOP FOR NIGHT. NOW MOTEL. VISIT DEAF CLUB. MET MANY PEOPLE AND THE KING. NOW VISIT WITH WOMAN—

SHAME ON YOU! THINK I BETTER FLY THERE NOW. DONT WANT YOU IN TROUBLE—

YOU KNOW ME! Lyson hastened to interrupt. YOU KNOW ME INNOCENT.

THAT WHY I MUST FLY THERE PROTECT YOU—

STOP THAT! SHE NICE! NOT TROUBLE—

SORRY! CANT HELP WORRY BECAUSE YOU DUXXXX INNOCENT, EASY FOOLED. MY FAULT! SHOULD TEACH YOU SECRETS ABOUT WOMEN—

The machine stopped and Lyson stared at it for such a long moment Sandy took notice and asked, *S'matter?* But before he could reply the machine came to life. PLEASE FORGIVE ME FOR WORRY FOR NOTHING. WISH BEATRICE NEVER TOLD ME THAT COWBOYS PREFER WHORES—

MARY MARY MARY, Lyson typed rapidly, impatiently, MARY ENOUGH! YOU KNOW THAT IA AM A GOOF XXXX GOOD BOY—

GOOFY YOU MEAN Q GA.

ENOUGH! GA.

The machine remained silent for about the time a sigh takes and resumed, IS SHE HEARING Q GA.

OH NEVER THOUGH ABOUT THAT. WILL ASK HOLD. Lyson turned to Sandy with the question, *Wonder want know if yourself hearing. Hard for me know, you sign same deaf.*

Really! Sandy was immensely flattered.

Uh? he urged.

Secret! She hugged herself coyly, happily.

Lyson returned to the teletypewriter, HARD SAY. PROBABLY HEARING. GA.

IS SHE PRETTY Q GA. The machine typed slowly, as if plaintively.

NEVER THOUGHT—WILL ASK—

NEVER MIND, the machine quickly interrupted. DUMB ME! DONT WANT CHASE YOU INTO HER ARMS. DUMB ME! CANT HELP—

Straightening himself in the chair, he pulled up his sleeves and like a pianist typed in what he felt to be a brilliant manner: I AM NOT SURE IF SHE IS PRETTY BUT I KNOW YOU ARE. LOVE LOVE LOVE—

STOP THAT! YOU MAKE ME MISS YOU! GA.

LOVE LOVE LOVE LOVE LOVE SK SK

SKSKSKSKSKSKSK

Inhaling deeply, triumphantly, he hung up the telephone, turned off the teletypewriter, reclined tipping back his chair with his feet on the dressing desk, and looked with dreamy eyes at Sandy. He was startled by her eyes huge with interest.

You married? she demanded with suddenly narrowed eyes.

Married? What's that? he asked innocently.

Put-on! She tossed him the jogging garments. *Let's go climb tree!*

In the park, by the River Platte that courses through the city of Obeke, stood a tremendous tree reverently verified by Sandy as a red maple. The trunk, to Lyson, seemed to be at least four or five feet wide, and the lowest branch was way out of reach, surely some dozen feet above the ground.

The crown of the tree had to be a hundred feet high and the longest branches stretched maybe thirty or forty feet, so that were it not for the lights of the skyscrapers across the river, it would be very dark beneath the tree. There was no moon and Lyson, to say the least, was very much concerned for their safety. It's not just that the tree was so huge. There were so many trees in the gloom, their trunks standing black against the darkness deeper in the park.

Beautiful! exclaimed Sandy. *Come!*

A heavy rope so thick he couldn't completely enclose his hand around it, hung against the trunk from a heavy limb. *Watch!* Sandy looped the rope under her armpit, behind her back and between her thighs. *Prevent slip-down. Can up but not down,* she explained, and started up hand over hand, her feet walking up the trunk. Before he could ask how they were going to get back down she was already straddling the limb, waving him up.

He gripped the rope bravely, planted a foot on the trunk, and pulled. But he only swung sidewise, bumping his head on the trunk. He blew heavily and tried again, this time getting both feet on the trunk. Exerting mightily he managed to work his way a couple of feet up when he realized he'd forgotten to loop the rope about his body. For an awful moment he hung there, strength rapidly melting from his hands, his body horribly heavy, Sandy so far beyond reach. Out of the tail of his eye he thought he detected a movement among the dark trunks; and before he knew it he was clinging to the limb with all fours, Sandy pounding his back gladly. She helped him up to the crotch of the next limb where he needn't cling so tight to his soul. *Relax! Relax!* she urged as she pulled up the rope, looping it over its limb. It was unbelievable to him how she could stand balancing on the limb while explaining, *When climbing you move only one hand or foot while other three hold. Never move two, same time. Understand?*

She felt his shoulders and found them rock hard. *Relax! You must relax!* She kneaded them firmly until they softened. He felt so good, so comfortable, and was beginning to enjoy his perch on the tree, his first tree! So high off the earth, the sensation of, well, being up in a tree thrilling him when Sandy squeezed his shoulder. *Watch!* and with lithsome grace of a cat disappeared up into the darkness.

This is plenty high! Lyson wanted to protest but again he spotted movement down below in the murky gloom among the other trees. He tried to get up but his feet flailed in empty air. Keep calm! Slowly, feeling his way, he worked his way up after Sandy. Everytime he reached a limb or two below her and thought the end was within reach, she climbed higher, drawing him ever higher. The trunk and limbs grew smaller and smaller as he climbed, groping, sweat stinging his eyes and fogging his glasses. Soon his hand met Sandy's and she helped him into a comfortable, secure saddle where the trunk split widely into two branches, wide enough for the both of them to straddle face-to-face, reclining against opposite branches, their knees touching.

For a long time they lay there, silent, way up there in the tree, swinging their legs, revelling in the cool breeze, the slow ponderous sway, the lights of the city blinking between leaves, the river drifting, twinkling below, its whirls and whorles reflecting innumerable sparkles of light. Sandy's knees felt reassuring, warm against his, and during lulls in the breeze he imagined he could feel her warmth radiating on his face. And her smell, delicious and female, coconut. Her hair and face glowed softly in the darkness, her eyes huge, almost floating. Very lovely. He was very happy. He allowed the moment to sink deep into his soul so that it would always be there, a wonderful part of his life.

Her eyes were soft and gentle on him, full of wonder, when she pointed to her ear. *Bird sing sing. Surprise! Most birds don't sing nights.* She tilted her head another direction. *Whip-poor-will. Their famous sing nights.* Her eyes brightened. *Ohhh! Mockingbird.* Her head turned, *Another mockingbird.*

Lyson enjoyed very much the pleasure lighting her face, the way it reflected joy at the sounds of birds. She gave him a wistful look but he was so happy she took his hand gently. She turned her head suddenly, amusement in her eyes, *Crows arguing.* Her eyes widened, *Owl O-O-O-O.* Lyson nodded contentedly at her descriptions of the sounds around them, his hand snug in hers so warm, feeling, quivering with life. He never wanted to ever get back down on earth. A most happy man.

So it was with extreme reluctance that, when she touched him that it was time to go down, though he trembled at her touch and wanted it to remain forever, he meekly followed her down, allowing her to guide his feet to lower limbs, if only for the touch necessary for such guidance.

Even the earth firm beneath his feet did not break the euphoria as she helped steady his balance that, he apologized, was nonexistent in the dark. She tugged him through the dread blackness of the forest toward the playground and seated him on a swing. He was feeling so good he fell off with the first push and, laughing, she teased him on to the merry-go-round. She pushed and pulled on the machine until everything, the dark trees, the city lights, Sandy herself, whirled into a dizzying blur and he allowed his limp self to slip off onto the grass, so freshly mowed it smelt like hay.

He lay there on his back staring up at the sky. Stars! The heavens so full and deep with countless worlds. He lay right there, enjoying every bit of the feeling of floating in space among the stars. Sandy's face appeared above him, her hands on his chest. The very fraility of her shoulders, the gentleness of her hands, the kindness in her eyes held such a tremendous power he lay there completely helpless, vulnerable, literally in her hands.

But something possessing great power derived from the good and strong earth intervened: ants finally found their way under his jersey and countless little pricks spread burning, stinging all over his back and neck. Lyson scrambled howling to his feet, bowling over Sandy, and ran leaping around in wild circles slapping his neck and shoulders. She followed around, anxious, trying to help but they tripped over each other and rolled down the bank into the river. He writhed in the shallow water, rubbing his back on the mud, much as a dog on a pile of manure.

S'matter? she cried, trying to restrain him.

"Burning!" he cried. "Help!"

She pulled up his jersey but it was too dark. She could feel little bumps along his back. With globs of mud, she rubbed his back vigorously. *Better?*

Oh much! he sighed with obvious relief. *Before burning, stinging. Now just itchy.*

She dragged him slipping, slithering, into deeper water, and washed the mud off him and rinsed out the jersey and his glasses. He just sat there on the bottom, the water cool up to his neck, letting the river caress his back. He was again happy. And enjoying very much being fussed over, like the way she put the glasses on his face. But something in the river, floating by, nudged him in the side and he jumped, feet and arms flying, and fled up the bank.

Sandy erupted from beneath the water, floundering and spewing water. "Lyson!" she cried, furious, shaking the water out of her hair like a terrier. Then she remembered he was deaf. Deaf as in deaf and dumb. She couldn't see him in the darkness, and wiped her face and searched again. "Lyson!" she called in spite of herself, panic rising in her voice. Frantic, she groped under the water for him. "Lyson!" Her hands caught something, but it was only the empty jersey. "Think!" she commanded herself as she saw how the river sped toward the east, the darkness. Quickly she swished through the water downstream but a sudden dropoff, the water swirling ominously beneath her struggling feet, forced her to swim to the bank. "Oh, Lyson! Lyson!" she sobbed on her way up. "My God, find him!"

A pale form appeared ahead of her like a ghost, sitting shivering on a bench. "Lyson!" she ran to him and hugged his head tightly to her chest. *So glad you O.K.* she exclaimed. *Thought you finish drown!*

"Why? What made you think that?" he asked, his voice quivering from the cold. "I thought it was a snake."

Snake! Her eyes were bright in the dark. *I look look for you. Thought drown. Yell, yell your name, then remember you deaf. Why didn't you call, let me know you O.K.?*

He looked up at her, his mouth agape, his eyes brimming so that little lights flickered, floating, quivering in them. *Didn't-know. Thought you playing, swimming. Sorry.*

She slumped, grasping his face in her hands and felt how hot, flushed was his face. Pulling his head to her chest she cried aloud, "Sorry I got so mad, forgive me." Though he couldn't hear her he could feel her voice resonating in her chest and the way her hands held him. He understood and hugged her in gratitude. He tried to apologize but she put a finger on his lips.

* * *

The first thing, the first picture that came to his mind when he awoke in the morning was Mary, her eyes bottomless with reproach. Lyson, what have you done?

He sat up like a bolt in the bed. Sure enough he was in his motel room, the ceiling and floor painted a flat white, the curtains a dark green backlit by the sun. He just remembered the promise to meet Sandy for breadfast downstairs. His watch on the nightstand said nine-fifteen. I'm late! He rushed to the curtains and poked his head through. Her car was right there in front of the restaurant. But his own Mercedes was blocked by an Oldsmobile. Looking closer, he could see a slumped figure in the driver's seat, the head seemingly wedged between the steering wheel and door window. Why, it looks like Tin! He looked again at Sandy's car. For some reason, in his mind, it looked like it had been there a long time, likely all night too.

He ducked back and confronted his room. The bed looked like a wrestling match had occurred on it, so mussed was it. He wondered if he had actually slept. His clothes hung neatly on the chair, his shoes lay under the dresser, but his underpants lay crumpled, wet on the floor, with the jogging pants and shoes, wet too, by the bed. He looked down and was aghast. Mary must never know! She'd be very, very upset if she ever learnt he'd slept without his pajamas this night.

In the mirror in the bathroom he saw a befuddled Lyson with bloodshot eyes. Disheveled, matted hair. Ugly gray jaw. Mud on shoulders. Couldn't recall taking a shower after coming in last night. He sniffed an armpit. Probably not. The tub looked clean, the soap still in its wrapper, the towels folded neatly in their rack. Conclusive evidence enough he decided, and took a shower and cleansed himself from the night past. And for good measure he washed his underpants too.

It was Tin, all right, sleeping in the Oldsmobile parked so close behind his car that Lyson couldn't get in between to put his suitcase in the trunk. Though he couldn't see the face the way it hung down between the steering wheel and the door, Lyson could see Tin was sleeping the sleep of the exhausted. He can use an extra hour, Lyson decided, and put his bag in the back seat of the Mercedes.

Already the morning was getting very warm and his watch said it was nearly ten. She must be late for work, he fretted, and hurried to the restaurant. Sandy was at a table by the window, already smiling at him although he didn't see her at first when he entered with a preoccupied frown and looked around. But he couldn't see her for the glare from the window and she had to get up and fetch him. *Oh, hello!* he grasped her hand and immediately felt very bashful. *Uh—myself very embarrassed about last—*

Aw, thought myself lots fun. Come!

At the table already was a steaming cup of coffee for him and it took only a sip to straighten him out. *Never will forget that tree.* Another sip. *And you.*

She smiled and toasted him with her cup. *Likewise me. River too.*

Lyson drained his coffee and wiped his mouth thoughtfully. *Oh!* he thumped his forehead. *Hope I not cause you late there work.*

Don't worry, she smiled with a twinkle. *Have other plans.* She poured him another cup.

Hope myself not interrupt your other plans.

The same mysterious smile but her eyes were now laughing. *Plenty time. You going California?*

His shoulders slumped. *Yeah but so-far! Not realize America huge! Oh may seem easy drive but—* He blew heavily.

California before you?

Oh yeah, twice. But airplane fast, less than five hours. But car! Now three days from Islay to here. And not-yet halfway!

She leaned forward. *Why not you take-easy. Relax, enjoy your trip, scenery, forget about time? Between here and California truly beautiful, worth driving slow, sightsee.*

His jaw dropped and he stared incredulously at her. *Can't! Must fast!*

Why not? Sandy was amused and rested her chin on the prop formed by her folded hands.

Lyson was astonished. *You don't-know?* No one had ever told him to slow down.

She rested her chin on her hands, a deep look in her eyes as she probed his, wondering. Finally she admitted, *Sometimes I don't understand you.*

His eyebrows arched up, *Well,* and glancing furtively about with a finger on his lips, *Shhh!* He confessed, *Me neither.*

Sandy laughed softly, *I can believe that.*

Breakfast arrived and disappeared quickly into Lyson before her very eyes. She very much liked watching a man enjoy his meal, but Lyson was rather unusual; when finished he sat back satisfied, wiping his mouth with finality and met her eyes. He thought she was very beautiful, her eyes which for the first time he noticed were green diamonds floating in a deep blue sea. Such lips. And the nose! Indescribable! *You eating?* he asked.

Oh, already, she said, glad to get back on everyday topics. *Before you came.*

But Lyson was not quite as ready to reenter reality and sighed, *I guess I have-to vamoose. Wish stay longer but California —*

Lucky you! She pouted. *Wish me go-with you.*

He stared at her wistfully and slowly signed, *Wish me too.* He was going to start the sign *But* when she interrupted with a regretful *Can't.*

This wasn't exactly what he wanted and his shoulders slumped. Although his head said he should be glad, he still felt, inexplicably, disappointed.

In her mind she knew full well that, with her he would really have the time of his life, really live for the first time ever. Yet she hesitated: she believed that a man is married only when his wife is around. Body, mind, spirit make no matter, just so she is around. She hesitated yet again: she knew he would never again be the same man if she went with him. *Lyson,* she said very gently, *Wish me go-with you, but have business here.* She carefully studied his face, which was blank with obvious confusion, and added, *And my son here.*

God, she's a mother! Lyson berated himself and exhaled loudly. *Will never forget you. Hope someday meet again.*

That mysterious, beguiling twinkle in her eyes again, and she agreed, *Impossible forget! Tree, river, night.*

They walked slowly, silently, to his car, loathe to part but knowing they must. Hey! Tin was still asleep in his Oldsmobile, blocking the Mercedes. Lyson stood by helplessly, hands in pockets, a crinkle on his brow. Sandy sighed at Lyson and tapped on the window of the Oldsmobile. But Tin slept on and she opened the door a crack and he nearly slipped out. He gaped at Sandy and at Lyson, back and forth. His eyes registered a connection that never was there.

Please your car move, demanded Sandy.

Can't! Tin jumped out of his car. *Have-to ask King permission first.*

Before Sandy could reply he locked his door and fled down the parking lot signing wildly over his shoulder, *Tell King! Tell King!*

Fuming, Sandy made for the motel office, telling Lyson to wait. In a moment she returned with a lopsided grin and asked Lyson, *By-the-way, which way you going California?*

It took a bit of a while for Lyson to recover his senses and fetch the map from his car. *Well, myself not sure, but seems shortest way,* he traced a finger from Obeke to Denver to Grand Junction to Las Vegas, thence to Los Angeles.

She could not help but frown. *You enjoy driving through mountains?*

He shrugged philosophically. *All mountains.* He ran his hand up and down the Rocky chain. *Decide shortest anyway.*

If me with you, that's best, most beautiful way, she said wistfully. *But you alone, I recommend,* she pointed from Cheyenne to Salt Lake City and down to Las Vegas. *Easier, less winding, not awful steep.*

Thank you! Thank you! he effused, pumping her hands just as a wrecker entered the parking lot. With casual experience the wrecker quickly towed the Oldsmobile ignominiously away by the rear bumper.

Lyson had very mixed feelings now that there was no honest reason to linger any longer as he belted himself down in his Mercedes and declared, *Thank-you very much for everything! We must climb tree again.*

Sandy looked down at him very affectionately and kissed him on the dimple. Again the mysterious twinkle: *We will! See you!* And she was gone.

CHAPTER 12

Along the Interstate in Wyoming grew Little Antarctica, a modern little truck stop that came into being because of its demonstrable need to be right there on the freeway, miles from anywhere, to serve the traveling public. Much like towns that grew up along the Mississippi River, preferably where stood slack water, a stand of forest, and if possible a tributary of clear water, to serve the growing fleet of river steamers.

There are no tributaries, of water or asphalt, and no forest at this little location along the freeway. Little Antarctica actually came into being only because a man once got stranded there during a blizzard and saw a need for modern amenities at that location, particularly a hot cup of coffee and a warm stove. That man had a bit of savings from a stint in Antarctica of which the locale reminded him, so it didn't take long to get the truck stop on the map.

In the early summer, although some green could be seen in scattered prairie grasses and sage bushes, the area was as bleak, nearly, as in the winter, and the traveler's eyes brightened at the veritable forest of soaring signs proclaiming an oasis of gasoline, meals, shops, restrooms, and hot coffee. Such a sight is hard to resist, particularly for customers such as Lyson C. Sulla who are overawed, intimidated by the tremendous emptiness of the vast landscape of Southwest Wyoming. Something like a last-chance service station where you must touch base before braving such desolation.

Such an oasis signifies an exchange of goods and services that results in a great deal of loose change, which travelers hardly ever count and which most everyone considers a nuisance to get rid of at first opportunity, at a vending machine, an electronic game, or anything else that digests coins. Now, the Reverie family was designed and well-oiled and tuned to gather as many such coins as possible before other machines got them. There were four members to the family: Arnold and Maude and Bonnie and their van. Some people might dispute counting the van as a member of the family but Arnie and Maude would get you just as dead if you scratched their van as hurt their little daughter Bonnie. And by all means the van received the better care. It had to. The better care the van received, the more territory they could cover. The worse care Bonnie received, the more coins she could gather.

The van had come out of the factory as a rather ordinary black Dodge Maxi-Wagon. Then a series of visits to various custom shops for fabrics, windows, sparkling paint designs, electronics, cosmetics, modern appliances, galley, toilet, everything, and it became their home, and their friend.

In the back was a bed inside a heavily carpeted cocoon where safe from the world could snuggle the Reveries. In little niches in the cushioned walls rested several tiny portable color television sets, of the size easily smuggled out of stores. And at all times a live radio listened in on the police frequencies. Bonnie had to always listen to the radio, to keep her parents abreast of any police attention focused on them. The radio was never, ever turned off.

After the van pulled off the freeway onto the exit ramp to Little Antarctica, the first thing to do was to get it full of gasoline. This was most important. There was no knowing how far they might suddenly have to go before the trail cooled behind them enough to stop for the night. Or they might even have to leave the state entirely. Plenty of gasoline, water, food, and maps; their bladders empty; the van backed into a parking space directly facing the ramp back onto the freeway. Nary a hint of a black van on the police airwaves; and they were ready to begin the coin collection.

Maude was a small, wiry, lithe woman with a face pointed as a coyote, and as crafty, as cunning. That's when her face was at rest, in repose. Actually she had many faces, as many as she needed to fit whatever situation they found themselves in. A face for each occasion. A complete range of expressions, from the angelic to the demonic. Indeed the devil could often be seen quite clearly in those pale grey eyes, particularly by religious people, those with enough religion to know intimately what the devil looks like. Maude studied with shrewd eyes the mini-mall at the side of the huge truck stop, and the people entering. No need to notice those leaving. They're gone, lost. Circumstances, she felt, best called for the face of a weary traveler and the dress of a sweet dear matron, including a flowery little hat. She doublechecked the contents of her working purse. All coins were emptied into a special pouch hidden behind a crease in the cushioned wall. A crying handkerchief. A pad and pen ready for a quick defense or retort. False identification. A few dollar bills. And a knife with retractable blade, ready to spring out instantly at any danger.

Arnie was tearfully afraid of that knife. He had a very good reason to be so afraid. Across his neck, under his chin, ran an ugly scar, a momento of a drunken brawl in which he had beaten her into submission, and afterwards had allowed himself to triumphantly fall asleep, a deep sleep of careless heedless male supremacy. He still shuddered at the memory of how his hand had reached inside the throat and touched the larynx, and also the frailty of the pearly white windpipe and throbbing red veins in the mirror she held up to him after putting aside the terrible knife. *That warning mere,* she had said with death in her eyes, *Next time, for real.* Like the Pope she had made the eternal sign of the cross in front of his eyes.

Because of that awful scar he had to wear turtlenecks. When working he used floppy-necked ones so that when confronted by store authority he could straighten himself up from his usual stoop, allowing the scar to show, to gain sympathy that would allow his escape.

For this job, Maude decided he was to wear the big military field jacket. He would be the decoy. Little Antarctica, with its scores of travelers bustling about with change jingling in their pockets, she divined, called for a beggar girl, a Cinderella lost, forsaken in the wilds of Wyoming.

They had just the dress for Bonnie. An old party dress, fading-pink silky nylon, with flowers embroidered along the hems and the bust. The dress was open at the shoulders, all the better to touch the customers with the frailty of Bonnie, with her narrow bony shoulders, painfully thin arms, and hollow face with deep-set tragic eyes. It was difficult to determine Bonnie's age. The size of the body was that of a child but her eyes were ageless, reflecting centuries of travails, yearnings. Silk dancing shoes, a fading carnation pinned at the temple, a bead purse filled with what Maude would insist be called merchandise, and she was ready.

The sun had just set, and the dusk was soft and mellow. People are their kindest at such moments. Arnie was the first into the combination store. Immediately he went to the electronics section, to the little portable televisions. Because his great coat was open, the televisions were out of sight against his chest as he pretended to examine them. Almost on cue, he soon drew the attention, cautious and watchful, of store personnel. The manager and the security guard edged toward Arnie, pretending to rearrange merchandise, as they worked unobtrusively toward the best surveillance stations around the suspect.

Her eyes bright as a coyote's, Maude saw all this and nudged Bonnie into action. Grabbing a shopping cart she followed her little girl up and down the aisles, a few paces behind, instantly ready to stumble the cart into anyone who interfered. The first items she picked off the shelves were always the breakables or spillables. Milk. Orange juice. Apple cider jug. Anything to arouse the cleaning instinct in store personnel, just in case.

Great soulful eyes just on the verge of tears confronted the shoppers as Bonnie handed them little cards and waited patiently, meekly for the little coins, shivering slightly in the cold of the air conditioning. The little cards were much like business cards. On one side were printed the alphabet and numerals as spelled out on fingers in the form of sign language called fingerspelling. On the other was this message:

Sign Language Instructional Card
Distributed by the Deaf of America
A Charitable Organization of, by, and for the Deaf
A most convenient way of private communication
with your family and friends!
A contribution of any amount will be much appreciated.

Very few people whom Maude allowed Bonnie to approach could resist the appeal in the soft eyes offered up by such a pitiful little girl. Truckers, commercial travelers, construction workers, and blacks were the most dear, ready and quick with bills, fives, tens, even twenties on a good day. Mothers were kind too, although rarely able to afford more than coins, probably because their husbands did not give them much, Maude judged. Ordinary people were always good for a coin or two, sometimes a bill too. Tourists in outlandish clothes were unpredictable; a few liked to make a joke, a game out of flipping a coin for Bonnie to scramble after. But Maude had her pride: Bonnie was never to pick up any coin dropped in jest.

To be avoided at all costs were people dressed to advertise their belief in a truth made indisputable, sacrosanct by the simple expediency of being in the right, on the side of respectability: that clothes make the person. Especially if their faces were tight, their lips pinched, their eyes dry. They were liable to believe Bonnie required the attention of Authority, Correction, Rehabilitation, Redemption. Besides, they counted their money carefully, down to the most humble penny. Bonnie was never, ever, to offer a card to anyone, male or female, in a suit and tie, their hair frozen by spray, without first a nod from her mother.

At the candy shelves was a short squat man in a suit and tie. Bonnie halted and looked over her shoulder at Maude. The suit was not middle-class but in good taste, thought Maude. The man moved aside politely and diffidently for a passing woman with a small child in a shopping cart. The man wrinkled his nose friendlily at the child. Had he had on a hat, he would have tipped it. Maude gave the nod.

Bonnie tugged at the man's sleeve and held up a card. The man gave a small start as he read the card and his eyes widened as he looked down at the trembling eyes. He hesitated a moment, confused, but gave in with a bill from his pocket, not even bothering to check its denomination. He held up a finger and from his wallet he took out a little card, which he gave her as well.

Just then Maude spotted Arnie being marched toward the office by two grim looking men. A flash in her eyes told Bonnie it was time to go and they pushed their cart toward the checkout counter, picking up some potato chips and snacks along the way. It might be a long night. Though anxious to hurry, she took the time and extra distance to obtain some raspberry flavored yogurt, for her stomach.

In the office Arnie stood stiff with righteous indignation as the two men frisked, patted, and probed him. Out of the pockets of the great coat came a thin tin box rattling with aspirin, a half roll of TUMS, an inhalant tube, a dirty comb, soiled crumbled Kleenex, a number of short pieces of pencils, scraps of paper, empty candy and gum wrappers, and a few lost dusty pennies which he sardonically thanked them for finding. The men slumped down on the desk, dumbfounded. Inexplicably, they had found nothing on Arnie. He knew it was vitally important to restrain his sense of triumph as he took out his wallet and found a calling card, which he handed the manager.

Jack Nelson
Attorney-at-Law
Specialty: Deaf Rights and Lawsuits
Nationwide Toll-Free Number:
1-800-322-9537

Consideration was all over the manager's face as he gave the card quickly back and pleaded forgiveness. Calmly, Arnie placed the card back in the wallet and stood his ground, his hands clasped behind his back. The manager and the guard exchanged unhappy glances and blew through clenched teeth. Finally, the manager offered a twenty dollar bill, holding it up, urging him to take it and be gone.

Arnie looked down incredulously, contemptuously at the twenty, his hands still clasped behind his back. The guard dropped his shoulders and found a fifty in his wallet. Arnie graciously accepted it and reclasped his hands behind his back, holding his ground again. The manager shook his head in defeat and came up with another twenty and two fives.

Good customers! Arnie felt a great sense of relief that he would not have to expose his awful scar. To show he had no hard feelings, he shook their hands and bought a pint of Tennessee Straight and a six-pack of beer in the store. At the door he offered each man a beer, but they demurred. They were glad to see him go.

Before going out to the van, Arnie slipped into the restroom and hid a twenty in a secret flap in his wallet. He earned it, he declared, toasting himself in the mirror with a swig from the bottle. The whiskey made him feel on top of the world and he skipped happily down to the van.

Maude was already at the steering wheel, and as soon as he entered, she drove quickly away down the freeway into the night. *Must hurry!* she yelled.

Eighty dollars! declared Arnie triumphantly, pulling out a tiny pocket television set through a secret hole leading to the bottom of the great coat. The picture was not much larger than a big postage stamp.

Splendid! chortled Maude. *Bonnie got 168!*

Really!

Look! Bonnie held up a crisp hundred dollar bill.

Man give, himself deaf! Maude said with awe.

Deaf?—Arnie was incredulous. *Can't-be!*

Yes! Look! Bonnie handed him the calling card.

ISLAY COMPANY
603 Grand Boulevard
Suffex, Islay

Islay—the Garden of the East
An Opportunistic Company for, or, and by the Deaf
Residential, Commercial, and Agricultural Properties
Employment, Investment, and Finacial Opportunities
Recreational, Social, and Athletic Activities for the Deaf.

Lyson C. Sulla
President and Chief Executive Officer
Chairman of the Board
Himself Deaf

CHAPTER 13

Lyson was alone again in his genuine leather-covered seat, wheeling rapidly on his way west. Already he was through the Rockies, hardly having noticed them, let alone Cheyenne and most of the other towns along the way, even when stopping for fuel and food. Even as the signs said he was approaching Salt Lake City, Lyson remained conscious of no time, in the usual sense, ever passing since the warm soft kiss implanted on him by Sandy, still warm and soft on his dimple, from way back there in Obeke. That morning seemed fresh still. Hey, which morning is this, now?

God, how long ago was that? The stubble on his face felt heavy and coarse as sandpaper. Must be at least two, three days! He looked back and, sure enough, the Rockies could be seen way back in the distance as the Mercedes floated down the canyon toward the Great Salt Lake Basin. After a very brief encounter with the desert, the automobile brought him to a paradise of prosperous, well-kept farms. So marvelous were the orchids and pastures, so straight the furrows, that Lyson felt a tinge of shame at the wildness of the Islay farms. Not even half as civilized, he thought. Even the cows here looked scrubbed, brushed, and milked by comparison. Ah, the horses. Such sheen. Such muscles. The tails and manes seemed to have been shampooed and air brushed. And forests like trimmed parks. Flowers around the houses. Fresh paint on houses and fences, even on the playground sets that every other house seemed to feature.

The houses grew closer and closer together. Before long he was in Salt Lake City itself, so modern and neat he had to stop over, if only to refresh himself.

Among a profusion of fast food drive-ins stood a Stars and Stripes Motel. He stopped right there on the road in front of the driveway, hesitant. He only wanted to freshen up and go on to California. But a bed! He reasoned it must be a Saturday, and he'd best keep those wheels spinning if he was to make Los Angeles by Monday and start the drums booming for the Islay Company. How many miles now? He was trying to look up the distance when he noticed stares from people on the sidewalk. Oh! Oh! Traffic was backed up behind him. The man in the next car had his head out his window, cursing him, no doubt loudly.

The motel manager was already at the door to the office when the Mercedes quickly pulled into the lot. Lyson had the feeling the manager didn't come to the door merely out of eagerness to be of service, and with studied dignity consulted his watch. It was a navigator's watch, a gift from Beatrice and the Captain for this journey. Little buttons not only for the usual time, day, and stopwatch, but also a calculator. The Captain jokingly regretted that the state of technology had not yet produced a watch that kept track of latitude and longitude. The digits showed that it was 9:27 A.M. Friday. Only Friday? Impossible. He checked the odometer. Nine-hundred and seventeen miles since Obeke. Twenty hours since Obeke now. The calculator came up with 46 mph. Must be right, then, he nodded, getting out to stretch. His legs felt stiff, wobbly as he staggered toward the door where the manager still stared at him.

"Excuse me! But I'm deaf—"

The manager continued staring, unmoving. He had on pressed blue slacks and a white shirt with a red tie. A healthy tan on his lean and hard features. Angular face made even more square by a flat top. Sinewy arms and hands. White shoes.

Apologetically, Lyson pointed at his ear. "Deaf!"

No response other than a glance at the offending ear.

Lyson sighed and pulled out his old pad. "Do you have a room, please?" he wrote.

The manager read the note and turned with the precision of a soldier, without a twinge on his face, into the office and took up position behind the counter.

The registration form was a shocker: it was practically an employment application form. It not only asked for his birthdate and place, Social Security number, employment record, marital status, schools attended starting with kindergarten, military record, financial status, and religious and fraternal affiliations, but also: did he smoke? Did he drink? Was he ever fired from a job, and why? Was he ever suspected of a crime? Was he ever a member of the Communist Criminal Conspiracy? If so, when, and where. Did he pledge Allegiance to the Flag of the United States of America?

Lyson looked up incredulously at the manager, who responded by pushing a pen under Lyson's hand. The man's face was as stone—still as Mt. Rushmore. Behind the manager, to the side, Lyson noticed a black box with a lens in front and a little sign: For your protection, a photographic record of this transaction has been permanently processed.

No way can I ever get to sleep in a place like this, Lyson decided, and stomped to the door. But it would not open. He whirled, furious, to confront the manager.

His eyes completely without expression, giving away nothing, the manager moved his lips very slightly, just enough that Lyson realized he was at last saying something.

"Look" Lyson cried, pulling out his ear. "Deaf!"

The manager remained rock still, immobile. Out again came Lyson's pad and pen: "I have decided I do not want a room here after all. Please let me out!"

The manager replied with such imperceptible lip movements that Lyson grunted and wrote: "Can't you see that I am deaf? Impossible to read your lips. Please write!"

Again the manager pushed the registration form a fraction closer to Lyson.

"No! I want to get out of here!" Lyson wrote furiously across the form and folded his arms stubbornly.

Still completely expressionless, the manager did an about face and marched out of the office to the back. Lyson was stunned. Unable to stand still, he began to pace back and forth in the lobby, like a caged animal. Suddenly, on impulse he tried the door and it opened as if it had never, ever, been locked at all.

* * *

Lyson slipped gratefully into bed, the sheets cool and smooth on his feet, and he allowed his body to relax and his toes to wiggle after their long cramped confinement in the shoes. The comforter pressed upon him as lightly as Sandy's knees in Obeke, and he liked being where he was very much. The room behind drawn curtains had a soft pleasing glow. It was a simple room, not just in the furnishings but in the way the walls and ceiling were plastered by hand to give an adobe effect, almost primitive. And so near Speed Burger too. The motel looked old, more like a motor court of the old days, the kind that used to be found along two-lane highways outside of town, before freeways and their phantasmagoria of motels, eateries, service stations, car lots, quick stop markets, animal clinics, recreational vehicles dealers, malls changed the character of the land, made the land seem an inconsequential part of the scenery.

But the light behind the curtains bothered him. Oh no, not just that it was in his eyes. It's just that it reminded him that it was daytime. And that the earth, no matter how still, solid, steady it felt on his back, does indeed move. Not just move, but hurtles! A thousand miles per hour! It goes around the sun like a giant clock, he thought uneasily, and because the sun moves too, never returns to the same spot again. And it's Friday!

"Time's wasting!" he cried and jumped out of bed. In the long list of names and addresses in his attache case, he found one for Salt Lake City: Anthony Pankey, Geneologist for the Deaf. *If I can't trace your lineage back at least five generations, your money refunded with my condolences.*

Just what we need! Lyson rejoiced. Hearing think us deaf have no family, no loved ones, no roots, no legitimacy.

Anthony Pankey ran his business in his own home, informally on the dining table with a view of his backyard. It was a very nice yard, surrounded by hedges and flowering bushes, with a gym set for children, not only his own but also his clients'. He didn't want little children to join in the search for their ancestors. As often as not, they ask disconcerting and inappropriate questions at the very time their parents were most vulnerable in their quest for identity. He thought too, people felt more at home at the dining table with its sunlight and view of distant mountains, than in his office with its cold, imposing computer remorselessly spewing out private information, totally heedless of the sensibilities of his clients. He was fully aware that his competitors in geneology considered his methods less than professional, particularly those who trade on their professionalism. They were apt to denounce his methods as unethical, but he was prepared to counter that doctors dropped quite a few notches in public esteem when they replaced the old custom of home visits with the new professionalism of insisting that patients, no matter how ill, drag themselves out of warm beds unto cold examining tables.

Coffee? his wife and partner Jayne offered Lyson as they settled down at the table. Anthony was still awed that he was her husband and never got over his wonder at her acceptance of him. Everytime she set a cup of coffee in the sunbeam on the table, the play of light on the down on her arm invariably drew him to brush it softly with his lips.

But Jayne was quicker and led his attention to Lyson's clothes. *Pretty clothes.* She felt the jacket appreciatively, running her fingers over the sleeve. To Lyson: *Where get?*

Oh! There, Fremont, he blushed.

She even fingered the shirt. *Soft! Compared here, starchy.*

That little touch went deep into Lyson and her eyes, strikingly hazel, caught and held his gaze.

Cute! laughed Jayne as she settled herself down on the opposite side of the table, telling Anthony, *Better find-out name their clothes.*

Can't remember. Lyson pulled out the lapels, looking for the trademark. *Ah! Says, quotation-marks, The Rake.*

Never heard.

In Fremont, near my home.

Jayne exclaimed to Anthony, *Wonder, have here?*

No idea. Will check. He too felt the jacket. *Like, myself.*

They sipped the coffee quietly for a moment before Jayne asked, *You say your last name S-U-L-L-A, right?*

Yes! Lyson was grateful to get off the subject of clothes and on to his favorite subject. *Formerly, Washington, D.C., now live there Islay.*

Where from? inquired Anthony with crinkled brow.

I-S-L-A-Y, between Washington D.C. and New York, Lyson spelled out.

No, no, I mean, where your family from?

Oh, New York.

Anthony could not help but laugh. *I mean, your nationality.*

My father, his parents from Italy, said Lyson. *My mother, her father two, three generations from Germany. But her mother many generations American, same my wife, her family many many generations there Boston.*

Anthony pulled up his eyebrows; it always awed him the way people got around; the situations that compel some to leave their roots for a faraway unknown land, to meet a stranger and produce offspring that otherwise would never have been. He shuddered at the immense odds against anyone ever having been born. In only 10 generations, over 2,000 couplings are required to produce the eleventh. Just one missed connection somewhere, maybe a great-grandmother sleeping that one night on her left side rather than the right, a burned dinner, an alien scent on grandfather's shirt, a headache, a late train, an ill wind on the ship coming over to America, a stray bullet, a noise at an inopportune time. Any one of these in your background, and you'd never have been born. *My God!* he exclaimed to Jayne. *Amazing!*

Lyson's face reddened and Jayne was quick to explain, *He think wonderful that people born from different different places, happen meet, never know why—or how—*

Anthony, realizing the embarrassment, jumped in. *Suppose your grandfather missed ship to America, or storm blew-up, ship sank, or force divert different port, meet different wife—*

But myself here! Lyson protested plaintively.

Shooting a sharp glance at her husband, Jayne soothed Lyson. *Wonderful you here! Marvelous!,* And sweetly to Anthony, *More coffee, please.*

Like a little boy ordered to the corner, Anthony disappeared into the kitchen. Squeezing Lyson's hand, Jayne reassured him with her free hand, *Don't feel bad. Just talk theory. Not mean anything.* And brightening, *Want cookie?*

Before he could respond, she slipped away into the kitchen.

Anthony! She confronted him imperiously. She folded her arms just long enough for that pose to register, and snapped, *Careful yourself careless talk!*

I know! Know! Anthony hung his head lamely. *Not intentional. Thought he knew what I mean—*

He won't, she said with the wisdom it seems only women have. *Never,* she signed slowly. *Can't.*

This intuition of hers, this ability of hers to see what he could never even imagine never failed to fascinate him. *Love you,* he declared and gripped her shoulders for a more intimate contact with her eyes. But he could see that her eyes saw something in him she would never tell him, at least directly. He would have to feel for it in her shoulders. She did not hold back, but allowed herself to be gathered in his arms. *Love you, love you,* said their caresses.

Lyson appeared at the door, befuddlement all over his face, even his posture. *Oh! Excuse me! Not intentional!*

Jayne waved quickly, *That's all right* and teased him by naively asking, *You starved for cookies?*

No! No! He had the most uneasy shamefaced look she had ever seen. At first she misread the way his knees rubbed each other until he finally blurted out, *Need restroom!*

It took her only a second to react, but to a man in Lyson's predicament it was a noticeably long one. She seized his hand and dragged him, stumbling because he was afraid to relax his knees too much, to the guest bath.

When she returned, Anthony was laughing uproariously. His infectious laughter started her giggling as well, but she could not let go entirely; she was too worried.

It was so unlike Anthony to lose his composure with his customers. A sixth sense, somewhere, told her to quiet Anthony's demeanor and she cradled his head in her arms. If done right, and briefly enough, he would be all right. The only problem was her sixth sense was a trifle too late. Lyson, looking greatly relieved, appeared at the door.

Oops! Excuse! he exclaimed, his eyes wide as he fled. She ran after him in haste, afraid they'd lost him. For a very brief moment they froze, staring at each other, then broke into sheepish smiles. She shyly inquired, *Ready for cookies?*

Back in the kitchen, Anthony was still trying to collect his wits. A darting glance from Jane fixed him. Soon they had the table laid with cookies, crackers, cheese, sausage, olives, coffee. Anthony took out a yellow legal pad and explained, *We need names your parents, grandparents, and if possible when and where arrive America.*

Lyson looked at the pad and at Anthony in mild astonishment. Jayne saw all this and corrected Anthony: *he didn't come for research his ancestry. I think for other reason.* Turning to Lyson, *Right?*

Lyson was surprised. *How know?*

She smiled a mystery, passed him the bowl of olives, and sat back expectantly, awaiting his reaction. But Lyson just simply ate a few olives with a frown of perplexity. She saw that Lyson entirely missed the whole point about the olives, noticing them only long enough to get them into his mouth. He probably didn't even recognize their significance, she thought ruefully. *Myself think yourself really looking for something,* she finally said. *Something very hard get, almost impossible get.*

Truthfully Lyson had noticed but wasn't quite ready to acknowledge her perspective, and plunged himself enthusiastically into the crackers, cheese, and sausage. He knew it is considered very impolite to disturb a man's meal and took every advantage of this quaint lovable little rule that seems universal everywhere among mankind. Anthony wasn't so quick so Jayne confronted him with a question in her eye that obligated him not to try and duck out of her intuition.

He tried anyway: *Maybe search for love.*

She surprised them all, even herself, by agreeing, *Kind-of.*

But myself married! Lyson's hands cried out in spite of himself. *Have wonderful wife.*

Jayne looked at him so tenderly that Lyson shrank back into the refuge of eating.

You love eating, Anthony joked weakly, risking the wrath of his wife.

Yes, of course, she had enough forebearance to reply. *Of-course all men do.* Again that imperious look: *You know what I mean.*

Anthony saw her hands perfectly clearly but managed to pretend not to notice the look in her eyes and helped himself to a cracker sandwich. He asked Lyson, *What your wife, her former name, before marry?*

Lyson was only too happy to divert into this pretended business and avoid the truth: *Barnclay, most important family in America, England too, very wealthy. That how help me buy Islay, try*—He stopped, suddenly aware he had said too much, and stared at the Pankeys with his hand frozen halfway through the last sign, half hoping they had not understood.

But the Pankeys weren't blind, least of all Jayne, who started her hands into action only to have Anthony interrupt, *Barnclay, that Boston eminent family?*

Oh yes! Lyson was quick to get back on track. *Most important family there Boston. Since two hundred years—everything—*

Jayne refused to be sidetracked and butted in, *You mean, hearing Barnclay own Boston, while deaf Barnclay own Islay?*

The completion of his last sign *everything* had left his hands wide open, palms up, so that Jayne's interruption caught him with his hands still in the position that inadvertently conveyed the gesture *helpless.*

So helpless did he look that Jayne grasped his hand. *Sorry! Not intentional. Just curious, why you here, your purpose.*

Hope you understand, Anthony explained earnestly, *that we—she, me—believe we really all brothers, sisters, one big family intertwined together, in unity—*

The sign *unity* can also mean cooperation, and Lyson saw it that way. *Right!* he declared enthusiastically. *All deaf true brothers, sisters. Feel close relationship, closer than hearing. Something special between deaf, very beautiful, wonderful. Good feelings related with deaf that makes me happy, feel comfortable—*

Anthony's face crumbled into dismay, his mouth open in protest, and Jayne knew exactly what he was going to say. *Wait!* she held her hands in front of the men's faces until they both diverted their attention to her. *I think you two talking about different things—*

No, no, we talking about brotherhood, Lyson said in all innocence.

Of Course! she patted his hand. *But different kinds—*

Me meant family, ancestry, Anthony interjected, but quickly put his hands under the table when Jayne glared at him. Besides, Lyson still seemed puzzled.

Like pulling a tight rein on a skittish horse, she held the men still by fixing each with a rigidly pointed finger in front of each man's face. *Let me talk! You, Anthony, don't-know what him, Lyson talking about. You, Lyson don't-know what him, Anthony talking about.* Again, her pointing fingers held the men in their places while she froze them with grave eyes. *I know what you and you mean,* she nodded at each in turn. *You, Anthony talking about blood. You, Lyson talking about spirit.* With that she sat back and gestured the men toward each other, like a boxing referee. The men continued staring stupidly at each other so she helped herself to the food.

But me talking about deaf, Lyson finally said.

Right, exactly right, agreed Jayne. *That what myself want talk about too, but,* rolling her eyes at Anthony, *he keeps dwelling-on family, blood, flesh—*

But deaf have those things—Anthony protested.

Jayne rolled her head and eyes back. *Yes! But you stubborn on ground, while he, Lyson, trying fly!* She grabbed each man's hand and dipped it into the crackers. *Eat! Now I go make soup. That will help clear your heads.*

She stood up over Anthony. *After we finish eat, you, me shut up, let him talk about himself, his idea about Islay, O.K.?* She put him in place with a tender kiss and, winking at Lyson, went into the kitchen.

Alone with each other, the men grinned at each other and chuckled. *Smart woman, right?* Anthony remarked. Lyson agreed heartily and they busied themselves with the task of clearing the table of all edibles.

* * *

MARY HERE GA.

LYSON HERE. MISS YOU VERY MUCH. HOW YOU Q GA.

HELLO! MISS YOU TOO. EVERYTHING FINE! YOU BE SURPRISED THAT MANY DEAF ALREADY MOVE HERE. VERY CONFUSING. WE VERY BUSY SELLING HOUSES AND BUILDINGS. MY PARENTS COME VISIT, SURPRISE, BUY HOTEL AND MANY APARTMENTS, NOW FULL! YOU BETTER COME HOME SOON, BEFORE OTHER DEAF TAKE OVER LEADERSHIP! WHERE YOU NOW Q GA.

Lyson stared at the teletypewriter, his jaw slack in surprise for such a long time that Mary lost patience. LYSON ARE YOU THERE Q GA.

OH YES! JUST BIG SURPRISE. DO YOU KNOW HOW MANY DEAF THERE NOW Q GA.

HARD SAY, BUT HUNDREDS FOR SURE, MAYBE THOUSAND. WALLY SAY ROOF FOR BOWLING NOW ALMOST FINISHED. START INSIDE ON MONDAY. 75 DEAF WORK THERE ALREADY. MANY DEAF WHO MOVE HERE WORK IN FREMONT. STILL COMING SO CANT COUNT. WHERE YOU NOW Q GA.

CANT BELIEVE! YOU SAID YOUR PARENTS BOUGHT HOTEL. THAT ISLAY HOTEL Q GA.

YES. WHERE YOU NOW QQQ GA.

SALT LAKE CITY. BEAUTIFUL TOWN. MANY IDEAS FOR ISLAY GA.

WHY NOT YOU CALL LAST NIGHT Q. I WAS VERY WORRIED. WAIT WAIT ALL NIGHT—

SORRY! DRIVE ALL NIGHT. NO SLEEP—

WHAT! DRIVE ALL NIGHT Q. NO SLEEP Q—

DON'T WORRY. I THINK I SLEPT—

WHILE DRIVING QQQ GA.

I THINK SO—

NO MORE DRIVING! YOU STAY THERE! I WILL FLY TONIGHT, MEET YOU AIRPORT. TELL ME, MUST! NAME YOUR MOTEL! GA.

WONT TELL!—Lyson blurted out and immediately felt ashamed and fell silent. He stared at the words glaring back at him from the teletypewriter, unmoving, accusing. He could imagine Mary staring at those same words printed on paper in her teletypewriter, dreadfully alone in the huge empty office in their castle in Suffex. Undoubtedly she's crying, very badly hurt, he thought unhappily, and his eyes teared. His hands remained posed over the teletypewriter, uneasy, wavering, trying to think of a way to erase those cruel words. But those words started moving to the left; slowly but surely as his name appeared in jerks, letter by letter. The ponderous slowness made him anxious, because Mary usually typed rapidly.

L-Y-S-O-N, NAUGHTY YOU! THIS IS BEATRICE. BE NICE TO NARY! DIDIT EVER OCCUR TO YOU THATSHE LOVEX YOU ANDHAS MISSEC YOU VERY MUCH. EZUSE MY TYPING PLEASE. THIS DAMN ARTHRITIS! HER PARENTS ARE HERE WITH US. SOGLAD! THINK WE NOW CAN BUY ENTIRE STATE! NW LYSON YOU KNOW YOU CAN SOEAK FREEKY WITH ME. WHY DONT YOU WANT MARY WITH YOU. The machine stopped and Lyson waited until he realized Beatrice forgot the GA ending.

BEATRICE SO GLAD YOURE WITH MARY AND CAN HELP HER. I APPRECIATE THIS VERY MUCH! IT IS JUST THAT I AM NERVOUS ENOUGH TRYING TO ATTRACT DEAF TO ISLAY WITHOUT HER CORRECTING MY STUPID TALK. ALL THE TIME. THIS WILL MAKE IT IMPOSSIBLE FOR ME TO DO A GOOD JOB

CONVINCING DEAF TO MOVE TO ISLAY. SHE LOVES ME SO MUCH THAT SHE WONT LET ME MAKE MISTAKES AND IF I MAKE A MISTAKE SHE WONT LET ME CORRECT THE MISTAKE MYSELF. THIS MAKES THE MISTAKE BIGGER IN OTHER PEOPLE'S EYES—He stopped with the sudden realization that Mary was undoubtedly reading over Beatrice's shoulder and groaned.

The machine came to life again:

LYSON I UNDERSTAND. PLEASE FORGIVE ME GA.

He stared at the GA and it took him a while to realize that Mary was back on the teletypewriter. THAT YOU MARY Q GA.

YES. DIDNT MEAN TO BE BOSSY. I JUST LOVE YOU VERY VERY VERY VERY VERY MUCH AND CANT HELP WORRY—

WORRY FOR-FOR Q. MANY DEAF MOVING TO ISLAY NOW. THIS MEANS I AM DOING OKAY. STOP WORRYING. THAT MAKES ME NERVOUS. GA.

PROMISE YOU WONT SLEEP WHILE DRIVING—

PROMISE! WONT TRY THAT TRICK AGAIN! GA.

NOT ONLY THAT TRICK. NO OTHER TRICKS TOO GA.

YOU KNOW I AM A GOOD HONEST BOY I MEAN MAN GA.

OKAY. IF YOU ARE GOOD AND HONEST TELL ME NAME YOUR MOTEL. I WONT FLY, I PROMISE! GA.

CANT REMEMBER—

DRUNK! GA.

NO NO LET ME LOOK AT SIGN OUTSIDE. IT SAYS WAGON WHEEL MOTEL GA.

MEET ANY COWBOYS AND INDIANS Q GA.

NO BUT SAW SOME ON HIGHWAY AND IN CAFES IN WYOMING. NO TROUBLE. LOOK MEAN THOUGH GA.

BE CAREFUL! MYSELF KNOW THAT YOUR WAY CARELESS NOT WATCH OUT FOR—

STOP SILLY! THINK COWBOYS ARE AFRAID OF ME. WONT LOOK AT ME STRAIGHT BUT THROUGH THE MIRRORS AT THE BACK OF CAFES—

KEEP AWAY FROM CAFES! PROMISE! EAT ONLY IN NICE RESTAURANTS GA.

O.K. TONIGHT AM INVITED TO DINNER WITH WONDERFUL DEAF COUPLE. HIMSELF HAVE OWN BUSINESS IN GENEOLOGY. WANT ME MEET OTHER DEAF LIVE HERE WHO MAYBE INTERESTED ABOUT ISLAY GA.

WOW! FAST WORK! THAT MEANS MORE BABIES, MUST BUILD MORE HOUSES. ALREADY HERE SEVERAL DEAF BUILDERS WANT BUILD HOUSES GA.

GREAT! NOW MUST BATH, CLEAN UP READY FOR DINNER. LOVE! GA TO SK.

DONT FORGET SHAVE AND BRUSH TEETH. BE CAREFUL! SKSK.

CHAPTER 14

The dinner party at the Pankeys' began under the stars, outside on the lawn softly lit by floodlights arranged among the shrubbery so that the light was filtered and indirect. This had the admirable effect that while the lawn and tables were lit up, the stars and sky formed a contrasting canopy above. Lyson was transfixed by the immense depth of the desert night. Why you could tell which stars are close, which are far away, he marveled to Anthony. Back East, the night sky looked shallow and featureless, somewhat smudged. Here you have the sensation that the earth is indeed right out there in outer space, drifting among the stars. Lyson kept scanning the sky until his neck hurt.

Jayne saw him twisting and turning his head to get the kink out of his neck and put her hand there. Lyson jumped and slapped his neck. *Oh! Excuse me!* he cried. *Thought bug, something.*

You mean I bug you? she teased him as she proceeded to work the stiffness out of his neck.

The expression, dinner party, always had a formal connotation for him back east, but here in the west it's so laid back, he was musing while Jayne's wondrous fingers caressed the muscles and sinews in his neck. On the jungle gym clambered numerous children in neat clothes. All around, at tables, on benches, on the lawn, were their parents in quiet conversation. He considered it bad form to eavesdrop on other people's signing so he allowed himself the luxury of vicariously enjoying the comradery passed around on faces and hands in little groups. These people seemed to have known each other for a very long time and certainly were in no hurry to meet everyone in the party, to seek out any particular individual. They were comfortable, content with whomever appeared in their presence. No one tried to be the life of the party. He very much liked this kind of party and wondered if this was possible in Islay. No, he thought regretfully, we Easterners crave attention too much, too aggressively. And he worried that the people here at this party might be too content with such amiable social life to move to Islay.

Suddenly Jayne stopped working his neck and called over a man. He was Doctor Hansel Fletcher. *Himself only one deaf doctor in USA,* she gushed, *Imagine, only one!*

Doctor Fletcher gave a brief, grave nod and, gripping the top of Lyson's skull, turned Lyson's head so that it faced forward for a neck examination. Lyson could not help tensing up, frustrating the examination. Jayne broke out laughing. *Him doctor said can't find what wrong.*

The doctor gave up and joined Lyson on the bench and remarked, *It seems you have been driving for a long time. That is why your neck is rigid.*

Lyson was startled. It is uncommon to see Sign Language bastardized to fit the English language, particularly at deaf gatherings. Such an anglicized illegitimacy of sign language is usually seen only at schools as a method to help hearing teachers achieve a modicum of respect from deaf children. Ninety out of every hundred deaf people abandon such signs as soon as they leave school and quickly adopt, if they had not already done so secretly at school, the natural Sign Language of the deaf, affectionately called Ameslan by the deaf. After all, Lyson always thought, such hearing-invented signs violate all rules of visual intonation. He could not help but find it difficult to draw close to, to enter into intimacy with, deaf people who persisted in using such a hearing oriented language in preference to a graceful language so ideally suited to the eyes, so beautiful, so perfect!

Still, Lyson had this weakness for people, or perhaps more truthfully for himself, but nonetheless he thought it unconscionable for any deaf person to treat another deaf person the same crude way an unenlightened hearing person would treat a deaf mute. After all, this guy was a doctor. Undoubtedly he never had a chance to play, to live, to be intimate, considering all the studying a medical student has to do. All that English can weigh very heavily on a deaf person's soul. Not to mention all that Latin, or is it Greek, that doctors have to learn.

It's never, ever, a mistake to be kind to people, no matter how alien, or obnoxious, his grandmother had taught him. So he replied in pure Ameslan, *Oh yes! Long drive since Islay, about two thousand miles, I imagine. Tired me.*

It surprised and pleased him that the doctor understood perfectly clearly, though he had the mildly disconcerting way of fixing his eyes on hands, instead of eyes, the way Ameslan is best, more intimately read.

Out of nowhere Jayne appeared with graceful glasses of champagne. Lyson was rather startled; he had not even noticed her getting up and leaving, something he certainly should have noticed right in front of his nose. But just the same, here she was, holding the glasses out to them. He thought she looked radiantly beautiful in the soft light, and congratulated himself for having enough self-control to grab the glass rather than her arm so fluffy against the night sky.

But the good doctor hesitated, pleading with his eyes for her not to tempt him beyond endurance. Jayne looked down upon him with such tenderness that the doctor manfully accepted the glass. She stood over him, holding her hands together against her stomach, her eyes immeasurably deep, and he sighed and acceded with a sip. Then she was gone, back into the house, leaving a star-filled void where she had stood just a second before. Again, Lyson was into stars and allowed himself to be borne bubbly headed among the heavens as the champagne lifted him up away from the earth. As he gazed at the stars, he thought how close she had been to him, near enough to envelop him, to render him tingling in a never-never spell all her own. Her scent still hung in the still air. He like it very much and imagined himself following it among the stars, sniffing like a bloodhound.

The doctor jarred him back to earth with a tap on the shoulder. Normally this would not have put him in good stead with Lyson, but Lyson realized that people who use bastardized sign language have a certain difficulty with their eyes, with coordinating themselves with their environment. The doctor presumably was unable to appreciate the aura Jayne had left them in, so Lyson silently but magnanimously forgave him.

Can you help me, please? the doctor asked urgently with half hidden signs and a quick furtive look at the house. *I need your help.*

Lyson was surprised and quite flattered that a medical doctor, the one and only deaf doctor in the USA, would want his help. The anxiety in the doctor's face that this be kept in the strictest confidence made Lyson all the more eager to be of service. Conspiratorially he shielded his hand from the others and spelled, *Y-E-S.*

Doctor Fletcher shook his shoulder appreciatively and, with a quick look around, poured the remainder of his champagne into Lyson's glass. *Thank you! Very Much! I really appreciate this.*

Lyson stared stupidly at his glass and at the doctor who hurriedly rinsed and filled his glass with water at a garden faucet by the house.

Never know when the hospital will call me, the doctor explained when he resumed his seat by Lyson. *Must keep my head clear, you know.* Lyson still looked confused, so the doctor pulled out of his pocket a small box about the size and shape of a pocket calculator. *See, this is a buzzer. Of course I can't hear it, but I can feel it. If it is for me, I mean if they are calling me, they use long and short buzzes, almost like Morse Code—*

Jayne came by and held out a large tray of hors d'oeuvres that she had to balance on their knees in order to free a hand to offer, *More champagne?*

Oh no, thanks! Doctor Fletcher demurred, holding up his glass and taking the compulsory sip.

She smiled approvingly and turned to Lyson and saw with surprise that he'd already consummed almost half the little sandwiches on the tray. *Naughty! Patience! Dinner soon!*

She jerked the tray away and, shaking her head, rearranged the little sandwiches so that they were spread more uniformly over the tray so the other guests wouldn't know of Lyson's gaffe.

Sighing, she squeezed Lyson's shoulder. *Sorry, my fault, putting-off dinner too-late. You can't help hungry, naturally!* She planted a very light, tender kiss on his dimple and swished away among the other guests.

Lyson sat in a most delightful stupor, staring up at where she had been, now filled with stardust, his dimple tingling from the kiss, still warm, and the close proximity. Ah! So close! He needed badly, even more than Anthony, he declared to his glass of champagne, to be gathered into her arms, into the most comfortable pillow possible on this earth. Yet, nagging in the back of his mind was Mary looking down tearfully, reproachfully at him. And there also was the knowledge, he just knew, that the good doctor would intrude, break this most sweet spell, almost as if at Mary's behest. Oh yeah, he was already nodding to himself when the doctor tapped his shoulder.

What is your business? I mean, the purpose of your trip? Doctor Fletcher inquired a trifle too politely, although his curiosity drew his body forward.

Lyson looked away up at the stars and thought for a long moment. Heather with her slightly askew face. Sandy—her eyes! And now Jayne; how he longed to be gathered in her arms. *Sometimes,* he finally said pensively, *sometimes I wonder.*

At first the doctor did not quite understand, but following Lyson's eyes to the stars, believed he did. *I think I know what you mean,* he said with a weary sadness. *When I was studying to become a doctor, my goal, my dream was to help deaf people, I mean, to be a real doctor for the deaf, but*—He looked bleakly at Lyson and his shoulders sagged.

Lyson was shocked. Here was a deaf man who had achieved one of the highest, most honorable and respectable positions possible in society and yet was still trying to fathom the same stars as Lyson himself. *Come on,* he urged, *I'm all eyes.*

Look, please understand I have to live here, said the good doctor. He drew Lyson's attention to the other people in the party. *These are my friends. I want them to be happy, to be proud of me. That is why I never told them*—He glared soberly at Lyson, as if assessing him before venturing any further.

I think every man feels same you, Lyson nodded slowly, gravely. *Naturally we want respect, love*—His face lit up with the dawning of a new truth. *Love itself blind, you know,* he chuckled and toasted the stars with his champagne before draining it. The champagne made him happy, more comfortable with whatever truth might be hidden among the stars.

Suddenly he seized Doctor Fletcher's glass, and dumped the water from it, and strode up to the house, leaving the doctor baffled on the bench, quite rebuffed, disappointed at the loss of an opportunity to unload his soul on a stranger from a faraway land, a person he believed he would never see again, who would never torment him with a knowing look. But before his despair became complete, Lyson returned with full glasses sparkling with the promise of a most enjoyable evening. The manner with which Lyson handed him the glass, and the way he held his own up, demanded a toast, not the kind easily satisfied by a mere sip.

In unison they both drained their glasses and Lyson again went to the house. The doctor felt much, much better; the stars looked so friendly he felt he was really out there among them, at one with them. Shortly, Lyson was on the bench beside him with fresh glasses, and the doctor knew he was at last free. He was very happy, unbelievably happy with this strange feeling of kinship, camaraderie.

Something tells me I can confide in you, he declared, holding his glass out to Lyson. At the click he drained the glass in one swig and stared at it, then held it out to Lyson. *Please!*

Anthony saw this and hurried over with a bottle. *Enjoying yourself?* he asked as he refilled the glass.

Oh yes! Your parties are always wonderful.

Anthony smiled modestly. *People like you, that why.* Before going off in search of empty glasses he assured them, *Eat soon!*

The doctor realized that dinner would come soon, and with it his opportunity would be gone, perhaps forever. Here he had a sympathetic stranger, practically a captive audience for his soul, in such a splendid setting under the true and good stars, his eyes wide open to anything he might wish to confess. *Look!* he urged as he slipped a leg over the bench so that he faced Lyson. *I must tell you that I am not a real doctor, but really just a butcher!*

The men stared at each other in horror for what seemed to be an eternity. Lyson finally got himself together long enough to break the spell. *You mean, you work there hospital kitchen?*

Kitchen? Doctor Fletcher could not help but break out in helpless laughter. *Kitchen! Ha! Ha!*

Jayne came by, pleased to see the doctor so happy finally, and hugged him. Lyson was too puzzled over the doctor's mirth to realize that a hug in those wonderful arms was again escaping him. She squeezed the doctor's cheeks and announced, *Dinner ready!*

Alarmed, he cried, *Wait a minute! Want to finish talking with this man, uh—what's his name again?*

Lyson. She tweaked his nose and went to call the others.

Lyson got up to follow but the doctor pulled him down. *Please. I must talk to you, I must tell you that you misunderstood me. I want you to know that I am a M.D., fully trained to heal people.*

Nodding gravely, Lyson urged him on. *Hope that doesn't mean you make mistakes, cut-off wrong pieces—*

You're a comedian, Doctor Fletcher laughed but then became serious. *Truth is because I am deaf, the hospital forces me to work only on dead bodies.*

Dead? Lyson said with the fear of someone afraid of the dead.

Yes! Doctor Fletcher seethed with disgust. *Pathology! Autopsy! I want to heal live people, to save lives! Not pull out guts!*

Jayne saw all this and rushed over. *You poor dear! We love you!* She gathered him again in her arms and shot Lyson a glance pregnant with urgency.

Don't worry! Secret! he assured her and left them alone, giving her shoulder a squeeze on his way over to the buffet. He sniffed his hand on the way. Some of her scent had rubbed off.

Lyson found himself seated at the long table on the lawn, under soft Japanese lanterns, on a bench between energetic consumers of food. Barbecued spare ribs, baked potatoes wrapped in foil and swimming with butter, corn on the cob, tomatoes broiled with mayonnaise, cheese cubes, celery, carrots, orange slices. And grape juice for those who believe that the word wine in the Good Book really refers to grape juice, although they would admit to an uncertainty just how Old Noah became drunk on such a refreshment. And wine, good wine for those untroubled by such semantics. A deep stunning red was the wine compared with the blood purple of the grape juice.

With such a bounty assailing his eyes, nose, and taste buds, Lyson was very happy. He attacked the food and gorged himself; soon he became satiated and aware of a warmth and dampness against his hips and in his thighs pressed tightly together. On his right was an enormous man, his second chin so large as to preclude the possibility of a necktie, his armpits drenched with sweat, a whitewall haircut that made his head diminutive in relation to his body. The man tossed a rib carelessly over his shoulder to be whisked away by a rotund, furry little dog that disappeared into the darkness proud with his prize.

Looking down, Lyson saw that he had to be at least three inches into the man's hip, and his pants were darkening with sweat, probably more the man's than his own. He squirmed away only to burrow deeper into a soft hip opposite. The hip wiggled back. It was a woman looking shyly back at him, quite pleased with his attention. By all the laws of nature and probability, the woman had to be the man's wife, or at least his sister. Even while tearing into a rib, the woman kept glancing very friendlily at Lyson and bumped his hip affectionately.

Excuse me! he cried, *My hands dirty, must wash!* He tried to extract himself but the woman squeezed him even tighter, giggling with great bouncings of her flesh as are the wont of the very fat.

Hands dirty! he pleaded and she let him go with an exaggerated pout. The man on the right gave no sign he ever noticed Lyson slipping away, for the woman did not have to move very far to close the gap, which she did as soon as Lyson freed his leg.

He hurried over to the garden faucet where cool water rinsed his hands and face. The inside of his thighs felt sweaty and clammy. He was concerned that this might emit an odor that others, but not he, could smell. He was wiping his hands dry on his thighs in the half-hope this would help when Jayne pounced on him.

Careful to keep her back to the party, and keeping her signs small and out of sight, she urged with a look of concern in her eyes that Lyson thought very touching, *Please help me talk Doctor Fletcher. Himself very depressed, imagine you-me look-down-on him because himself not true doctor—*

Lyson stopped her hand with a squeeze and slowly winked a vow that he would handle things just fine. *Bring him food and wine, O.K.? And for yourself, too.*

The doctor was sitting on the grass, his legs straight out, his feet held vertical by some sense of demeanor not entirely absent even in his condition of abject dejection. He held his back and head upright as befitting his position of trust and respect. There's no holding this man down, Lyson thought admiringly, knowing full well it was only because of Jayne, her wondrous feminine instinct, that got him as far as the earth, not to bring him down, really, but to draw upon the earth for strength.

Earth wonderful! Lyson remarked cheerily as he plopped down by the doctor on the carpet of grass. Doctor Fletcher nodded bleakly, pointing up at the sky. *Can almost see the stars moving, slipping away.* He turned from the stars to Lyson. *You know, can feel the earth moving, spinning very fast, but the funny thing is, I feel like I myself am not, have not been, moving at all.*

Lyson was entirely sympathetic, yet felt so inadequate. He knew that only a woman could adequately comfort the doctor, bring him off his slump. A certain tea cup-like juxtaposition of tiny stars reminded him of the purpose of his trip, and how very little he had actually done so far. Good thing, though, he did not know that up there in the sky also soared Pegasus, an actual constellation very visible if he only looked. He never knew Pegasus could actually get up and fly in the vast sky right among actual stars, and that she had living, breathing stars for her garment. If he had, his butt wouldn't have retained its contact with the Good Strong Mother Earth. He'd have blown it. And, thank his lucky stars, he didn't know the true bloody history of how Pegasus arose from the blood of Medusa, the beauty whose hair turned into snakes because she couldn't or wouldn't keep her knees demurely together. That would've really set him on his ear. Instead, the starry cup rising in the east transfixed him and he innocently asked, startling the doctor, *You want work on live people?*

Of course! Doctor Fletcher exclaimed, exasperated at the prospect of going through the subject again. *But I am deaf!*

I mean deaf people, Lyson explained, trying to soothe the doctor.

Work on deaf people, you mean live deaf people? the doctor asked calming down. Lyson could see a flicker of interest in his eyes.

Yes! Myself attracting deaf people flocking there—he pointed at the little tea cup low in the east—*Small state, secret! Won't tell because—because*—he stopped, unable to finish his spiel because, for one thing, he realized how wild his story surely seemed to such a learned man. For another, the doctor seemed incredulous, his jaw slack, pulling his mouth open. And he turned rather vacantly back to the tea cup of stars.

Let me explain again Lyson cried, rising up on his knees so he could make better, fuller use of his hands and arms.

Just then Jayne came with a tray and tossed Lyson a tablecloth, indicating that she wanted it spread on the grass. She too came down on her knees and as she set the tray down she saw her friend's confusion. *What have you done to him?* her furious look demanded of Lyson.

Tried encourage, Lyson defended himself meekly, *but myself, my fault, not explain clear enough—*

Explain not necessary! she shot back. *Encourage, enough! That's all he needs!*

The doctor interrupted with a tug on Lyson's sleeve. *Exactly what do you mean by those stars? What do the Seven Sisters have to do with medicine?*

Told you! Explain not necessary! Jayne scolded Lyson, and saying to the doctor, *Eat! Helps your head clear.*

Lyson sat back, dejected, and watched the two eating, the doctor almost desultory in the way he picked at his food, as if it were only a biological function necessary to the maintenance of his body. Jayne's appetite was none too good either, and she glared at Lyson. But she saw the glistening in his eyes and was immediately sorry and stroked his dimple with a light finger. Lyson looked down at the hand, ecstatic at the touch and saw how fine it was. He liked it very much and wished he could keep it forever, looking adoringly up at her, the way a dog does at a person so good enough as to deign to give it a pat.

Wine? She offered him her glass, putting it in his hand, and gripped his shoulder as she rose to her feet.

He drained the glass gladly, his eyes closed, his head back, enjoying the surging of the wine in his mouth, stomach, and body. He opened his eyes and saw Jayne looking fondly at him. Exhaling decorously he looked down at his shoulder and put his own hand there and kissed it.

Jayne laughed, took the glass, and the doctor's as well, and caressed his hair. *Funny you!* She left the men alone, promising to be right back with more wine. And to Lyson: *Be good!*

Lyson sat very still, his eyes tightly shut, though under the lids he was looking up, still savoring the remembrance of her hand on his hair. He reached over and gingerly examined the evidence of her touch, tracing the course of her caress.

The doctor tapped his knee. *Here!* He held out a comb under his nose. If only Jayne were holding that comb! And combing him! That would—

Jayne returned, read Lyson's eyes, and took the comb; with one hand on the back of his neck as if he were a child, she straightened out his hair. Tilting her head, she looked thoughtfully at him. *Maybe you should let your hair grow more.* With her fingers she traced the length she thought best on him, along the lobes of his ears. Her touch was so light on the fuzz of his ears that as she withdrew her hand he leaned forward, trying to keep in touch.

Naughty! She giggled and filled the glasses.

Anthony saw all this and stood sternly over them. *Jayne! Not good separate from party. Should associate!* His eyes indicated the other friends in little clusters around the lawn.

Doctor needs help, encouragement! Depressed, must help! she told Anthony firmly. *You go ahead, mingle.*

Anthony glared at her and at Lyson whose ears immediately became flushed.

Jealous, silly you! Jayne said severely to her husband. *Your way, jealous jealous. Finish! please.*

Lyson was shocked, stunned at the ferocity of this woman who just a few seconds ago seemed the warmest, softest person on earth. The doctor was apparently unmindful of all this, for he held out a glass, calling for a toast. In a flash, Jayne had Anthony down on his knees beside her, returning the toast. The glass drained, she held up a finger to the doctor and Lyson and turned to Anthony.

Satisfied? She gripped his ears and brought his face closer to hers. *Still jealous?* she asked imperiously with clear lips. His eyes wavered in confusion and she sighed and gave him a kiss.

A young girl in a nightgown, Lyson thought maybe 6 or 7 years old, ran up and tugged at Jayne. *Mama! Little Andy bother, bother me! Refuse let me sleep!*

Lyson was dumbfounded again. Here's this beautiful woman. She's sweet, loving, but also fierce. She can be dangerous, even a vixen. Yet, a mother too! A wife is sacred, of course. But a mother! A bit too much he thought, and discovered a glass filled to the brim under his nose. *Drink!* Anthony urged.

Jayne was gone, no doubt tending to her role as mother. Doctor Fletcher seemed lost to them, sitting like a sack of flour, intent upon the Seven Sisters in the sky. It was not certain whether the doctor was sober or merely in a stupor because of Jayne, or perhaps even transfixed by the stars.

You talk about those stars, the Seven Sisters, I believe called Pleiades by the Greeks of long ago. The doctor directed Lyson's attention toward a tiny group of stars arranged in a lovely cluster among the great constellations. *That name Pleiades means the 'Sailing Stars'. Sailors long ago, over there in Greece, named them because in the spring those stars become visible, after winter, when it is safe to sail. Myself, starting to wonder if that is what you have been trying to tell me? I mean about your secret state?*

Lyson felt a strong hand pushing his glass up toward his mouth. It was Anthony, his eyes wild and dangerous. So insistent was the pushing that he had to drink or else have wine spilled all over his clothes. As soon as his glass was empty, Anthony immediately refilled it. Lyson couldn't move, or the wine would spill. Again that push under his nose and the devilish look.

Just in time, or more truthfully a bit too late, Jayne returned and Anthony retreated quickly into the posture of a gracious albeit overly generous host. But Jayne saw and was furious. *Anthony! Trying make them drunk! Shame-on you! Jealous, hope them drunk, look stupid!*

They want more. Anthony protested innocently.

True? Jayne demanded of Lyson.

But Lyson hadn't noticed her presence yet, and was saying to the doctor, *Myself don't-know story Greek about those stars. Didn't-know called Seven Sisters or that name Phila—what? what?*

Pleiades, the doctor spelled helpfully.

Pleades, O.K., Lyson thanked him. *Don't-care about name, but look, their shape, similar tea cup. See?*

Ah, I see, the doctor nodded, holding his glass out to Anthony who was only too glad to refill it, glancing at Jayne: *See!* Lyson thought he had better be polite, keep in step with the party, so he drained his glass and held it out a bit unsteadily. Anthony was quick to comply and looked smugly at Jayne, but she had caught his eagerness and took away the bottle.

I see, the doctor repeated, tugging at Lyson.

Right! Lyson cried, warming into his dream. *Over-there, east, near New York, Transylvia, there very small state, its name, name, name*—For some reason he couldn't remember the name. He panicked and looked helplessly to Jayne, his hands working, trying to find the name.

Your fault! She lashed at Anthony, and gently to Lyson, *Islay.*

How know? he asked dumbly.

You told me, this morning. Remember? she said gently.

I told you secret? Lyson's hands were weak with shock.

Islay? Doctor Fletcher tugged again. *What?*

Islay, right! Lyson jumped as if out of a trance. *Myself taking over, become Governor, will! Similar King of Deaf! You can doctor there!* He tried to get up upon his knees to better be able to use his hands fully, floridly, but couldn't manage. His legs were too soft, like wet noodles, and he sank back upon his back. As he watched the stars receding into the blackness of the heavens, rapidly as if the earth were rushing backwards into the night, he thought he saw Jayne above, gathering him into her arms.

* * *

While still groggy so early in the morning, Lyson felt something being pulled out of his mouth and something else inserted. This startled him into full awakeness. A terrible headache hurried the process and he saw a face in front of his.

It was the little girl of the night before, who with a motherly frown of disapproval scolded him, *You wet last night.*

Now fully awake he took bearings and found himself on his stomach under a quilt blanket on the sofa. He was hugging the pillow tightly. A corner of the pillow was thoroughly chewed and wet. Whatever was in his mouth felt soft and rubbery and he spat it out. It was a pacifier.

Bad boy! the little girl snapped and put it back in his mouth. She was down on her knees by him. *Be-good!*

An even younger boy beside the girl was very amused and clapped his hands. The girl spoke sharply to her brother and he made a face. She seized him and tried to spank him but they rolled on the carpet, he twisting to avoid the spanking.

They were still in their nightclothes and Lyson saw it was light behind the drawn curtains. It was still early, though. On the floor across the room, the living room he now realized, was a sleeping form in a sleeping bag. The boy freed himself from the girl and dashed toward the sofa, leaping and landing on Lyson. The girl pulled on the boy who clung tightly to the blanket. Lyson held on to the blanket and managed to break the boy's grip, and the boy fell back upon his sister.

A light flashed. The girl jumped over to the telephone and the boy rushed back upon Lyson again. The girl put the telephone on the teletypewriter and hurried down the hallway. The boy rode roughly on Lyson as a horse. Lyson's neck ached as did his head. He managed to pull the boy off from behind and hold him down wriggling on the floor. The boy tried to bite him but Lyson jerked his hand away so abruptly it clobbered the boy on the nose. Hollering, the child ran away down the hallway, where he bumped into his sister. They both fell down and bawled on the floor, the boy covering his now twice-banged nose; the girl seemed to be trying to catch any teeth that might be falling out of her mouth.

Lyson wanted to go over and comfort them but couldn't find his pants anywhere nearby, though his shoes were by the sofa. He was appalled with the thought he'd lost his pants in a strange home the night before, possibly outside, and grimaced at what the Pankeys must think of him now.

Out of the dim gloom of the hallway Jayne appeared, still swollen with sleep so that her face reposed in the softest, most appealing feminine appearance Lyson thought he ever saw. Disheveled hair and billowy pink nightgown made her all the softer, more beautiful. Especially now that he did not have his glasses and everything fuzzed in a soft outline. She stepped crossly over her children; Lyson liked the way she frowned. Pulling out the chair, she plopped down at the teletypewriter and with just two fingers typed rapidly on the machine.

Her elbow fascinated him: so tiny in relation to her upper arm which jiggled ever so slightly as she typed. And her feet! As finely shaped as her hands, long and well-arched. Her back, though strong in appearance yet soft by the fact her skeleton did not show through, sloped down from narrow shoulders to pleasingly plump hips squashed on the hard chair. He found something in his mouth and realized he was chewing the pacifier, the whole of it, and he spat it out.

The children, still bawling, clamored for her attention, tugging at her arm, but she, not even looking up from the machine, jabbed out her arm, pointing down the hallway. Lyson felt a powerful urge to burrow his face into her armpit and moaned, burying his face in the sofa instead, behind the still warm soft pillow. He hid there for a long time, the vision of that armpit digging his face even deeper into the darkness.

After a while he felt a refreshing, cool hand on the back of his neck. It was Jayne leaning over him, a look of soliticous concern over her face. *How feel, you?*

Terrible headache.

Bad boy. A corner of her mouth lifted in amusement. *Make coffee now me. Want aspirin?*

As she retreated toward the kitchen, the way she walked, he thought was as maddingly soft as her appearance, possibly because she was barefooted on the carpet and freed of the constraints of street clothes. He sank back down into the pillow, clinging it ever tighter.

Then he remembered the loss of his pants, and since he was now alone, other than the sleeping figure on the floor, he thought it opportune now to look for them. He wrapped the blanket tightly about himself and struggled to his feet. But the pants were nowhere to be found in the room or under the sofa. He was upset and anxious when Jayne returned with a steaming cup of coffee and a bottle of aspirin. The way she leaned over to put the cup on the coffee table nearly drove Lyson out of his mind, now that he was standing up with no where to hide.

She saw his discomfort. *Wrong?*

Pants! he pleaded, *Can't find!*

Lost?

He nodded desperately, confused in her aura that enveloped him.

Thought you still have-on, she said gravely.

He stared dumbly back.

Last night you go bed, still wear.

Really? He patted inside the blanket and to his relief found the pants. He removed the blanket and there they were on him, as good as ever, though a bit wrinkled.

Didn't-know you still wear? Jayne asked with growing amusement.

He shook his head slowly, soberly.

Cute! She burst out laughing, hugging herself in such a manner that Lyson was extremely hard put to keep his eyes up at the socially mandated level; that is, level with hers. She saw his difficulty and quickly discerned the reason. *Excuse me!* She blushed and fled giggling down the hallway.

Lyson was very glad that she blushed; otherwise he might have gotten into trouble with Mary. Now that he was alone again, with nothing to distract him, his headache manifested itself and he became ill and queasy. He hoped three tablets of aspirin would do the trick and tried to wash them down but the coffee was too hot and he gagged, the dry pills sticking in his throat. He ran to the bathroom. There were no cups or glasses; however, the cap from a spray can was big enough, and the water from the tap was cool and delicious. He drank many capfuls, the sensation of life-giving water replenishing his body with the essence of life.

Finally feeling much better, with just traces of the old headache lingering still, now more on the surface of the brain than the interior, he confronted his image in the mirror. He did not at all like what he saw, least of all what he imagined Jayne saw earlier. Pale face, all the paler by the black stubble on the jaw. Bloodshot beady eyes. Greasy matted hair. An ugly grimace caused by the foul taste in his mouth. Jayne must never see me like this again! He drank some more water.

A bit of rummaging under the lavatory yielded a half-empty bottle of the shampoo, an old razor, and a worn toothbrush. No toothpaste, so the bar of soap had to make do. No brush or comb, so his fingers had to make do, and finally he was ready to face Jayne. His clothes were at least on straight as best can. It was unfortunate he had to use the same old underwear, but he hoped the spray from the air freshener would work well enough. Everything seemed clean and in its proper place in the bathroom. He'd even wiped the tub clean and dry: mustn't let Jayne know he's losing his hair. He pulled himself straight and opened the door and immediately his headache returned.

Jayne was kneeling on the floor kneading the neck and shoulders of the man in the sleeping bag. It was Doctor Feltcher in the throes of a hangover. She saw him and said something with her mouth.

Excuse me! Can't see! Glasses! Lyson came over closer.

"Can you help me?" she mouthed the words while still massaging the doctor.

Of course.

She nodded him down and deftly started him massaging the doctor without a hitch. She rose unsteadily to her feet, and as she made for the kitchen remarked, *Good thing I have only one husband, not three!*

Lyson was continuing the massage the best his hands could, his brow crinkled at how it all happened when suddenly the doctor grabbed his wrist and rolled so that Lyson fell into his grasp and they were face to face much too close for comfort. They stared in amazement at each other for an awful moment, the pucker fading slowly from the doctor's lips. The doctor finally pushed him off roughly and rolled back on his stomach and banged his forehead on the carpet.

Lyson wasn't too keen to resume the massage and fled to the kitchen bright in the morning sun. Jayne was at the table wearily urging her children, *Eat, please!*

Lyson was so diffident, so shamefaced that she softened and beckoned him over, oh no, not the chair, but to her.

You so sweet, she said, and, pulling on his tie, drew his face down and implanted a light kiss on his dimple. *Not your fault! Shame don't, please.*

Drink too-much, me should not, he apologized.

Blame Anthony! she replied with icy disgust. *Very silly! Easily jealous when other men become friends. Try make them drunk.* She paused and sighed. *Sit-down, please. Coffee? Orange?* With swift, sharp tugs at her children's hair in front of their ears, she got them back to eating, and served Lyson and herself coffee and orange juice.

I love Anthony very much, truly wonderful man, she resumed, sitting again. *But needs growing-up!*

Lyson sipped his coffee thoughtfully and then diplomatically admitted, *When I saw you rub doctor there, myself surprise, felt jealous, same Anthony.*

Jayne dropped her shoulders, tilted her head, uncertain whether to laugh or not, to be pleased or not, and lamented, *Why?*

Lyson pulled up his eyebrows and blew, *Well,* and sighed, *Can't help! Something very special yourself. Very powerful.* He raised the glass of orange juice, toasted her, and drained it.

For a long while they were very quiet, Jayne musing over her coffee. The children were strangely quiet and busy with their cereal. Lyson was breathing heavily and drinking his coffee, afraid to intrude on her thoughts. He very much liked the golden down on her cheek bright in the sun from the window. And the way she'd wrapped the pink bathrobe demurely around herself. Their eyes met and they giggled. He was very happy that she liked him. Maybe not as much as he liked her, but at least she liked him. That's quite something, considering last night, he congratulated himself. Maybe she liked him enough to drag Anthony and the kids to Islay.

In the entrance way, like a ghost out of the realm of the dead, appeared Anthony leaning against the wall, in crumpled pajamas, ghastly pale and ill-appearing. He looked bleakly down on them, the way a homeless stranger might look upon a warm and cozy domestic scene from a distance, resentful of happiness beyond his grasp; perhaps he had known the woman at one time, long ago, and had lost her but not his longing.

Swiftly Jayne shooed the children outside with the explanation that their daddy was sick and asked them to please play and behave in the backyard. She left the sliding door open, apparently to let out the stale breath of three hung-over gentlemen, and helped Anthony stumbling and staggering to the table. He belched so hard that at first she took fright and grabbed a bowl but he waved it away.

Finish, stomach, he gestured the flushing of a toilet. *Now empty,* he grumbled.

She insisted a glassful after glassful of water, with aspirin, on him until he felt better enough to withdraw the bowl from under his chin.

Very sorry, cause you headache, he apologized to his wife.

Sighing like a mother over an errant child, she took his head in her arms. Her eyes met Lyson's and rolled. She kissed Anthony on the top of head with such tenderness that Lyson became rather confused. Hadn't his mother-in-law explained in no uncertain terms that a woman is only impressed with sturdiness, steadiness, sobriety, sanity, and other such laudable traits and totally repelled by the slightest flaw in a man?

As if to confuse him further, there was a sad but kind look in her face as Doctor Fletcher came crawling in on his hands and knees in his underwear. Lyson didn't think it possible for a man to sink as low as the doctor, and yet there Jayne was, trying to help him, holding the bowl in a helpful manner. She even caressed the back of his neck as he made an animalistic, ugly face trying to purge himself of the consequences of the previous night's intemperance.

His mother-in-law must be old-fashioned, out-of-step with the times, Lyson decided and went over to help. Jayne was surprised and grateful as she allowed him to hold the bowl while she went to fetch a glass of water. Doctor Fletcher was surprised too but Lyson was uncertain as to the level of his gratitude because the doctor promptly began to struggle to his feet. Lyson helped the doctor to a seat at the table. So solicitious was Jayne over the doctor that Lyson decided it was time to get going to Los Angeles. Besides, the people here seemed happy. Better luck over on the West Coast where certainly there were some among the thousands of deaf who wouldn't take so much time and persuasion to relocate in Islay. A kind of letdown, leaving through the back door, he thought helplessly, but . . .

Excuse me, he declared sadly to Jayne. *Have-to go now.*

She seized his wrist and with a ferocity that startled him. *No! Not-yet! Need talk first. Patience!*

The doctor grabbed his tie and wrestled him down to a seat, in spite of the anguish from the headache evident in his face and the way he kept one eye tightly shut as he peered back at Lyson with the other, startlingly red and out of focus. *Wait, please!* he signed clumsily. *Bear with me. Want talk first.*

Me too! chimed in Jayne. *Besides, embarrass me if you leave quickly. Must eat first.*

And—the doctor interrupted, the one eye still tightly shut, *you haven't yet given us your address.*

Right! Jayne enthused. *You must tell us more about your dream, goal for deaf take over Islay.*

Did I say that? Lyson was aghast.

Jayne looked sharply at him. *Can't remember you? Yourself plan become Governor, right?*

Governor? Lyson tried to appear innocent.

Doctor Fletcher laughed and thumped him on the back. *Wine powerful, eh? Ha, Ha.*

Suddenly serious, Jayne asked Lyson, *That talk about yourself becoming Governor, true? Or just cheap talk, drunk blah, blah?*

Lyson bit his lip, feeling his face redden. *Drunk, but true.*

Anthony slapped his head, remembering something important and tugged at the doctor's arm. *Thought you supposed go work there hospital this morning?*

Staring back at Anthony with his one open eye, the doctor declared, *Quit! Never again death!*

CHAPTER 15

The Most Dear Reverend Calvin Dowie was down on his knees in the morning sunbeam flooding richly through the tall narrow window into his study, as it did every morning before nine-thirty, before the sun rose above the eave, plunging the study into quiet shade. The sun felt wonderful on his uplifted face, penetrating his closed eyelids, so intense that his eyes filled with an astonishing fiery golden-red, quivering light. The Reverend was a natural optimist: this light gave the delirious feeling of being in the presence of a beneficence, rather than in the throes of hellfire. Having tried and failed all too often before, he knew it was futile to search for actual words in the message he knew was intrinsic to the pulsating rays. Instead, he allowed the light to overwhelm the barrier of language into his very being, to pour into the deepest recesses of his skull so that his entire soul became aflame and floated off into the ecstasy of Paradise Galore Up There.

A sudden shadow shut off the light and brought him crashing back on Palms Galore, California. Right away his face felt cold and his soul forsaken, stranded. He opened his eyes slowly, reluctantly, and saw that someone was at the door, so close to the window that he cursed the design of the parsonage. He had thought of putting up a little sign directing visitors before 9:30 A.M. to the back door, but his good wife Geraldine thought that would be inconsiderate to his parishioners, though quite appropriate for the tax and bill collectors. Besides, wouldn't it be awfully untenable if they ever saw the contents of the garbage cans?

Rising heavily to his feet, he saw, now that his face was out of the glare of the sunbeam, that there were two men at the door. He was intrigued: those men had to be here on some sort of business; yet they were dressed too elegantly, in sport coats too, to be coming to a parsonage for anything he could think of. Quickly he went to the desk and hid the bottle of whiskey in its drawer. His shot glass was already filled for his morning toast. He hesitated: he didn't like to rush the toast; he liked it to be leisurely and thoroughly enjoyable. But this morning it couldn't be helped, and it would have to be out of the way quickly or else Geraldine would have another disappointment added to the many, oh too many, she already suffered in him. This maneuver was completed just as the door opened and Geraldine led in the two men.

The Reverend Dowie could not help but be astonished at them. Not just that one was short and hefty; the other tall and gaunt. However ashamed he was for such a thought, he couldn't help but think Laurel and Hardy. The saving grace, he decided, was that he couldn't recall which was which; who was the short, who was the tall. So he was safe from an unconscious and unconscionable comparison unbefitting his dignity as a judg—that is, helper of souls. He stretched himself to his full length and could already feel himself recouping, recovering his demeanor, as he extended his hand.

Hello! Welcome here Deaf in Christ Church! My name first, The Most Dear—I mean, he rubbed his forehead, shaking his head, *Calvin. Last, Dowie. Minister—professional, NOT amateur.* He pointed out impressive diplomas on the wall behind the desk.

The short man was suitably impressed, thought the Reverend Dowie. He knew full well how impressive he, the Most Dear Reverend, looked: snowy white mane and goatee, erect bearing despite a slight paunch, granny glasses, crisp business suit as black as sin—uh, as black as sobriety itself, with no flaw visible anywhere, except of course to the good wife. If this demeanor didn't inspire awe, respect, or trust in a person, then the only option left for that person would of necessity have to be, of course, the Devil Himself.

The problem was the tall one: he had such a silly look on his face—wild, reckless, so deliriously happy—as to be quite irreverent, almost unworthy of the great presence of the Most Dear—The Reverend Dowie rubbed his forehead again and reminded himself of the Humility of the Christ.

Go sit-down, he urged the two men quickly, before the tall one could get out of hand. And something told him to escort Geraldine to the door quickly before he himself lost his own demeanor. But not quite: something about the tall man was so persuasive that the Reverend couldn't help but pat his wife in exactly the way that made her jump out the door.

C-A-L-V-I-N! she cried, *Matter you?*

Happy, happy, he replied with a silly grin of his own and shut the door after her, still having enough of his wits about to lock it good and solid.

Regathering what was left of his demeanor, he put on a serious grave face and went around his desk to his seat, swiveling the chair around to try and face the two men. But the silly reckless grin on the tall one was unsettling, disconcerting, so he focused his energy on the short one. He couldn't help but marvel at the brightness of the eyes that met his own. The intelligence was there of course, but there was something else too, something so uncanny that he was unprepared to face it quite yet. He had to shut his own eyes in order to be able to figure just what that something was. But he was unable to, really, so he began his professional discourse, still keeping his eyes tightly shut. His signing was graceful, grandiose, earnest, with many solemn pauses.

I myself truly mere humble servant his up-there Christ; myself have imperfections but will do my best help-you with obviously awful problem that brings you here, to me for me intersect with up-there Christ help solve for you. Don't worry, up-there Christ can understand Ameslan, can com-

municate with deaf. Not necessary hearing can talk with up-there; deaf, all-of-us can, because him up-there died impaled for all-of-us, deaf too.

He opened his eyes slowly, still avoiding the tall one. The short one spoke up, *My name first, Lyson. Last Sulla. My wife her name Mary. Before marry, her last name formerly Barnclay.*

Mary Barnclay! exclaimed Reverend Dowie.

Yes, she told me, when myself arrive here Palms Galore, California, must come here, visit you.

Mary Barnclay! repeated Reverend Dowie, delirious with surprise. *Long time since no see! Let me think—about 15, 20 years since last time saw her!*

Yes, Lyson said brightly. *She herself told me, never forgot you, your preaching, and commanded me, must visit you, say hello.*

You, her husband?

Yes. Married since twelve years.

The Reverend Dowie sat stunned. He remembered Mary Barnclay very well, when he was just starting out in the business in Boston, trying to establish his credentials as a professional. Of course he didn't quite succeed, considering that he made the mistake of insisting that Christ could understand, and furthermore approve of, Sign Language in an area where many of the deaf prided themselves on their unfamiliarity with such a crude method of communication. Mary, she was different. She thought the Lord's Message far more important than any mode of communication used to convey it. Why, even English was so inadequate to express the intense, exquisite agony of the Crucifixion! He remembered well and gratefully how she, a mere child, stood up for him and, in defiance of all who knew and loved her, learned Sign Language. Not just any sign language but the Ameslan so natural to the eyes but foreign, even archaic, to the ear. There were times he thought she was the only sheep he would ever find until, of course, economic realities drove him to the more fertile fields of California where the people, it seemed to him, were more willing to accept the image of a signing Christ, outside the more established method of orally preaching a wooden Christ. Let's just say, he nodded to himself, Californians are more receptive to a more vigorous method of preaching than people in more traditional areas.

Mary! Can't believe! his hands cried. *That little girl married now! Children?*

Lyson was so shamefaced that the Reverend felt for him and changed the subject. *How herself?*

Fine! She say hello.

The Reverend shook his head in amazement, and in the course of shaking his head his eyes met those of the tall man, and his head stopped. There was something about that man, his evident happiness, deliriousness, that brought the bottle of bourbon out of hiding.

Excuse me. No glasses. apologized the Reverend as he offered the bottle to the tall one, whose eyes leaped with joy and who was only too happy to take first honors with the bottle.

His name, Doctor Hansel Fletcher. Lyson helpfully introduced them. *Himself first and only doctor, deaf himself, in USA.*

Really? Reverend Dowie asked of the tall one.

Doctor Fletcher raised the bottle and grinned. *Lyson will help make me real, honest doctor,* he said boastfully. He toasted the Reverend with the bottle and took another long swig.

His life fouled-up, Lyson cautioned Reverend Dowie hurriedly before Doctor Fletcher lowered the bottle enough to see. *Myself going help-him—*

The Reverend Dowie caught Lyson's hand and bowed his head, his eyes shut in humility. *Understand! Understand! Remember when myself, my life fouled-up, thought myself no-good, my life worthless, long ago there Boston.*

Lyson squeezed back. *Don't worry. Mary told-me yourself wonderful, most fine man she ever-since knew.*

The Reverend softened, smiled, and took an immediate liking to Lyson. *Thank you! I knew she would find wonderful husband—*

Lyson saw the doctor taking another long swig and became worried. He grabbed the bottle. *My turn!*

Sorry, not intentional, the doctor apologized. *Thought you busy too-much for drink.* The speed with which the doctor was learning Ameslan was astonishing, thought Lyson approvingly, now that he is free from the clutches of the dead.

The Reverend made sure he didn't miss his own turn and, after a good and luxurious swig, remarked jovially to Lyson, *If Mary, and my wife too, saw this, you and me will have-to live there desert!*

Lyson took the bottle quickly before the doctor opened his eyes long enough to see he was missing his own turn and chuckled, *Men! Can't help.* He shrugged and, after a quick swig, urged the Reverend to put the bottle away. *Too-early.*

Right. Should know better myself, the Reverend ruefully acknowledged and would have put away the bottle except that he noticed it was already practically empty, there being barely enough to wet a thirsty tongue. *Well!* he shrugged and finished the bottle before hiding it.

For a while the three sat quietly, content for the moment with the sensation of a new, budding relationship, each lost in his own private thoughts, or perhaps more truthfully, stupor, relishing the power of the bourbon coursing through their veins. The sunbeam was long since gone, and the room was already very pleasantly cool and quiet when the Reverend finally asked Lyson, *You come here California, for-for?*

Lyson stared back, almost as if surprised at finding himself in California. Reverend Dowie couldn't help but chuckle, *Seems yourself maniac wild, roam around, wake-up here California.*

Yes! said the doctor perking up, *Before him show-up, myself O.K. but bored, dead. Ever-since my mind worthless, flipped. Travel around crazy, happy.*

Truth! Lyson cried defensively. *Myself going help-him become real doctor.*

And myself going help-him become real Governor, the doctor laughed maniacally.

The Reverend was rather disquieted, and wondered if he wasn't in way over his head with these two lunatics. Lord, please help me, he pleaded silently, get rid of the whiskey in our veins. He couldn't very well ask for Geraldine's help, and as for his daughter, his beloved Evangeline—how he hated those doubts! Somewhat as if attempting to answer his prayer, Lyson patted his arm and assured, *Don't worry! Know that seem crazy, but true!*

Governor, Governor, mused the Reverend openly. *California itself very big state—*

Right! the doctor agreed happily. *Thousands deaf here,* he gestured gathering and picking them up en masse and moving them faraway. *East, small state where few hearing live.*

The Reverend looked quickly at Lyson and saw with alarm the same dream in the happy eyes. *Obviously you-two need my help,* he declared after an uneasy silence. *Myself trained, expert in psychology—*

Hurrah! the doctor exulted to Lyson, *our first day in California, our first customer!*

Alarmed, the Reverend tried to demur but Lyson was already shaking his hand. *Welcome to Islay!*

The doctor shook his hand too. *Person like you with your skill with people, will big help for us.*

Never drink with your cust—I mean, patients, the Reverend groaned to himself. You old fool!

Let's toast! the doctor suggested enthusiastically, his eyes bright with wildness, and fished out a shiny brass flask from inside his jacket. To Lyson he toasted, *You sure have powerful pull-in people!* To the Reverend: *Your quick intelligence, can spot good idea!*

Reverend Dowie meekly accepted the toast, acceding to his defeat philosophically. The Lord sure moves in wondrous ways.

Fortunately, very much so, the flask was less than half full and was empty soon: this gave the Reverend an opportunity to bolt for the door to call for coffee. But Geraldine was much too upset to want to help. He dared not approach her too closely lest she smell the booze on his breath, so he got the coffee himself. It took him a while to find the cups, so that

Lyson and Doctor Fletcher, to pass the while, had nothing better to do than to examine the wall decorations: diplomas from various schools, framed sayings from the Good Book engraved on ancient looking parchments: Thou shalt not curse the deaf. And the ears of the deaf shall be unstopped. They are like the deaf adder that stoppeth her ear. This last verse mystified Lyson, and he diverted his mind toward something he hoped was more concrete, such as the portrait of the Christ crowned in full glory by thorns. This too was beyond him, as also was the fact that such a juxtaposition seems common, rather compulsory in religion.

Oh! Hello! Lyson cried, his face reddening as the Reverend returned with the coffee. He quickly resumed his seat and tried to be nonchalant. *Fascinating room.*

Seems like you plan stay long time, sighed Reverend Dowie as he served the coffee. Then more seriously, *How, really, is Mary?* He tilted his head in signal of expecting a frank, honest answer.

Wonderful! Best wife I ever had, Lyson exclaimed with enthusiasm. *Miss her lot.*

Reverend Dowie nodded slowly, satisfied that the compulsories had been met with. He leaned forward, in an attitude that reminded Lyson of the confessional, and crinkled his brow. *I mean, how is she, truthfully?*

Fine! Lyson declared, but seeing the Reverend still frowning, fell silent, his hands tucked into his lap. Something is funny here, he thought uneasily, but then he too realized that when you start off on the wrong foot, it sometimes helps to backtrack and start over on the right foot. *Mary and myself, two-of-us, married since twelve years—*

Know that! The Reverend threw up his hands.

Lyson married? Honest? the doctor asked playfully.

Obvious need more coffee, said Reverend Dowie rubbing his eyes and again reminding himself of the humility of the Christ. *Sorry! Please forgive me. Something funny this morning.*

The Reverend's mood, his quest for the hidden truth, affected the doctor so much that he jumped up, his hands agitated. *Listen! Myself true doctor. Not false! Deaf but still doctor. M.D.! You must honest with me; think you; me real doctor?*

Reverend Dowie stared bleakly back at the doctor, quite abashed, and crossed himself although he knew well it wasn't kosher with the dictates of his faith; it's just that it's such a convenient way for a deaf person to express himself, Lord, have mercy on us! No thinking, no verbalizing required: just cross yourself from deep inside and the Lord will understand. This act of crossing disquieted the doctor, and he sat down heavily.

Reverend Dowie was the first to come to his senses and held up a palm: *Best medicine for all-us, I believe, coffee.* Lyson looked down on his cup and saw that it was still full. He tasted it and had to agree it was cold. *Please.*

Suddenly the Reverend gripped Lyson tightly by the hand and pleaded, *Help me please! My wife, wonderful woman! But she must understand! Can you, please, tell her that Mary your wife said hello? Please—*

Lyson stared back, not quite comprehending. He did not know ministers could need help with their wives. He was not sure he wanted to debase himself of this notion, but quickly brightened, *O.K. don't worry! Myself adept, know how handle—*

Good! Reverend Dowie jumped to his feet, still holding Lyson tight to his word, probing deeply into his eyes. He pulled Lyson to the door and, laying a hand firmly on the back of his neck, took him out to the kitchen.

There Geraldine was standing, her arms crossed, at the window over the sink, her eyes sad with hurt as she contemplated the beautiful morning sparkling over the garden behind their house. The Reverend set Lyson a bit off to her side, a comfortable signing distance, and with a wink at Lyson to be patient, put a hand softly on her shoulder.

Geraldine held still long enough to sink her husband ever deeper into the defensive, and for Lyson to appreciate the fineness, the goodness, the strength in her features which he thought were the very embodiment of a woman thoroughly in command of her role as a homemaker, mother, wife—especially a minister's—so that she possessed a certain power over her husband, all the stronger because she used it wisely, not for herself, her own sake, but for the sake of Good.

You remind me my wife! Lyson's hands blurted out almost subconsciously, in spite of himself, and Geraldine turned to face him.

Remember Mary Barnclay? Reverend Dowie jumped in with anxious hands. *Long-ago there Boston, your favorite little girl—that one always help care for Evangeline—*

Mary! Geraldine's eyes leaped with joy. *Yes!*

This her husband!

Husband! She turned to Lyson, seeing him for the first time. *Really!*

Yes, my name first, Lyson. Last, Sulla—

Husband! She became excited as a little girl opening a present. *How is she? Where now?*

Fine, fine! Lyson said happily. *Now live there Islay. Formerly Washingt—*

Islay? Where? A comfortable level of intimacy and rapport had been established enough to allow the Reverend to suggest they sit at the table. She gushed, *Children, any?* Already she was holding Lyson's hand as Reverend Dowie clumsily set the table for coffee and cookies. *Calvin! Relax. Everything OK now, can wait until tonight, then we can talk, O.K.?* Her imperious look melted immediately on turning to Lyson. *Wonderful! Hard believe, finally meet you!*

For a pleasant while Geraldine and Lyson sat at the table talking about Mary, consuming cups of coffee kept refilled by the Reverend who remained standing, hovering over them like an oversolicitous waiter, ready and anxious to be of instant service. Lyson learnt what a remarkable young girl Mary had been, gracious and helpful to her elders, although shy with anyone who exhibited the slightest forwardness. Geraldine was glad how well that little girl had turned out, and made Lyson bashful with compliments that Mary couldn't have found a better husband.

Your blush, cute! she laughed, *still little boy, you!*

Lyson tried to divert attention from his reddening ears by glancing at Reverend Dowie and pointing at his cup though it was more full than not.

Excuse me! Dream, me! the Reverend apologized as he brought the percolator over the cup. But he suddenly stopped and gapped at Lyson. *Forgot doctor!*

He dashed to the study and found Doctor Fletcher in a happy stupor behind the desk, his feet up on the mess of papers littering the desk top, a new bottle of bourbon already more than half consumed on his lap. With a whiskey connoisseur's unerring nose he had found a case of the stuff hidden in the ottoman that had successfully served the Reverend so well until now. Quickly, the ottoman was shut before Geraldine and Lyson entered the room.

Geraldine! This doctor needs our help. Reverend Dowie pleaded to his wife in panic.

Drunkards can't enter Up-There, she replied icily, fully prepared to evict the doctor.

That for up-there Lord his decision. The Reverend tried his best to be resolute, to assert his authority, and found it helpful to assume his sermonic stance, the way he imagined the Lord giving the Sermon on the Mount, his head slightly bowed, eyes closed for better, more intimate contact with Up There, a finger raised while the other hand did all the signing. *Our responsibility very grave, must help, show love, understanding—*

He opened an eye a crack to assess his audience and found them gone. Already Geraldine and Lyson were helping Doctor Fletcher down the hall toward the spare bedroom. The Reverend gave out a great sigh and dropped his finger. The sunbeam of course was long since gone from the window. He wished it were still shining there. The thought of having to find a new hiding place for the case wearied him very much. He really needed that sunbeam right now. Lord, don't forsake me now!

He couldn't help but be very much concerned. There just wasn't enough time to find a new hiding place. True, Geraldine was busy right now setting up the spare bedroom for Lyson and Doctor Fletcher. Even now she was tucking the doctor in bed. But he couldn't very well lock the door long enough to transfer the case to a new hiding place. Also, his mind was too agitated for successful thinking. And he certainly couldn't lock the door when leaving the study. That was certain to arouse Geraldine into calling a locksmith. Finally he decided it best to leave the ottoman strictly alone, as it was, where it always had been, as if nothing had ever happened, as if it had nothing to do with the doctor. Even the open bottle of bourbon on the desk would be better left alone. At least Geraldine probably thought it was the doctor's. The only thing he could hope for, really, was mercy. He knew it was true that the merciful would always be shown mercy. The trouble was, Geraldine was too good, or too smart, or both to allow herself to get into a situation where she herself needed mercy. Otherwise, it might be possible to induce her to show him a little.

Best stop staring at that ottoman! he cautioned himself and fled the study, remembering to carefully leave the door open as was his custom. He hurried to where he belonged, helping settle the guests into the spare bedroom.

More baggage? he asked Lyson who was helping Geraldine pull out the doctor's pants from under the blanket. Lyson was having a bit of difficulty so Reverend Dowie pitched in to help. So helpful did he try to be that Geraldine had to hold the blanket fast as he pulled at it.

Stop! she commanded with a hiss. She was the only one in the room with any intelligence whatsoever and already knew the problem. The doctor still had on his shoes. Scram! She shooed the two men away and shut the door after them. The Reverend and Lyson retreated quickly, sheepishly to the kitchen.

Forgive us, Reverend Dowie pleaded, *this not really our natural way. Just happened—feel silly.*

All right, Lyson assured him. *Not your fault. Happen myself too, once-every-while.*

The Reverend sat with such dejection and anxiety at the table that Lyson took pity and fetched the coffee and cookies himself. After all, no breakfast yet this morning. Close to noon, too.

The coffee and cookies did Lyson a great deal of good but not Reverend Dowie, who kept glancing at the doorway as if something dreadful was certain to come after him. He hated this, this feeling of being cowed, intimidated, but could think of no strategy that had any possibility of averting the crisis unquestionably coming his way. He was just too drat guilty, that's what! Lyson tried to make small, jovial talk but the Reverend kept glancing at the doorway. This worried Lyson very much and he too stared at the doorway.

A saving grace arrived through the flashing of a lamp. After a momen't confusion, Reverend Dowie jumped up. Door! and hurried to answer it.

It was Jewell Cameron, her three children, their little dog, and all their worldly possessions piled up on the doorstep. The children were in tears, and Jewell was exhausted and distraught. *Cab mad me!* She held up a department store credit card. *Won't accept! Need money, pay cash.* The taxicab was in the driveway, the driver sitting on the hood smoking a cigarette. After all, he was blocking three other cars in the driveway, including Lyson's Mercedes. He'll outwait 'em, no sweat.

Calm. Faith. the Reverend bowed his head and prayed with great swings and sweeps of his hands. *God up-there, our beloved Lord, hear this humble prayer, please. Help this dear little family, so innocent and helpless! Please send-us someone good, dear heart who can and will help from greatness his heart. Please, in his name our Sweet Lord up-there. Amen.*

He turned his head and looked over his shoulder. Ah! Here was Lyson staring at them all. Their eyes met and Reverend Dowie glanced expectantly at the taxi. It took Lyson some seconds to get the message, but when he did, he was quick to go over to the cabbie. The wallet was quick out of his pocket too, although he was stunned by the fare: $68.45, plus tip, please. He'd been driving them all around, all over, all night, the cabbie explained. And he even had to walk the dog for her several times while she changed diapers. What do you know, he even had to trash the diapers for her too. Lyson let him go with a crisp new hundred dollar bill.

Quite a crisis gripped the parsonage when Lyson returned. Not only was Geraldine upset at what Doctor Fletcher had said before dropping off to sleep, not just about the ottoman, but that Reverend Dowie had agreed to relocate in Islay, which meant she would have to leave her friends, her garden, and her beloved California. But also there were only three bedrooms in the parsonage. One belonged to their precious daughter Evangeline and was strictly off limits, particularly to children, because of the delicate and fine furniture and mementos. The room was made up in a wonderful pink, and the draperies were so fragile, so costly. Even Reverend Dowie feared to tread into such delicateness.

Myself, and doctor, not mean stay here, just visit. Lyson tried to explain, but Reverend Dowie would have none of that. Once a guest, always a guest, he declared with bowed head and shut eyes. Swiftly, before Geraldine could protest, he had Lyson help him carry the doctor, still dead asleep, to the divan in the study. The Cameron children and dog were fed, washed, and put to bed on the floor in the guest room.

Must talk! Geraldine tried to corner her husband.

Patience! Later, he pleaded. *Must counsel this pity woman.*

Geraldine and Lyson were left alone at the table in the kitchen. There burned such anger in her eyes that Lyson hung his head in guilt. *Sorry, cause trouble,* he apologized, *not intentional.*

She looked strangely at him and took pity. She put a hand on his. *Not your fault. My husband!*

Not really, he shook his head. *Can't help, thing happen fast, wrong time—*

True, she sighed, patting his hand. *His trouble, his softhearted, don't-know how say no. Sweet, true.* She thought it best not to mention the awful ottoman.

Wonderful man, he agreed eagerly, *minister life not easy.*

They remained quiet for a little while, her hand still on his even while they sipped coffee, not wanting to disturb this most comforting amity. But a disturbing thought returned to her. *Doctor say, my husband agree move there Islay, and yourself will become Governor—*

Lyson blushed. *Really*—he began but caught himself. Not my business to mention the whiskey, he reminded himself. *Happen fast! Can't help—* he finally explained lamely, his hand whirling aimlessly.

She looked curiously at him. *Tell me! Have right know, decide myself!*

Doubt myself, that he understand everything, decide yet, Lyson began carefully.

Oh! up went her eyebrows.

You see, we not finished talking, but doctor jump conclusion, think minister already decide—

I see, she nodded with obvious relief and gratitude. *Thank-you, but what this story Islay about, yourself becoming Governor, true?*

Lyson could feel his ears turning red. She saw them and laughed, liking him instantly. *Bashful, cute you!* She reached over and playfully poked his dimple. Just then the Reverend returned, stared at them, and crossed himself.

Silly you! she laughed and pulled him down upon her lap and squeezed his nose. He was clearly shocked and looked from Lyson to his wife and back again.

Man like you, he finally said, almost reverently, *should be Governor.*

CHAPTER 16

Lyson was very impressed with the new two story building that housed Silent Electronics. Tastefully modern, with a mixture of brick, cedar, glass, and solar panels worked into a series of geometric shapes, mostly cubes, hexagons, and wedges, arranged so that no one pattern was repeated anywhere; so that it gave the impression of several buildings, a village instead of the single immense building it really was. The landscaping was first-rate, with palms, willows, eucalyptus, pines, hedges, flower beds, and crisp lawns worked into the grounds all around—instead of one large broiling parking lot, several smaller lots lay hidden among the greenery. No car need become an oven here. The walkways were pebbles set in concrete—they looked like a real trail in a forest. Lyson was already thoroughly convinced that all this could only be the work of a deaf architect, and determined that this was the man to redo Islay. And any company that would hire such an architect belonged in Islay too.

Beautiful, eh? the Reverend nudged his elbow.

Fantastic! Lyson declared with awe as the glass doors slid open at their approach. Instead of a frigid blast of sterile air conditioning, they were greeted by a gentle mellow atmosphere of potted plants—palms, banana and rubber trees, hanging fuchsia and begonia, even vines climbing up the walls toward the skylight. This then, is what would be called the main lobby, or even the great hall, with doorways all around, with a reception room created tastefully in the middle of the hall by walls of plants.

The receptionist at her desk was very pretty. Lyson and Reverend Dowie stared at her for an unseemly moment. The very informality of her Mexican peasant blouse that she allowed to drop down her shoulders, revealing the fineness and clarity of her amber skin, the delicacy of her collar bones, gave Lyson the idea he would like Monte Guthrie very much. She stared back, not entirely displeased but calm and composed. Finally Lyson patted his coat pockets apologetically and, speaking as clearly as he knew how to, asked for a pencil and paper. She glanced down at her desk where already lay a pen and pad.

"Excuse us!" he wrote, *"but we're deaf and—"*

Her touch on his hand was so delicate it sent a shiver up his arm. He gasped and looked up into her dark but laughing eyes. She cocked one eyebrow and pointed at her mouth. "Can you read lips?"

The words came out of her mouth so startling clear that he was stunned. She patted his hand again and pulled up her eyebrows. "Well?"

"Excuse me, but my speech is not too good," he explained, speaking very carefully. "Most people can't understand—"

She burst out laughing, so uproariously that the Reverend, shocked and offended, stepped up fully prepared to reprimand her callousness toward the handicapped. What unseemly behavior for a woman working in an organization supposedly serving the deaf.

Silly you! Ourselves deaf here! her hands signed with the grace and verve that only the deaf possess. The men stared at her so stupidly that she laughed again. *Seem you never saw signs before.*

Lyson slapped his forehead. *Dumb me! Old habit! Can't help!*

Worst me. Reverend Dowie interjected. *Myself live here, should know better.*

I-see, no wonder, she quipped. Then to Lyson, *You not live here?*

Oh—oh, my name first, Lyson, last, Sulla. Formerly live there Washington, D.C. Now move there Islay. Lyson was very glad to get back on track, back to business. *Here, my friend, name first, Calvin—*

Hold-it! the Reverend interrupted, demurring with eyes closed and head bowed sidewise. *My full, true name: The Most Dear Reverend Calvin Dowie. Minister there, Palms Galore, The Deaf in Christ Church.*

She noted how red Lyson's ears were turning and teased, *Yourself minister too?*

No, no, he denied with more vehemence than intended. *Businessman.*

The teasing was too successful, too much fun to let up now, and she pressed, *Your business, selling church things, supplies?*

The Reverend stepped in firmly. *We came for very important business with Mr. Monte Guthrie.*

Oh. She glanced at Lyson for confirmation.

*Yes! Important secret—*He stopped quickly, too quickly, and already her face showed curiosity. He groaned and thumped his forehead.

After an awkward silence she asked graciously, *Appointment?*

Please, Lyson nodded, and was surprised at himself, at his uncanny ability to come up with the correct answer, even after a gaffe.

Let me check, come. She saw them to comfortable chairs in a foyer enclosed by walls of plants facing a large planter's window dazzling with its profusion of tiny flowers growing in the sun. A table was set for coffee and tea and held bowls of nuts, chocolates, mints, and what to Lyson looked like birdseed. He picked up the bowl of chocolates but she slapped his hand and put it back, scolding, *One each! Your health!* Lyson tried to apologize but she was already gone.

The Reverend was at the window, examining it with the closeness of someone who would buy it right off the wall, were it immediately for sale and not nailed to the wall. *Wonder where can find, buy for myself, he exclaimed, perfect for my office.*

Lyson was more intrigued with the variety of pastels in the mint bowl. He picked out a white, a green, a blue, and a pink and commenced a testing program. The colors made no difference at all in the flavor: they all tasted equally minty. And his mouth felt good, refreshed. His breath would not offend anyone, that's for sure. He had a little debate with himself: were the mints made available to put visitors at ease regarding their breath or was it a defensive tactic on the part of Monte? Either way, it was still an impressive show of hospitality that the Islay Company would do well to emulate. He slipped a few mints in his pocket for future emergencies and jotted on his handy pad: "A mint bowl on every desk." Also: "Find out who architect Silent Elec."

The receptionist was already back, so quickly that Lyson out of habit hid the pad behind his back. Her eyes widened and she teased, *Spy?*

No, no, Lyson protested, his ears reddening. *Just copy good ideas—*

Like my ideas? She was very pleased.

Yes. But Lyson was perplexed. *Your idea?*

Oh yes, boss here very good, allow everyone invent ideas ourselves.

Lyson was impressed and looked around the waiting room. Just then he noticed the wall paper was actual burlap. *Excellent! This room perfect idea for myself, my own office.*

Where get that? the Reverend held his hand out to the planter as in beholding a miracle. *Want for my study.*

Oh, easy find. Common all-around. Lumber stores.

Beautiful, beautiful, his hands signed softly.

You eat, eat candy? she suddenly accused Lyson, who was flustered and tried to explain but she laughed, *Can smell,* and motioned them to follow her. She guided them, weaving around and through staggered walls of plants, like a maze, behind which reposed exhibits of electronic devices for the deaf, starting with the original Baby Radar that began it all. Its microphone caught the cries of babies and flashed a lamp to awaken deaf parents. It also caught the doorbell, telephone, and alarm clocks. All around were various models of teletypewriters from the earliest mechanical monsters up to the modern digital types. Teleprinters. Television phones. Even an experimental earphone that emitted, instead of sound, electronic impulses directly into the brain in hopes of emulating the same signals normally carried by the auditory nerve. In a niche were arranged a display of current teletypewriters, one of which Lyson recognized as a Silent Communicator, just like his own. Already he felt on more familiar grounds and more anxious to meet the founder.

At the very end of the hall was a door marked New Ideas. Inside was a confusion of computers, blinking lights, flying digits, and flickering screens on which danced strange lines representing some mysterious computations. Whirling discs. Jumping dials. Wires snaking all over the floors, machines, countertops, everywhere. A heavy electrical smell permeated the room. The receptionist flicked on a switch. *He always forget, must fan suck-out smell.*

Behind a bank of computers stood a tall, slight man in a laboratory coat stooped over a teletypewriter, watching a digital screen, a hand gripping a wrist behind his back, the free hand spelling out the message streaming across the screen in bright green letters. KAND EEOO THINGK UF A BEDUR—

He stamped a foot and signed in exasperation to himself. *Wish hearing improve themselves speech.* Lyson liked him immediately. The man was charmingly unaffected. The hair had once been reddish but now was a dull brown with numerous white strands and unkempt: it appeared that it hadn't been barbered or combed lately. His white laboratory coat showed ink stains, solder splatterings, cigarette burns, and tears from sharp pieces of machinery, the sleeves blackened by the handprints of others tugging for his attention. Baggy pants, blue shirt, and striped green and brown neck tie. A general appearance of having slept in his clothes. Horn-rimmed glasses speckled with dust, dandruff, and various dried sprays, possibly grapefruit too. Lyson was awestruck and had a feeling of being in the presence of a great genius like an Einstein or Edison.

There was reverence too in the gentle way the receptionist tugged at the man's sleeve. Even then, the man was startled and stared at them with wide eyes tremendously magnified by his thick spectacles. With the speed of a computer the man saw his opportunity and, dispensing with introductions, seated Lyson at one of the teletypewriters over which stood a television screen. The man sat at another machine and began typing rapidly with two fingers. HELLO MY NAME MONTE GUTHRIE. YOURS? said the screen in front of Lyson.

Lyson typed: HI! LYSON SULLA HERE. GEE AYE. At the GEE AYE he was startled and examined more closely the keyboard. It looked no different than any he ever saw. Just a G and an A. The screen was already now registering what Monte was typing in response: WELCOME TO SILENT ELECTRONICS. THIS MACHINE GIVES PERFECT SPEECH THROUGH ITS SYNTHETIC VOICE. IT RECEIVES VOICES AND TYPES OUT WHAT THE VOICES SAY. ONLY PROBLEM IS SPEECH MUST BE PERFECT FOR THIS MACHINE TO TYPE OUT ACCURATELY. VERY FEW HEARING PEOPLE CAN SPEAK ACCURATELY. CAN YOU? PICK UP TELEPHONE AND SPEAK.

Lyson glanced quizzically at Monte who pointed earnestly at the telephone cradled over Lyson's machine. *Talk,* he motioned. The receptionist helpfully held the telephone to Lyson's face and urged, *Talk. Idea-hearing same.*

He took a deep breath and began. HALOU MBAE NAEMB IZ LIESHUN—declared the screen over Monte's machine as he spoke. Lyson stopped, his ears reddening, and looked over at Monte who mentioned him to replace the telephone on the machine. Monte picked up his own phone and spoke. HALLER MBE SBEDSHT ISD WOORSD.

The great inventor shook his head and shoulders laughing as he put down the telephone. *People speech can't equal machine speech. Even hearing!*

Lyson slumped back in his chair. *Myself not sure exactly for-for this machine?*

Monte stared back with the same incredulity he would at someone who didn't know the purpose of a telephone. *TTY before see you?*

Of course, Lyson protested innocently. *Have one there home, made here.*

With the weary patience of someone who has made the same explanation again and again Monte explained, *O.K. This TTY purpose for deaf type to hearing, typing convert to voice for hearing. Then hearing speak to telephone, convert to sentences there.* He pointed at the screen.

Good idea! Lyson nodded enthusiastically.

See, machine can speak to hearing perfect, no problem, Monte continued with the air of a man only half satisfied, *But hearing can't speak clear enough! That why machine print hard for us read. You see, it print phonetically, exact way people talk. Look!* He turned on a television set and a soap opera came on. A woman was berating a man in a hospital bed. Monte held a telephone up to the television. EEAU HAHD NRO RIET TOO GAO LAK DAD AN GEED EEURSEEF BUSHJD—

See! Monte said, putting the telephone down. *That woman movie star, you know that movie star always better speech than common people—*

Not true! Reverend Dowie declared, stepping forth. *Hearing preachers have best speech!*

Lyson winced and was about to tell the Reverend to hush when Monte calmly replied, *You before here on Sunday?*

No, admitted Reverend Dowie, abashed.

You see, this machine for many purposes, Monte went on. *First purpose I already told you, for use on telephone with hearing world. Second, can use for captioning any TV, radio, even hearing people talking here. Third, can use for speech training. First thought,* he chuckled, *can use for teaching deaf speech, but now know should use for teaching hearing people how can pronounce words right.*

Always thought hearing speak clearly, perfectly, Lyson remarked soberly.

Me too! agreed Monte. *That why I use TV for testing, but still problem, problem, until I ask some hearing friends come, help. That how proved machine O.K., nothing wrong, really work perfect.*

Lyson nodded sympathetically. *Do? Do?*

Well! Monte sighed, *impossible force hearing improve their speech, so myself thinking about invent other computer that can convert phonetic, or wrong speech to correct spelling, even different dialects—*

Lyson became excited. *Ask you, can convert bad deaf speech to perfect speech?*

Monte was intrigued with this new idea. *Interesting! Interesting! But not now. Maybe eventually, future.*

Lyson was sold. Why, with such a machine he could go to Congress! He could easily picture himself, with a miniaturized version hidden in his clothing, standing up in the Senate and making an eloquent speech on the behalf of the deaf, the downtrodden, the victims of the hearing world! And a wrist television, or perhaps a tiny screen ingeniously hidden in his glasses, and no one would ever guess he was deaf! Everybody knows the hearing never take the deaf seriously, no matter how reasonable, how intelligent. Seems they only listen to a good listener! *Need investor, you?* Lyson asked Monte fervently, almost pleading.

Investor? Monte was puzzled. *You mean money?*

Yes! Have money! Lyson could hardly contain himself, his excitement. *Myself want invest, help your company grow, spread, invent new things—*

Well, well, Monte mused, *money not my area. That belong my wife.*

Your wife?

Yeah, there, he nodded at the receptionist.

Lyson stared at Exota, his mouth dropping open in astonishment. Exota smiled an amused smile, picked up her eyebrows, and curtsied with her head: *Indeed so.*

CHAPTER 17

WONDERFUL DAY! SUCCESSFUL MAKE AGREEMENTS WITH THREE DEAF COMPANIES. SILENT ELECTRONICS SAY OK BUILD NEW BRANCH IN SUFFEX. DEAF PUBLISHERS AND CAPTIONERS AGREE LET US REPRESENT EAST USA. BOND AND SCHAFFER ARCHITECTS DEAF INTERESTED IN NEW BRANCH OFFICE THERE SUFFEX. PLEASE TELL ANDY AND CAPTAIN SAVE SOME LAND FOR THAT. GA.

GOOD FOR YOU! SURPRISE YOU SUCCESS. NEVER DREAM YOU COULD—

YOU KNOW I CAN! Lyson butted in, his typing speed a measure of his indignation. GA.

ARE YOU STAYING WITH—

THE DOWIES OF COURSE! YOU KNOW THAT! GA.

LYSON! ARE YOU MAD AT ME Q GA.

YOU ALWAYS THINK ME DUMB, CANT DO ANYTHING GA.

SORRY. NOT MEAN TO. JUST SILLY ME. CANT HELP WORRY BECAUSE I MISS YOU VERY MUCH. SHOULD KNOW BETTER MYSELF THAT THE DOWIES CAN TAKE GOOD CARE OF YOU. HOW ARE THEY QQ GA.

The Reverend urged Lyson aside and took the seat himself and typed: THE MOST DEAR REVEREND CALVIN DOWIE HERE. SO GLAD TO FINALLY MAKE CONTACT WITH YOU MY MOST DEAR FAVORITE PARISHIONER! HOW HAVE YOU BEEN MY MOST DEAR Q GA.

The machine was silent for a long moment and resumed life: CALVIN! SO GLAD LYSON IS IN YOUR HANDS. I AM FINE. JUST LONESOME FOR MY HUSBAND. SILLY ME WORRY ALL THE TIME, BUT NOW DON'T HAVE TO. DID HE GIVE YOU ANY PROBLEMS QQ HOPE NOT! GA.

LYSON IS A MOST DEAR WONDERFUL MAN. I AM VERY PROUD OF YOU FOR FINDING SUCH A MOST DEAR HUSBAND. IT HAS BEEN MY GREATEST PLEASURE HAVING HIM HERE WITH US AND DRIVING HIM AROUND TO VARIOUS DEAF BUSINESSES. REALLY, IM AFRAID IM MORE TROUBLE THAN HE IS. HE IS THE SUCCESSFUL ONE, FULLY QUALIFIED CAPABLY AND MORALLY TO BE GOVERNOR. HE DOESNT NEED MY HELP EXCEPT FOR DIVINE DIRECTION GA.

DIRECTIONS! I KNOW HIS WAY, ALWAYS NEED DIRECTIONS, EASY GET LOST. I'M SO GLAD YOU ARE THERE WITH HIM.

HATE IDEA HIM GET LOST IN LOS ANGELES. NEVER FIND HIM AGAIN. GA.

I DONT THINK HE IS THAT EASILY LOST. I JUST HELP HIM SAVE TIME NOT HAVING TO SEARCH ALL OVER LOS ANGELES. BY THE WAY, MY MOST DEAR, WHEN CAN WE SEE YOU Q GA.

WHY NOT YOU MOVE HERE Q. HAVE HUGE LOVELY CHURCH. TALL STEEPLE HAVE OFFICE HIGH UPSTAIRS. MANY COLUMNS. HAVE BIG APARTMENT. DONT TELL LYSON, ALREADY BOUGHT CHURCH FOR YOU. MANY MANY DEAF ALREADY MOVE HERE. NEED YOU! GA.

Reverend Dowie looked quickly over his shoulder. Lyson had seen, but didn't mind at all. Lyson was a good sport and smiled encouragingly. Think votes. Think votes, Lyson chuckled to himself as he rocked himself on his heels, his hands clasped behind his back, watching the Reverend typing: LYSON THINKS ITS A GOOD IDEA TOO—

DIDNT KNOW HE IS INTERESTED IN CHURCH. HOW HAPPEN Q GA.

DONT KNOW. THE WAYS OF GOD ARE MYSTERIOUS AND WONDOROUS, the Reverend typed happily, feeling right in his own element. MAKES YOU VERY HUMBLE. AGREE Q GA.

IF GOD CAN DO THAT, MAYBE HE CAN BRING YOU HERE AND MAKE YOU THE TOP DEAF MINISTER GA.

THE FIRST SHALL BE LAST, Reverend Dowie hastened to type, THE LAST SHALL BE FIRST. GA.

RIGHT! FOR YEARS YOU HAVE BEEN LAST. WE SHALL MAKE YOU FIRST. GA.

NAUGHTY YOU! THAT IS GOD HIS JOB—

SORRY! I MEAN WITH HIS HELP. GA.

CORRECT. CORRECT. NEVER FORGET THAT, MY MOST DEAR FAVORITE PARISHIONER. WITHOUT GOD WE ARE TOTALLY COMPLETELY THOROUGHLY ABSOLUTELY HELPLESS AND NOTHING WE DO CAN HAVE ANY GOOD. ALWAYS ASK HIM FIRST, THEN OBEY HIM. GA.

IM WORRIED NOW. MAYBE IT WAS A MISTAKE TO BUY THAT CHURCH WITHOUT FIRST ASKING GOD HIS PERMISSION GA.

NOT NECESSARILY. DID YOU BUY IT FOR COMMERCIAL PURPOSES Q GA.

COMMERCIAL QQQ WHAT DO YOU MEAN QQQ GA.

I MEAN WERE YOU THINKING OF WHAT THE LORD TOLD ADAM AND EVE, TO GO FORTH, BE FRUITFUL AND MULTIPLY THEIR PROFITS GA.

NO! NEVER! I SAID I BOUGHT FOR YOU. GA. The machine typed so furiously that the Reverend immediately felt ashamed.

GOOD. GOOD. THEN GOD CAN LOOK WITH FAVOR UPON THAT CHURCH. I WILL PRAY WITH GERALDINE AND EVANGELINE AND SEEK GOD HIS WILL AND GUIDANCE, AND LEARN IF HE THINKS I DESERVE SUCH A WONDERFUL CHURCH. THANK YOU MY MOST DEAR SWEET MARY. GA.

THANK YOU FOR YOUR KIND WORDS. NOW FEEL BETTER THAT NO MISTAKE BUYING THE CHURCH. REMEMBER IT IS FOR YOU. BY THE WAY WHERE IS LYSON Q. IS HE UPSET Q GA.

Lyson shooed the Reverend away and began typing: BRILLIANT BRILLIANT OF YOU! DID YOU KNOW THAT THE REV. DOWIE HAS ABOUT 300 MEMBERS HERE Q. THEY WILL VOTE THE WAY HE TELLS THEM—

LYSON! LYSON! L-Y-S-O-N. . . . .

* * *

Lyson wanted to treat them all to dinner but Doctor Fletcher was not fit to go out, it was agreed. And Jewell was loathe to go out: she did not want her awful husband Mer to find her and she did not want the children to see their father with someone who was not their mother. Too much blood and guts, she declared, for such tender youth.

You mean, he's violent? cried Geraldine.

No, Jewell replied with such icy calmness the subject was dropped promptly.

It was then decided to order pizza by telephone. Evangeline was not yet home from work, and would not be for another hour or so. The PIZZA SHACK refused to take orders from children over the telephone. So finally they had to fall back on TTY Referral Service as a roundabout way of placing an order. The TTY service charge was two dollars, explained the Reverend. It used to be free, but Reaganomics. . .

The children were very hyperactive and would not let Doctor Fletcher have any peace. They liked him very much and thought he was cute when he groused and brushed them from their perches on top of him on the hide-a-bed. All three of them, the girl about 7, the boys 5 and 4 or 3, would pick themselves up from the floor and pretend to leave the study. As soon as he closed his eyes, they would dart back and leap upon him.

Jewell wanted to be left alone, strictly alone. The Reverend had too much dignity to have much effect on the children. Geraldine was too frail. So it fell upon Lyson to entice the children away with a game of peek-a-boo through the house and out the back door. There were enough shrubbery and trees in the backyard for a good hide-and-seek. Lyson obliged them for a while, until the girl asked him to help her climb a handsome pine tree, the nearest branch some seven feet above the ground. The boys wanted up too and he was only too happy to see them disappear up the tree, pieces of bark and needles raining down on him. Brushing off his clothes and hair he figured it was a good chance to slip into the house for a drink, perhaps an iced tea if Geraldine didn't mind.

When he entered the kitchen, the Dowies were at the table, visibly distraught, an air of helplessness over their features, wringing their hands.

Wrong? Lyson asked in alarm.

Can't do anything, cried the Reverend. *Spirit maybe strong but flesh true weak.*

Lyson turned to Geraldine staring at the wall in shock. He waved his hand in front of her face and she turned slowly to him *Can't believe. Can't imagine,* her hands signed weakly. *Our own house! C-H-U-R-C-H house, imagine! Can't imagine.* A tear appeared in her eye and Lyson hastened to offer a handkerchief and a squeeze on her shoulder.

Well, well, Reverend Dowie sighed philosophically. *Themselves young, maybe can't help.*

Lyson put two and two together and dashed for the study. Jewell was straddled over Doctor Fletcher's back, giving him a long, luxurious massage. Lyson watched for a few moments, more envious than he ever remembered feeling. The doctor seemed unconscious, although his face had a happy look, as in a pleasant dream of a Turkish harem, Lyson thought ruefully. Jewell stared straight ahead, a faraway look in her eyes. Lyson couldn't see any reason why the Dowies should be so upset: the doctor at least had on his pants, though he was shirtless. He sat on the ottoman and watched, fascinated with the life in her hands. Again he felt a twitch of envy: he hoped the doctor had enough sense, consciousness, to enjoy such magnificent hands. Already his mind was scheming a way to get his turn.

Jewell turned her head his way, though her eyes weren't focused directly on him. She opened her mouth and said, "I feel so sorry for him. He's so confused." Lyson looked down at the doctor who looked peaceful enough. "I want to help him, to take him into my arms," she continued slowly, in what to Lyson's eyes seemed to be sotto voce, "but he's so bad, so wicked."

She frowned for a moment, looking down at the doctor sleeping like a baby under her hands, and turned to Lyson, this time looking directly at him. "No, I shouldn't think he's bad. I don't think he can help himself."

Jewell noticed the bafflement in Lyson's eyes and sighed. "You just don't know him. He's really, really fouled up. I'm afraid there's no help, no hope for him."

Lyson looked with alarm at the doctor. But he looked all right. All right, indeed! He's in heaven!

"Listen!" She was glaring at him. "There's no hope for him! He's thoroughly wild, irresponsible, immature! He'll never, ever, grow up!"

Again the faraway look came over her eyes as she fixed her gaze ahead, and her hands became more vigorous in their work on the limp man. She seethed, "You'll never be a man! You never were and never will be a man!" Her fingers gripped the skin, digging in, and she shook hard. "Never! Never!" The doctor bellowed and flailed his arms in alarm and pain. Lyson thought she was going to rip off the skin and grabbed her wrists.

Jewell started at him, like breaking out of a trance, and looked down. She saw for the first time the doctor's skin pulled up in her hands. She opened her hands and there on the skin ran scratches long and deep, tiny beads of blood welling up like rubies along a necklace. She couldn't believe her eyes. She put a finger tenderly on a big red drop. It collapsed and spread over her finger. She tasted it and found it was real.

"Oh! Poor you, poor you!" she cried and soothed the moaning doctor, running her finger tenderly up and down his back alongside the scratches. "I'm so sorry! So sorry!"

"What happened?", Doctor Fletcher cried in bewilderment.

Not intentional! she signed for the first time. *Dream!*

Dream? the doctor exclaimed, trying to get up. But she held him down and hissed at Lyson, *Hold him! Be back!*

What happened? the doctor demanded of Lyson.

No idea! Lyson confessed. *She herself said yourself very bad, wild, responsibility none—*

Doctor Fletcher was too amazed to reply and slumped back on the divan. Jewell returned quickly with a new disposable diaper and first-aid kit. She was rather agitated and lashed at Lyson. *Go get something drink. Lemonade, tea, coffee, no matter. Get!*

In the kitchen the Dowies were still at the table, slumped in their chairs, sick with worry. Either sensing Lyson's presence, or feeling the footsteps through the floor, Reverend Dowie looked up expectantly.

Have lemonade, you? Lyson asked urgently.

Lemonade? asked the Reverend dumbly.

Everything O.K.? Geraldine inquired hopefully.

Lemonade, pleaded Lyson.

Many? The Reverend went to the refrigerator and found the pitcher.

Two, I think.

Two? Only two?

Lyson shrugged, *Three.*

Good! The Reverend filled three glasses. *Three better than two, you know.* His humor was returning. *Three too-many crowd, you know. Ha-Ha.*

Everything O.K.? Geraldine asked more insistently.

Apparently, Lyson tried to be nonchalant.

Apparently? She was not too convinced.

I think so, he sighed, *but myself puzzled. She accused him, bad, wild, responsibility none.*

Oh! Geraldine broke out in relieved giggles. *You right, everything O.K. now.*

A light blinked in the hall. *Pizza,* announced Reverend Dowie. *Tell them, better come eat.*

Jewell had already covered the wounds with the diaper and was solicitously helping the doctor with his shirt when Lyson returned with the lemonades and the news about the pizza. Confronting him fiercely with grips on the lapel of his coat, she commanded Lyson to keep his mouth shut about what had happened. *Understand?*

He feigned injured feelings. *Me? Always mum, me.*

Good. She looked hard and deep into his eyes and sealed his lips with a fierce kiss. *Remember!* intimidated her eyes.

Lyson nodded weakly and they all went to the kitchen where already on the table two huge pans of pizzas steamed, heaped with bacon, bits of ham, peppers, onions, and black olives. Rev. Dowie urged Lyson toward the front door where the pizza man was impatiently waiting.

Finally they were all seated around the table. The Reverend held up his hands in prayer and looked around, the kindly blinking of his eyes reminding them all to please prepare themselves for prayer. Satisfied, he bowed his own head, closed his eyes, and prayed with flourish: *Lord, our most dear wonderful God up-there, we ask your blessings on this table, our food and fellowship, this house, and all-us here—*

Lyson couldn't help but notice out of the corner of his eye that the doctor and Jewell were sneaking furtive glances at each other. He was confused: there was warmth, even fondness in her glances!

—We beg, beseech you, have mercy on us, on our horrible sins. Crush our flesh, please. Itself so weak, so powerfully weak it overpowers us—

Jewell slapped at something under the table and the doctor jerked his arm back. They laughed with their eyes.

—Look over us, please. May your angels always sit guard over our right shoulders, keep devil away—faraway—

There was some kind of commotion outside that Lyson could see through the fine curtains on the lower half of the window. He couldn't resist raising his head for a better look. Policemen were running all over the yard!

Oh God. Lyson remembered the children and dashed outside, leaving the others in confusion. Police officers surrounded the tree where he could see the children bawling and hanging on for dear life. Quickly with professional efficiency, the police had the children back on the ground, safely in Jewell's arms.

Over the fence, in the next yard, an old man with a mean, sour face was yelling at the officers, pointing straight at a very shamefaced Lyson. The dozen or so officers looked quizzically at Lyson, so that it seemed to him they were wondering whether or not to run him in. Even the children accused him with the terror in their eyes as he tried to apologize to them. One of the officers, in a white helmet and jackboots, with a huge revolver on his belt heavy and bristling with bullets, came up to him and said something, evidently a question by the inquiry in his eyes. Lyson sighed loudly and held up his wrists in resignation, for the handcuffs. The officer looked down at the wrists and back up at Lyson, a flicker of amusement in his grey eyes. He said something again, only slower this time.

Fortunately a young woman came running to his rescue; it was Evangeline, daughter of the Dowies, and a professional Sign Language interpreter too. Her skill got the officers happily on their way, the mean old sourpuss shut up or else get in trouble for disturbing the peace, and Lyson forever in her debt. For reasons of her own, she never explained to Lyson that, really, he was never in any trouble at all.

* * *

Because he was so thoroughly in her debt, Lyson couldn't help but study Evangeline minutely, trying to fathom her, the extent of her hold over him. The Reverend had whispered to him that she was 27 years old and they were worried. For one thing, she was so professional that no man dared want her. And age wasn't helping any. Look at her poor legs! Rather thick, don't you agree? Also, she insisted on dressing in tweed businesswoman's suits even in hot weather, even on weekends. Neckties! Can you imagine? Oh, it's because she's toying with the idea of going to law school, yes to specialize in the law for the deaf, so she wanted to dress the role now. Imagine! We tried our best for her, but it seems we did too well, groaned the Reverend, shaking his head bowed in repentance.

Funny, though, Lyson thought to himself, she seemed to be stealing glances at him and looking quickly away when he tried to catch her eye to express his gratitude. He sighed. Maybe she was afraid he would consider the debt payable in full by a mere word of thanks. There she goes again! She turned her head swiftly from the doctor on the left to her mother on the right. Lyson lifted a finger but was too late, though he'd have sworn her eyes stopped very briefly at him, a tiny sliver of a second, long enough for a look at the dimple, but not to acknowledge his gesture.

Pizza cold! she said to the Reverend, urging a slice on him. Munching on the pizza that now had the texture of rubber and cardboard, Lyson tried to think about the problem. Maybe something was amiss in his appearance. He wanted very much to examine himself in a mirror. But right now Jewell was giving the kids their bath, their second today. He had promised to go to the Dairy Bar and bring them some goodies after their bath: kids naturally need some tangible form of an apology.

He would offer to treat Evangeline to a Dandy Slush too if she would only look at him. Before he realized it, his hand was at his face, picking at and probing his nose, examining it for possible causes for Evangeline's aversion. Looking at her again, he was startled: she was looking straight at his nose. His hand went quickly under the table; her eyes were just as quick off his face.

He felt rather low, poorly. He wished he'd had the foresight to have checked first into a motel before stopping by here. Why, by now he'd be soaking in a tubful of hot bubbly water! Pretending to search for a dropped napkin he ducked under the table to sniff at his armpit. It upset him. No wonder! Now his face was flushed hot and he hesitated: maybe he could just say it was hot under there. He made motions as if groping for the napkin. A foot slid along the floor under his nose and waved. The shoe was a businesswoman's type. The ankle was thickish. Evangeline! Get up, Lyson, red face or no!

He rose too fast and bumped the table. Everyone's eyes were on him as he emerged rubbing the back of his head. He could sense the triumph in Evangeline's eyes as he avoided her. Why, she's trying to sink me!

Hurt? Geraldine was at his side, squeezing his shoulder.

No, no. O.K., he assured her. *Just need wash-face.*

Come, come. She took him to the kitchen sink, apologizing, *Sorry, have only one bath.*

He was in such a hurry to wet his face that he forgot his spectacles. He pretended they needed washing too. His face felt much better, less greasy and less red, though he wished for a mirror. His nose felt a bit itchy, but he wasn't about to touch it again, no, not in public view. For some weird reason he could feel Evangeline's eyes running up and down his back, stopping at his armpits. He kept his arms very close to his body.

At long last the children were out of the bath and it was time to go to the Dairy Bar. But he made the mistake of asking the Reverend for directions in front of Evangeline. He recalled seeing the Dairy Bar on the way to the Dowie house that morning, but wasn't sure he could find it again, now that it was dark.

Evangeline was already at his side. *Know where, can guide.*

Help! Can you help? he blurted out at the doctor who was quick to beg off, *Need bath.*

Geraldine had to wash the dishes. Jewell said Mer cruised the Dairy Bars too. The Reverend needed a quiet moment alone in the study. The children were in their nightclothes. Besides, they were still afraid of him.

Evangeline was triumphant. Lyson felt cornered like a rabbit, but without the courage. He sank to his knees clinging to his stomach and rolled writhing over on his side. *Stomach ache!*

* * *

The ploy worked very well. Perhaps too well, admitted Lyson, but here he was safely bedded on the divan. His conscience did not bother him at all that he had knocked the doctor off to the pad on the floor. In the first place, Doctor Fletcher had been more concerned with himself, being first in the tub, than in helping Lyson with his problem with Evangeline. Tough! Too bad the doctor had to go in Lyson's place with Evangeline. He didn't owe her any debt! Didn't Jewell go along with them after all?

The children were happy with their sundaes, although he suspected they credited them to the doctor, not their true benefactor. No matter, he had his bath. And now the divan. Besides, he did all the driving from Islay, didn't he? And Evangeline got the message, he was certain. Unless she was as dumb as the doctor, or himself, he sighed.

He was happy too that the doctor was a good sport about it all; he even let Lyson in on the secret of the ottoman. Lyson pretended to be sleeping but could not avoid opening his eyes everytime Doctor Fletcher held a shot glass under his nose. Bourbon smells too good to pretend not to smell it.

As long as Jewell and the doctor were there, on the floor with their legs crossed, he was safe. They of course suspected he was only pretending to sleep. Not that he was sneaky. True, it was nice watching Jewell when she thought he was not watching. But, honestly, he wished them all the privacy they wanted. That was the only reason, really, he pretended to be sleeping. Even though, he couldn't resist cracking a lid open. It was just so good watching the rapport developing between them.

No question about it, he'd had it, he confessed happily to himself. Too much bourbon. Too congenial company. But Jewell's hands were too nice to ignore. Such a fine shape. The power of ideas, feelings they could express!

Tried my best, the hands were saying, *thought if myself patient, husband would feel enough, change for better, learn truth about love, not dwell-on flesh—*

Hope myself can, will find that truth, Doctor Fletcher replied, rather morosely thought Lyson. *Only truth I know, that's can't separate woman from body. To be woman, must have body.* Jewell's eyes widened dangerously. The doctor didn't notice as he continued innocently, *No body, no woman.* He gave out a hugh sigh. *Really difficult understand love in relation to medicine—*

Love nothing related medicine! declared Jewell angrily, shaking her head so vigorously her hair flew back and forth. Lyson had to chuckle, if that didn't hit the doctor right in the throbber, then he'd been too long in the lab. *Love itself, most important, most magnificent mystery since history.* Jewell insisted with graceful forceful sweeps of her hands, *Science, medicine, psychology, religion, politics, economics will never find secret. Never find truth! Only heart can, will understand.*

Doctor Fletcher nodded amiably. *Mystery, for sure.* A quick furtive look at the door and the bottle was out of the ottoman. Lyson gave up the pretense of sleep and held out his glass. Jewell turned on him furiously, *Matter you? Never before taste love, you?*

Of-course, nodded Lyson grunting as he drained the new glassful and held out for more. *But love belong woman, her job—*

Jewel was furious. *M!C!P!*

No, not true, Lyson shook his head slowly, sleepily. *Myself prefer women. Think women wonderful, better than men.*

Love best! She was deathly angry, her nose flaring, eyes blazing.

Please, please. Lyson brought up his glass and emptied it. *Understand please, us men busy, busy*—The whiskey was so good: his nose turned numb, his eyelids became very heavy.

* * *

It was dark, very dark. Something very nice, cool was on his forehead. It moved down to his cheek and down around his jaw to the other side and found the dimple. It was gentle, delicate, wonderful. It went over to his ear and lightly played with his ear lobe. Lyson turned his face toward it, the way a dog positions its head under a hand for a better petting, and it caressed his lips. He finally realized it was for real. His eyes opened. Looming over him was a figure soft, almost luminous in the dark.

He tried to get up but the figure held him down by the shoulders. A mouth, the lips full and rich, fell warm and moist upon his eyebrows, eyes, nose, dimple. He struggled against the grip on his shoulders only to be smothered by something warm, exquisitely soft rubbing across his face. It was so tremendously delicate and silky smooth he was rendered weak and helpless. He took the bait and began nibbling.

Suddenly the figure jumped off him. Frantic motions rearranged the blanket over him. It rushed over to the lamp by the divan and the light came on. It was Evangeline. She looked worried, and leaned over, solicitous over him. *You O.K.?* She put a hand on his forehead, *fever?*

The door opened and Reverend Dowie entered, a look of extreme exhaustion over his features. It was clear he had just gotten out of bed: he was still tying his bathrobe over the pajamas.

Lyson seem sick, Evangeline was quick to explain, *Heard cough during night.*

The Reverend looked kindly, tenderly upon Lyson. Lyson coughed. *Excuse me! Can't help!*

Evangeline looked sharply at Lyson, her eyes wide with gratitude. *Myself concerned, come help.*

Sitting on the divan, the Reverend patted Lyson's chest. *Don't worry. You will O.K. We here, help.* To Evangeline, *Have cough medicine?*

Go get, she nodded and was gone.

Feeling Lyson's forehead, Reverend Dowie declared, *Fever. Must rest, you.*

Just little bit, Lyson assured him. *Think smog—*

Smog awful here, agreed the Reverend. *Myself have problem, cough, cough, sometimes, same you.*

Evangeline returned with a bottle and spoon and sat on the opposite side of the divan. *Here!* She filled a spoon and helped it into his mouth. Her hips were soft and warm against his.

Mary will never forgive me, the Reverend told Lyson, *if I don't watch over-you, make sure you O.K., not get pneumonia.*

Daddy! You look tired! Evangeline protested. *Let me watch, care him for you—*

Thank you, thank you, I appreciate that. Reverend Dowie gripped her hand affectionately, bowing his head, his eyes shut in humility. *But Mary most special dear to me. Feel my personal responsibility. My own personal cross, must bear myself.*

But, Daddy! You must sleep! Your health!

My most dear sweet daughter. Tears appeared in his eyes. *You too-much wonderful for old man like me.*

Evangeline glanced hopefully at Lyson, whose terror she read the way she wanted to read. *You can't hear his cough. I can.*

True, true, the Reverend allowed, *but myself have hard time sleeping anyway. Might-as-well me watch, care him. You have-to work tomorrow.*

Worried me! she pleaded.

Go bed, go bed, he urged gently, taking her by the hand to the door. She threw a wistful look over her shoulder at Lyson, and the door shut after her.

Moving slowly, from the years, not just of age but also of responsibility heavy on his bones, the Reverend checked the supine doctor, out cold on the pad on the floor, turned on a smaller lamp on his desk, and turned off the big lamp by the divan, so that the light was softer, more subdued in the room. Reverend Dowie rolled the swivel chair up beside the divan. Yawning widely, he eased himself down on the chair and put his feet on the divan. He and Lyson looked at each other for a long affectionate moment.

Tomorrow, he finally said, *you and me fly there Islay.*

Fly? Lyson was incredulous.

Yes, fly tomorrow, the Reverend nodded with the finality of a man whose mind was made up.

But my car—Lyson tried to protest.

Worry, don't, Reverend Dowie waved carelessly. *Doctor, Jewell can drive. No problem.*

But business here not finished—

God will care for that, believe me, the old minister affirmed slowly, his eyes drooping. *I know, know God will help.*

Lyson was speechless, and kept still. After a while he realized the Reverend was fast asleep, chin on chest. The man looked so old, so careworn that Lyson was touched, ashamed. Slowly, gently he removed one of his blankets and covered the old man's shoulders. He settled himself back in bed careful not to bump the feet still propped on the divan.

And before closing his eyes, he saw the door opening a crack. But it shut quickly before he caught sight of who it was.

CHAPTER 18

The airplane began dropping and terror arose in Lyson. He could feel the ball of fear, heavy in his stomach, growing rapidly, sucking at the vitality of his body so that his limbs became weak and his mouth dry. No more would they be high above the world, a pie in the sky remote from affairs of man upon the ground. Very soon they would be discharged from the rarified atmosphere of the airplane onto the tumult of the street, the travail of life. It had been a good trip, he thought regretfully. But now Mary was certain to have questions. He was not certain he knew how to answer them.

He did not know how he should call that which he encountered in Palms Galore, in the Dowie's house, on the divan just the night before. Of course he knew the name for it but was ashamed to name it, because to name it would make it true. Hey, he never even got to see it. The only thing he could really say about it was that it was nice and soft and smooth. Yes, that's what it was, really. He shall henceforth refer to it as Something Nice and Soft and Smooth.

The ball of fear robbed his body of its heat and he shivered. Gotta confess, he cried to himself, and get rid of that ball. Then he could be comfortable about that Something Nice and Soft and Smooth. He even could be smug about it. The Reverend was right beside him, happy in a nap. Lyson tugged him awake. *Want confess!*

Confess? The Reverend blinked around to reorient himself, and stretched.

Yes, must confess.

Excuse, sleepy, Reverend Dowie rubbed the sleep out of his eyes behind his glasses and noted the seat belt light. *Finally, landing. Excited me see Mary and new Church.*

Yes! Church! Lyson nodded vigorously, anxious to get started on necessary business. *Want confess now, before landing.*

Confess? Reverend Dowie was at first puzzled but then a light came to his eyes. *You mean confessional, similar church?* he said at last.

Lyson nodded impatiently. *Ready now, me. Hurry! Landing!*

With troubled regret the Reverend demurred, *Can't! Very sorry, but can't.* He squeezed Lyson by the hand. *Not my job, that God up-there His job.*

Lyson was crestfallen, so much that Reverend Dowie felt bad and suggested, *Why not we pray silently, secret to God up-there. You can give him your heart, confess, and He up-there will clean-it, give-back.* Immediately his head dropped, his eyes shut, lips quivering.

God, don't anglophiles realize the power, the beauty of the confessional? Lyson wailed to himself deep inside the ball of fear, anxious to be rid, free of it.

* * *

Mary met the airplane at Fremont and Lyson hoped she did not notice the ball of fear huge in his stomach. But the Reverend got to her first and they hugged and kissed and exchanged greetings and news while Lyson stood aside, the ball of fear inside him heavy as a rock. Surely gossip about that Something Nice and Soft and Smooth must have already hit Islay, or else why would Mary ignore him? Another thought squeezed the ball ever tighter that maybe now people were whispering, *Imagine Lyson climb tree! There Obeke! With Woman!*

Behind Mary were the Qualeys who seemed so glad to see him that he felt a sense of relief. Here were some people he knew would never hold that Something Nice and Soft and Smooth against him, not even the tree in Obeke. "Welcome home, Lyson! Good to have you back with us."

"Yes."

"How was the trip?

"Wonderful."

"You must be glad to be back home."

"Yes."

"Lyson! You're bashful!" laughed Beatrice.

"Embarrassed," he tried to giggle it away. "Forgot many things—my toothbrush, the TTY, the car—"

"Not the car!" Beatrice teased, and rolled her eyes, "Lyson, you'd never believe it, you'd never recognize Islay now."

"Thousands here already," the Captain added. "Andy is going crazy, can't keep up. Barrels of money, haven't the time to count yet."

A kiss was warm and moist on his cheek. It was Mary. He leaned to return the kiss but she recoiled. *Your breath!*

Sorry. Forgot toothbrush. His face reddened and the ball of fear manifested itself again. The Something Nice and Soft and Smooth hadn't yet been washed from his face this morning; he thought he could still taste it. Maybe Mary can smell it as well.

"Here!" Beatrice slipped a Tic Tac in his mouth.

Lyson, Mary narrowed her eyes in mock suspicion. *Good, you?*

After a long uneasy moment he shook his head so slowly and shamefacedly that Reverend Dowie was quick to explain, *He imagine himself not finish his job there California, but told him, don't worry, God up there will care. Himself feel bad, want confess—*

Lyson winced so openly that Mary turned sharply to him. Her eyes were so wide that he was quick to explain, *Many people I want meet, talk about Islay—*

Rumors already all-over USA, she marvelled, rolling her eyes. *Everyone now know—*

Lyson was frightened and nearly said, That Something Nice and Soft and Smooth, but caught himself. *About what?* he asked innocently.

About you!

Me? Tears began in his eyes and he dropped his hands.

Matter, you? Mary demanded. *Hordes here already! Deaf all-over USA know already. Thousands, thousands, moving here!* She put emphasis behind her signs by gesturing countless hordes of lemmings scurrying toward a common objective.

Lyson was stunned. Not only was he off the hook for the moment, but Mary's body language brought home to his senses the full enormity, the whole panorama, the overwhelming mass, of what she had been trying to tell him over the TTY. It was way ahead of his wildest dreams. It was scary on top of his confusion about the need for a confessional about that Something Nice and Soft and Smooth. He was almost afraid to go to Islay himself now.

And some new deaf bigheaded, try establish leadership, she suddenly snipped. *You know Gene Owles? Himself already establish club, plan newspaper—*

Me here first! He was indignant and afraid at the same time. *Unfair!*

Must home now! Mary grabbed his elbow. *Busy, work!*

* * *

The Sports and Recreation Mall had gone so fast that his sense of time was thrown off. Why, it was only a short while ago when all this was wilderness. The bowling alley and the theater roofs were up already and other walls were rising everywhere for the other shops and restaurants. It was much bigger than he ever envisioned in his mind. Even the plans hadn't looked so large.

Whenever deaf show-up, buy house, give job, Wally explained. *That why so-fast. And Beatrice fast work get permits, loans. Wink eyes, pull, bamboozle, that why easy get permits, her. Thank her!*

Cranes, forklifts, bulldozers, cement mixers, trucks were everywhere raising dust, not one idle. Piles of lumber, bricks, gravel, dirt, steel, other building supplies. Heavily muscled workmen. Surveyors. Bricklayers, cement finishers, iron workers, carpenters, plumbers, plasterers, wiry electricians, superintendents in bright yellow hard hats. Even hot dog and refreshment stands, some manned by enterprising little children, for the construction project was the biggest show in Suffex right now and did not lack for sidewalk superintendents and rubbernecks drawn from sleepy Suffex by the commotion and dust.

Working on the walls beside the theater was a familiar figure. Lyson and Wally went on over and found it was Dottie. She had on a hard hat and a carpenter's belt, and was helping build her own new coffee shop. Darcy was with her too, very proud of himself, his mother, their hands, their shop.

"Hi Dottie!" Lyson cried. "What a surprise!"

She hugged him warmly and looked up at him with a sly grin and a tease in her eye. "Well, now what!" Lyson giggled. "Something up your sleeve, eh?"

Dottie laughed, "How apt! Watch!" With florid theatrics she rolled up her sleeves, rubbed her hands, flexed and wiggled her fingers, and began signing. *Myself can sign similar deaf. Surprise you see sign?* With that she hid her hands away behind the front of her overalls and threw up her eyebrows the way a magician does when a rabbit disappears in his hat.

Lyson stared on at where her hands had disappeared and would've continued this unseemly staring had not Darcy got in on the act too. *Myself can sign too, better than mom. Faster than speed of light.*

It took an act of Wally to get Lyson back together: a forklift was approaching with a load of sheetrock for the shop, and Wally had to pull Lyson stumbling out of the way. The kid operating the forklift needed help, and Lyson and Wally steadied the load as it was deposited and the forks pulled out from under.

Thank you, your help, Dottie signed with a grace that was so pleasing it was astonishing.

Good signing you, Lyson heartily complimented her. *Where learn, you?*

She shrugged, pointing around at the other workers around the construction site. *Just watch everyday and pick up little by little everyday, have-to use.*

It dawned on Lyson that physical work breeds a physical way of doing things. The signs wrought by construction workers are large, robust, three dimensional, very alive. A sharp contrast to signs usually seen among white collar workers: signs that portray ideas behind words rather than the physical world of words. One worker in particular, up on the rafters, shirtless with a muscular tanned sweaty back, was signing down to someone on the ground. His back muscles rippled and jumped along with his signing, so that you could sense raw power in his signs. Lyson felt his ears growing warm: he was conscious of how effete his own signing must seem by comparison with such a splendid specimen of the male species. He well remembered the awful struggles of his friends at the old office in Washington with even the simplest, most rudimentary signs. Why even the basic signs *go* and *come, sit* and *stand, up* and *down* were difficult for some office workers, so sedentary was their life at the office. Not that ideas and abstracts were that difficult to sign. Just that people need to learn the three dimensions first. He became very excited with this new discovery and hugged Dottie and Darcy. *Magnificent! Myself very proud yourself learn yourself.*

Myself surprised too, Dottie signed robustly. *Just sudden happen while watching workers while working—*

Signing FUN too, Darcy's hands leaped.

Tears welled so dramatically in Lyson's eyes that Wally and Dottie agreed it was best to get him in the car, quickly before any hard-boiled construction worker saw and became ashamed of the future Governor. Remember Muskie!

* * *

ISLAY BOOM FLIES IN DEFIANCE OF REAGANOMICS

A veritable building boom, visible to practically everyone who lifts his head up from the gloomy economic pages, is exploding right here in our Islay, in the southern environs of Suffex along Interstate 297. A tremendous new mall is sprouting along nearly half of the industrial belt just south of I-297. Out-of-state industries have been buying up all the rest of the properties zoned industrial. One in particular, Islay Company, is believed to be the principal force behind this resurgence in the fortunes of Islay.

No one in authority appears to have any idea of the reasons behind this strange boom in the middle of the Reagan Depression. The Chamber of Commerce said it was happening all so fast they don't yet have the statistics they need to explain the activity. Mayor Dada said he'd never seen the likes of it since the end of the big war. Beatrice Qualley of the Islay Department of Commerce would only say that business is boomin', boomin'. Governor Slappy Wenchell was furious he hadn't been told and promised to send over a man as soon as he returns from an urgent investigation of a Federal agent posturing as a deaf mute who suddenly disappeared a while ago.

Your reporter went out to interview people directly responsible for this new economic activity but has not yet been able to find the proper officers of Islay Company. The workers appear to be Deaf mutes. They refuse to speak to this reporter but communicate with each other by means of dexterous gestures too swift for mortal eyes.

Your newspaper, the *Islay Itemizer,* believes something big is afoot and will endeavor to utilize all its resources and investigative capabilities to get to the root of the matter. Publisher Bob Honeser divines that something sinister must be behind all this activity. How else can we explain the employment of an entire work force either unable or unwilling to speak with reporters? The *Islay Itemizer* promises to ferret out the truth of this matter and present a more comprehensive story next week.

* * *

You would have never known anything was different about them as they entered H-Street Elementary School. Just a mother bringing in two children new to the area to register early for the autumn. Oh, it was noticeable that they were very quiet and standoffish. Actually a most becoming shyness, thought the principal.

They had wisely come, too, for the school offices were just starting up after the summer slumber for the new year. Still a month yet, but the principal liked it when the parents thought enough to come early. Children of such parents do best in school, that was his experience.

"Welcome to H Street School!" the principal graciously greeted the mother on her way to the registration table.

Then she did something astonishing: she squeezed her children's shoulders, pointed at a pile of children's books scattered on a low table surrounded by lounge chairs, and made gestures that the children obviously understood instantly: not only did their eyes register cognition but also old familiarity. The principal stared at the children picking out some books and setting themselves down, sprawled as are wont children, in chairs. He turned to the mother with his mouth open and saw that she was looking patiently up at him, waiting for him to get his arithmetic in order, to get two and two together and get down to the business for which she had come. There was something about her eyes, their alertness, the expectancy clear in them, that fascinated him so much that he noted also that they had many colors, graduating from grey in the very center to hazel speckled with brown diamonds along the rim of the iris. They were eyes that commanded respect and he was quick to seat her at the table and to slide the registration form up at a convenient and comfortable position in front of her. He was about to place a pencil on the forms but caught himself. He looked very thoughtfully at her and at the children and again at her. Finally, he said something to which she replied with a frown and a shake of the head.

She took the pencil from him and began turning over the papers on the table until she found a blank piece. "We are deaf," she wrote. "Let's communicate on paper, please."

It took the principal quite a few moments to rearrange his mind to this new way of dealing with a parent, so long in fact that her patience was tried. He looked up and saw that she was waiting. "Excuse me!" was what she could recognize on his lips but the rest she could not catch so she pointed at the pencil and paper with a suggestion in her raised eyebrows.

"Are the children deaf?" he finally wrote.

Of course! said her impatient nod.

"You should take them to the Institute for Communicative Disorders in Crewe," he was writing when he noticed the look of distaste on her face. He quickly added, "That is where all deaf children of Islay go to school."

"No way!" she wrote vigorously. "I'm enrolling my kids here, near our home."

"Impossible," he began, but she shook her head resolutely. "This school does not have any facilities for the deaf." She lifted her brow at this so he explained, "We do not have any auditory devices—"

The mother slipped the pencil out of his hand even while he was still writing and wrote with a firm hand: "Those things are for the hearing impaired. My children are deaf."

"We do not have anyone here who knows how to teach the deaf."

"My kids are still coming to this school," she insisted. "You'll have to hire somebody who can teach them."

"We are sorry," he was becoming exasperated. "We cannot take your children. You must take them to Crewe where the teachers are."

"You must accept them." she wrote firmly, and tossed over a booklet titled *Public Law 94-142 and the Deaf Child.* "Federal Law, you have no choice."

The principal stared at the booklet. It was evident he had never heard of such a law. He was going to write his reply when two other women entered with more children. And the air was filled with gestures and signs as the women all greeted each other and began a discussion that even he could see concerned him and the school. He had a sinking sensation that they were taking command and that he was becoming the outsider, even in his own school.

* * *

Governor Slappy Wenchell was sitting upright in his rocker, stiff with displeasure. He did not like to be bothered. He believed in the Eisenhower System, where problems were the direct responsibility of the department heads, freeing the chief of state to enjoy the pleasures of the top job. When a petty complaint managed to break through and involve him directly and personally, he did not like it one bit. "What the hell do they think I know about them deaf and dumb!"

The man responsible for this latest disturbance was stopped on his way up the steps, so that he had to stand in the sun, just below the porch, inches away from tantalizing shade. Doctor Hermann Masserbatt, the Superintendent of the Institute for Communicative Disorders, was dressed for the kind of environment he was accustomed to operating—in air conditioning. A few seconds in the August sun was enough to render his elegant shiny blue suit dumpy and sweat drenched. Even his neck tie was rapidly losing its lustre.

With grim satisfaction the Governor watched the superintendent wilting like a flower cut off from its roots and remarked dryly, "I presume you know why you're here?"

The sun heavy, oppressive on his brow knitted in desperation, Doctor Masserbatt confessed, "I've been away all summer, to all those meetings, conferences, conventions, workshops, you know, to keep up with all those advances in the service to the deaf and the hearing impaired—"

"Hearing impaired—what's that?" the Governor said under his breath, making a face that the superintendent, half-blinded by the sun and the salty sweat running into his eyes, couldn't see. "Hearing that is impaired—" the superintendent began.

"That's better," the Governor cracked sardonically. "Watch your grammar."

"All this travel, you know. St. Louis, Boston, Portland, Los Angeles, Washington—"

"D.C., eh?" The Governor narrowed his eyes, which the superintendent missed.

"Oh yes, sir. A very important meeting—"

"Federal, eh?" Governor Wenchell and B-52 exchanged quick glances. "Should I assume you spent State money—"

"Oh no, sir!" Doctor Masserbatt shook his head too defensively, scattering drops of sweat in the bright sun. Governor Wenchell smiled. He was beginning to enjoy this very much. "It was Federal money—don't ask how it got out from under Reagan's nose, but the Feds paid for all those meetings, travels—"

"Jelly beans!" the Governor remarked wonderingly to B-52. "Why do you suppose they would do that?"

"Beats me!" B-52 whirled a finger around his ear. "Thought Reggie wanted out of the Fed business."

"And furthermore—" Governor Wenchell was speaking to B-52, but his eyes worked over the sweltering Doctor Masserbatt with the same relish a cook would baste a roasting goose. "—I thought it was understood that contacts with the Feds were to be kept to an absolute minimum—"

"Absolutely yes! Absolutely yes!" cried Doctor Masserbatt who was beginning to sway dizzily in the heat. "But we can't allow the Islay Institute for Communicative Disorders to become obsolete! Gotta keep abreast—"

"Is that a Federal outfit?" snapped the Governor.

"What—what do you mean, Federal?"

"That big name—Institute of Commune, communist—whatever you spell it, it's too Federal sounding for my taste! Where'd you get that fancy name, anyway?" Snappy Wenchell winked at B-52. Is this getting to be fun!

Doctor Masserbatt was on the verge of a sunstroke, wavering, unsteady on his feet. B-52 was quick to catch him before he fell over. B-52 cocked an eyebrow at the Governor, who gave a short nod. Let's keep this game going: not much fun to be had with a comatose heap anyway. The superintendent was helped up the steps out of the sun into the welcome shade. As he was eased down on the top step of the porch, he cried out in a quavery voice. "Thank you! Your excellency, thank you!" His face was soaked and flushed, and he searched his pockets for a handkerchief. At a wink from the Governor, B-52 went and fetched a frosty glass of mint julep for the Governor, and a plain glass of water and a paper towel for the superintendent.

"Thank you! Thank you!" Doctor Masserbatt dampened the towel and wiped his face. "That sun is a killer!"

"Don't mind if it does," Governor Wenchell shrugged. "Experts on the deaf and dumb are a dime a dozen."

Doctor Masserbatt pretended he did not hear, and drained his glass on one swing. He screwed up his mouth. The water was lukewarm and, he thought, a bit salty. Must be to replace the salt lost through sweat, he decided to magnanimously think, and said, "You're so thoughtful, your excellency!"

"You're most welcome," the Governor nodded grandly. And then innocently, "Just what were all those meetings about?"

"Oh, the various aspects of deafness." The superintendent was happy to get back to his area of expertise. "Sociology, psychology, medical, rehabilitation, physical therapy—you know, there is an investigation into the possibility of restoring hearing through vigorous rubbing of the ears—very possible in 3.2 percent of cases—but mostly they were about new fads—I mean, trends in Special Education for the deaf. Speech, hearing aids, auditological equipment, that sort of thing that helps improve the service of the deaf and the hearing imp—ah, uh—that is impaired."

The Governor nodded slowly, sipping his julep, as if earnestly mulling over those words, and grunted, "Didn't know that deafness was that complicated. Thought they just wiggle their fingers and make funny faces—"

"Not here on Islay!" declared Doctor Masserbatt, his finger straight up in the air. "We have the finest, most advanced educational system for the deaf and the hearing—that is impaired. There is absolutely no reason other than mental deficiency why a deaf person couldn't learn to speak properly and to read lips!"

"That so?" Governor Wenchell shook his head in disbelief. "How so?"

"First of all," cried the superintendent enthusiastically, "You get a hearing aid powerful enough to overpower the deafness, and the rest comes easy. Absolutely, totally no reason why a deaf person should have to use sign language!"

"Is that what is called the things they do with their fingers?"

"Oh yeah! A stupid way of communication if you ask me. A disorder! The single most important reason why as soon as the deaf learn sign language, their English is ruined! This has always exasperated educators of the deaf over the last hundred years. All over the world, millions upon millions of people, some of them even primitive savages in the jungle, use English naturally, easily as a matter of course. Everybody but the deaf! It's that blasted sign language!"

The Governor coughed politely. "Never could understand, exactly what's a hearing aid? Isn't that kinda like putting eyeglasses on the blind—"

"Easy!" cried the superintendent, agitating his hands. "You know how a magnifying glass gathers the sun's rays and focuses them into an intense beam. The blind can feel that hot beam and know the sun's shining. The same way with hearing aids! If you make them powerful enough, the deaf can feel the sound waves vibrating inside their skulls. Believe me, there's absolutely no reason why the deaf can't use hearing aids!"

"Funny, most of them deaf and dumb I've seen lately don't wear hearing aids. How come?"

"Stubbornness!" huffed Doctor Masserbatt. "The deaf are just about the most intractable people you'll ever encounter!"

"I see, I see," mused Governor Wenchell, leaning back in his rocker. He sipped his mint julep thoughtfully and asked, "Now, how is it that all of sudden Suffex is crawling with them deaf and dumb?"

The superintendent wasn't certain he heard the Governor correctly and was suddenly conscious of his position on the top step of the porch. "What do you mean?"

"Just look around," the Governor waved his hand and returned to his julep.

Everywhere visible from the porch of the Governor's Mansion were people, on the sidewalks, in automobiles passing by on the streets, in the park, under the trees, picnicking at the tables, people that were talking with each other by means of manual dexterity. Even the smallest child used his hands with his parents. In the Bandstand was some kind of pantomime show that elicited much laughter and applause from the crowd in the park. The color drained from Doctor Masserbatt's face. He did not look at all well. "Outrageous! How'd all this happen!"

"Right under your nose," commented the Governor with a touch of irony.

"Impossible!" screeched the superintendent. "Not in Islay!"

"Theoretically, I presume." Governor Wenchell and B-52 exchanged wry glances.

"Where'd they come from?" Doctor Masserbatt demanded of the air in front of himself. "We never had this many deaf and hearing—ah -uh, impert—uh! impertinent!"

"That question is your department." Governor Wenchell yawned decorously. "You're the expert."

"Don't blame me!" cried the superintendent. "I had to go to those meetings!"

"And left the store wide open, didn't you?" roared the Governor.

"And they refuse to let their kids go to your school," chimed in B-52 tauntingly.

"Listen!" seethed Doctor Masserbatt with ice glinting in his eyes. "Don't worry! We got an ace behind our ear!"

Governor Wenchell remained skeptically silent, sipping his julep. B-52 spoke for him, "Call it."

"There's a law in Islay," Doctor Masserbatt chortled. "It's illegal to use sign language in Islay!"

The Governor looked sharply at B-52 who shrugged that he never heard of such a law either.

"It's in there somewhere," insisted the superintendent, "Some big numbers like Code 73, Section 504—like that—"

"The year 1973, must be," mused the Governor.

"Absolutely! Absolutely!" clapped the superintendent.

The Governor looked up at B-52 and shook his head uncertainly. "Must be getting old, me. Can't recall signing any such thing—" B-52 made a face it was all new to him too.

"I'll look it up!" Doctor Masserbatt rose in triumph. "I'll send you a copy and show you!"

His brow furrowed dubiously, the Governor remarked, "If that's the law, it's your department."

"Right! I'll enforce it to my utmost!" The superintendent dropped to his knees and made a motion to grab the Governor's hand to kiss it, his pucker out.

"Don't," bellowed B-52 like a bull and picked up Doctor Masserbatt bodily and set him back on his feet. "Illegal to touch the Governor!"

"Oh sorry! Didn't know—"

"Never mind! You better get going and start enforcing your law!" growled B-52.

"No fear! I will! You can count on me to defend to the utmost the integrity of the Great State of Islay, our beloved English heritage, and our great Governor!" Doctor Masserbatt hurried down the steps and walkway toward his car at the curb. Passing by on the sidewalk was a couple engaged in animated conversation, their hands alive with expression. Indignantly, Doctor Masserbatt grabbed their wrists and forced their hands down. He said something, a rebuke by the set of his face, wagging his finger and pointing toward the Mansion. A sharp nod, a hiss, and he got in his car and was gone.

The couple stared after him in amazement and at each other and at the Mansion.

Slappy Wenchell sank deeper into his rocker, his ears furiously hot.

"A-hem," began B-52 looking down at his toes.

"Sha-at up!"

* * *

Lyson wanted a moment alone with Mary, so that he could prostate himself at her feet, make his confession, and perform the act of obeisance so necessary to restore his self-esteem. He couldn't get that Something

Nice and Soft and Smooth out of his system. And there is this matter of the tree in Obeke. Must confess!

But Reverend Dowie was there. So were the Quayles, the Tupers, Dottie and Darcy Smida, Crystal and Trent, and the Ballingers. Even Professor Donald Vought had come from Gallaudet. Doctor James Shooner: *You'd be surprised, even hearing come me for psychiatrist help.* Byron Windecker was tickled pink with his new factory, already roofed. And Gene Owles! In lovely blue surrounded by half the women in the party, explaining his plans to establish a newspaper and television station, you know the deaf must have a leading voice, and we deaf must cooperate and shove the hearing off! Everytime a woman looked at him, her eye brightened with admiration of the sort almost always reserved for pop stars and men of such disrepute as to be beyond all reproach, any redemption; remorseless and self-possessed, such men sleep well and peacefully the sleep of the innocent even after performing the most dastardly acts known to mankind, and live on to a ripe old age, their badness unabated to the very end. So unburdened by guilt are such men that even the Devil himself must quail at the thought of receiving such men to be administered their just and everlasting punishment. Such men also have the sort of luck that will find their souls their way to the Pearly Gate. "Aren't you guys supposed to go to hell?" St. Peter would rebuke them.

"Yeah, we tried but the Devil wouldn't let us in."

"Blast! St. Lucifer has never been the one to keep his end of the bargain," St. Peter would grumble. "We'll have to let you in, I suppose, but just for a little while. Remember, just a little while until we see the Lord about this."

Once in, it'll be the very devil to get them out again.

That sort of luck.

Lyson blanched at this invasion of his turf and looked desperately around the ballroom to see if by chance his old friend Robert Altman of DEAF magazine might not be present. Must talk to him! A hand fell on Lyson's shoulder. It was Lester Lieseke. *Hello! How your trip?* He winked naughtily, as if sharing a secret joke.

Crazy! Lyson's finger jumped to his ear and just as quickly fled down. Think before you sign! he scolded himself and bit his lower lip.

Know what you mean, chuckled Lester. *Myself long-ago travel for business. Meet many people all kinds. Interesting! Different, different experiences. Love America, travel, myself.*

Lyson smelled something and his nose sniffed the air: it was a familiar smell and he tried to identify it. The tobacco smoke in the ballroom was strong; yet he could still smell the scent. Coconut oil. The tree of Obeke! Sandy! She was right behind him, standing shyly with her feet primly together, her hands behind her back, her eyes laughing mischieviously. Lyson's knees nearly buckled but Lester and Sandy caught him. She looked even more wonderful, more golden, more glowing in a pleasing orange dress cut simply so that its folds and creases were natural, where they belonged. He became even more dizzy and gave his head a vigorous shake. Sandy was very pleased and giggled.

Good taste, women, you! Lester jostled him playfully. *Introduce!*

Mary came quickly. *Lyson! Your face pale! Sick you?* She put her hands on his cheek and forehead. *Cold!* She dragged him speedily through the party to the kitchen.

Must tea you. With anxious hands she fixed him orange spice tea. *Too-much travel, travel you. Not realize me, forgive me.*

He saw that, now that they were alone, here was an opportunity to rid himself of that ball in his stomach. *Mary! I must tell you—*

I know. she scolded, pushing his hands down. *My fault, forgot about jet lag—*

Not that, he managed to pull a hand free. *Something else must tell—*

Mary caught his hand. *Not now. Must rest, you. Tired, pale you. Your eyes red, cockeyed.*

Reverend Dowie burst in. *Someone there door, said important business—*

Can't! Mary stamped her foot. *Must rest. Look!*

You're right, the Reverend had to agree, squinting at Lyson's face. *Pale.*

Lyson mimed cigarette smoking. *Makes me sick, dizzy—*

Drink! Mary urged the tea on him. It made him feel immediately better. Already he could feel the color returning slowly to his cheeks. Impulsively he stood up. *Outside, me.*

Mary tried to dissuade him but he surprised her with a kiss on the lips, so passionate she sat down in confusion.

Lyson went to the door. Outside on the porch under the soft yellow light was a woman, very thin, so thin she clung tightly to a shawl around her shoulders despite the warmth of the summer evening. In the dim light her eyes shone, intense as beacons. He froze like a deer stunned by a spotlamp.

You Lyson Sulla? She stepped up, leaning closer to him in an attitude not unlike a cobra about to hypnotize a mongoose. Lyson stared at her eyes in a fixation. They seemed to float in the air in front of him, unsupported and disembodied.

The eyes moved closer, and the face became more visible. *You Lyson Sulla?* she repeated more in anticipation than inquisition.

Lyson nodded slowly, his eyes glassy under the spell.

You Governor? she queried again.

Lyson gulped and shook his head slowly.

Deaf all-around told me, she leaned closer, *said yourself Governor here state Islay.*

His mouth dropping, his eyes blank, he shook his head. *Deaf say that?*

Funny! the woman tilted her head. *Everyone said Islay now belong deaf and yourself Governor. That why myself come, want establish business.* Out of her purse she extracted a business card. He read it slowly, as if for the first time, and finally snapped out of his stupor. It was his own calling card, the Islay Company. *Where get?*

There Wyoming. She handed him another card. It looked faintly familiar, like the one he recalled receiving somewhere in Wyoming. She continued, *My company name:* Deaf of America. *We distribute sign language educational matter. Want establish printery here, make many different different things for sell, about sign language, fingerspelling—*

Wonderful! Lyson pumped his palms in the air. *All deaf companies welcome, establish here. Can help-you buy, or build for your printery. Come tomorrow, can you? Then we can show you, look for establish—*

Good! Will here tomorrow, the woman clapped happily. Out of the darkness and up the stairs floated a ghostlike figure, a frail little girl.

Mama, Daddy waiting! pleaded the child, her eyes bent with fatigue.

O.K.! See you tomorrow, said the woman, who then with the child disappeared into the darkness. Lyson stared after them. The girl looked vaguely familiar, and he tried to place her. He again looked at the card in his hand, and saw the drawings of the fingerspelling. Now I remember! Somewhere there Wyoming! He looked up and saw them entering a dark van that immediately drove away.

Another figure lurking in the darkness caught his eye. It was a large man in black, only his hands and face visible in the night. The man ran up into the circle of light and pointed at him and triumphed. *Saw! Caught you! Peddler!* The figure came up closer and Lyson saw it was Tin.

Peddler! Tell King! Tell King! Tin ran whooping to his car and sped off into the night. Probably back to Obeke, thought Lyson incredulously. Just then another face floated up out of the dark and mesmerized him. It was working its mouth, saying something like "Tell Governor! Tell Governor!" As it flitted off into the night, the recognition hit Lyson that it was P-51.

This is too much! Too much! Insane! He turned to the door of his castle and realized he was loathe to go in just yet. He could feel his face taut with horror, the wideness of his eyes as the ball of fear stirred in his vitals. Can't let anyone see me in this state! He walked rapidly away from the castle, lest someone suddenly come out and see him. Almost instinctively he turned toward the park, the Bandstand. Ah, the Bandstand. Just the place!

He hurried his feet down the sidewalk like a man escaping from a nightmare. Must not run! Running would only attract new nightmares, he had enough presence of mind to caution himself, he congratulated himself. The night was wonderful, the street lights enveloped by foliage of the trees along Central Promenade so that the light came down soft, subdued, transparent, yet with substance, almost like walking under water.

The Bandstand came into view, its roof silvery in the night. His heart quickened and his steps picked up. Emerging from under the trees of Central Promenade he crossed the open space of Tenth Street, quiet and solitary at this hour; so open was it that it did not at all seem in the night like a street but a void to be crossed into the trees on the other side. In this open space a breeze brushed his cheeks, soft and refreshing. The conical roof loomed above gaps in the trees, floating in the night, ethereal, arresting. Then sharp and unworldly in the flashes of lightning.

Climbing up the stairs the nightmare shed away as he disappeared into the darkness under the roof, into a refuge where he could dream his dream, as happily as he dared. He fell down and prostrated himself spread-eagled on the clay and started at its faint odor of ammonia. Quickly before it overwhelmed him, he gave out his confession. If this be only a dream, he thought aloud to himself, let it at least be pleasant. When I wake up, he begged, let this ball be gone from my guts, and do let the dream be good and true, please. Everyone is saying I'm the Governor. If that be only a dream, do let it be good.

Thunder resounded under the roof so that he felt the booming sharply all over his body. Sparkling in the lights from the streets, water was pouring in torrents down from the eaves of the roof, a solid rippling mass. The very air was pungent, electric with the fresh scent of a summer rain, washing away the aura of ammonia from the clay so that he rejoiced in its sweetness, its vibrancy. The unearthly sensation of being surrounded, isolated by vibrant cleansing water, like in a cave behind a waterfall, heartened Lyson very much. He would have been content to have remained there, in that dreamy never-never land forever. At least that much was true, real, he knew.

PART III

CYMBALS

The truest lesson . . . resided not in intellectual fact but in spectacle . . .

—William Kennedy

CHAPTER 19

It took some doing, and the help of some friends including a carpenter skilled with compass and saw, but they finally got the big table, the one with the map of Islay and rivers painted on it, up on the roof and into the top room in the turret. The table had to be recut and two legs relocated to fit snug against the inside curving wall of the turret. But it was well worth all that fuss and dust. The table fit perfectly so that the map pointed true north out the arched window directly toward the Merry Bandstand. Of course because of the trees only the lantern could be seen, but for Lyson this somehow had the effect of drama, more so at night when the lantern glowed mysteriously from city lights all a round. And because the walls were very thick, the sill was deep. Just the right spot for the model of the Bandstand. It looked really pretty; belonged exactly there in the shadow, so to speak, of the real Merry Bandstand.

Lyson was very delighted with his office. No longer need he be ashamed of the model. He was free to put it on display for all the world to see. He was so tickled he bit his knuckles.

Fist on hip, he surveyed the office with the air of a proprietor, as was his wont every morning ever since the move from Washington last year. The desk was directly across from the table, against the other window facing south. Thanks to the ideas he'd picked up from Silent Electronics in California, the deep arched recess of the little window had been turned into a mini-greenhouse and filled with a profusion of tiny flowers and plants so that the sun filtered through soft and pleasant. Every morning seemed new, everything new anew because of this, and a sense of timelessness permeated the office. Lyson was very happy.

The desk of course had to be recut in the back so that it fit flush against the wall under the window. He used to have to crawl on all fours across the desk in order to be able to water his little plants. Not anymore. Beatrice had found him a neat brass sprinkler with a slender spout some two feet long. Watering the little plants the first thing every morning brought him an inordinate sense of pleasure and well-being—now he knew why the movies often depicted the mighty captains of industry, particularly the immensely successful ones Hollywood wished to have seen in a favorable, lovable light, performing a similar trifling little chore with plants around the office. To show they've not lost touch, are still people. Such as what he was doing now, Lyson thought contentedly as he gave each plant its morning drink. He didn't know a daisy from a kalanchoe; they were all lovely to him. In particular, though, he liked those tiny blue flowers that looked like exquisitely tiny musical bells. Also, the star-shaped blue ones no bigger than an asterisk. Must ask Beatrice their names, he hummed to himself. Would be interesting to know, wouldn't it?

Just like the movies, he thought irritably when the telephone rang, triggering a flashing lamp by the telephone in a dark corner. Resolutely he ignored it and gave each plant his affection. It's lackeys that jump at telephones, he said to the little flowers. The lamp was insistent and irritated the tail of his eye with its unpleasant blasts of glare. With the stiff upper lip he'd often seen and admired at the movies, he unscrewed the bulb a bit and returned to the plants.

At the third window, the one facing east, full in the morning sun was a tiny tree, a fully grown pine, some kind of Japanese bonsai. This dwarf tree was really something, a gift from Beatrice and the Captain, and looked exactly like those trees in Japanese paintings with long contorted branches artfully scattering dense green tufts of leaves. It was very old, the salesman had said, older than Islay itself, older perhaps than the United States. Lyson smiled with affection at Beatrice's taste and eye, for the tree filled the recess exactly right, not touching the walls or intruding into the room, nor entirely blocking the view of the street down below.

Something down on the street disrupted his communion with the bonsai and he squinted for a better focus. Mary was down there waving frantically in a great arc over her head. Her face was toward him, though her eyes were not quite focused on where he was. A searching look on her face prompted Lyson to put his hand around the bonsai and wave close to the window. There she could see him better against the sky he knew to be reflecting off the window, having himself been down there trying to see if the bonsai and the model of the Bandstand were visible from the street.

Mary saw, and exclaimed with agitated hands, *Why didn't you answer phone! Important business! Come-down immediately!*

In his haste, Lyson nearly knocked down the bonsai and he bit his hand while the other rescued the tree. He blew, and screwed the telephone lamp tight and scampered down the stairs to the Great Ballroom and into the living room.

There huddled a frightened little family staring at him with such astonishment Lyson nearly buckled at the knees. The father was short and stocky, rather like Lyson though less beefy and dressed in the universal grey khaki of professional janitors. He held a grey cap crumbled in his hands at his chest, his mouth open as he stared at Lyson. The mother was short too and so disproportionately large that Lyson had to blink rapidly to keep his eyes on the level. Her mouth too was open as she gaped at him. Her great mass hid their two children, who peeked from around her chemise. Lyson's ears began burning at this inappropriate moment. He brushed his hair down to cover them.

The door flew open and in rushed Mary. Seeing him, she abruptly stopped in her tracks and took slow, small measured steps toward him, sidewise in the cautious manner of cats closing for a fight, a fist on the hip that was thrust out in his direction, a maneuver which by some inexplicable feminine instinct she seemed to figure to be effectively intimidating to Lyson. The mere knowledge, entirely intuitive, of that line of reasoning and also the set of her face set Lyson quaking although her face could have been said to be quite expressionless. But the way it was set, with her eyes large and all pupil, her mouth full and soft at the very beginning of a reproach, her nostrils flaring, struck Lyson as more dangerous and ominous than he'd ever seen her. As often happens in such situations time seemed to hold still, to hold its breath as it must for a bird hypnotized by a cat, and Lyson had ample time to read fleeting messages in her face, none very complimentary. Disappointment. Accusation. Shame. Reproach. Disapproval. An intense anger seething within her, about to lash out. He blinked.

Never dreamt! her hands finally broke. *You my husband!*

Lyson's hands hung dumb by his sides.

Never dreamt you would d-a-r-e d-i-d DO!

Not that, the woman and man were saying to each other, shaking their heads at Lyson. *Not that him.*

Mary and Lyson stared at each other and at the couple.

Man sold us house, the man explained to Mary, *not that him,* pointing at Lyson.

Different person, someone else, his wife interjected.

Shorter, more fat—

Black hair, wavy, similar—she nodded at Lyson, *but shorter—*

And clothes different, cheaper—

Sweater, turtleneck regardless hot day—

Mary interrupted, *You mean, not that him,* indicating Lyson.

The couple agreed, *Not that him.*

Lyson's hands hung uselessly by his sides.

Smells different, perfume cheaper than his, the woman added.

Let's see card again, Mary waved. She studied the card carefully and looked up at Lyson. *Yours?* she asked.

Lyson stood by dumbly and she had to bring the card up to his face. *Yours?* she repeated. Lyson nodded weakly, his eyes wild with bewilderment.

That one sold you house, his name? Mary demanded of the couple.

Lyson first name. Last name Sulla, the man said as his wife nodded in confirmation.

That him? Mary jerked her head at Lyson.

No, no, not that him, the coupled demurred, vaguely puzzled at Mary. *Different person.*

Mary turned intently to Lyson and, with raised eyebrows, nodded significantly. Lyson stared back dumbly. Mary took a deep breath and explained to the couple, *That Lyson C period Sulla. My husband.*

The man and his wife stared at Lyson, and at each other and back at Lyson. *Can't-be!,* the woman cried, pounding her husband on the chest. *Impossible!*

The husband gripped her by the shoulders, turning her with such vigor the children had to scurry to keep hidden behind her from Lyson. He thrust her at Lyson. *He fooled us! He cheated us!*

The woman hit Lyson with her handbag. *You thief! Deceive deaf!*

Money back! demanded the man, drawing courage from his wife.

Money give-us! The woman tried to hit Lyson again but he threw up his arm and the strap got caught and she lost her grip. She recoiled away. *Thief! Thief!*

Lyson tried to calm her with pats but because she was so large, and retreating, he could not help but offend her. Her husband took offense as well, who withdrew as from a snake and ducked behind his wife, joining the children.

Mary was furious. *Nonsense!* She grabbed the purse from Lyson. *Dumb you! Pea-brain!* Restoring the purse to the woman, she sizzled, *My husband NOT thief! Himself always heart for deaf!*

The couple retreated ever further and clung to each other. The children wailed, grabbing their parents around the legs.

Taking deep breaths as if this would calm down the messy situation somehow, Mary commanded, *Everyone sit. Must talk sense!*

* * *

It was a difficult passage but Mary managed to get everyone quieted down around the dining table with coffee and cookies; even the children were successfully mollified with some ice cream, though they sat away from Lyson. The man and woman were Russell and Vivity Score from Clinton, Ohio. They had heard about this new deaf state of Islay from a salesman, they said.

Same person that sold you house? Mary asked.

Yes, that one call himself Lyson C period Sulla, the man nodded his fist. Lyson cringed. *Said, come with me, you can have real home in deaf state, only deaf allowed. Will sell us house in true deaf community, all deaf, no hearing—*

Two thousand! Vivity wailed.

Down-payment? Lyson inquired.

Yes, and showed house outside. Told us can't go-in for three days until present owner finish move out.

Dumb you! Vivity berated her husband. *Should first look inside before giving money—*

Not me! You that gave money! I told you—

Your fault! You gave-me money—

Gave you because thought you knew better than me, would hold—

Should think twice! She was about to pound the table but Russell quieted her by thrusting a cookie in her mouth like a pacifier. She sat back and began munching away, her eyes absorbed with the cookie.

Ask you, did man say himself Lyson C—Lyson began anxiously. Russell nodded his head and fist at the same time.

You said, he look almost like me? asked Lyson.

No, not really. Short, plump, black hair similar you, but face not. Seems puffy, pale, not healthy. Now realize I should know better. His face looks not honest—

Told you! chortled Vivity who was rewarded with another cookie.

Seeing that Lyson wasn't carrying the ball, Mary stepped in, *House where?*

Somewhere near river, about three blocks back, Russell said vaguely. *Thirty-first street, I think.*

Address?

Can't remember exactly. Somewhere, he indicated some vague direction to the south.

Ask you, got papers, signature? Mary asked, her eyes narrowed.

No, no! Dumb him! interrupted Vivity. *He crazy, just give money, no proof!*

Not so! Yourself that give money!

Oh, oh, that's right! Vivity reddened, rolling her eyes up. *You see, husband and myself very close, similar one person. That why sometimes think he did, sometimes think I did.*

Russell nodded vigorously. Mary nodded slowly.

How-much down-payment? Lyson asked. Mary kicked him under the table.

Three thousand! Russell began but Vivity slapped his hands and said, *No! Dumb you! Two thousand, remember?*

Oh yes! That's right! Confused me, Russell knocked his head. *You see, at-first man that call himself Lyson—*

Enough! Lyson flicked a hand in front of Russell's face. *That man NOT L Y S O N,* he said firmly. Mary kicked Lyson again.

Go-on, finish your story, Mary encouraged Russell with a pretty smile.

That man, at-first want three thousand, but wife successfully reduced to two thousand.

Vivity nodded with her entire upper body. *That's right, that's why confused.*

Mary sat back and released all the air in her lungs in a long exhalation.

You gave money, then—Lyson wanted to know.

Man told us wait in car, be-back, Russell said shaking his head. *But never showed-up.*

Waited, waited all-night. Vivity did the night sign slowly: it was a long night. *This morning not-yet show-up, that why came here, thought man live here.* She looked at Lyson. *Not that him.*

No, not that him, agreed Russell holding up his cup. *Coffee?*

Mary sighed again and refilled the cup, and shot Lyson a glance. But Lyson was shaking his head, bemused, lost in thought. He made as to reach for his wallet but she stopped him with a squeeze of the shoulder.

Excuse! Will back few minutes. She dragged Lyson to the kitchen and set him against the counter, out of sight of the Scores. She stood herself where they couldn't see her from where they sat at the table, but if they got up from the table she would see that immediately.

Weak-headed you! she remonstrated him. *Wrong you? Can't you see that's them themselves really deceiving you?*

Impossible! Lyson cried. *They're from Ohio!*

Ohio? Mary wrinkled her nose.

Yes! Ohio people famous honest. Likewise Iowa. Ohio always honest, you know that yourself.

If Lyson weren't her own husband, she would have laughed. Instead she turned an ear toward him and whirled a finger in circles around it.

Not crazy! Smart politics!

Mary mouthed the word smart as if it were the funniest word she ever saw.

Not funny! Lyson insisted. *Help those two, have two votes for sure.*

She cocked her head at him, a mixture of amusement and bemusement softening her features. *You mean, two thousand dollars for two votes?*

Not so! He denied hotly. The force of his denial sign lifted his torso in a little hop. *Help! Not buy! Think you, me dumb? Think you, I would throw-away two thousand USA dollars? No way!*

How? Mary wanted to know.

Simple. Lyson narrowed his eyes craftily and tapped his temple. *Help them buy another house. Just tack-on two thousand.*

CHAPTER 20

Spring had been rather slow in coming, and when it finally arrived it yielded almost immediately to summer. Lyson was elated. Now he could implement his plans for the Bandstand. First it had to be cleaned out: it had been a messy winter. He'd take a mop and bucket and do it himself, except that he knew he would be in full view of Governor Wenchell.

The only solution he could think of was to go to church with Mary this fine morning. The church Mary had bought for the Most Dear Reverend Dowie was right on Tenth Street, facing the park strip, a couple blocks west of the Bandstand. A grand old church that sparkled with the devotion of its congregation. How did Dowie ever get his parishioners to clean out those tall arched ceilings, Lyson thought happily. They stood perhaps three stories high.

Why, my dear beloved Lyson, no problem! said the Reverend Dowie at lunch with the Sullas. *Jesus did his preaching outdoors, sun among people all-around.*

Lyson tried hard not to frown. This was not exactly what he had in mind. *Splendid! But not so obvious, please. Remember, the Bandstand itself, public property—*

Perfect. Perfect, chuckled the Reverend Dowie helping himself to a drumstick. For all the world he resembles Colonel Sanders, fretted Lyson. Tough old bird.

Eat, hurry, Mary prodded Lyson. *Chicken, cold.*

* * *

A few days later Lyson was driving down Tenth Street and braked hard. He could hardly believe his eyes. The Bandstand actually glowed. Shone! All the grime was gone that had hid its outer beauty; of course nothing could ever mar its inner beauty: a bandstand is beautiful from its function whatever its decorations, of course. In the first place, the Merry Bandstand was an architectural masterpiece in its own right and so therefore beautiful in any condition, Lyson nodded to himself.

But today all the grime dumped by pigeons was gone, as was the soot brought by the prevailing westerlies from the mills of Fremont across the river. All scrubbed and hosed down, the Bandstand literally glowed in a fresh coat of pure white paint, and its roof shone as silvery as a new dollar so that the breath went out of Lyson. My God it is beautiful, he exulted in the exuberant manner of a connoisseur of art.

A tapping on the window jolted him. It was the Reverend Dowie. *Better move! Park over-there.*

Lyson looked and saw he had stopped right in the middle of the street, stalling a long line of cars behind him, motorists shaking their fists out their windows. He was so hurried to park out of their way his tires bumped the curb. There goes the alignment! Practically a new Renault LeCar. Although it had been a year since he'd left the Mercedes with the doctor in California, Doctor Fletcher had never shown up as promised. He had disappeared completely with the Mercedes, along with Jewell Cameron and her children and their dog. Lyson was sorely disappointed: the deaf really need a doctor of their very own right here in Islay. Mary was sorely disappointed too: it was her car. She and Beatrice agreed that, considering his loose way with automobiles, the cheapest of the cheap was all he deserved. Besides, he didn't need to travel very far anymore, did he? argued Mary. With Islay filling up rapidly with the deaf from all over the country, the LeCar was just fine, Beatrice assured him, for his image as a daring entrepreneur, yet cheap enough for a populist. Lyson was disturbed for only a day or two about this, though, and henceforth was too busy with the new Islay to notice anymore that the car was a Renault. Otherwise he might eventually have made the connection between the perpetually damp seat of his pants and the cheap vinyl upholstery of the car.

He kept his face averted so that the passing and cursing motorists would not know it was a Future Governor that had inconvenienced them. The Reverend Dowie opened the door on the right and soothed, *Don't feel bad, happens same-all-us. Naturally this Bandstand surprised you.*

Lyson did not reply but stared at the Bandstand, glistening white silver ivory and pristine in the sun. The Reverend Dowie chuckled and motioned him out of the car. It was no ordinary whitewash but actual house paint that brightened the ceiling. Gone were the spider webs, bird and wasp nests, and the old gloom. It was so bright and airy that Lyson gave a little dance as he stared up into the lantern overhead. Little birds entered the lantern but departed in a flash.

Paint smells strong, theorized the Reverend.

The platform was a stone floor polished smooth, and Lyson registered surprise. *Used-to-be gray, white, kind-of chalky,* he remarked.

Oh, that's bird droppings real thick—the Reverend held a finger and thumb an inch apart. *We scrapped and collected for fertilizer there our church.*

Lyson examined the soles of his shoes and began brushing the seat of his pants. Reverend Dowie laughed, *Silly you. Clean now.*

Lyson raised his hands to say something about that dark and stormy night but thought better and instead scratched the back of his neck.

No birds now. Look. The Reverend laughed and gestured around the ceiling so white in the shade there was no shadow, even among the rafters.

Hard believe, Lyson managed to say, running his hand over one of the columns. It was marble: an ivory white with whiter and less white streaks, joined together so neatly that he could just barely feel the joints as his finger glided over them. *Nice and smooth same woman, er, baby,* Lyson said blushing.

Remarkable, agreed Reverend Dowie, fingering the column himself. *Marble itself formerly living things, dead long-ago, crushed-into rock. Alive now in different way, similar*—He straightened himself into a stance more becoming a sermon but Lyson caught on quickly, *How much altogether?*

Reverend Dowie was rather disappointed. He liked giving sermons but under the circumstances relented. *Seven hundred dollars for paint alone—*

That cheap! marveled Lyson.

Free labor, remember! Then four hundred for wax and polish. Floor, columns, roof—

Islay Company will pay, Lyson said quickly. *Just send bill.*

Oh no, no. The Reverend waved magnanimously. *We ourselves glad to help improve our city, never asked for money. Anyway, cost us around five hundred more for various supplies. Altogether sixteen hundred. Not bad, eh?*

Lyson knew he was beaten and made a mental note to tell Mary. He shook his head in amazement at how she so quietly and unobtrusively maintained the real control over the finances of his company. Hey, she was the de facto president!

Not bad. Lyson assured him. *Worth every penny. Beautiful! Thank you very much!*

No problem. Glad serve you anytime, you know that, the Reverend Dowie said grandly, although Lyson thought he could detect a slight uneasiness, unsureness in his manner. Lyson was tickled happy that the matter got where it could best be left up in the air, in the clouds, in the hands of Providence.

I know I can always rely—he began but his hand was suddenly seized and slapped.

Four men were on the platform with them. One was Governor Wenchell, all white in the white light of the shade of the Bandstand. The Governor was frowning gravely as if Lyson had done something very naughty. Beside him on either side were two muscular men, one of whom Lyson recalled as the bodyguard who served drinks at the mansion. The other he recognized as the party-crasher—P-51.

But unfamiliar was the man gripping his wrist and even now still slapping it, if Lyson so much as twitched a finger, as if he wanted the hand good and dead. Lyson could not recall ever having seen him before. This man was dressed rather too nicely to be out-of-doors, in a severely tailored, dark blue suit although the color was more suitable for ordinary everyday business occasions. Lyson's eyes traveled all the way down to the shoes, which had been taken from the tender part of an alligator, and up along the fine weaving of the suit, to the huge tie with its shiny pin; he cringed to think how he himself used to dress in the same pretty way, to the same standards of respectability and reputability. By the time he returned his gaze to the man's face, he already disliked him and saw him differently. Lyson winced at the thought how others must have viewed him in the bygone days when he himself favored such pretty suits.

Lyson tried to withdraw his hand but the man tightened his grip and slapped harder. "No signing!" the man's lips seemed to be saying.

"What's the—" Lyson began to bellow.

The man released Lyson and turned jubilantly to the Governor. "There! I told you!" And he said something Lyson and Reverend Dowie couldn't follow on the lips. The Governor nodded gravely and looked intently at Lyson's mouth and ears, and down at his hands which hung limp at his sides.

Turning to Lyson the man declared, while holding up his hands curled into beseeching claws, "You can talk if you want to! Sign language is bad for your speech." He tapped his mouth and wagged a finger. "And it is against the law in Islay to use sign language." He slammed a fist into his hand.

"Law?" Lyson and the Reverend asked incredulously.

"Yes!" the man clapped. "Most assuredly yes! The State of Islay will not tolerate sign language in any form." He wagged a finger in front of Lyson's nose.

Lyson and the Reverend gaped at each other. With a hand down low behind his hip out of sight of the man, Reverend Dowie asked, *Who's that?*

In a flash the man seized the Reverend's hand and slapped it. "I'm not blind!" he declared indignantly. "You deaf people think you can fool us hearing people. You can't hide your hands. Sign language is too obvious." His hands flapped like an ostrich's fluffy wings.

The two deaf men looked down at his hands, and the man followed their stare and saw his own hands flapping. He became furious and slapped his own hands, one after the other. "You think you're so smart, eh? I'll give you just one more chance—" He held up a finger and pointed at it and glanced over at the Governor, evidently to make sure the Governor noticed his great skill at handling these deaf renegades. But the Governor was looking with a puzzled wrinkle in his brow at the finger being held up and at the one pointing at it.

His face reddening, the man slapped his own hands again and jammed them into his pockets. Through tightly clenched teeth he said something to the Governor as he led them all away. Lyson and the Reverend gawked after them as they went down the stairs. The Governor stopped suddenly in the manner of a man who just remembered something he'd forgotten he'd come to do in the first place. He half turned toward the deaf men and, keeping his hand hidden from the man, pointed up at the Bandstand. He smiled his appreciation, and made the O.K. sign.

The man made a motion toward the Governor's hand with the intent of slapping it but the big bodyguard grabbed him first. The Governor chuckled, shaking his head, and they all went their way toward the Governor's Mansion. Lyson and the Reverend stared after them and at each other.

* * *

"See what I mean!" Doctor Hermann Masserbatt was saying indignantly to the Governor as they were walking from the Bandstand toward the Mansion. "Sign language is dangerous! Contagious! If we don't watch what we're doing around deaf people, why—" he waved his hand around and seeing his hand waving around, threw it down in disgust. "Why, we'd lose our speech."

Governor Wenchell coughed politely. "You said you'd bring me a copy of that law—"

"Oh, certainly! It's just that I've been so busy in the service to the deaf, no time! I mean, I've not had the time."

"Well, well," the Governor arched an eyebrow and turned to B-52 on his right. "It's been a year since—?"

"Nearly a year," nodded B-52. "Last summer."

"That long!" exclaimed the superintendent. "I've been extremely terribly busy, what with all these deaf people moving in and taking over the schools. They refuse to enroll their deaf children at the Institute for Communicative Disorders."

The Governor stopped abruptly. "Why would that be?" he demanded.

The man threw up his hands. "Because we would not, ever, allow any sign language in any form at our institute. You see, it is our job to cure communication disorders. You can't very well do that if you allow sign language. Why, that's like fighting fire with fire! Our mission in life, I mean at the institute, is to teach the deaf to talk. To speak like you and me." He make a choking gesture. "It's so frustrating! Those children pick up sign language so fast, like wildfire it's all over the place and next to impossible to stamp out. That's why we have this law to forbid sign language, to give these kids a chance to learn to talk!"

Governor Wenchell frowned pensively. "This law, exactly what does it say?"

"No deaf person shall at anytime use his hands in a gesticulating manner to convey his communications, or in any other manner than the accepted mode of speech by manipulation of the mouth and vocal cords—"

"Does this mean they mightn't even write—" B-52 asked incredulously.

"Of course!" The superintendent stamped his foot. "If we allow them to write, they'll never use their mouths!"

"Not even to eat—" B-52 began jokingly but the Governor shot him a sharp glance.

"Not funny! The mouth is a magnificent device wonderfully designed for speech!" the superintendent shot back indignantly, pulling out his lips to display his entire mouth and its wonders. "You only eat an average of thirty-eight minutes a day but you use your mouth in a communicative manner an average of fifteen hours and twenty one minutes a day—"

"Including snoring—" B-52 bravely ventured and ducked playfully at the Governor's writhing eye.

"This is most serious—" the Governor began.

"Absolutely!" interrupted Doctor Masserbatt. "The deaf are invading! It's a disease!"

Governor Wenchell held up his hand in a commanding manner. "Exactly where can we find this law—"

"I tell you! It's in there somewhere—"

"Exactly where?" demanded the Governor imperiously.

"Can't remember just now," pleaded the man knocking his forehead. "Saw it once, a long time ago. Something like Code 73, Section 504, paragraph—" He shrugged helplessly.

"Look it up!" ordered the Governor stiffly.

"It has to be there somewhere! It's so right, so natural it has got to be—" He froze, staring at an old couple strolling by gesticulating with their fingers. "Stop that!" the superintendent yelled and ran after them and slapped their hands. He scolded them and looked back to check if the Governor had seen this fine performance of a civic duty.

But the Governor and his bodyguards had vanished.

* * *

Lyson had wanted to flee but the Reverend Dowie restrained him. *Courage. Courage,* urged the Reverend and they watched from the Bandstand the commotion between the Governor and the strange man.

Wonder who's that man? asked Lyson.

No idea! Something funny about him, remarked the Reverend. *Can tell himself prominent, important, but what, no idea.*

Forgot tell you, introduce you, that man clothed white, white mustache, that's himself Governor here Islay.

Really! exclaimed the Reverend. *Didn't know!*

Thrill? Wonder why those four came here, and man slap, Lyson gestured his hand being slapped. *Thrill? Wonder what Governor do-do with that man?*

Apparently something do with—The Reverend tried to think, but gave up. *Can't imagine.*

They saw the man bolting from the Governor toward the gesticulating couple and slapping their hands. The Governor and his bodyguards ducked behind some hedges and scurried away toward the Mansion.

The man noticed the disappearance of his friends and became agitated and dashed about in aimless circles, like a dog chasing his tail. When he realized his abandonment he became frightened and ran toward the Mansion. But the door was locked and would not open to his knocks.

Even from the distance of the Bandstand, Lyson and the Reverend could see the man's face turning red as he fretted about the porch, rattling the door and windows. Lyson and the Reverend turned toward each other and when they looked back again, the man was slinking away down the walk toward his car. He drove away in a huff and a cloud of exhaust.

"Wonder who could that be?" the Reverend exclaimed aloud, catching the attention of the old couple who waved gaily and came toward them.

"Beatrice! Captain!" Lyson cried, bounding down the steps. "He slapped your hands!"

Hi Lyson! Beatrice signed, proud of her hands although awkward.

"Yeah!" the Captain laughed. "We were just practicing our signs and—" He slapped his own hand humorously.

"Crazy man!" the Reverend made a cranking motion around his ear.

"Wonder who was he!" Lyson threw up his hands.

"You don't know?" Beatrice exclaimed in surprise.

"No idea!"

"Really!" she declared with a big wink to her husband. "Isn't that something? They don't even know their own Savior!"

The old man on the bench continued tossing nuts to his pals the squirrels and pigeons, minding his own business. He's not saying. Seems he doesn't want to get involved.

CHAPTER 21

Mary woke Lyson the next morning by slapping his chest with the morning newspaper. She had never done this before: if there was news she wanted him to see, she always simply folded the paper to the proper place and left it by his plate at breakfast. This was her gentle way of letting him know she had seen the news, and that she would not let him slip away without first a discussion.

But this morning she was not so gentle. *Why didn't you tell me!* She thrust his glasses on his face before he so much had raised his head and worked his eyes into focus. She thumbed her nose. *Secretive men! You know better than not tell me!*

Spectacles have never been made that fit just right when someone else puts them on for you. Lyson had to readjust his before picking up the newspaper. The lead headline screamed across the top:

ISLAY ITEMIZER
NOW IS DEAF!

The *Islay Itemizer,* a venerable Suffex newspaper dating from the eighteenth century has been purchased by a group of deaf investors.

Lyson flipped around on the bed and fell to the floor with a thump. He stood on his head but fell over on his back. Dauntlessly he rolled and again stood on his head, legs flying in the air for balance. Mary folded her arms and twisted her lips.

The door flew open and Mortima and Evangeline rushed in still in their nightclothes. *Thrill? Felt floor thump!* cried Mortima.

S'matter, Lyson? Evangeline tried to go to his aid but Mary stopped her.

His fault! declared Mary imperiously, pushing Mortima and Evangeline back out the door. Just because they lived in the house did not mean they were family. They were employees—Evangeline was their resident interpreter; Mortima had been invited to be their housekeeper so Mary could gain a modicum of control over the famous wagging fingers.

Lyson failed to maintain his balance upside down and fell again. He lay there biting his knuckles. Mary was not amused and stepped on his toes. *Tell me secret now! Thrill?*

Didn't-know! Truth! Lyson pleaded from the floor. He rolled to his knees and attempted to kiss her feet, but she pulled away.

Disgust, you! If there was one thing that didn't impress her it was attempts to kiss her feet. Anyhow, that's not where she liked to be kissed. *Get-up!*

But Lyson continued crawling after her. She seized the newspaper from the bed and laid it on the floor under his nose.

> "Thanks to the great and vigorous leadership of Gene Owles—"

Lyson grabbed his hair and would have pulled out fistfuls had Mary not grabbed his wrists. "I was here first," he wailed.

She resorted to the old trick of pinching his ears. *Read more!*

> —Gene Owles, a renowned writer and editor of deaf publications, namely, the DEAF Magazine, Athletics of the Deaf, National Newsletter of the Deaf, and the Deaf and National Affairs, it was possible to acquire an already established and respected newspaper and begin immediate publication. His entire professional life has been devoted to the cause of the deaf, and therefore he has dismissed the entire hearing staff of the newspaper and replaced them with deaf people, themselves having been displaced by computerization of newspapers all over the country.
>
> Editor Owles does not believe in pulling any punches and has declared the Islay Itemizer the entire province of the deaf. He says that there is an abundance of newspapers and periodicals devoted to satisfying the ignorance and prejudices of hearing people and so, therefore, the abruptness in changing the goals and hopes of the Islay Itemizer.
>
> Our Distinguished Editor Owles says that since the deaf population of Islay is rapidly approaching the majority mark—

Idiot! Lyson threw the newspaper up in the air. *Hearing not supposed know until November!*

Mary watched her husband beating the floor with his head and sighed, somewhat mollified that he clearly had had no part in this game. But still she had to keep up her disappointment that he had not kept on his toes. *Lyson, thrill? You not tell me?*

Didn't-know! Tell you truth, myself didn't-know!

She sat on the bed, chin on fists, elbows on knees, and studied Lyson with an air of such detachment that he cried out, *I knew nothing! Honest!* He crossed his heart with such vigor he nearly tore his pajama top.

The icy calmness with which Mary continued contemplating her husband obligated Lyson to get his act together; he collected the scattered sheets of the newspaper and resumed reading:

> —thanks to the efforts of numerous efforts of deaf investors and leaders—

"Thanks Gene," Lyson uttered between clenched teeth and signed for Mary to know exactly what he said, so she would not misconstrue the way "Gene" reads on the lips.

> —who put their faith in the supposition that the future of Islay lies entirely in the hands of the deaf. These hands Gene Owles has declared to be his own—

Thief! Lyson tore up the newspaper. *Me here first!*

First, but maybe last—Mary began wryly.

Lyson stared at her the same way any man would at an awful truth, one he was loath to allow, let alone face. He was on his knees, hands on lap, mouth open. She was sitting on the bed exactly as before, her chin comfortable in her hands as she continued looking at him with a certain blank look that was not so blank.

Do-do? he finally stirred.

Simple! She made a series of gestures that could literally be translated: grip your left buttock with your left hand. Grab your right buttock with your other. And take a deep breath and LIFT. She actually by this means raised herself to her feet.

So graphic, so out of character was her gesture, that Lyson was stunned. *Mary! Can't imagine!*

She arched up her eyebrows and nodded. *Oh yes, you can.*

* * *

That same morning Captain John Quayle saw the newspaper at his morning coffee before breakfast. "Beatrice," he called out. "Bet Lyson flipped this morning."

"Flipped! What do you mean?," Beatrice turned the eggs in the simmering bacon fat.

"Come see this paper and you'll see—"

"Just a minute! The eggs—"

The Captain read the entire article and chuckled. "Bet this set Lyson on his ear."

"Coming! Coming!" She brought in the breakfast and read over his shoulder. "Isn't that something!" she exclaimed.

"Yeah, it's enough to make a man howl—"

"Eat your breakfast!" cried Beatrice. "Today is the day!"

* * *

The Reverend Dowie was kneeling reverently in the sunbeam, his eyes shut so that his eyeballs filled with the astonishing red light that he loved so dearly. Against the red background he could see a faint mosaic of mysterious amber lines. They have always been a puzzle: he was never quite certain whether they were cells on his eyelids or in his retina. He tried rolling his eyes and blinking his eyelids to detect any movement in the mosaic, but there were always those worrisome little flecks floating inside the eyeballs, or was it the outside? He could never tell for certain. They looked very much like those little bacteria swimming under the microscope, except these were quite lifeless. For a long time they worried him: some of them actually looked like little segmented worms. He dreaded the thought they could well be a harbinger of some eye disease. But they never wiggled nor so much as moved a twitch. If they ever did—he shuddered and clutched his hands against his chest.

He sought to allow his mind to go blank, to surrender his soul to the sun warm on his face and overwhelming in his eyes. Just be still and the little flecks will settle down out of sight. Ignore them and they will blur away. Ah, here's just this one pesky little microbe—no! Mustn't call it that! The Reverend Dowie gave up and opened his eyes slowly, reluctantly returning to the environs of his study.

A newspaper half-slipped under his door was frantically waving on the floor. He grabbed at it but it pulled away under the door. As he unlocked the door, Geraldine burst in shaking the newspaper in his face. *Good news! Deaf finally have own newspaper!*

Really! The Reverend Dowie took the paper and saw it was indeed so.

Can imagine Lyson and Mary excited, enthused Geraldine. *Islay becoming more and more ours—deaf.*

Yes, yes, the Reverend was nodding as he turned the pages. But she could detect a hint of disappointment.

S'matter?

Yes, very exciting—he continued turning the pages.

S'matter? she insisted.

He gave her a sidelong glance and saw that she had seen. He took a long breath. *Well, big surprise for sure—*

Come-on, tell me! she urged impatiently.

Another deep breath. *No-one told me. Seems Lyson would tell me beforehand.*

Oh.

Lyson ever-since always kept me informed—

Maybe he wanted surprise you? she ventured hopefully.

The Reverend looked at her sadly. *Doubt. This too important for that.*

Oh. Geraldine sagged. *Maybe just forgot. You know himself very busy, have many things thrill happen, happen—*

He rolled his eyes. *Hope not! Rather he thought none my business—*

Impossible! He knows your interest.

The Reverend looked again, closer at the newspaper. His eyebrows shot up: *Gene Owles new editor.*

Owles? she searched her memory. *Never heard.*

I think you did. DEAF Magazine.

Ah, yes! Remember now, she slapped her hip. *Famous women women famous.*

Right, he nodded significantly. *Believe myself that Lyson surprised, like you and me.*

* * *

"But I didn't know!" protested Doctor Masserbatt.

"Exactly what I meant!" retorted Governor Wenchell. "Them deaf people are your responsibility."

"Those people never went to my—our school."

The Governor grunted, "Remember you said you'd take—"

"I know!" pleaded Doctor Masserbatt. "It's just there's so many of them and they're just so—so overwhelming—"

"You say you're a leader of them deaf—"

"Exactly! But these are the signing deaf!"

"Signing?"

"Yes! You see, I'm the leader of the speaking deaf. I've nothing to do with the signers."

"Nothing, eh? " the Governor fixed him with such a new look in his eye that the superintendent hastened to explain the difference between the two kinds of deaf.

"You see, the speaking deaf are normal like you and I. They can speak, see? By means of propulsion of air through the vocal cords and thence through the—"

"Shattup!" The Governor threw a hand. "That's your area. I don't care for no nit-pickin' details. What I want to know is what the hell is going on. And just what do you mean, you've got nothing to do with it!" The Governor curled his lips the better to bristle his mustache and glared at the man in the pretty suit. "And exactly what you do mean, Leader of the Deaf?"

"I can explain!" implored Doctor Masserbatt. "But it's really a very long, involved, convolved, complicated—"

"I see!" Slappy Wenchell leaned back in his rocker and signalled for B-52 to go fetch a drink. "You've been remiss," he aimed a finger at the superintendent. "Them deaf are your responsibility, or maybe 'were' would be a better word," he narrowed his eyes threateningly.

"Don't worry—"

"Let me finish!" shot back the Governor. B-52 returned with a tall glass filled with ice cubes and a lovely amber liquor. The fact did not miss Doctor Masserbatt that one and only one glass was served. Indeed the Governor made a big point of taking a leisurely sip, wincing, pulling his lips away from his teeth and shuddering before continuing. "Firstly, you allowed the situation to become too complicated to manage. My family, my grandfather, my father, and myself, we made damn sure things stayed simple! Easy to manage. We never allowed things to get out of hand. Troublemakers were simply marched to the bridge and shown out."

"But this is the twentieth century—"

"So? You said you'd handle it! Had I known any better I'd have done the job myself. Before things got out of hand, thanks to you!"

"Things can't be that bad," Doctor Masserbatt tried a new tack, smoothing the Governor's ruffled feathers.

"What you mean, can't be that bad!" demanded Governor Wenchell, tapping the newspaper with the back of his knuckles. "Them deaf are taking over!"

"Impossible!" cried the superintendent, scanning the newspaper. "True, there're many but I've not noticed all that many in Crewe!"

"Exactly! You were down there in that little village, your head in the sand, your ass in the air, when—" But he suddenly felt tired of it all and turned to the comfort in his glass.

"But I've been so busy in the service to the deaf—"

"Very good, very good, I'm glad to hear that," the Governor interrupted and returned to his drink.

"It's the type of work you never leave, and the work never leaves you—" Doctor Masserbatt held up imploring claws. "To succeed in this type of work requires total dedication and single-mindless—'scuse me, mindedness! Which means complete absorption in one area—"

"Just what are you talking about?" interrupted B-52. "Governor Wenchell is a busy man. Speak plainly!" He looked smugly at his boss and was rewarded with a wink.

"I'm just a country boy," the Governor yawned and scratched his armpit. "My old brain can only chew a few words at a time."

"Right! I mean O.K.! Here's it in a nutshell." Doctor Masserbatt wrung his hands earnestly. "Here's this two kinds of deaf people: the speaking and the signing kinds. The speakers communicate by means of emitting sound waves through the air whereas the signers seek to communicate by means of propagation of symbols, shapes, graphics, pictures, and other signals in the medium of light waves rather than the English lang—dumb me, sound—"

He stopped uneasily, for the Governor had turned his attention elsewhere, across the street. A crowd was gathering around the Bandstand where a television crew was already setting up their equipment.

Doctor Masserbatt spied some of the people in the crowd using Sign Language. "I'll stop this nonsense!" he cried to the Governor and began running toward the Bandstand.

* * *

Lyson was petrified. In front of him were the steps leading up to the platform of the Bandstand. Despite its brightness, the sunlight flowing through the open lantern above and reverberating around the fresh white paint so that the interior of the Bandstand was as fully bright and airy as the outside, the television crew insisted upon adding powerful spotlights. For the color, they explained, otherwise you'd look as pale and gray as Nixon.

"You're pale!" Beatrice cried and put her hands on his forehead and cheek. "And cold! Poor Lyson!" She squeezed his cheeks.

The Captain tugged him into the television van and poured some warmth and comfort into him from a hip flask. Lyson shivered, bared his teeth, shook his head, and blew.

They stepped out of the van and immediately Beatrice, Evangeline, and Mary were on Lyson. They straightened his jacket and tie and combed his hair. Mary refitted his glasses but they didn't feel right and he had to restraighten them himself. Beatrice brushed lint and dandruff off his shoulders. Evangeline rearranged the fake handkerchief in his breast pocket.

Don't worry. I'll interpret faithfully, perfectly, Evangeline reassured him.

If he says anything dumb, Mary admonished, *don't interpret so perfectly! Make him sound smart!*

Can't, Evangeline said apologetically. *Professional ethics, must interpret exactly.*

Lyson, Mary confronted her husband, *memorize your speech perfectly, you?*

He pulled the Captain back into the van for a bit more warmth and comfort. He shivered, bared his teeth, shook his head, and blew. "Lyson old boy, just relax and enjoy yourself," cheerfully said the Captain. "You'll do just fine."

"But the lights." There was a hint of panic in Lyson's voice. "Can't see with them in my eyes."

"All the better," the Captain patted his shoulder encouragingly, "to see what a great guy you are. Let's go."

Lyson was conducted—with much patting, shaking and pulling of his hand and many words of support and encouragement—to the foot of the stairway. *Don't worry, I'll interpret you faithfully,* sweetly repeated Evangeline. *I'll be right with you every word all way.* The Reverend Dowie squeezed his shoulder, rolled his eyes up out of sight so that only the whites showed, and sent up a prayer. Wally hit his back and said, "Go get 'em!"

Mary moistened one cheek with a kiss. Beatrice kissed the other. Crystal came and did her bit. Dottie, Sandy, Exota, even Geraldine left their mark so that his cheeks glowed rosily. Maybe like a clown's, he fretted to himself. Up popped Heather with a smirk. Her eyes slightly askew as ever, she put her mark of approval on his dimple. Not that dimple again!

But behind her Mortima lay in wait, eyes intent and lips parted in anticipation. And before he knew it, he was bounding up the stairs into an intensely bright void.

Like a deer stunned by a spotlight, Lyson stood stock-still in the center of the Bandstand, his arms stiff by his sides. The brightness hurt his eyes and made his nose ticklish, threatening to sneeze. He rubbed his nose with his upper lip to suppress the sneeze. Barely visible among the lights were the television camera and a man in earphones beside it whirling a finger in the air. It took an awful moment for the signal to register in Lyson's mind and he opened and closed his mouth. He could not remember his speech!

He looked helplessly over his shoulder and spotted Mary at the foot of the stairway. *Forgot speech!,* he motioned frantically with a hand behind his back.

"Forgot speech!" interpreted Evangeline faithfully into the microphone.

Lyson motioned again to Mary. Evangeline interpreted helpfully, "Help me!"

Announcement about TV for deaf! Mary cued desperately.

Lyson thumped a finger on his hip and Evangeline translated, "Right!" He turned and bravely faced the camera in the glare of the lights. But again the lights brought forth the tickle in his nose which he massaged with his upper lip. Evangeline saw this and earnestly interpreted into the microphone, "Oh, well!"

Hearing people in the audience broke out in applause and appreciative laughter. The deaf looked at each other in puzzlement and shrugged. Lyson saw none of this of course and puffing up his chest courageously began.

Myself, name Lyson C period Sulla, President of Islay Company. That's me that one who started, invented here state for deaf one year past. Amazed myself how happened, now state of Islay filled with deaf, approaching majority. Evangeline interpreted perfectly sign for sign and Doctor Masserbatt blanched at the grammar.

Finally have own state! Have bowling, movies captioned, TTY factory, printers, many business belong their deaf. Nothing hearing. Now have newspaper belong their deaf! Because he was concentrating on his speech he never saw the thunderous applause at this last statement. Instead his nose itched and he rubbed it again with his lip.

Funny thing thrill happened, myself not sure exactly how happened but Islay Company, that one start here state for deaf, bring deaf here, anyway, that one just recently, about one hour ago bought TV station! Channel number—number—

Lyson snapped his fingers trying to remember the number. The heat and the intensity of light in the Bandstand brought forth beads of sweat on his forehead, and a drop ran down his nose. He wiped it, unobtrusively he hoped, with his upper lip. Evangeline translated, "Oh, well!" The powerful lights overwhelmed the darkest recesses of his skull so he gave up searching for the number and looked over at Mary for help. A whole forest of hands held up the sign eight. The Captain helpfully drew a big figure eight in the air.

A blue like the seas of the Caribbean so wonderfully blue it caught his eye appeared behind the crowd. Gene Owles! He smiled that little half smile of his and folded his arms as he leaned against a tree, his legs scissored elegantly.

Lyson was shaken and quickly forgot the number. But fortunately some people still held up the eight sign. "Oh, that's right!" He again faced the lights and held up the eight sign high for all to see. He knew there was a crowd behind the lights and rotated his wrist so that everyone would know for sure it was an eight. He held it up for a rather long time. He couldn't help it: he was trying to remember what he was supposed to say next.

Captioned! Mary cued him when he finally looked her way.

Oh, that's right! Captioned news, movies, sports, cartoons, plays, everything captioned! he happily resumed his speech. *Not only captioned, but also signed news. I don't mean interpreted; I mean signed by deaf themselves news people for deaf all us. Channel—channel*—a quick glance at Mary for help. "That's right!" *Eight!* He held up the sign eight for all to see. Doctor Masserbatt shook his head at the grammar as conveyed by Evangeline.

Enough speech! Mary cued when he again faced her direction.

Enough speech! he announced to the lights. *Thank you very much! Hope you enjoy our new deaf TV Channel 8.* Again he held up the sign eight very high at an arm's length above his head. He wasn't exactly sure how now to extract himself, to withdraw gracefully. He searched his mind for a way out, but could only recall Johnny Carson's masterful entrances. He'd never seen that show to its end: it was all talk, talk, talk. Trying to lipread was such work that he had always fallen asleep before the show ended. So he had no idea how Carson left the stage. He thought maybe he could simply do the Carson entrance in reverse. Holding out his hands, he walked backwards, smiling his best smile.

Just when he thought he had reached the safety of the stairs, a man seized him. It was the same man who had slapped his hands some time ago, in the same place. The Hand Slapper!

Before Lyson could pull free, the Hand Slapper snapped a handcuff on his left wrist and reached for the right one. Lyson jerked his free hand out of reach and hopped around to the right so that his hand would remain far away enough from the handcuff to make this sign: *Thrill?*

Evangeline interpreted: "Thrilling!" But then something told her she hadn't interpreted quite right so she hastened to correct herself, "Thrilling, isn't it?"

The Hand Slapper, in his endeavor to reach Lyson's right hand, tripped over Lyson's foot, knocking him down and landed on top of Lyson. Through great effort and singlemindedness he managed to subdue Lyson's right wrist long enough to latch the handcuff on it. Now Lyson was in his power!

Trent and Wally pulled the Hand Slapper off Lyson and shook him like a terrier worries a sock. "What's the joke?" Trent roared at him.

"He's under arrest!" trumpeted Doctor Masserbatt authoritatively, dusting off his jacket.

What's he say? Lyson beseeched Wally despite the handcuffs.

In a flash Doctor Masserbatt slapped Lyson's hands and gripped the chain, holding it down so Lyson couldn't raise his hands again. Trent roared "Let go!" and wrapped his huge hand around Doctor Masserbatt's neck and lifted him bodily off the floor. "Let go!"

Legs flailing in the air, Doctor Masserbatt tried to speak but only made a choking sound. He waved desperately and pointed at his neck and whined.

"Need any help?" Evangeline appeared in their midst out of the blue, speaking and signing simultaneously. "I'm a professional certified interpreter."

Doctor Masserbatt pointed frantically at his mouth. Evangeline interpreted, "He cannot speak."

Trent eased his hold on the superintendent's neck enough to allow emitted this sound: "You mean you use your hands?"

Evangeline nodded politely, almost in the manner of a geisha. "At your service."

Doctor Masserbatt straightened himself as best could be done while suspended above the floor, Trent still holding him by the neck, and stiffly announced, "Don't you know it is absolutely forbidden to use your hands in a gestical manner in the State of Islay?"

"You mean a bird?" snorted Trent.

Evangeline gasped, "You can't mean interpreting!"

"I most certainly do!" hurumphed Doctor Masserbatt waggling a finger. "Any and all gestures up to and including the bird!"

Evangeline was furious. "There's more to interpreting than a bir—bir—that!"

Doctor Masserbatt chuckled as happily as could any man under the circumstances. "Really?"

"Like this?" seethed Evangeline thumbing her nose. The Reverend and Mrs. Dowie gasped.

"That's illegal!" cried the superintendent, scandalized. He attempted to slap her hand but she was faster; instead he slapped her where never ever can a woman be endeared by such a manuever. The Reverend and Mrs. Dowie gasped again. Beatrice and the Captain laughed.

The bad thing, the awful thing about it all was that Doctor Masserbatt was not at all apologetic about it. He even had the nerve to chortle, "That's the law, like it or not!"

With icy disdain she demanded, "Prove it!"

For emphasis Trent held the superintendent still higher in the air. There was no slackening in the grip around the neck; instead there was an implication in the way Trent's fingertips were eased ever so lightly over Doctor Masserbatt's jugular. "If you put me down," cried Doctor Masserbatt, "I can supply the proof!"

"No way!" roared Trent. "Release Lyson first!"

"Can't" explained Doctor Masserbatt. "Don't have the key!"

Trent tightened his fingertips ever so powerfully and motioned to Wally. A frisk produced, among the usual pocket paraphernalia, a ring of keys. Wally tried them all but none would open the handcuffs.

Lyson was visibly upset.

Trent squeezed until a choking sound escaped the superintendent and he pointed, jabbing at his neck.

"Key!" was all Trent would say.

Doctor Masserbatt waved his hands desperately. Trent cracked, "That seems to be a surrender signal." And eased his fingertips enough to allow Doctor Masserbatt to croak, "No key!"

"What you mean, no key?" Trent moved in his fingertips again. Doctor Masserbatt tried to run but his feet were too far off the floor for any such success.

Wally finally found the key in the breast pocket of the jacket and held it aloft. Everyone looked at it and at Doctor Masserbatt who tried to giggle, but Trent tightened his grip. Wally made sure the television camera saw the key before he released Lyson.

Trent deposited the superintendent on his feet on the railing of the Bandstand, so that Doctor Masserbatt had to utilize the energy inherent in his hands much as a cat's tail to maintain his balance. Trent positioned himself where a mere jab of his finger could topple Doctor Masserbatt off his precarious perch.

"Don't use your hands!" scolded Evangeline smugly.

"I wasn't gesturing!" denied Doctor Masserbatt hotly.

"How was I to know?" shot back Evangeline.

"How do you like this?" Trent solicitously handcuffed Doctor Masserbatt by the ankle to the railing. "Comfy?"

"Explain this law, please," Evangeline asked sweetly, respectfully in the manner of an eager pupil, diabolically urging the teacher toward a trap.

Doctor Masserbatt nearly lost his balance but one of his flailing hands hit on and found support on the beam above. "Let me explain," he began, thoughtfully running his free hand in little circles, almost in the manner of snapping fingers but without actually snapping them, and almost as if by such a gesture the facts would be more readily summoned to mind. "You see, the law comes in such funny numbers—well, something like Code 73, Section 504, paragraph—"

"That's the Vocational Rehabilitation Act!" cried Evangeline.

"Exactly! That's it!" Doctor Masserbatt agreed, giving his pointing finger such a sharp shake he nearly lost his balance. He grabbed again the beam above and seeing that he'd stunned her, gloated, "See, the law is on my side."

"Charlatan!" seethed Evangeline. "That law is for the deaf! You're twisting it around to your own advantage!" She gave him a sharp poke in his side and he lost his balance and began falling backwards. Lyson seized the leg that was handcuffed to the railing. Trent grabbed Lyson to keep him from being pulled over the railing too. So Doctor Masserbatt's fall wasn't as violent as it would've been. They eased him down so that he hung upside down by the ankle.

"Whew!" Lyson wiped his forehead and flicked off the sweat. *Didn't want-break this,* he patted the railing soliticously.

Something caught his eye. A blue so startlingly blue it exploded when it entered in the lights for the television camera. It was Gene Owles. He came up beside Doctor Masserbatt and looked up at Lyson with that half smile of his. He held up an open palm and wiggled a finger. *Key, please.*

Lyson stared, his mouth open, his hands on the railing. As in a trance Wally handed down the key. Gene Owles held up the key toward the camera and smoothly, calmly remarked with his other hand, *This key, that's our deaf future!* With that half smile of his, he slowly dropped the key in his own breast pocket and patted it. The upside-down Hand Slapper attempted to slap Owles' hand but missed.

Gene Owles chuckled and sauntered away through the crowd wild with enthusiastic applause and waving handkerchiefs. He stepped into a waiting limousine with a flourish and drove away. All the crowd, even the upside-down Doctor Masserbatt stared after him. Only the old man feeding his squirrels and pigeons didn't notice. Or seem to. He's not saying. Could be he's too polite to say.

Not until Owles was gone did any hearing person realize that his little remark had gone uninterpreted, so that only the deaf understood.

CHAPTER 22

To be with Lyson at a most historical moment, many of his friends crowded into his office up in the turret. Due in a few minutes was the very first newscast on WZPO Channel 8, entirely in Sign Language. The atmosphere in the office was electric with excitement, and literally warm, as well as infused with the better kind of warmth that only friends can give. Wally opened the door to the roof for some air.

There was yet another source of warmth that Lyson would have to face up to but it wasn't on just yet. Right now it was not yet 5:30 P.M. and the soap opera had yet to culminate in a murder or a kiss before the news came on. The soap opera was terrible, of course, but there are people who revel in its very terribleness. Besides, it was being captioned by WZPO Channel 8 so that everyone, deaf or hearing, could appreciate its terribleness.

Before captioning, Professor Vought was marveling to Lyson and all the crowd, *I used-to think hearing people themselves naturally smart. You know how intelligent, how worldly people seem while they're just moving lips. But when you finally find-out what they're really saying*—He rolled his eyes and threw up his hands.

Similar, my dog, agreed Wally amiably. *Himself shut mouth, never talk, that why I think himself intelligent.*

When myself not fully understand my hearing husband, chipped in Undresa, *thought me that himself wonderful, brilliant. Then he learnt signs—*

Were the news not to come on in just a minute or two Lyson would have been tickled happy. He only managed a tight giggle.

Hearing, deaf, no real difference, Mary nodded ruefully at the television. The hero was clutching at his heart and crying out to the star, "You broke my heart, you bitch!"

The crowd in Lyson's office laughed. *Horrible, eh?* giggled Mary. The crowd laughed again and nodded their fists.

"I know I'll rue this moment even if I spend the rest of my life in prison," the hero was saying to the star as he was choking her, "but this is the only right thing to do, to prove my undying love for you."

"I love you, too, darling," the star said in spite of being choked, thereby making things right again. And preserving the show for another day.

Then the commercial flashed on and a man in white explained, holding up a little bottle for stomach acid relief, "There are three good things about Awayacid. The first two are: this bottle is doubly sealed against tampering. Third, it works!" A cartoon appeared with a sinister figure in black cape, wide-brimmed black hat, and black halloween mask over his eyes. Try as mightily as he could, the bottle steadfastly resisted his attempts at tampering. "See! This bottle is completely safe!" flashed the caption.

"Isn't that something?" remarked Beatrice to no one in particular. All the deaf understood from her expression and gave their heads that half shake that is more appropriate where words would be trite.

Then the room quieted. The screen lit up with a notice in orange letters against a background of the state flag of Islay: "For the first time in history, since the first man came down from trees and noticed his hands were fully capable of signalling messages, have the deaf ever had their own television station." Laughing applause rose in the room, thunderous to the eyes as well as the ears. The screen rolled on, "Islay Company under the leadership of its president Lyson C period Sulla—"

Lyson shrieked. "Evangeline didn't have to be so damn literal!"

"—has appropriated WZPO Channel 8 for, of, and by the deaf of the Great State of Islay.

"It is unconscionable that an audiovisual media like television would so neglect the visual aspect as so many stations do; for this reason WZPO Channel 8 shall endeavor to emphasize the visual aspect for the deaf. Of course, accomodations will be made for the hearing over the audiological capabilities inherent in television. The key element of television is, of course, the picture; therefore television should be more for the deaf than the hearing—"

Lyson remembered Beatrice, the Captain, Trent, Dottie, Crystal, Andy, Sandy and last, but not least, his mother. His ears reddened.

"—Like all history-making episodes, there may be some confusion at first, as you'll notice in the following news program—"

"Doesn't Evangeline know what and what not to interpret?" wailed Lyson. Then the scene at the Bandstand came on.

Lyson saw himself stumbling up on the platform of the Bandstand. He saw the silly grin and the squint. He saw the grin collapse and watched himself looking left over to the rear. He saw himself nod dumbly and turn back to the camera and rub his nose with his upper lip.

Lyson bit his knuckles. Everyone in the room was heartily laughing.

He saw himself giving the speech. He never saw the signs. Just his upper lip rubbing the nose. The helpless shrug and the look again over his shoulder.

Lyson remembered there was no bathroom in the turret. He saw his mouth open in amazement at something out of camera. He saw his head snap and jerk toward the camera. He saw his arm held high so that his hand was out of camera. He winced as he saw his wrist rotating around the stage, his hand invisible. No one could see what his hand was saying. He saw himself looking again over his shoulder and nodding and resuming his speech.

He never saw the signs. Only his face, earnest at first, then sagging and looking again over his shoulder, then brightening and returning to the camera: *Enough speech!*

Everyone in the room laughed. Even Mary. Lyson sank to his knees, biting his knuckles.

He saw a man snapping handcuffs on his left wrist. He saw the hopping around and the *Thrill* sign. Everyone in the turret couldn't stop laughing except Lyson. He saw himself falling under the man, his legs thrashing in the air.

He shut his eyes tight. He kept them shut for a long time. He could feel the floor thumping and rocking from the amusement of the crowd. He hated them all. Not funny! Suddenly the floor grew quiet. Not a foot stamped or stirred. No one joustled him.

His eyes opened reluctantly, afraid. On the screen was Gene Owles holding up the key besides the Hand Slapper hanging upside down by the ankle. He saw the sex in Gene Owles' eyes. The half smile.

In the background above Gene Owles, he saw himself gripping the handrail, his mouth open foolishly, staring at Gene Owles. A chuckle and a slow wink, and Gene Owles departed suavely. The camera zoomed in on Lyson C. Sulla biting his knuckles.

* * *

It took some doing to get Lyson out of bed. Mary tried with all her might and all the entreaties she could muster but she couldn't get him out of bed. Beatrice tried tickling him but he only burrowed deeper under the covers. Evangeline hoped for a chance but Mary insisted it was no use. Let him be.

Frankly, it took Mortima to get him out of bed. Not directly of course. It just happened that Lyson had to go to the bathroom one dark night when everyone else was asleep. After accomplishing this necessary function of the body he was on his way back to bed when he bumped into someone in the hallway. This would've been no big deal for most of us except that that someone attempted to put her hands on Lyson's face. Not just put her hands on his face but give him a message with her clumsy little fingers. Mortima! He tried backing into the bathroom, but as he tried to open the door after a few tries he realized he was pushing when he should pull.

He panicked and fled down the stairs and up the spiraling stairway to the turret. It was some time before they could get him down again. Mary could not figure it out but decided to at least be happy he was out of bed.

* * *

Myself one of most impossible people I ever knew! bewailed Lyson.

It's-all-right, all-right, soothed Pamela as she rebalanced the block on his head. *Calm yourself, then easier control yourself.*

Lyson looked up and the block fell off. *Don't look up!* scolded Pamela. *Watch my eyes.* She replaced the block on his head and he whiffed her perfume. The block fell off again. She frowned and felt the top of his skull. *No wonder; pointed.* Out of her kit came one of those little round leather cushions filled with shot normally used as paperweights. It helped keep the block from slipping off his head.

After lengthy practice over the next several days, Lyson was able to sit, stand up, walk around, and bow without dropping the block. Pamela was very pleased. When he was able to slip a key into his breast pocket, chuckle, wink, and saunter away without toppling the block, Pamela promoted Lyson to the next program.

It wasn't as easy, though. He had to learn to descend and ascend the steps in the turret without losing the block before Pamela would graduate him. All of his many close friends attended the ceremony at the foot of the steps. They applauded and patted him on the back.

He was out of the turret.

The next program, Mary announced, would be speech.

No way! said Lyson who would have none of it. *Oralism detest me!*

She realized she had used the wrong sign and tried to explain she did not mean speech THERAPY but Lyson was already out and running.

Sandy insisted on redoing Lyson's hair. *You can't look like Benny Hill forever.* She shook his head gently in her hands. *Be still!*

To be honest, Lyson enjoyed it very much. He liked her cool hands fussing over his head. And her warm scent, coconut oil. He was very happy and submissive in the chair. It was the first time in a long time that his body relaxed so luxuriantly. He dreamt of the tree in Obeke.

All too soon, Sandy patted his cheek and held up a mirror. At first Lyson did not know who confronted him. For one thing he did not have on his glasses. *That me?* he shrieked.

Sandy, Mary, Beatrice, Sally, Dottie, Crystal, Evangeline, Mortima, and Heather laughed and applauded. He reddened. He'd not known that Mary had allowed in such a crowd of witnesses. His ears blushed but in the mirror he noticed they were now covered by the new coiffure Sandy had conjured up. His eyebrows lifted: he liked it.

Mary remembered and put his glasses on his face. He rearranged them and looked again at his ears in the mirror. Only the lower lobes were visible. He studied his new haircut, turning his head this way and that for a thorough view. He saw how prominent was his dimple and was about to ask Sandy to erase it with makeup when Evangeline held up another mirror behind his head so he could see the back. He stared. He'd never before noticed that little bald spot where his whorl used to be. Evangeline realized her gaffe and pulled away the mirror. Too late. He patted the bald spot, visibly upset, but Sandy brushed off his hand and did some deft combing and fussing.

"There!" She said brightly, patting his dimple. Everyone in the salon patted him too. Beautiful! Handsome! He was flattered and tried a half smile and a slow wink. Sexy, wow! He was very happy now and rose to his feet, his fist thrust high. Gene Owles look out! Eat your heart out!

Lyson began sauntering toward the door before Sandy stopped him. She pulled off the sheet and brushed off his jacket and trousers. She pinched his dimple; then he was guided to the waiting car where Trent and Wally held the door open.

All of them, in a long line of automobiles winding through the streets of Suffex, made their way to the Merry Bandstand. For another go. Lyson wanted to impress the largest possible percentage of the voters.

The television van was already there, the crew setting up the camera and lights. Monte Guthrie was in charge of the crew this time. The hearing crew chief and camermen had been fired, of course, as had the news editors at WZPO. Only his friends, deaf and deaf, would he trust to do the job right this time. But Monte convinced Lyson that they needed a hearing person to do the audio part, so Lyson relented and kept on the sound engineer. After all, he was learning Sign Language, feverishly as if his life depended on it. The Captain, Beatrice, Sandy, Dottie and particularly Andy had assured Lyson that the engineer was a good one to keep aboard.

The engineer attempted to say *Hi!* but his fingers clumsily spelled *I H* while his tongue worked the side of his mouth. Lyson laughed and gave him a thumbs up.

He was ready this time, he grunted to himself. Mary seized the lapels of his jacket. *Remember speech?*

Of-course! Think you, me dumb? he replied curtly. He could feel his haircut moving in response. It was a new sensation and he shook his head just to get the sensation again.

Remember, just that one sentence—Mary admonished.

Don't worry!, he growled and worked his way toward the stairs.

Pamela stopped him for a moment. *Remember, pretend have block balancing on-your head.*

He smiled a half smile and winked a slow wink. At the foot of the stairs he paused and took in a deep breath and awaited Monte's signal. He felt calm, really. After all, he only needed to say just this one sentence, and it'd be easy coasting from then on. The Merry Bandstand loomed over him. Looks great, he thought, examining the details that combined to make the whole lovely. He glanced over at Monte. Still fiddling with the camera. Lyson didn't mind the slowness; at least Monte wanted the job done right. Evangeline stood by, ready with the microphone, her eyes smiling at him. Lyson quickly turned his attention to the Bandstand and this time studied the structure by which the lantern was held aloft so spectacularly. A little signal told him he shouldn't have left Sandy's salon without a visit to the restroom first. Too late now, he shrugged. Besides, only this one little sentence and—

A heavy booming sound reverberated against the back of his neck and shoulders, and he whirled to see where it came from. A band was marching toward them. Uniforms, drums, horns, cymbals, flutes, all the works. A drum major led them, strutting, kicking, leaping and hopping, clapping and snapping, whirling like a ballerina, and pretending to spin a baton though he had none. This drum major was not in uniform but had on an expensively tailored suit. As he approached the crowd he began, without any pause at all in his antics, slapping any and all hands visibly moving.

The Hand Slapper!

Monte signaled Lyson to hurry before it was too late. But Lyson stood there petrified. Bumping Lyson aside, Doctor Masserbatt bounded gleefully up the steps and pranced about. Without missing a beat, the band followed him up the steps and formed a circle facing the crowd all around.

The crowd stirred and hand messages of confusion flew all about. The Hand Slapper saw this and, without a letup in his prancing, came down and bounded his way around the crowd, slapping hands along the way. But the hands kept fluttering among the crowd. He at last gave up his prancing and shook his head wearily; with a great sigh, he began the earnest task of stilling those blasted hands. He worked his way around and around the Bandstand, slapping any and all hands, moving or not. His face was set with the resigned determination of a man who knows he has a mighty long row to hoe and might as well get on with it. Hand after hand he slapped and slapped. One after another. A rather tiresome chore, Doctor Masserbatt lamented to himself. Don't people know what their hands are doing! Slap slap, dear me, slap slap.

Lyson wailed, "My announcement?"

Mary dropped her head on his chest and sobbed. Suddenly Exota seized his hand and dragged him in a flurry around the Bandstand to the waiting camera. There, Monte explained that all wasn't lost by any means. *Just stand there in-front and make announcement. Show hearing we deaf don't give-up easy! Imagine perfect picture, deaf defiant in-front-of hearing trying-to suppress deaf!*

Lyson was elated and squeezed Monte's cheeks and kissed Exota. He was ready. Let's get rolling! But Sandy stopped him. First she had to redo his hair. He stood meekly while she fixed his appearance and wiped his face. Exota guided him to a position off-camera and coached, *Monte snap fingers, you walk there, see that paper on ground? Give announcement, then thumb-up and walk back here, O.K?*

The Captain, behind the shield of his jacket, gave him a quick nip of comfort and happiness. Andy thrust a fist high.

Hurry! Monte gave the camera a final check and snapped the signal. Lyson was too slow and needed a prod. Pamela reminded him of the block on his head. The band played on, playing its heart out. Very calmly, almost in slow motion Lyson sauntered to the paper on the ground and faced the camera, smiling the half smile and winking the slow wink.

Doctor Masserbatt lunged like a fullback toward Lyson, but Trent was a better linebacker and seized him by the neck and held him up off the ground, kicking thin air. The superintendent slapped the air in the direction of Lyson, earnestly and singlemindedly determined to get at Lyson's hands. Trent was disgusted and would have snapped his neck except that Crystal ran up and stopped him with great eyes. Trent growled and tossed Doctor Masserbatt aside like a rag.

Myself announce, myself will become Governor here Islay. State our own Deaf! Lyson signed happily toward the camera. Evangeline interpreted politely into the microphone, "I declare my candidacy for the Governorship of Islay!"

Doctor Masserbatt charged Lyson again but Trent made a good stop and dumped the superintendent on the ground.

Exota and Monte urged Lyson to move off-camera. *Thumb-up!* Lyson held up a thumb, smiled the half smile, winked the slow wink, and departed suavely off-camera. The band went into an even more fervent beat, booming off the ceiling so loud it felt like a screeching wail to the deaf assembled around.

With dizzying swiftness Trent and Wally carried Lyson under the armpits to the waiting automobile, the crowd streaming behind like lemmings. By the time Doctor Masserbatt had shaken his head clear and struggled to his feet, everyone deaf was gone. Only the band still played on, its sound reverberating throughout the park. Doctor Masserbatt looked around in amazement.

"Hurrah!" he cheered. He leapt high and danced and jigged and clicked his heels and whirled around the Bandstand. "I've done it!"

The Governor came up with his bodyguards and watched, frowning at the leaping and prancing. Doctor Masserbatt saw the Governor and pranced up. "Hi Governor! I, Doctor Hermann Masserbatt, finally did it! I've driven them deaf away! Hip! Hip! Horray!"

Aghast, the bodyguards picked up the Governor by the armpits and whisked him away to the Mansion.

CHAPTER 23

From dawn til midnight, day after day, the bands played on in the Merry Bandstand. Doctor Masserbatt saw to this, arranging for relays, substitutes, meals, an ambulance, and Porta-Johnies so that the beat would not cease from dawn till midnight. No way was he going to let the deaf desecrate such a fine structure dedicated solely for the celebration of sound!

Everyone in the city of Suffex that could hear, from the freeway to the rivers, woke to this earnest music every morning and did not fall asleep until it ceased at midnight. Even as far away as Fremont and over in Sutherland, the rumble could be heard because of the huge amplifiers set up around the Bandstand. The sound drew people to the park, day in and day out. The old man and his squirrels and pigeons were nowhere to be seen.

So thunderous was the beat that late every afternoon a cloud would form over Suffex and grow into a thunderstorm, scattering the crowd. But the band dauntlessly played on and after the cloud drifted away to the east, the crowd would return with sheets of plastic and tarps to throw on the grass. Picnics went on all day and evening, attracting vendors of all ilks bearing their wares in vans, pushcarts, display stands, wooden crates, and even overcoats. They would have become wealthy: business was that brisk, except there were so many of them, too many for any one to become rich. Perhaps because of the excitation of molecules in the air by waves of sound, the very air was filled with scents of all sorts: hot dogs and mustard and buns, cotton candy and popcorn and butter, perfume and sweat and body odor, tobacco and tobacco smoke, grass and freshly mown grass. It was later claimed that fully half the alcoholism and other such deliriums in Suffex got their start that summer. Little children collected a fortune in bottles and beer cans and found many lost pennies. For the Reveries, Arnie, Maude and Bonnie, each day was a field day: fingerspelling cards sold like ice cream on a hot day. Pickpockets became so embarrassed by their loot they had to also pick up valises, picnic baskets, or whatever was handy to haul it away. Even Doctor Masserbatt passed the hat. "All in the service of the deaf," his placard explained, and to make it all the more legitimate he flipped it like magic to the reverse side where it added, "Of course it is deductible."

Just then something caught his eye.

At a nearby intersection was a policeman in white gloves directing traffic. Never before did Islay have such a sight. But now the Merry Bandstand was drawing traffic from all around, so that for the first time in history Suffex required a traffic policeman.

The Hand Slapper saw the gesticulating white gloves and began running toward them.

* * *

Lyson was dismayed and showed it. He did not know there were so many hearing people still in Islay. All those cars! Those crowds! He paced to and fro waving his hands. *Truth! We bought most houses here Suffex, and sold deaf only, you know that!* he bewailed to everyone around the conference table.

It was a grand table that ran in a long oval around the room so that everyone was equally visible from each seat. Deaf people need their eyes to know what is going on: long, straight tables are not convenient where they need to see and be seen by their leader. The Islay Company is of, by and for the deaf, as Lyson insisted, and everything therefore had to be designed for the deaf. The seats had arms placed low and out of the way of elbows while signing. And padded velvet so that the audience would not squirm from discomfort and distract the speaker. On the table conveniently in front of each seat was a handkerchief standing next to little placards that read: "For applause only please. Not for blowing nose or interrupting." Lyson was extremely proud of that little touch; it had taken him two full weeks of hashing it out with Wally, Mary, the Captain, and other members of the board to work out the precise wording in those little placards. The deaf are easily distracted by sudden flashes, you know, and it is extremely important those handkerchiefs be used only in the way indicated.

Enough! Mary closed the subject. *Understood!*

Exactly, thrill? Problem? Lester Lieske was asking. *Insurance business growing fast, zooming! Many deaf buying, buying insurance for life, home, car, health—*

Bowling, movies, arcade, crowds deaf, added Wally. *Country Club now almost all deaf. Hearing moved away.*

But did you see crowd there Bandstand? Lyson hopped without his feet actually leaving the floor. *Thousands hearing! More coming everyday!*

Thousand deaf there my church, soothed the Reverend Dowie. *Hundreds in nursery.*

Three hundred deaf carpenters work for me, said Byron Windecker. *Plus their families. Hundreds children will go school here, need deaf teachers.*

Me and Walt have over 200 workers, chipped in Steve Kinyon. *Our construction company growing fast, building 50 new homes, 7 new business.*

Monte Gunthrie threw up his hands, *Wife told me, can't catch-up her figuring how-many TTYs in state, how-many deaf work there Silent Electronics. Too-many!*

Three thousand deaf children in public schools next fall. Doctor James Shooner arched his eyebrows significantly. *Twenty deaf now there mental hospital.*

The room quieted thoughtfully. Doctor Shooner lit his pipe. Byron fired up his cigar. Cigarettes flared here and there. The Captain nodded. Evangeline nudged him awake and interpreted, "Smoke time." Wally and Steve dipped snuff. The Reverend Dowie blanched. Lyson paced to and fro. Mary folded her arms and crooked her mouth in amusement at her husband.

Lyson stopped suddenly, chin in hand. Mary could see the thoughts rolling in his eyes. She waited until they stopped rolling and held her hand out and waved in his face. Lyson jumped as struck by electricity.

Excuse me, she said, suppressing a chuckle. *Beatrice told me most those people, hearing, themselves from out-of-state. Nothing worry about.*

Lyson stared at her, his mouth open.

Understand? she asked gently, inquisitively.

Lyson sat down heavily. This jarred him back into the room. *Outside?* He confused the sign for *outside* with Mary's for *out-of.*

Those people themselves from out-of-state, Mary repeated patiently. *Hearing, I mean those there Bandstand.*

His eyes widening Lyson exclaimed, *You mean, hearing moving here?*

A big chuckle popped out of Mary. *No! I mean, attracted music, just visiting.*

Sure?

Of Course! Beatrice saw license-plates, talked them.

Lyson jumped to his feet. *How know they not moving here? Maybe they will like here, stay, idea-same us deaf!*

Doubt that. Mary drew his attention to the others shaking their heads in agreement around the table. *When they try buy houses and find deaf, and when they take kids school and see signing, they will vamoose, same other hearing live here before.*

Suppose more more hearing come, crowd us deaf out? Lyson hopped. *Must do something now!*

The room was still for three or four moments and Wally asked, *Do? Do?*

Must out hearing! Must stop music now—Lyson froze and stared at something in the back. All eyes turned too.

Resplendent in a baby-blue suit, leaning against the doorjamb, his legs scissored elegantly, was Gene Owles smiling that half smile and winking that slow wink and biting on a toothpick. He wrinkled his nose, in effect saying *Don't mind me. Go on.* He looked straight at Lyson with sleepy, chuckling eyes.

Everyone turned to Lyson. He was biting his knuckles. Everyone turned back to Gene Owles who looked calmly, serenely, around. *Mind if I join?* his eyes seemed to ask.

Mary glanced over at Lyson from the corner of her eye and saw his hand still at his mouth. She sighed, and waved in Gene Owles. Lyson glared, scandalized at his wife. She shrugged back.

Lyson right, hearing must leave, Gene Owles finally said when he had all the attention of the room. *All hearing!*

A stir flew around the table. Gene Owles shot a challenge at Lyson. *When I say all hearing, I mean A-L-L hearing. Must none remain here.*

Mary saw that Lyson was too dumbstruck to be of any good. Disappointment rippled across her face, changing quickly to disgust. She jumped to her feet and demanded, *Exactly what you mean, A-L-L?*

Still leaning jauntily against the doorjamb, Gene Owles said easily, *I thought we, all-us deaf here, want deaf state.* He paused to allow nods to go around the table. Lyson bit his lip when their eyes met. *You?* Gene Owles asked with his eyes. Lyson nodded slowly, still biting his lip.

Well! said Gene Owles stepping into the room. *Deaf State means NO hearing, right?*

Lester Lieske stood up. *My children themselves hearing. Must they leave?*

My wife hearing, Byron Windecker said simply.

Excuse my signing, the Captain moved his hands with the awkwardness of a person who learns Sign Language late in life. *I am hearing but I have a deaf son and believe in you deaf people.* He sat to enthusiastic applause and waving of handkerchiefs.

Lyson took courage and thrust his chin at Gene Owles. *My mother herself hearing!*

Handkerchiefs flew around the room. Mixed emotions worked across Gene Owles' face. He wanted to laugh but knew he must put on the correct face. This struggle lasted only two or three ticks of the clock but all the deaf saw. He saw them watching him and flashed his teeth. *Wonderful! My mother also hearing.*

Lyson cocked his head like a rooster that had just laid an egg. He was about to begin strutting when Gene Owles said quietly, his hands small by the very way he used them: *But my mother never understood me. Herself wanted me copy hearing, pretend hearing. Not allow me express myself naturally, freely. Not all me myself. I want her love but she love hearing more.*

Every head including Lyson's, Mary's, even the Captain's nodded sadly. It was not that difficult to understand Mother. Mother means well, she loves you, you know, but she cannot help but want to hear you say Mother. She loves you still even when the best you can utter with that deaf mouth of yours is "Murdah."

Lyson dropped to his seat and bawled. The entire room sniffed with him. The only dry eyes belonged to Gene Owles and Mary Sulla. They glared at each other. She looked cooly back. He ducked his eyes and made an attempt at sobbing. Mary simply folded her arms and twisted her lips.

Evangeline came around to Lyson and comforted him, patting his back and squeezing his shoulders. Lyson twitched in his seat. He saw Mary watching them and he jumped to his feet. *Nothing wrong with hearing,* he cried out with his hands. *Nothing, really. That why upset me when—when we have-to—have-to—*

Right! Must push-off hearing! declared Gene Owles. Lyson's wince seemed to say not so fast! *We want deaf state,* Gene Owles continued vigorously, *This requires all hearing leave. Only deaf allowed here.*

Love thy enemy, stood up the Reverend Dowie, his face earnest with sincerity. He saw the stir around the table and held up his palms. *Don't misunderstand me, please. Myself minister, therefore must love all people.* Gene Owles tried to interrupt but the Reverend Dowie shook a firm palm. *Let me finish. True, true, hearing always ever since suppress deaf, control schools for deaf. Even churches for deaf, myself very sorry have-to admit. Deaf start or establish something like school, club, church—*

Then hearing take-over! roared Gene Owles with triumphant signs. *And push deaf aside! And don't forget Alexander Graham Bell! Hearing say he's best friend us deaf ever had, but he tried destroy our Ameslan and culture, forbid us deaf marrying; he even proposed sterilizing us deaf—called "eugenics"—his best "cure for mutism!" Hearing still honor him. Imagine, still honor him! Me trust hearing? Ha Ha, No thanks!* He grabbed his crotch by way of declaring, "I'm holding on to my jewels!"

Reverend Dowie and Evangeline gasped. Mary laughed.

"Is this true?" exclaimed the Captain.

"I'm afraid it is."

"I never knew!"

What's more, Gene Owles announced with a flourish, *This state, Islay itself one of several that Bell convinced, passed law that all deaf must—* He finished with a graphic gesture of castration.

Impossible!

Gene Owles laughed and tilted his head toward Jack Nelson, *Ask him, himself lawyer.*

Knew that several states—about 16—did pass that law long ago, Jack Nelson said with a slow shake of the head, *but most repealed later on.*

Check Islay!

Will, but hearing probably forgot about that law—

Check anyway!

Statistics say ninety percent of deaf children are the products of hearing parents.

Alexander Graham Bell was an active member of the American Stock Breeders Association which put to successful practice eugenics—the science of selective breeding—which proved successful in eliminating tits too small for milking machines, and steers not beefy enough for Wendy's. We now enjoy turkeys that taste like bologna, hams in tin cans, eggs that do not chirp. And potatoes that do not explode in the oven.

All this reminded the Captain of a favorite joke of an old uncle of his—the one that chewed and spat tobacco in the presence of ladies for the sheer pleasure of inciting their displeasure—"If only women were as easy to make happy as cows: just milk 'em and feed 'em oats twice a day and they're happy."

The man guffawed. Mary and Evangeline twisted their lips.

Anyway, so successful was eugenics with livestock that this American Stock Breeders Association, with an avid Alexander Graham Bell, strongly urged and lobbied for the sterilization of socially unfit classes—that's us deaf, mind you—to purge the United States of America of its "burden of undesirable germplasm."

Fancy term for deaf semen, commented Doctor Shooner.

Not exactly—began Reverend Dowie.

Enough! Enough! commanded Mary.

Hearing and deaf. How is this possible?

Deaf see with eyes. Hearing see with ears. With eyes if they will.

Plato said, I think, therefore I am. Deaf say, I see, therefore I think. Hearing say, I hear, I hear.

Deaf say, my hands are me.

Hearing say, Jesus said out of the heart comes forth the mouth. Hearing say, must speak for the deaf. Must help deaf, guide deaf, show deaf, hug deaf.

Funny thing, noticed two odd things about hearing, Doctor Shooner held up two fingers and tapped one, then the other. *Hearing either too-much interested in us deaf. Or nothing interested none.*

When the twain meet, have you noticed, the first question a hearie asks a deafie almost always is an insult, if not stupid?

Yeah, the old guilt trip.

Deaf and hearing. How can this be?

Why are hearies so afraid of hands, hands alive with life and power, power incomprehensible to the ear, yet perceivable as the invisible wind that flies among trees, rousing and swaying the limber and bringing down the stiff, down to the roots of fear. Why are hearies so afraid, Captain?

Evangeline nudged John Quayle awake. "Afraid?" mumbled the Captain. "Who's being afraid?"

"Never mind."

For a while the room was very still, sober, not a finger stirring. Then Doctor Shooner raised a hand slightly, looking over at Lyson for permission to speak. Mary nudged Lyson who started as from a trance and looked around. Mary nudged again and pointed her eyes at Doctor Shooner. *What?* Lyson asked with the innocence of confusion.

One thing bothers me very much, said Doctor Shooner sadly. *Seems to me same old story: majority always suppress, thrust under table minority second-class citizens. You know that we deaf ever since always second-class, interested only in equality. Now we're thinking about making hearing—*

No problem! countered Gene Owles. *No hearing here, therefore no second-class.*

Byron Windecker stood up with a growl audible only to the Captain and Evangeline but clearly visible to the deaf. *Thought this supposed important meeting, not absurd bull-shooting contest!*

The room burst out in laughter, applause and waving handkerchiefs. Gene Owles was not amused. Mary saw. He saw her watching him and he made for the door. She stopped him and guided him to a chair. Even she was puzzled at herself: some kind of intuition made her do this. She did not know why, but something told her it was the thing to do. Right or not.

Lyson glared at her. She made a face back. He looked quickly away and wailed, *Do? Do? Hearing already took-over Bandstand from us deaf!*

Bandstand? Lester peered at Lyson comically. *Thrill, important?*

Lyson blanched.

Bandstand really theirs hearing, agreed Doctor Shooner. *Nothing connection with deaf—*

That building very beautiful but for music, nodded Jack Nelson. *Let hearing have—*

Look-at-me! Lyson jabbed seeing fingers at himself. *We must take that bandstand from hearing. Important that we deaf control it. Bandstand itself built for pleasure, for nice things life, for joy. Happiness, beauty that gather people closer together. Unity and—and—*He blushed. He didn't quite know how to say such an awkward word.

Power, Gene Owles mockingly finished for him, his eyes exulting in triumph.

No! No! Lyson protested, flustered. *Not that! Another word, another—*

Love, the Reverend Dowie suggested solemnly. *Idea same church.*

Deaf club! Lyson hastened to say, his ears burning cherry hot. *In other words,—*

Music. Gene Owles said, dryly playing a violin.

Not talking about music! Lyson's hands yelled back. *Talking about deaf community!*

Then why you talk talk about Bandstand Bandstand? asked Gene Owles, sitting back and putting his feet on the table. *Bandstand their hearing problem, not ours deaf.*

Exactly! interceded the Captain. *It is keeping us hearing awake nights!*

Everyone laughed but Lyson. He was popping mad. *It's attracting more more hearing back here Islay!*

Gene Owles watched him and noted the flushed face dripping sweat, the shaking fingers, the growing rings under the armpits, the wildness about the eyes. *Idea!* he said artfully. He put his feet down and leaned over eagerly so all in the room could see him. *Burn down Bandstand!* He blew ashes off his palm, *Bye, bye.*

Lyson glared at him as a bishop would at a heathen using for a hoe a consecrated gold and ivory cross off the altar. There are times when deep anger produces a terrible calm and a clear head. Lyson was surprised to discover this, and at the smooth whirling and meshing of the gears in his brain. No sane, right-thinking human could fail to find Gene Owles' remark highly offensive. I've got him this time! He straightened up in triumph and looked around the room.

Every last single one of them were laughing. The Captain was resting his face on a hand, his shoulders bouncing. Wally was slapping his thigh. The Reverend Dowie was doubled over. Even Mary was smiling.

Tears threatened to burst out and spoil his countenance so he roared, *Not funny!*

The room found that even funnier. You could almost feel the floor bouncing with laughing. Lyson sank slowly and crumbled into his chair, eyes glazed and running, face ashen and damp. The Bandstand a joke, a joke.

Mary and Evangeline fell on him, wiping his face, patting and soothing. *Can't help. Truly funny your face. Your expression!* Mary tried mightily to keep her face straight and concerned but couldn't. She buried it in his chest so he wouldn't see—the mirth bursting over her face. But he could feel her shoulders jumping.

A joke! A joke! Some Pied Piper I am! Pied Piper. Pied Piper. Pied Piper!

CHAPTER 24

The Federal Building in downtown Suffex on the corner of Fourth and Great had only three tenants and intentionally so. The United States Postal Service was on the lower floor. The Internal Revenue Service and the Treasury branch of the Selective Service took three or four offices upstairs. Actually there was a number of empty offices, never manned since the day the building was completed during the Depression.

The Post Office of course was a natural: everyone wanted it and it was quite handy for receiving Social Security and Veteran's checks. Of course nobody wanted the IRS and Selective Service but the Government insisted. As for the other empty offices, one would have expected to find various agencies such as Commerce, Agriculture, Employment, Health and Welfare, Legal Aid, Civil Rights and other useful services available from the Government. But the Wenchells had always prevailed. States' rights, you know, and all that. They argued that those same services were, at any rate, available at the State Building and so forth. The people did not mind and the Government paid no mind. When Lyson first came to Islay he was appalled but eventually saw that this state of affairs would only serve to make his task all the easier once he moved into the Mansion. No entrenched Federal bureaucrats to uproot.

As you enter the main lobby from the street by going up the long stairs through the tall, heavy polished-brass framed doors, you find on the left corner a newsstand. Horace half-leaned against and half-sat on a tall stool behind a glass counter, something like a meat counter only it was stocked with magazines, newspapers, candy bars, chewing gum, and the like. Normally at such an establishment you would also find cigarettes and other tobacco products but Horace did not like smoking. In the bad old days before the Surgeon General's determination that smoking might be hazardous to your health, Horace innocently, like everyone else, stocked all brands of cigarettes and cigars and a few major chews.Not anymore. Anyone so foolish as to inquire was scowlingly pointed to a notice in bold print on the wall: NO SMOKING—FEDERAL LAW.

Horace meant it. He was serious and saw and noticed everything going on, to, and from, the lobby. The Post Office was the old type with little caged windows along one wall over which proclaimed little signs: STAMPS MONEY ORDERS PARCELS GENERAL DELIVERY. In the grand old days when everyone had a job and no one minded the red ink at the Postal Service, each window was manned by a clerk, line or no, busy or not, the rationale being that while stamps may lose the government a penny, the sheer volume of commerce through the through the mails recouped for the government hefty profits upstairs at the IRS. These days, however, the Grand Old Party wanted each and every little stamp to turn a pretty penny, so only one harried clerk flitted from window to window to perform whatever service required. A customer who inquires at the wrong window is referred politely to the correct window behind which the same clerk would pop up before the customer finds it.

On the far wall a portrait of the President of the United States watched. Above him a little two-way mirror watched also. Horace watched too. The clerk was careful to avoid his eye. Horace was a taxpayer and as such exercised all the rights and responsibilities therein. No less.

Horace was happy and proud for many years. He had his own little corner in the Federal Building. People came to him for an important service. Newspapers, magazines, cough drops, aspirin. They spoke to him. He was an expert lipreader. So long as he kept his mouth shut most of them did not even know he was deaf. He was very proud of this. People would come up and say something. He would, if their lips weren't clear, watch their eyes closely and discover where they pointed, what they wanted. He would run his hand under the counter to where their eyes would give a subconscious signal. This was how he could so readily know just what merchandise the customer desired. He was an expert lipreader. A solemn and learned look was always on his face. He was not deaf and dumb. He was the only deaf man that stayed in Islay after graduation . . . the others departed immediately and never returned. Sean Quayle, for instance. They even learned Sign Language! Deaf and Dumb.

But lately his face hung long and heavy. A disquiet had come over him. People coming up to the counter did not all speak to him but pointed at whatever they wanted. If they did not see what they wanted they would write on a little pad something like Pall Mall? He would point indignantly at NO SMOKING and run them off with full confidence they would never know he was deaf too. This part made him ten feet tall. Still, there was this disquiet. There were more and more such people. People who did not speak to him but pointed or wrote on bits of paper. Sign Language was everywhere now. In the lobby, out in the streets, in the cafes and restaurants, everywhere. A man even offered to sell him a little card teaching people how to form the alphabet on their fingers. He tried to seize the man but was suddenly confronted by such a hideous scar across the man's throat that he nearly fainted. When the blood returned to his head—he could actually feel it rushing up inside his skull—the man was gone.

And Channel 8. At first he was overjoyed to see the subtitles and captions and to finally find out the hearing don't really talk as smart as they had always seemed. But then there were more and more programs that were in Sign Language so that the captions were really for the hearing. Everything including the commercials were now captioned so that he found himself incessantly watching Channel 8. He tried to restrict himself to the movies, which of course were not in Sign Language but fully captioned. He tried to force himself to watch other channels but had to admit to himself that even an expert lipreader gets tired of lips all day long. The captions were so much nicer, so much more complete that, in spite of himself, he felt a part of the program, so well did he understand what was being said.

But the blasted Sign Language! And the people using it were so happy. No shame at all! Don't even know they are deaf and dumb. And demonstrating it for all the world to see. Horace was disturbed. Sign Language was everywhere he turned. There was no avoiding it. Even the newspaper had gone to the deaf. He needed to go down to the Bandstand and talk to Doctor Masserbatt about it. Surely the good superintendent would know what to think about it. Horace put on ear protectors, just like all the hearing in Suffex who did not like the music shaking and thumping the entire town. Even the deaf couldn't help but take notice, so thudding were the vibrations.

He put on a learned look, locked up the counter, and started for the Bandstand.

* * *

Governor Wenchell was extremely displeased. He'd tried plenty of mint juleps but had too many. Not only did they do no good in blocking out the horrendous noise, but they seemed instead to magnify the terrible sound. The Governor was incensed. Instead of the pleasant glow he only had this nasty uneasiness that he had had too much, and he still required the help of ear protectors. But so percussive was the booming that it still got through his skull to the drums in his ears or whatever activated the awful banging in his head. No respite, no way.

If you asked him, Doctor Masserbatt was a complete, total fool to be walking up the stairs at this very moment, just when he, Wenchell, discovered that aspirin was no proof against the all-pervasive sound booming and shrieking from the Bandstand. And just when he should be settling into a delightful stupor, with the sun warm on his face tingling with the buzzing in his nose. A drunk does not at all like to be reminded of his diminished capacity, his disability. The hair on his head, eyebrows, mustache literally stiffened as the superintendent bounded up the stairs.

B-52 and P-51 noted the bristling hair and patted their coats, feeling the guns and blackjacks and handcuffs and whatever makes for a compleat law officer. Satisfied that they were fully equipped, they allowed their hands to hang limp by their sides even as they guarded the Governor's flanks.

"Get rid of that sound!" hissed Governor Wenchell.

"What?" said Doctor Masserbatt extending out an ear.

"Shut up that sound!" seethed the Governor with hands over his ear protectors.

"Oh, oh, thought you liked it," apologized the superintendent.

"What?" growled Slappy Wenchell taking off an ear protector to hear better.

"Thought you liked it," yelled Doctor Masserbatt in his ear.

Governor Wenchell tossed aside the ear protectors in disgust and thumped the side of his head with the heel of his hand. "You'll make us all deaf yet!"

"Uh?" grovelled Doctor Masserbatt working a finger in an ear.

"I said you'll turn us into deaf mutes!" roared the Governor slapping at his ears.

"Right! Right! Lovely music, isn't it?" clapped the superintendent.

Slappy Wenchell seized Doctor Masserbatt by the ears and shook hard. "Get rid of that blasted band! Immediately!"

"Oh—oh, you want me to turn down the volume?" The superintendent was down on his knees clasping his hands.

Slappy seized the doctor by the nose and twisted. He pointed at the band and flung away his hand.

"I see! I see! You want them to go away."

The Governor again thumped the side of his head and shook a finger in an ear. "Git!"

"Let me try turning down the volume a bit—" Doctor Masserbatt made an attempt to kiss the Governor on the hand but P-51 slapped the pursed lips and shoved him. The superintendent slithered down the stairs in bewilderment and hightailed it toward the Bandstand, his heels kicking. "Git! Git!" called the Governor and his bodyguards after him again and again, knowing full well he couldn't hear them. It just felt good doing it.

* * *

The air was taut, electric with coiled energy as the Petite Pipers limbered up like ballerinas before the dance; restless as sprinters shaking limbs loose before the call to blocks. Spirited horses stomping, straining at the bit. A dog running full bolt at the end of his leash. A leopard pacing its cage. The Petite Pipers were no turkeys, for sure.

Lyson was so excited he required being held up under the arms by Wally and Trent. He was so sweaty his glasses kept slipping down his nose.

Actually the Petite Pipers were Gene Owles' idea. Lyson had wanted to play the Pied Piper himself but support in the boardroom was for something more delectable introduced by Gene Owles, so much that Lyson had to hustle to gain some credit for the idea. In the confusion, the excitement, it no longer mattered whose idea was whose. At least Lyson had managed to emerge on top of the heap.

All around him were dazzling, spirited women in the very prime of their womanhood. All of them eager, jumping, kicking, and hopping in sparkling tights and white boots and whirling batons. It's not everyday you get to see a woman give herself out, full and rich, to the power and glory of being woman, Lyson enthused to himself. All those long legs dazed Lyson. Wally and Trent shook him.

Waiting, for-for? Lyson asked Wally.

Patience! Important, everything must mesh.

Finally the television-crew van arrived, Monte perched on the roof with a huge camera, his hair blowing in the wind, Exota holding him fast, her hair flying wild in a way Lyson liked very much. Everyone drew together at the stairs of the Bandstand where the musicians played on and on, bombarding the very air with swirling molecules of sound palpable to the deafest of the deaf. Everyone expected was there except Gene Owles. Lyson could not help but fret at this absence, for it could only mean Owles was up to something, something no good for Lyson, for sure.

The Petite Pipers took up station along the bottom of the stairway and began gyrations designed to do no less than attract the attention of the band. The band stared back over their instruments, mesmerized. The bandmaster's baton nearly faltered and the music with it but Andy and Lester bounded clapping up the stairs and whirled around him, urging him on with claps, snaps, jugs, clicks, winks, and kicks. The astonished bandmaster whirled around along with them and was soon borne along with their enthusiasm down the stairs, drawing with him the band blowing, drumming, plucking strings, and marching right along.

Doctor Hermann Masserbatt still in full run, highballing from the Mansion, saw the band departing and fell flat on his face.

The Petite Pipers fell in place and led the way down the park, toward the west where the sun hung fat and heavy. The Petite Pipers, about a dozen of the finest female specimens Gene Owles could gather up in Suffex, were absolutely magnificent in their kicks, prances, hops, spins, thrusts, bump and grinds in that ritual so immortalized and sanctified by the Dallas Cowgirls. The drummers banged their drums. The trumpeters blew until their ears popped. Cymbals crashed, fifes shrieked, strings rang and resonated. Andy and Lester danced the way old men dance, urging the befuddled bandmaster after the Petite Pipers. Batons caught the sun. The tights sparkled from thousands of little jewels. The Captain gripped Beatrice on the hips and they hopped after the band. Marlene gripped the Captain, Doctor Shooner caught her, and they all hopped along. Dottie, Darcy, Crystal, Byron, Beanpole, caught on and so began the hopping snake dance. The Reverend Dowie and Geraldine even joined in and away went the snake, slithering after the band booming, roaring, and shreiking. The snake hopped and kicked and grew and grew. Men grabbed hips and their wives seized them and were borne along and grabbed themselves. Women grabbed men and their husbands seized them and were borne along and grabbed themselves. Mortima wanted to join in but was afraid she would lose her purse and hat and so fell away. The snake grew and grew and trailed after the band and Petite Pipers, drawing all the people in the park into itself and out of the park.

Doctor Hermann Masserbatt sped around and outflanked the Petite Pipers and made a stand courageous, arms folded, face stern. But the Petite Pipers jumped, hopped, kicked, twirled, and marched right on by him. Furious, he ran up and outflanked them and began slapping hands. Only he missed and slapped some thighs. A fury of batons felled him and the band marched right over him and the Snake, each and every leg of it, knocked him down again and again.

Swiftly, Wally and Trent carried Lyson under the arms to a big black convertible and tossed him into the back seat and jumped in. A big sign taped to the sides of the car announced: LYSON FOR GOVERNOR. Mary just managed to get in the front seat as Sandy stepped on the gas and the automobile sped down Ninth Avenue toward Wrong Road. They got there before the Petite Pipers and slowed down. Along Wrong Road the automobile led the procession, Lyson perched on the shoulders of Wally and Trent, waving at the crowd cheering all along the road. Lyson saw that the crowd was more interested in the Petite Pipers behind. He waved all the more frantically but the crowd waved and cheered more wildly at the Petite Pipers.

The television van came abreast, Monte intent on the Petite Pipers. Lyson waved and waved but Monte was deep into the camera. Exota saw and tapped Monte. Look!

Oh! Monte turned the camera to Lyson and waved. Lyson waved happily. Wally and Trent waved. Mary waved. Just as quickly Monte turned back to the Petite Pipers. Exota shrugged an apology and gave a small wave.

A flash of electric blue suddenly materialized out of Twelfth Street and took up a position in front of them. Highly polished chrome wire wheels caught and directed the sun into the eyes of everyone. Gene Owles! He stood in his Porsche and flashed a grin back at Lyson and began waving small, modest waves at the crowd. Red, white, and blue signs on his car proclaimed: GENE OWLES FOR GOVERNOR!! Gene Owles looked back and smiled that half smile of his. Lyson nearly lost his perch and pounded Trent and Wally on the head. *Do-do?* he demanded.

Mary pinched Lyson just where she knew it would quiet him quickly. She looked around at the crowd, shame on her face, and her hand sizzled, *Calm yourself!*

Many in the crowd recognized Gene Owles and waved enthusiastically.

Do-do? Lyson shrieked.

With swiftness of mind over matter that is the bread and butter of a professional linebacker, Trent set Lyson down and jumped out of the convertible. Long easy smooth strides and superb timing carried him to the driver's side of Gene Owles' car. He gripped the wheel and swung the car into a side street before the driver knew what was happening.

Sandy nearly followed them but Mary grabbed the wheel and they cruised on down Wrong Road. The applause had by now spread among the crowd ahead so that Lyson was insanely happy. Hands, handkerchiefs, and little green, blue, and yellow Islay flags flew and waved. Tears came to Lyson's eyes and he waved as hard as he knew how. The ultimate honor that could ever befall a politician occurred: a mother thrust her baby at him. He pecked at it but it smelt of milk, and other baby smells, and he gave it quickly back. He hoped the mother didn't see and that Wally didn't notice his wiping his hands on him.

Trent bounded back in the car and flourished a ring of keys from the Porsche. Mary took them greedily and kissed them. Trent and Wally rehoisted Lyson on their shoulders. Lyson thrust up his arms in a triumphant "V". The crowd waved wildly but it seemed to be more directed toward the Petite Pipers behind.

With the grace and quickness of a feline, Gene Owles had figured his options and joined the Petite Pipers. He hopped, jumped, kicked, twirled, thrust, bump and grinded along with the best of them. The crowd went wild.

A smile as good as any Cheshire cat could ever muster spread across his face as Gene Owles looked directly at Lyson. *You just wait!* his eyes seemed to say. Lyson again nearly fell off Trent and Wally.

Soon they were going up the ramp toward the freeway bridge over Wrong Turn toward Fremont. The freeway was blocked by Gene Owles' men, and traffic backed up as far as the eye could see to the east. The road and bridge to the west remained clear and bare. The air was thick with helicopters. Channels 2 and 7 from Fremont. Channel 4 from Trenton. Channels 5 and 11 from Philadelphia. Channel 8 had Monte hanging out the door, is camera straight at the Petite Pipers.

Lyson looked over his shoulder at Gene Owles who looked smugly back, step in step with his Petite Pipers, never missing a beat. Gene Owles waved at the helicopter and said ha ha to Lyson.

The camera, Monte's face deep in it, was pointing yet at the Petite Pipers. Lyson waved wildly but Monte was too into the Petite Pipers. Gene Owles laughed and waved gaily at Lyson and matched his entourage kick for kick, jump for jump, bump for bump, grind for grind. Lyson waved harder at the helicopter. Finally, Exota saw him and, reaching over her husband, pushed the camera toward Lyson.

With a double victory sign at the camera, Lyson shot a triumphant look back at Gene Owles. During the rest of the procession across the bridge

Lyson did not again look at the helicopter or look back. He was happy now and kept his head straight ahead, the double V's high in the air and his balance on Trent and Wally. Already they were over the hump and on the Transylvia side of the river. They marched resolutely on, the Petite Pipers prancing and the band blasting and the Snake writhing behind.

The bridge began bouncing up and down, resonating from the hopping snake dance. Up and down, back and forth the waves spread across the bridge. Terrified, the band played harder and harder. The Snake hopped harder and harder, writhing, coiling, undulating up and down its entire length. The bridge responded and began gyrating too.

Mary stepped on Sandy's foot and the car raced down the bridge to safety. The Petite Pipers broke and ran, Gene Owles screaming after them. Andy and Lester knocked the instruments away from the band. Everyone ran madly down to the shore, the Snake hot on their heels, slithering like a frightened snake.

Safe on shore, everyone stared back at the bridge waving, weaving and swaying. It took a long while for it to settle down, its vibrations traveling in waves back and forth along its entire length until wrung out completely. Never again did anyone, least of all Lyson who saw all this, ever trust that bridge.

Lyson prudently returned home on the WZPO helicopter.

* * *

All was quiet around the Merry Bandstand under the great elms and maples. Birds came again and perched in the trees and the lantern and hopped among the litter, pecking at crumbs, popcorn, chips, whatever looked edible. Squirrels scurried everywhere and hurried to seize their share. Newspapers, lunch baskets, blankets, strollers, bicycles, even little portable television sets lay abandoned, strewn all over. Some of the televisions were still on, and tuned to the Petite Pipers. It was eerie.

Horace saw this and was mystified. He saw no people anywhere in the park. A parade was in progress on some of the televisions under the Bandstand. He had no idea what parade. There was a close up of drum majorettes kicking, strutting, bump and grinding. He blushed and furiously turned off the pictures. A movement in the far distance under the trees caught his eye. A man was struggling to his feet only to fall down again. Horace gasped and ran over to the figure laying face down like a broken doll, his clothes wrinkled, disheveled, dirty.

A drunk, Horace huffed and was about to walk away when the man lifted his head. The eyes groped for focus and the jaw hung slack but Horace immediately recognized him. "Doctor Masserbatt!" Horace cried and dropped to his knees, putting a solicitious hand on the man's shoulder, "What happened?"

The eyes searched blearily and finally found their focus. The jaw flopped like a dying fish but Horace could not understand the words. "What happened?" he cried. Doctor Masserbatt struggled to his knees but nearly fell again. Horace helped him to his feet.

"Here!" Horace said, pulling out of his hip pocket a whisk brush. "I never know when I will get dirty. That is why I always carry this brush." With great love, and his eyes tender and solicitious, he brushed off the superintendent, the jacket and pants, the shoes and collar. The hair was an awful mess. Horace took out a comb.

"There!" he announced as he put the finishing touches on the hair, careful not to hurt the bumps. "You are fine now."

"Thank you, thank you," Doctor Masserbatt nodded weakly, patting Horace on the head. "You are a good boy."

"You are welcome!" Horace was filled with pride and joy at being of such good help to so important a man. "Yes, I am a good boy."

Doctor Masserbatt gripped his elbow. "Can you help me get down there?" He nodded in the direction of the Governor's Mansion.

The Governor! Horace was astonished and overjoyed. The Governor! "Yes! Yes! I will be very happy to help you!"

Gently as a nurse at a nursing home, Horace helped Doctor Masserbatt over and around the blankets, newspapers, baskets, televisions, hot dogs, through the trees to the sidewalk. Slowly they made their way, Doctor Masserbatt avoiding the cracks in the sidewalk, and as they were crossing the street toward the Mansion, Horace saw some people in the park. They were stooped over picking up things.

A little girl, painfully thin with great eyes, scooped up lost coins. A woman, also thin but with a sharp face, looked through baskets and purses. Picking up and loading televisions into a stroller was a man. Behind them was another man, professorial-looking, sweeping the grass with a metal detector. Whatever the detector found he picked up and examined closely and recorded carefully in a little notebook: pennies, rings, keys, pull tabs. He was puzzled only to find pennies. He did not know about Bonnie with her sharp child's eyes and Maude with her hawk-sharp eyes far ahead of him, and after silver only.

Horace was enraged. He hurried Doctor Masserbatt across the street and ran roaring toward the man with the stroller. He seized the man by the collar and jerked him around. Eyeball to eyeball Horace confronted the man with bared teeth. But his grimace faltered and collapsed. Horace released his grip and fled from the terrible scar.

And the old man came but his squirrels and pigeons were scattered throughout the park after tastier pickings. He scratched his head. But he's not saying, though. No doubt he wouldn't like to confess he missed the Petite Pipers.

Governor Slappy Wenchell in his rocker sipped mint julep with a new kind of happiness, a kind of celebration as he watched Doctor Masserbatt limp up the stairs. "Well done, well done," muttered the Governor.

"But—" Masserbatt tried to explain and catch his breath at the same time.

"Never thought you had it in you," remarked the Governor benevolently.

"Let me explain—"

"Want a drink first?" interrupted the Governor. "Plenty of time. I can see you've had a hard day. It's nice and quiet here now, just like the old days before them deaf and dumb came. Good job!"

Doctor Masserbatt was so astonished he nearly fell down the stairs but a grab on the bannister saved him. Repressing a smirk, P-51 brought the ice-cold drink white with frost.

"Much obligated!" cried the superintendent. He was so thirsty he drank the entire glass before he realized it was extremely salty.

CHAPTER 25

GENE! OWLES! REMOVES NOISE POLLUTION!

Thanks to the leadership of our candidate for GOVERNOR GENE! OWLES! a major source of annoying noise was removed from Suffex. A band was playing 18 hours a day from 6:00 A.M. in the morning to 12:00 Midnight at the Merry Bandstand everyday and shook Suffex with heavy noise. A series of amplifiers set up around the Bandstand threw the noise across the rivers into surrounding states, attracting countless hearing people and annoying the deaf of Islay.

Even the deafest of the deaf could feel the noise. The noise activated signaling lamps in deaf homes. Hearing children complained to their deaf parents. The noise vibrated pictures loose from walls and interfered with TTY's so that messages were scrambled over the telephone. Headaches were reported everywhere by everyone, deaf and hearing. Dr. Schonner expressed concern that powerful vibrations could destroy brain cells.

Something had to be done and our candidate for GOVERNOR GENE! OWLES! took leadership action! He organized a fantastic group of marchers called the Petite Pipers and personally led them, drawing the band and all the hearing out of the park, out of Suffex, and across the bridge to Transylvia.

Our candidate for GOVERNOR GENE! OWLES! hit two birds with one stone! He stopped the noise and got the hearing out of Islay!

ISLAY FOR THE DEAF! is the avowed goal for our candidate for GOVERNOR GENE! OWLES!

Lyson dashed the newspaper down and stomped on it.

* * *

Lyson resolutely refused to watch the evening news. He knew full well where the camera was pointing the entire time. He ate alone at the table while Mary, Mortima, Evangeline, Beatrice, the Captain, Wally, Sally, and Trent watched the news in the TV room. The ham and sweet potatoes and corn bread made his stomach glad. He helped himself to more. He ate on and pondered what to do about Monte Guthrie. He liked Monte very much, and it made him sad to think about it in this way. Monte was important to Islay. The Islay Company. The Deaf. Yes, very. But Monte was having too much fun with the camera, yes too much, if you ask Lyson.

This ham is so delicious! And the sweet potatoes, melted butter, and marshmallows! He helped himself to more. Now this Monte, such a wonderful inventor, belongs in the lab. Can't rightly blame him, his infatuation with camera, helicopter, and women. Ah the women! A fine and valued friend, the women, I mean Monte! Lyson tried his best to be magnanimous. Monte worked so hard, so long, all his life. Certainly understandable he wants to play with his inventions now. Lyson sighed and licked the marshmallows off his potato. All work and no play . . . true, true. Lyson nodded at what little there was left of what undoubtedly had been a most healthy pig in the very prime of life. But play, play, no work?

Mary came running. *Good news! Beautiful!*

You mean Gene Owles beautiful? Lyson inquired mildly.

No! No! A happiness, a sense of gratitude filled her. *Exota true fantastic editor! Put-together good news, cut-out bad. You should've seen.*

Really? Lyson sat back and folded his legs and wiped his mouth daintily with a napkin.

You looked brave, true leader! Gene Owles looked foolish, silly—

Then why Monte—

Let me finish! When bridge started shaking and bouncing, remember? TV pictured perfectly how happened! Remember, at-first helicopter side-by-side with car? Then it moved front. Perfect! Bridge waving similar ocean, your arms high V shape. Through V can see Petite Pipers running-after car, abandoning Gene Owles, leaving him alone by himself. So funny! Made me laugh! You should've seen him panicking, his hand grabbing for balance and him running behind girls, like drunk on boat!

Beatrice and the Captain returned laughing and thumped Lyson on the back. "You should've seen the snake dance!" Beatrice cried, and laughed. "Crazy!"

"And the close-ups of the Petite Pipers!" the Captain guffawed. "That Monte—ha ha."

Mortima, her mouth moist, came in scowling and immediately noticed the table and sounded the alarm. There weren't any sweet potatoes or corn bread. All that was left of the ham was a bone, and there only was a bowlful of brussel sprouts, now cold and drab without the warmth of the ham and sweet potatoes.

Lyson! shrieked Mary and Beatrice. *You've eaten our dinner!*

For the first time Lyson noticed the ham was gone. He stared at the bare bone and cried, *Impossible!* But his stomach said it was all true; its weight was so great he could feel it swaying as he tried to rise.

Beatrice and the Captain laughed and pushed him down. "It's alright!" They then hurried off to the store where could be bought a ham-to-go, all heated and ready for immediate eating when they returned.

Lyson, Mary's hand called with such gentleness he looked quickly away, pretending not to see.

Mortima folded her arms righteously.

Lyson, Mary was repeating when the doorbell lamp flashed. *Lyson,* she said again with the implication she wasn't going to forget this business by no means, and went to the door.

Mortima refolded her arms indignantly but Lyson studiously ignored her.

After a few moments Mary returned with thin lips and said with a careful calm, *Woman there wants you.*

Lyson remained heavy in his seat, his mouth and eyes agape, his head shaking slowly in the beginnings of a denial. Mary pulled him to his feet and marched him stumbling, his legs wide apart to the door.

Hi! Lyson! cried the woman at the door. Though her figure said she was young, her cotton print dress thin and wrinkled and soiled, her eyes wild and unsteady from lack of sleep, her face thin and pale and haggard, her feet black and long and bony in sandals, her hands careworn and scrawny, all her features told of the travails of motherhood, of nights over sick children, of endless diapers, dishes and laundry, a demanding husband.

Don't know you!, recoiled Lyson ducking behind Mary. *Deny Remember!*

The woman glared back at Lyson reproachfully the way people do when confronted with a blatant refusal at recognition, when there was really no valid excuse for such nonrecognition, or any pretense at that kind of behavior. Lyson cringed behind Mary.

Lyson C period Sulla, the woman spelled out precisely, between long slow inhalations. The manner by which she spelled his name, the style and form of her hands, he finally recognized: Jewell! She saw the light in his eyes and brightened, *Remember now?*

Another woman came up bearing a tiny baby. Lyson gripped Mary's shoulders so tight it hurt. Mary whirled and confronted him, *S'matte you? Tell me, who?*

The golden down glistening against a handsome tan and the warm brown eyes were unmistakable. And Lyson remembered the softness and deliciousness of her hips squashed against that hard chair in Utah. She of course was Jayne and she held out the baby for Lyson to . . . to . . . He didn't know what to do and sought refuge behind Mary, but she grabbed him by his tie and forced him to face the child.

Jayne and Jewell looked at each other and at Lyson and back at each other and burst out laughing. Lyson tried to slip out of the tie but Mary pulled it tighter. Lyson's eyes quivered almost uncontrollably. Jayne saw this with a start and looked quickly down. The top button of her blouse was undone. No much, really, but enough to unsettle Lyson. Blushing, she redid it.

Suddenly children were everywhere, dashing, scampering, hopping around and through them. *Fast work, eh?* Mary said to Lyson with mock admiration.

Lyson tried to deny it but she gave the tie a jerk.

Thrill? she demanded of Jewell and Jayne still laughing. Jewell jerked her head at an automobile at the curb. It looked familiar. Dented and dusty, with some of the chrome missing and the antenna bent at a crazy angle in defiance of the windstream. The windows smeared dirty and oily and the rear window piled high with toys, discarded clothing, candy wrappers, and diapers. The color was familiar though faded. It was a Mercedes. The Mercedes!

A tall thin man stumbled out of the backseat, blinking the sleep out of his eyes and smoothing the wrinkles out of his clothes. A very married look hung about him, shoulders stooped, arms long from the tasks of parenthood, face screwed by anxiety, eyes not quite focused, hands pale from dishwater or perhaps diaper pail disinfectant. Swaying with disorientation he steadied himself against the Mercedes and yawned. Something disconcerting about that yawn. Lyson stared at him. Doctor Fletcher!

Doctor, Doctor, Lyson cried to Mary.

Doctor? Silly you, not necessary. Mary scowled, still holding fast to the tie.

Lyson tried to sink to his knees but Mary held him up by the tie. Jayne and Jewell moved to help but Mary slapped their hands away. *His fault,* she hissed. *Eat, eat Pig!* She noticed their bewilderment and narrowed her eyes. *You-two that borrowed car?*

Yes! Lyson nodded his fist vigorously. *Let go! Will explain.*

Explain, explain, wonderful! sneered Mary.

Truth! protested Lyson against the tie.

The doctor came up the stairs and put his hand on Mary. *Truth, yes. All my fault,* he explained.

Doctor! Told you about him. Lyson bucked against the grip on his tie. *Remember, told you, himself first and only deaf doctor in USA? That's him!*

Oh? Mary wiggled her little finger suspiciously and let go of the tie. Lyson began to sink to his knees. She grabbed the tie again.

Yes! Honest truth! True doctor, himself deaf.

Mary looked closely at Doctor Fletcher who bowed his head humbly and crossed his heart. *Yes, true myself doctor, name Fletcher, M.D. but lately not enough practice—*

Himself wonderful with children, Jewell interceded. *Children now healthy, happy, playful—*

Children? Mary cocked an eyebrow at Doctor Fletcher.

The doctor bowed his head. *True, but most my life, people dead—*

Mary's eyebrow rose even higher.

Oh no, no. I mean pathology, the doctor hastened to add. *Autopsy.*

Oh, you can help? She patted Lyson's stomach big and round.

Doctor Fletcher made a move to examine the stomach but Lyson fled into the house.

* * *

"We got a call! A call!" Beatrice exclaimed wildly excited as she burst in, the Captain on on her heels grinning broadly. "Sean is all right!"

Lyson and Mary stared at each other and at the Quayles.

"It was a woman that called," said Beatrice. Turning to the Captain, she asked, "Think she could be a girl friend?"

"Could be," said the Captain unable to contain his smile. "Must be."

"Such a darling. So soft, so sweet, her voice over the phone," enthused Beatrice her hands describing in circles a voice coming smoothly out of a fine woman. "And her name is Suzanne. Lovely name."

"Susan?" mumbled a dumbfounded Lyson. Mary looked sharply at him.

"No," *Suzanne* spelled Beatrice. "Oh! We're so glad he's okay!"

"Well, we should've known he would be—" The Captain began to boast.

"Of course, we knew he was! We just wanted to know where he was."

"Alaska, that's where he is," he said to the Sullas, whipping his finger.

"So far!" bewailed Beatrice. "Our fault!"

"Well, well, he's a Quayle, you know—"

"He has my genes too," snapped Beatrice.

* * *

FINALLY A DEAF DOCTOR!

For the first time in history we have a deaf doctor. Hansel Fletcher, M.D. formerly of Salt Lake City, Utah has opened his practice in medicine here in Suffex. His office is at his home on 1386 J Street. All deaf patients are welcome.

Dr. Fletcher came from a prominent medical family. His father is Dr. Stanley Fletcher, world-famous ear, nose, and throat specialist. His mother is Dr. Dorothy Fletcher, a psychiatrist who made significant contributions to the research of the trauma suffered by hearing parents who discover their deaf children are using sign language.

At press time Dr. Fletcher had yet to receive accreditation to perform surgery at University Hospital, but for now he can see patients at his home. He has already seen several, the first being Lyson C. Sulla who required a delicate treatment that was very successful. Mr. Sulla is very happy now.

Welcome to Islay, the Deaf State, Dr. Fletcher—the first deaf doctor in the world!

Mary saw Lyson's face working as he read the article at breakfast. Quickly she whisked him back to bed, drew the curtains, and tossed him a towel to bite on. She commanded Mortima to leave him alone, strictly alone, and sent Evangeline to fetch Doctor Fletcher. Immediately.

* * *

I never said anything to anyone about any shaft, the doctor said as he paced, stomping aimless, helpless little circles in front of the bed. Lyson stared back with hurt brimming in his eyes, the sheet pulled up under his eyes. Mary leaned against the bedpost with arms folded and lips pulled askew by conflicting degrees of disgust. *Honest!* The doctor stopped several times during his wild pacing to make the Christian cross, the Moslem sign of servility, the Buddhist prayer of peace, the Hebrew stab of contrition, and the Italian slap of the head. *Don't know, truth, where Owles got that information! You know that myself, oath must keep confidential all secrets about my patients!* He made a huge cross from the top of his head to his knees and implored with his eyes.

Mary's shoulders drooped and she turned to Lyson unfolding an arm to ask, *Think, possible Owles has someone spy here?*

Lyson widened his eyes in horror at such a thought of treason in his own house.

Must be! Doctor Fletcher snapped his signs with obvious relief. *Myself don't even know Owles, never met him, never seen him. Don't know what he looks like.*

Mary sat down on the side of the bed, facing Lyson, and motioned Doctor Fletcher to the opposite side. *Lyson, myself feel that Mortima that her!*

Lyson blanched.

Know that, for sure, Mortima herself not involved, Mary said staring above Lyson in an effort to reconstruct the scene, *but she knew what happened. Fact, herself too-much enthusiastic wanting join, help—*

Lyson shrank deeper into his pillow and bewailed, *Now I feel like everybody in Islay involved, watching—*

Doctor Fletcher turned suddenly to Mary with eyes bright with inspiration. *Maybe Owles has hearing spy outside, heard screams—*

Didn't scream! protested Lyson.

Yes, you did, Mary said sadly the way a parent would at an errant child. *My ears hurt.* She put a finger in an ear. Lyson tried to pull the sheet over his face but she pulled it back down. *Really embarrassed me,* she insisted.

Doctor Fletcher held up an open hand and counted the people involved. *Right leg, you Mary. Left arm, Jewell. Right arm, Jayne. Now, who else—can't remember—*Lyson pulled the sheet over his face. Mary let him. *Now, who held rubber—*

Wait! Mary started. *Realize that we don't have any rubber bag, its purpose only for shaft. You used rubber bag, right? Where you get?*

Car, Doctor Fletcher said simply, his shoulders sinking.

Who got it?

Bleakly, he sighed, *Samathana, Jewell's girl.*

They sat silently for a while, looking down at Lyson hiding under the sheet. *Samathana, ask you, she bring bag in box or what?* Mary finally asked.

No box, the doctor said weakly. *She playing.* He mimicked Samathana whirling the bag by its hose in the air as she fetched it from the car, where anybody could have seen it.

CHAPTER 26

Doctor Masserbatt was all set to protect the Integrity of Education in the State of Islay. "It is extremely important," he pounded on the table, "that the very principles on which education is founded not be violated by those who have so little education as would dare politicize it, make a mockery of it, or worse, cheapen it to the point it became readily available to any and all who thought it could be had just for the asking. Education has to be earned! And to be earned it has to be absolutely complete in all its aspects. Leave out one aspect, just one, and something is missing, all the same missing. What them deaf and—and—uh hearing imper, no, hearing that is impaired, don't realize is that sound is the most vital aspect of education. The key cornerstone! Sight is of course important, vital, but sound—sound—I just wish they would realize." Doctor Masserbatt threw up his hands. "What do you expect, how do you get the deaf to listen?"

"Enough, enough," Governor Wenchell muttered as he tore the meat off of a drumstick.

"The best scientific evidence indicates that the ability to speak is directly related to the level of intelligence of the speaker. If a deaf person can't or won't speak, how can one be expected to measure his/her intelligence? No way! We have no recourse but to conclude a lack of intelligence in such a person regardless of other evidence to the contrary—"

B-52 took a slight shift forward toward Doctor Masserbatt in an unmistakable intent to silence him if he so much as spoke another word. The superintendent dropped his shoulders in a sign of submission and awaited the Governor. The ferocity with which the old man stripped the bone bare gave the impression he would soon growl and insert the bone in his nose. Disregarding the glass already filled with a stunning red wine the Governor took the bottle and swigged from it. He held it up a long time, so long Doctor Masserbatt fretted and cried out, "Please!"

The Governor stubbornly held it up until the bottle ran good and dry and then slammed it on the table. "This ain't the Sabbath!"

"Oh, oh," the superintendent was quick to appease, "of course! I mean, please don't—don't—uh, I mean today, this day of all days you gotta—"

"I know that! When I want a sermon I'll send for Reverend Dowie!"

"Not Dowie!" shrieked Doctor Masserbatt.

"I do not discuss my religion," said the Governor icily. "And I do not want to hear any!"

"Of course! Of course! But—"

B-52 advanced an inch or two and the superintendent shut up. Governor Wenchell took the glass and held it up to the light. He smiled in admiration and drank it all. He pursed his lips meditatively, "My guts must be a lovely color by now. What time would it be, now?"

"Twenty minutes yet," said B-52 promptly.

The Governor nodded, still pursing his lips. "All right. Another bottle, please."

Doctor Masserbatt was aghast and opened his mouth.

"Hush up!" growled Governor Wenchell. "Plenty of time yet."

* * *

Hurry! Hurry! urged Mary, prodding Lyson down the stairs. *Twenty minutes!*

Plenty time, Lyson bravely said, clinging to the bannister, his legs unsteady.

Important day! she urged.

His legs collapsed but Trent caught him and carried him down to the Great Ballroom. "Good luck, Lyson!" cried Beatrice and he shivered. "Don't worry." The Captain laid a hand on his shoulder and Lyson wobbled. "Go for it!" Wally thrust a fist through the air. Lyson nearly fainted.

Wally and Trent had to help Lyson like an octogenarian to the car. In the short drive down to the school, Beatrice held his left hand and Mary his right. They remarked how cold his hands were. Trent turned in the front seat and grunted. Lyson smiled desperately.

* * *

Suffex Middle School was located in the central part of the residential section of Suffex, at Central Promenade and Twenty-third Street. Across the street was the high school. On the opposite side of Central was the elementary school. A good location for schools, within reasonable walking distance of every house in Suffex so that there was no need for a bus system. Obviously it was an intelligent man who had thought all this out. A committee could never have managed to come up with this concept.

The Middle School was the target today, where Governor Wenchell would make his stand. Doctor Masserbatt had convinced him it was the best, most logical place: "The elementary school is out. You know it wouldn't do to be seen running off little babies. The high school is dangerous. The kids are too big. Besides they're liable to laugh in your face, if not shove it in. So it has to be the Middle School. The kids there are about your own size, I mean they're not so small you'd look bad. They're at that bratty age, you know; you'd look great staring them down, putting them down. Why, even the parents won't mind, or shouldn't. If they do, you wouldn't want their vote, anyway, would you?"

"Shattup! Here they come."

Four children stood with the stillness of the terrified on the sidewalk in front of the walkway leading up to the entrance to Middle School, the doorway where in front stood the Governor of the State of Islay and his entourage. He looked dramatic in his whites, standing out among the dark clothes of his bodyguards, the Superintendent of the Islay Institute of Communicative Disorders, National Guard, State Police, Administration of Middle School, the members of the Legislature, the Rotarians, Chamber of Commerce, Secretary of Education, and Horace, resplendent in his new suit and hearing aid. Flanking them were the Boy Scouts in uniforms bristling with Merit Badges, holding aloft flags of the United States of America, the State of Islay, the Boy Scouts of America, and of course the School Flag. It was an imposing scenario: the avenging angel among the heavies. The four children backed away, eyes wide, lunch boxes clutched tight to their little hearts.

Doctor Masserbatt grinned toothily at the Governor: see, it was easy, wasn't it? Governor Wenchell made a point to ignore him as he stared, his brow furrowed, at the four children, their eyes wide like children lost in a dark wilderness filled with glowing yellow eyes. His ears turned a smoldering red.

Lyson's eyes were wide too as he peeked over Trent's shoulder at the standoff. Trent whirled to get a hold of Lyson but Lyson skipped around clinging to Trent's waist. Trent made a complete rotation grabbing for Lyson but they were back where they started, Lyson still behind peeking over Trent at the Governor, imperious with arms folded and feet wide apart, so white among the heathen. Lyson wished he were wearing whites too instead of the camel and buff everyone thought so becoming.

Captain Quayle put a hand on his shoulder and nodded with a big wink. Beatrice seized his hand, "This is it, Lyson. Go for it!" This gave Trent his opportunity and he grabbed Lyson.

Listen, You must, Mary exhorted, jerking at the lapels of his jacket, *Courage!* Lyson blinked, swallowed, and ran his tongue over his lips. Beatrice poked his dimple. "Lyson, we'll be right behind you!"

With powerful grips on his upper arms, Trent picked up Lyson and carried him bodily over to the tiny huddle of shivering children. Beatrice squeezed their cheeks one by one, and Lyson's too. She took their hands and clasped them together. Lyson in the middle with two children on either side. Beatrice, Trent, the Captain, Mary, and Wally turned the little group around so that they faced the walkway up to the school and the Governor with his army. Beatrice patted their bottoms and shooed them into a march up the walkway.

They were a pretty, endearing sight, the children in their Sunday best and Lyson in his camel and buff, their shoes brightly polished and their hair neatly brushed. Slowly, haltingly, timidly, they made their way up toward the huge arched doorway beneath which flared the Governor's nostrils. Flashbulbs popped. Monte stumbled around with a television camera on his shoulder. Handkerchiefs flew among the crowd all around. The Governor raised his chin ever so slightly and Lyson felt his hands sweaty and trembling in the tight clasp of the children. The steps up toward the Governor seemed inordinately high and Lyson nearly stumbled but Wally caught him under the arms and held him up slightly on his toes as they made their way up the stairs.

Finally there they were, on the portico facing the Governor and his men, flashbulbs popping in the bright sun and Monte intruding with that big camera, getting all the angles. The Governor raised an eyebrow and Lyson tightened his grip on the childrens' hands. The Governor spoke; Lyson became dizzy but Wally caught him.

Governor Slappy Wenchell began a speech, thumping his cane on the concrete. He said something, thrusting his cane at Lyson, but his lips were unreadable and Lyson looked helplessly over his shoulder at Mary and Beatrice. With a strong grip on the back of head, Wally turned Lyson around to face the Governor and held it there, giving a quick little squeeze that said, Don't blink!

Shaking his cane at Lyson, the Governor said something in the manner of making an irrefutable point. Horace saw this and nodded vigorously. Applause erupted among the people surrounding the Governor, even the soldiers who put their rifles between their legs in order to free their hands for clapping. The Boy Scouts couldn't very well commit sacrilege with the flags by letting them drop but they still managed to join in by slapping their thighs. Sweat ran into Lyson's eyes and he blinked. Governor Wenchell saw and nodded triumphantly. Applause again.

Mary succeeded in finding Evangeline among the crowd on the street and dragged her up to the school and inserted her on the side where Lyson could see. He rejoiced and cried, "What's he say?"

"Your Honor, excuse us please," Evangeline bowed her head toward the Governor, signing and speaking simultaneously, "I am a certified interpreter of the deaf—"

Doctor Masserbatt pounced on her and slapped her hands down. "Illegal to use your hands!" he roared. Horace held up a victory fist. Furious, Governor Wenchell caned Doctor Masserbatt on the head. "This is my show! I am Governor! I can handle this myself!"

Horace was shocked and covered his mouth.

Monte bounded around joyously working the camera from all angles. P-51 seized Doctor Masserbatt and roughly pulled him back in line.

"I wish to apologize on behalf of this great State of Islay," Governor Wenchell said consolingly to Evangeline. "The Hand Slapp—I mean, Doctor Masserbatt, you see, is not native to Islay and rather ignorant of our great tradition of chivalry to the fairer sex. Please pardon us."

Evangeline had a word or two she wanted out on the subject of sexism but instead smiled graciously and bowed her head and turned to Lyson and interpreted the Governor's words. The Governor watched her hands flying and was fascinated. "What are you doing, my lady?"

"Interpreting what you said."

"Oh, you mean deaf and dumb gestures?" asked the Governor.

"I may be deaf but not dumb!" Lyson shrieked.

They all looked at Lyson. He gulped. The Governor was puzzled, tilting his head to the side for a better look at Lyson's ear. "I don't understand all this deaf and dumb, deaf and not dumb business, I must admit." He shook his head and rolled his eyes by way of saying all this was beyond him. "This is rather confusing. I don't know what's going on, really, and what the hell you want—"

Lyson was about to say something but Wally crunched the back of his neck.

Pointing his cane at Doctor Masserbatt, the Governor declared, "This man is responsible for everything that has to do with the deaf and dumb in this State of Islay. He is the superintendent and is supposed to tell me exactly what's going on. But it seems," he glanced snidely at the cringing superintendent, "He's got some kind of communication disorder himself."

Applause and waving handkerchiefs burst out among the crowds on the street as interpreters spread his words up and down the street. This surprised and pleased the Governor. He looked around with twinkling eyes and joked, "I guess all these years fooling with the deaf and dumb somehow rubbed off on him somehow, y'know. Ha Ha!"

The only applause this time was among his own entourage— the officials, soldiers, cops, Boy Scouts, and the befuddled Horace. The crowd on the street was still and quiet. People put away their handkerchiefs. Governor Wenchell fell silent too, a puzzled frown on his brow. Interpreters allowed their hands to drop. Everyone saw the Governor strangely silent, and sensed something funny in the air, and shifted their feet.

Governor Wenchell pulled his lips one way and the other, scratching his head, surveying the scene about him. "Really I dunno what's going on, believe me," he finally said. "All I know is that Doctor Masserbatt tells me this here school was set up by the people of Islay for their children. He says that because it is impossible to teach, I mean accommodate the deaf and uh, not dumb, in this kind of school, the State of Islay has had to set up a special school down in Crewe." He saw how silent everyone was, only the interpreters were moving at all, and sighed. "Don't get me wrong. I got nothing against the deaf, or for that matter the blind, the idiots, the crazies, or the niggers. It's just they don't fit in this kind of school."

Everything was still. If there were any birds about they weren't singing. Even the wind seemed to fall silent. Interpreters saw the anger boiling in the faces of deaf, particularly the deaf blacks, and stilled the anger with forewarning waves. One put a hand gently on the chest of a huge black who had stepped forward.

Governor Wenchell could not understand any of this. "Could be I am old-fashioned but it seems all for the best if those deaf kids—" he waved his cane at the children and Lyson.

One of the little girls opened her mouth to protest but Doctor Masserbatt leapt and tapped her mouth shut.

"Shh! Mind your manners!"

The crowd roared angrily; swiftly the soldiers seized the children and Lyson and carted them off to a waiting bus. Wally and Trent tried to hold on to Lyson by his shoes but they came off and they lost him. Mary jumped on a soldier's back and they fell wrestling to the ground, her feet kicking at him. A policeman snapped handcuffs on her ankles and carted her off to a paddy wagon. Beatrice bit the cop but her teeth fell out. She was shoved into the wagon with Mary, sans her teeth. Another paddy wagon came up and took in Wally, Evangeline, the Captain, Reverend Dowie and Geraldine, and others. Trent beat off each and every cop and soldier thrown at him except a meter maid who led him docily into the wagon. Monte was insanely happy filming it all.

It happened all so quickly that the crowd was still on the street, every mouth agape, every hand hanging limp and useless. By the time the crowd came to its senses and surged forward, everyone was gone but for one figure in the doorway. Someone turned Monte and his camera toward that figure. It was Gene Owles. He stood there laughing, fists on hip. He was a pretty sight: the baby-blue suit, the neat hairstyle, the laughing eyes, the teeth white and flashing in the sun and flashbulbs.

He announced to the crowd, and to Monte's camera, *Success! We deceived hearing! Hurray for deaf here Islay! Fooled hearing!*

* * *

All the way down to Crewe in the bus, Doctor Masserbatt and Horace sat with the children and Lyson. The children cried all the way, afraid of Doctor Masserbatt and his sidekick. Whenever a child opened its mouth it would be tapped shut, gently yet firmly. "Not now! Wait until we teach you to talk properly. I can't abide bad speech!" Masserbatt would say. They were not so gentle with Lyson, however, and the taps were sharp for him. His hands were handcuffed behind his back and his wrists hurt. He was terrified too but the longer it went on the more ridiculously silly it became and he giggled. Horace slapped his mouth and scolded, "Be a good boy!"

Horace was dead earnest. He watched, with the sharpness of a hawk, all the hands and mouths for the slightest movement; a tremor on a lip, a twitch in a finger, a spasm in a wrist was enough to get an instant tap or slap. Horace was so conscientious even Doctor Masserbatt was embarrassed. He reached over to put a calming hand on Horace. Horace slapped it.

"Oh! Excuse me please!" Horace cried. "Thought—"

"That's alright. Just calm down and don't be so—"

A boy opened his mouth desperately. Horace instantly slapped it.

"Horace! Relax! Not so hard!"

"I did not mean to. I—"

The boy beseeched Doctor Masserbatt with tremoring eyes. Horace tapped the eyes. "You fool!" Lyson yelled. "He's trying to tell you—" Horace clamped a hand over the offending mouth. Lyson bit back.

Horace stared at the tooth marks. "He bit me!"

"Calm down, calm down," Doctor Masserbatt soothed Horace.

"Listen!" Lyson roared. "Look at that boy! He's—" Horace stuffed Lyson's mouth with a handkerchief. The boy whined. Horace tapped his mouth. The boy wiggled desperately, a certain discomfort that mothers instantly recognize in their hearing but, inexplicably it seems, not in deaf children, though the wiggle be exactly alike, just the same, arising from the same discomfort.

Horace spanked the boy and recoiled. The pants were wet. "He is wet," Horace said dumbly staring at his hand. "My hand is wet."

"That's what happens!" Doctor Masserbatt declared to the boy. "That's why you must learn speech! We are going to teach you how to speak, so things like this won't happen."

The boy tearfully opened his mouth. Horace tapped it.

Lyson didn't know how Monte did it, except perhaps by helicopter, but he was already there, camera perched on his shoulder and trained at them as they emerged from the bus. Yes, it must have been the helicopter because of the new and tall fence around the school. The gate was locked and the bus driver had to push a special button on the dashboard to get the gates to swing open.

"Mr. Sulla," Doctor Masserbatt put an arm consolingly around his shoulders. "Believe me, this is all for the best. We're doing this for the sake of the deaf."

The handkerchief was still stuffed in his mouth, so Lyson could only roll his eyes in an unmistakable cynicism.

"That attitude won't help you at all," Doctor Masserbatt said sternly. "The sooner you cooperate, the better, the sooner you'll learn speech."

Horace hopped around the superintendent in the manner of a puppy around a larger dog. "The children have all wet their pants!"

"Tsk, tsk, they all do the first day of school. Don't worry, Horace, the school will provide them with uniforms. And—" a significant pause—"teach them how to tell us with good and proper speech when they have to go to the bathroom."

"Yes! They must learn how to do that and not embarrass us."

"Exactly!" Doctor Masserbatt patted Horace on the head. "And they will be smart like you."

"Right!" Horace enthused. "The ability to speak and read lips will make them smart and not wet their pants."

"Very good! You are a fine boy."

Lyson thought he had better first case the joint before it swallowed him into its bowels, perhaps never to emerge again, at least whole. Again, there was something disconcerting about the place even though it wasn't his first time there. Still something very strange and discomforting. Everything painted government gray, even the brick walls of the buildings. The shape and look of shoe boxes at least have some color and variety, to give them a bit of attraction for customers. Here windows narrow and in precise rows, like Sing Sing. Two stories to each box, with doors only at the ends. Each door double, and metal. Lyson couldn't discern what metal, though, for the gray paint was thick and pervasive on each, even the hinges and handles.

No trees, no shrubbery, no flowers anywhere. Just neatly mowed lawns broken only by perfectly laid down sidewalks. It was all designed for efficiency and economy by some penny-pinching architect.

"This way, please, my dear children." Doctor Masserbatt led them down a walkway around a number of buildings to one with the correct tombstone: Communicative Disorders. "Listen, you may not realize, or understand, but you are about to begin a wonderful new adventure. You will be disinfected and given nice new clothes and a new personality. And what's really great," the superintendent thrust a fist deliriously, "brand new hearing aids!"

"See!" Horace pointed out his hearing aid. "This makes you just like normal people. It improves your speech. You will be happy we brought you here." A small child opened her mouth but Horace put a hand over it. "Wait until you are fitted properly with your hearing aid! Then you can speak."

"Exactly, exactly," Doctor Masserbatt rubbed his hands. "Without hearing, speech cannot possibly be good. You'd only make funny noises. People would look, laugh at you. Don't worry, we'll teach you proper speech. I promise!"

"You obey him," expounded Horace, "and he will help your speech. And your pants will never be wet."

Slowly, ominously, the doors swung open and out marched nurses and orderlies, dressed in official white, a pure white you dare not soil with a fingerprint. The nurses of course wore white stockings. Most likely rolled down and fastened just above the calves but below the knees, thought Lyson, as do nurses who take their jobs more seriously than the patients. He giggled through his nose that such an intimate thought would appear to him at such a time. Doctor Masserbatt tapped his nose. A nurse wiped it with a fresh and clean Kleenex. "Mind yaself!" She scolded. "Din't ya old school learn ya nothin'?"

Lyson worked his eyes at Monte in a desperate appeal but Monte was having too much fun filming all this. Exota wrinkled her nose for him not to worry, it'll all come out for the best.

"Promise me one thing," said a heavily muscular orderly stepping up, his white T-shirt stretched taut by a powerful chest. "That you'll behave and not use your hands, and I'll take off them cuffs."

His mouth full of handkerchief, Lyson could only nod. Horace slapped Lyson's head but Doctor Masserbatt cried, "Don't! That was not a sign."

"Oh, I am sorry. I did not realize—" began Horace as Lyson was freed from the handcuffs. Lyson began rubbing his wrists and Horace slapped them.

"Enough, Horace!" the superintendent intoned. "You've done a fine job today. Now you may go home."

"Are you sure you don't need me?" asked Horace, crestfallen, his eyes on Lyson's hands massaging his wrists.

"Oh yes, this is a job for trained professionals," Doctor Masserbatt patted Horace on the head. "Thank you very much. We'll call you when we need you, for certain!" As Horace turned and walked reluctantly away, his head low, Doctor Masserbatt patted his rump. "You are a good boy."

Now Doctor Masserbatt was the happiest man in all Islay, rubbing his palms like starting a fire with sticks. His grin was wide and benevolent toward Lyson and the four little children. "Today is the most important day in your lives. Today begins your edific—I mean education. Will you please—" One of the little girls opened her mouth. He tapped it promptly. "Please go with these nice people—" The nurses and orderlies smiled sweetly and nodded. "They are here to help you. Believe me, they are your friends. They really truly care, as they were trained to."

The nurses offered their hands to the little children and Lyson but they cringed. Miffed, the biggest and broadest nurse, most likely the head nurse from the mustache on her upper lip, put her fists on her hips. "Ef ya don come, we'll tak ya!" She lunged and grabbed a child and was promptly bitten.

"Tsk, tsk," scolded Doctor Masserbatt. "That's not nice." He grabbed the child by the neck and delivered him to the nurse. All the children and Lyson were caught fast.

Lyson shrieked at Monte who was deliriously happy behind the camera. Exota jabbed a finger frantically in the air. *Look! Look!* A huge, shiny, beautiful blue helicopter swooped down on them. On its sides in loud script was painted boldly Islay Itemizer—!GENE! OWLES! Its long blades cut a terrible swath through the air above, blowing a rushing wind down on them and popping the air like a machine gun as the blades slashed the air. Majestically, slowly, dramatically the helicopter came down over them and hovered a couple of feet above the ground.

Doctor Masserbatt ran away. The nurses dove on the ground. The orderlies holding Lyson stood fast, rigid, defiant at the blowing downdraft. A photographer from the Islay Itemizer leapt out and backed away to suitable photographic distance. Gene Owles stepped out to the landing skid and smiled lovely and waved gaily at the photographer busily clicking away at them. And at Monte asininely aiming the television camera right at him! Lyson was furious and struggled against the orderlies but they held him fast.

At a signal from the photographer, Gene Owles leapt dramatically to the ground and gathered the children in his arms. "Sweet dears," he said toward the television camera even though he knew they couldn't hear because of the roar rushing all around them from the helicopter. One by one he lifted the children up to the waiting arms of a crewman in the helicopter, all resplendent in blue coveralls and helmet, just like the professional rescue crews of the Coast Guard. With all four children safely in the loving hands of the Islay Itemizer, Gene Owles gave Lyson that half grin and jerked a thumb up and leapt agilely into the helicopter. The photographer began dashing for the helicopter but Lyson tripped him.

Furiously Lyson tried to pull free but the orderlies held him in an iron grip. Suddenly Exota attacked, scratching at their eyes; Lyson was free and running for the helicopter. The pilot saw him coming and jerked the machine up but Lyson managed to grab the skid. Up they went, Lyson struggling, kicking against terrifying G-forces to get a leg over the skid. Gene Owles kicked at his hands to break his grip but Lyson finally wrapped a leg securely around the skid and was able to shift and slip his hands to escape the kicks. Angrily, his lips pulled tight exposing his bright teeth, Gene Owles reached down to pry Lyson's fingers loose. Lyson bit his hand and clamped on tight like a bulldog.

The pilot tried to shake him off with wild gyrations but nearly ran into powerlines. He sobered up and made a beeline for Suffex.

* * *

A TREMENDOUS VICTORY FOR
GENE! OWLES!

Yesterday GENE! OWLES! outfoxed and foiled the attempts of hearing people to block the integration of the public schools of Islay. Hearing people thought the four children coming to school at Suffex Middle School were deaf, but GENE! OWLES! outsmarted them. The children were actually hearing!

The children were seized and taken to the State Institute for Communicative Disorders at Crewe and nearly imprisoned but GENE! OWLES! made a daring rescue in the Islay Itemizer helicopter.

CANDIDATE for Governor Lyson C period Sulla was there for some reason, probably for some corrective work on his speech. GENE! OWLES! was under the impression Mr. Sulla was helping put the children into the institution because Mr. Sulla attempted to hinder GENE! OWLES! efforts to rescue the children.

Our candidate for GOVERNOR GENE! OWLES! suffered a wound on his hand (his fingerspelling hand!) in the fracas but he says it's nothing. The service to the deaf is far more important. After all, those hearing children belong to deaf parents.

GENE! OWLES! is modest about his role in all this and declines to demand any explanation whatever from Lyson C period Sulla. Mr. Sulla has a lot of fast explaining to do, GENE! OWLES! agrees, but the facts are self-sufficient.

CHAPTER 27

The battle lines were drawn sharply, though Lyson didn't quite know just where. They were just there. He could feel them sharp as a knife. He was nervous and would have rubbed his knees had not Mary insisted he empty himself before coming. He couldn't go at all of course, and the Captain intervened with a solution. A bottle of Gorlesch's beer would do the trick, he declared. Just enjoy the bottle and relax a bit, and it will all come out. He was right and so now Lyson was dry, though very nervous and uncertain just where he was.

He gasped over his shoulder for help. Mary crinkled her nose lovingly. Beatrice beamed. The Captain saluted with a Gorlesch. Wally and Trent grunted. Andy whooped. Crystal, Sandy, Jayne, Dottie, Jewel, and Heather blew kisses. Evangeline raised her hands in preparation to interpret. The Reverend Dowie and Geraldine crossed themselves helpfully. Mortima's mouth was wetly open. Lyson looked up at the peak of the Bandstand, up into the lantern for better help and he sent up a silent prayer. Little birds cocked their heads and looked back down at him.

The debate was here and now. It was never in the scenario. Lyson was upset and uptight. He'd thought becoming Governor would be a pretty thing. But the way things were going wasn't so pretty. Gene Owles was fighting dirty, ugly now. And Governor Wenchell was the only pretty boy in all this. He wasn't even involved, keeping himself aloof, above it all, pretending there wasn't even an election. Blast Owles! Us deafies are besmirching each other and Wenchell is going to win reelection without even trying, without even knowing there was an election on! Thanks to Owles!

Gene Owles was across the Bandstand, floating like a butterfly, stinging like a bee, surrounded by gregarious legs. Legs that were never still but forever kicking, prancing, scissoring. Pretty as only the Petite Pipers could make pretty. Of course, of course. It made Lyson sick to go over this again and again, but he had to face it that blue was a very pretty color and that legs were, after all, legs. Gene Owles really understood what they did for him, for his image. And what they did to Lyson! It upset Lyson to find this was so, that a color could be exploited as much as mere legs, especially in contrast to his own. I mean color. Suddenly he felt inadequate—his own camel and buff. Those were the colors he liked very much. Solid and honest as the fields. But the way Gene Owles exploited blue! Sky blue, baby blue, the blue of a blond's eyes, name it and he did it. The blue of dreams. He hated to admit it to himself, but he had to admit that Gene Owles managed to make blue more than it was ever meant to be. Blue is supposed to be peace, musing, the sky. But Gene Owles made it sexy as moonlight. Restraining an urge to hop, Lyson felt stiff as a wooden doll, a plastic Barbie. He cringed and gnashed his teeth even though he knew that this was the day of days. The day he must soar! Soar above the matchbox automobiles, trucks, tanks, and the dollhouse. Get on with it, Lyson! He would've collapsed except he was so stiff.

Drums boomed. The sound reverberated through Lyson's skull, most keenly felt on the back of his head where the neck held it up, like a head on a pole poised to absorb heavy thumping. Drums boomed, trumpets blared, cymbals clashed. Lyson saw all this, insisted on this: Us deaf aren't dumb: we can see drums booming, trumpets blowing, cymbals smacking. Of course we can't hear them but, like fish in water, we live in a medium of sound and so are not totally ignorant as some hearing assume us to be. Certainly we miss the finesse but not everything.

The band was arriving but was not about to press them out of the Bandstand. Instead, the marchers encircled and enveloped the Bandstand, all the while playing some tune that felt good to Lyson although he couldn't identify it. He didn't quibble: If it feels good it must be good. Of course he only knew what feels good, not what is what. Oh, he could tell Beethoven from the Beatles, but not Beethoven from Chopin. Nor Presley from Jagger.

However good it felt, it all seemed suspicious and he searched for Doctor Masserbatt. There he was, off to the side with the Governor, in the back of the crowd. But his mouth was hanging open, so he wasn't the one that sent the band. Governor Wenchell was confused as can be, so it wasn't him either. Everyone in the crowd seemed puzzled too. Lyson looked sharply across the Bandstand at his opponent. Ah! It was Gene Owles. The smile was smug and knowing. So it had to be him! What treachery can this be?

Though his knees were wobbling like wet noodles, Lyson was astonished to find his nostrils flaring.

"Exactly, what's going on?" Governor Wenchell insisted again.

The superintendent pulled straight the way a man does when he wants to make his voice authoritative. "You see, the deaf love elections. Can never get elected to actual positions in the real world. So are forever making up various organizations—"

"Bogus?"

"Oh no! Perfectly legit. Just their own little world...they call it the Deaf Culture, a kind of subculture, you see. They even have a President of the United States in their own little world. Here they're having an election for their own little Governor—"

"How quaint!" the Governor chuckled.

"Yes, even Congress! Must humor 'em, ya know."

"Well, I hope you know what you're doing," the Governor said half jokingly, "allowing all this. The schools, y'know—"

"Can't help the schools!" cried the superintendent. "Too many of 'em. And the schools are real—"

"If the schools are real, what's Islay then—"

"Don't worry! They're not even interested in the world outside their own little one where they're with their own kind. Except of course those areas where they must perchance come into contact with reality. Schools, for example."

The Governor nodded musingly. "And the banks, the grocer, the employer, the welfare office, the barber—"

"Look at them girls!" Doctor Masserbatt nudged him. "They can't be serious, don't you see?"

"Ah so," Governor Wenchell pursed his lips appreciatively. "Some girls."

"Yes! Girls. Children, that's what they are."

The Petite Pipers restlessly and in unison scissored and unscissored and rescissored their long legs, Gene Owles beaming among them.

"That man over there," the Governor inquired, "that one in the blue, isn't he the one that made an ass of you?"

"You see, they're not even serious," Doctor Masserbatt said soothingly, like a father evading an embarrassing question from a child. "Dancing girls at a debate!"

"This other one, the one you let get away," Governor Wenchell pointed with his cane at Lyson, "he seems dead earnest to me."

"Exactly! You know there's always a sore loser in every poker game, the guy that keeps the exact score at golf, the one with a ball in one hand and the rules book in the other—"

"I see, I see," the Governor gave the Petite Pipers a final going over and turned away toward the Mansion. "Well, guess I'd better get going."

"Wait!" Doctor Masserbatt ran after him. "Aren't you watching the show?"

"Why should I," Governor Wenchell said over his shoulder. "You've seen one, you've seen 'em all. Besides, you yourself said it's only a sham."

"But—"

"Good night."

Lyson saw the Governor leaving even before the debate began. He wasn't quite sure what to make of it all but had seen the cavalier way the cane had been pointed at him. He could sense fuses popping in himself even though he didn't know the entire score, and looked over his shoulder at Mary for her opinion. She blew a kiss.

Soft as a ghost, Sandy appeared beside him and put a nice hand on his arm. His eyes widened in surprise. Positioning herself close in front and slightly to the side so that no one could see her signs, small, unobtrusive, and urgent in the shadow under her breasts, she quickly explained that Beatrice had sent her up instead of Evangeline who, Beatrice claimed, had a whining, grating voice that made him seem small, weak, and indecisive. Besides, she interpreted too damn faithfully, too damn precisely, gaffe for gaffe.

A gentle breeze lifted a few golden strands of her hair and Lyson remembered the fine wind in Okeke. He looked at her and the down on her arms that was as lovely, as glowing as ever against the rich darkness of her tan. She squeezed gently and their eyes met. He understood and looked over at Beatrice with appreciation. She wiggled her fingers gaily. The Captain, Wally, and Trent grunted. Andy whooped. So did the rest of his retinue except Evangeline, who folded her arms sullenly, and Mortima, whose mouth was open and moist. The Reverend Dowie and Geraldine were on their knees in prayer. Lyson turned to Sandy and mouthed, "You are lovely."

She laughed. "Let's climb a tree," she whispered mischievously. My kind of interpreter, Lyson thought happily.

A Petite Piper intruded with a plastic smile and glass eyes and announced it was time to begin. Lyson wasn't sure whether her star-sparkling red and white striped tights were a leotard, swimsuit, or maybe a kind of uniform like that of cheerleaders of professional football teams, but it was so tight he had to struggle to keep his eyes level with hers. Won't do to be caught by a photographer with his eyes bugged. The tights were so tight, an amusing anomalous thought occurred to him, but he quickly dismissed it and compelled his mind to the task at hand. Now he knew Gene Owles' game. Finally! He stole a snide look over at Gene Owles.

Though the image of a debonair man of the world—a man of many women was what everyone saw—a flicker flashed across the long lashed eyes of Gene Owles that only Lyson detected. The smile was toothy, reptilian, that Lyson returned mockingly. But Owles was more the reptile, and the smile he flashed was sweet, so sweet as to chill even his own mother. Something truly beautiful in its function, precise as a shark eyeing us without the slightest regard for our sensibilities.

The Petite Piper in front of Lyson scissored and unscissored her long legs and Sandy touched him. This broke the trance, the riveting grip of the eyes of the cobra, and Lyson shook his head clear. The television lights exploded on and he staggered. Sandy caught him by the elbow and led him to his podium. The lights held him tight, blazing inside his skull. Sandy tugged his attention to her hand hidden under the podium, visible only to himself. The hand said, *Calm yourself. Do your best, concentrate on deaf. I will make you sound great to hearing. O.K.?*

He nodded gratefully and squeezed the hand on his forearm. The lights struck across her face and he saw how soft and downy it was. He very much wanted to touch it. He knew he could safely do so, all eyes being on the Petite Pipers. Everyone except, of course, Mortima. And maybe Mary. He wanted to also run his fingers over the down on her hand, which rested still on his arm. It struck him that he was toying with disaster, on the verge of ruination. He chuckled sheepishly to himself. He patted her hand and turned to face the music.

The Petite Pipers began forming a line between him and Gene Owles, linking up, arm over shoulder, and throwing their legs high in the air in precise kicks in unison like the Rockettes of Radio City. Kick, kick, went the long legs, the white plastic boots flashing in the lights, their gold tassels flapping at the top of each kick. Lyson examined their buttocks and was surprised to discover they did not jostle or bounce. They were as firm and lean as, he decided, an athlete's. They seemed more an extension of their long legs than as separate entities, as on most of us. Gene Owles and I have different tastes, he huffed to himself. He likes his women plastic and I like mine in the flesh, he congratulated himself. His mouth twisted as disdainfully as a Calvinist preacher's when the village harlot weeps and gnashes her teeth in church.

Kick, kick, went the Petite Pipers as if hooked up to a machine, a master brain. Lyson yawned openly before he realized what his mouth was doing. He surprised himself again, and it delighted him to discover he was getting bored. He turned jaded eyes to Sandy. She saw the look and squeezed his arm in agreement. He loved her, he decided, if Mary wouldn't mind, and understood it's only art for art's sake, not for real. Sandy squeezed his arm again, harder this time.

The line had broken, scattering around the Bandstand, and the girls began a bump and grind routine. It was insane. No, a sacrilege! Gene Owles was among them clapping encouragement, step for step, kick for kick, grind for grind, bump for bump, obscenity for obscenity. One by one the girls came up to Lyson with lips suggesting kisses and upthrown buttocks suggesting kisses too. Lyson reacted as a preacher would at catching the harlot caressing the figure of the Lord. He announced as much to Gene Owles as to the camera, *Enough absurdity! People came for watch important debate, not gape-at pretty girls!* Gene Owles laughed in his face and turned his backside. Lyson booted him. The ensuing struggle had the passion of a dance as he and Gene whirled around and around in Lyson's effort to evict Owles from the Bandstand. Around and around they went in a death grip, knocking down Petite Pipers and the podiums, endeavoring to trip each other, eyes locked in hate, lips pulled taut over teeth.

The Reverend Dowie bounded up the stairs and scolded the hysterical girls one by one. *Tsk, tsk,* he told them. Geraldine led the girls out one by one with the assurance that the Lord would forgive if they'd come along. Trent and Wally pulled Lyson and Gene Owles rudely apart. Trent rapped his knuckles on Owles' skull. Wally shook Lyson to his senses. Monte deliriously filmed away. Andy whooped.

Mary, arms folded and lips pulled down, confronted Lyson. *Congratulations! Very interesting debate.*

Talk cheap, action worthy! he retorted.

Action worthy?

Yes! He thrust out his jaw.

She replied with the kind of look a wife gives when her husband arrives home in the wee hours, *Wonderful, wonderful.*

Want debate? Gene Owles interceded defiantly.

About what? Lyson shot back in the manner of saying we've said enough!

You! seethed Gene Owles.

What about you? said Lyson wearily.

You started!

So-what.

You cheat deaf!

Lyson would've dropped on the softest part of his anatomy were he not sheltered by his guards. *Prove-it!*

With a gay wave, a smile full of perfect teeth, a triumph in the eyes, Gene Owles said, *We can debate in my newspaper,* and disappeared into the crowd. The bright blue was there all along, working its way among the crowd to the baby-blue convertible waiting on Ninth Street; but for practical purposes Gene Owles had disappeared, out of reach, out of reproach, out of refutability. Lyson's legs worked for purchase on the ground but he was held up out of reach by Trent and Wally.

Calm, calm! You've won!

I'm not finished, he shrieked kicking in the air. *Many things still need debating!*

CHAPTER 28

Lyson still felt cheated, deprived. *Debate not finished! Still must debate!*

With the weariness any wife would toss at a husband that insists on playing the harp, Mary rolled her eyes. *Listen. New game now.* She threw the newspaper on his lap.

It had been some weeks since the so-called debate, the one where the future of Islay was to be identified for the edification of the voters, where the future of the deaf in Islay was supposed to be defined clearly, their relation to the hearing, to the schools and the college, to the creation of a state for, by and of the deaf, with the hearing as auxiliaries, like the Ladies Auxiliaries of the Rotarians. Lyson had been up in the air since the fiasco; there were still so many unresolved questions. He was as confused and frantic as a dog with an itch who couldn't find the flea. And now here was the newspaper sitting on his lap.

He didn't want to know. All he wanted to think about was how it all came to be. This great debate was supposed to clarify the issues between himself and a pretty boy. Mary had grabbed one ear and Beatrice the other, and together they made him watch the television. The Petite Pipers kicking. The superior look on his own face as he looked down on their rumps. The smooth suave grin on Gene Owles' face as he urged them on. The melee. The Petite Pipers disappearing tearfully down the way to salvation pointed out by Geraldine and the Reverend Dowie. It was all so confusing. The struggle, the hatred, the kicking and near bites.

Lyson, time grow-up, said Mary with the patience of someone urging a last spoonful on a protesting infant. *You gotta get-up and—*

Lyson held his head in his hands as if it were a separate entity and rocked it. He had been so happy with his dream. The swell little match-boxes. The Knight on his Pegasus!

Mary picked up and slammed the newspaper down again on his lap. *Lyson, you must read!*

You know that, he cried, making a huge gesture where a simple fist would suffice, with both his hands far apart twisting his nose as large as a barrel: *Bull! his Gene Owles! Nothing his newspaper worth reading!*

Read! insisted Mary.

Don't want! I'm happy myself my own mind!

He says you cheat. You must read. Must respond! He says yourself using the deaf for your own benefit, that you're taking-advantage—

Don't want hear.

He says he won debate.

Not true!

Yourself that one tried disrupt debate and cloud issues. Myself not saying this. The newspaper! You must read and respond!

Lyson fell to the floor helpless as a fish out of water and banged his head on the wooden boards. Mary fell too, she had to, to reach him, to get down to his level where she could make herself seen, understood. *The newspaper says you that one who fraudulently sold houses then leave people holding bags on sidewalk—*

Not so!

But that's what newspaper said. You and I know that's not true but that's rumor going around. You can't prove-it here floor, you must get up and read!

GENE! OWLES!
CATCHES
LYSON C period SULLA

Our candidate for GOVERNOR GENE! OWLES! has caught one Lyson C period Sulla in an act of fraud. This Lyson C period Sulla has been cheating innocent home buyers out of their down payments on houses supposedly for sale but actually occupied by innocent homeowners who never knew their homes were for sale.

Dirty Bastard!

Get-up and fight!

Lyson kicked on the floor and Mary, her heart knocked to pieces, gathered him up into her arms and proffered of herself something so soft it renders a man, any man, senseless. As Lyson partook of its softness she thought it wondrous how it could bring the strongest of the strong to his knees, to the cradle indeed. Nothing so strong it won't yield to the softness. She held Lyson to herself like a babe, and he reveled in the tenderness as would a babe; she marveled at the insanity of some of her sisters, those who despise their own softness and instead seek to imitate what is so despicable in the hardness of the opposite sex in pursuit of an equality where indeed no man dare venture, so that they render themselves angular and bony, powerless. Lyson, like a babe of course, knew nothing of the scheme in her mind and heart. He instead indulged himself, completely intoxicated, mindless, his eyes sunk into his head. Mary wondered at his impotence, at her power simply because she was soft and smooth where he was hard and hairy. She saw how helpless he was and held him tighter.

The door opened slowly, tentatively. It was Evangeline. She saw what was happening and was very sad to see it. Over her shoulder were the beady eyes of Mortima, bright at what she saw. Mary met their stares levelly and with tight lips and flared nostrils.

Excuse me, Evangeline said with some embarrassment. *Someone there door downstairs, wants see Lyson. Woman with baby.*

Not another one! Mary looked down at the huge baby in her arms. Evangeline and Mortima tilted their heads for a more upright look at the supine Lyson. He looked so happy and secure Mary was loathe to disturb him, to interrupt her power over him. But there's this woman with a baby wants to see him. Why? Does anyone ever know for sure? She patted his cheek. Slowly his eyes emerged from the depths of his skull and he looked about. He saw where he was, his situation and audience. He looked at each of them in turn: Mary, Evangeline, and Mortima. And Mary again.

Woman with baby wants you, Mary said evenly, with a tiny hint of accusation. *Another baby.*

Not true! His body jerked in denial. *You only woman!*

Let's-see what she wants. The severe formality of her manner and the strange distance in her eyes yet so paradoxically close was enough to compel him shakily to his feet and downstairs, his hands tight on the bannister all the way.

He hesitated at the door and bit the back of his hand. Mary gripped his elbow and opened the door for him. The opening brought in the full force of blinding sunlight. He tried to shrink away but a greater force from behind propelled him out onto the porch.

There stood a woman young and dirty blonde in cut-out jeans and white cotton shirt, sleeveless and shoulderless, not really a shirt but rather a band of cloth about her torso, laced together in front like a shoelace so that she was bare over an area a couple of inches wide from throat to navel. She was entirely barefoot and Lyson would have fallen back except for Mary right behind taking it all in over his shoulder. Before he had all his wits gathered together the woman thrust a bundle in his arms and cried out with excited hands, *Kiss!*

Lyson stared in horror at the bundle in his arms. It was a baby howling and struggling to get out of his arms. It was entirely bare except for very heavy diapers sagging around its hips. It smelt strongly of unfamiliar milk and wet diapers. Lyson tried to let go of it but the woman pressed it against him. *Kiss! Kiss!,* she commanded imperiously. A fierce tug at his ear forced his lips against the baby. The stench nearly made him faint.

Hurrah! triumphed the woman and she snatched back the baby and bounded away bearing high her prize. *Kiss successful!* she exulted to her baby.

Lyson sagged backwards on weak legs. This time the force behind relented and he landed on his rump, his legs straight out and numb. *More babies coming?* Mary inquired politely.

Can't help! Women won't stop birth, birth!

* * *

On his side lay Lyson, one ear snug in the soft pillow, the other up in the night. His ear felt cold and exposed. He restlessly pulled the sheet over it and wiggled deeper into bed.

Mary responded with a spasm of exasperation. Lyson lay still as could be. Mary must have her sleep. He gripped the edge of the bed, the better to hold still. The night was black as only dreary autumn nights can be, so that visions came to him as vividly with his eyes open as closed. In this black void floated and glowed Gene Owles, bright and merry in that sky-blue suit, clapping laughing pointing and slapping his thigh. Lyson bared his teeth and clamped shut his eyes.

Gene Owles saw this and with quick waves all round summoned a great number of faces out of the dark, all merry and ugly with mirth and pointing at him. Lyson ducked under the blanket. So nice and warm under there in the cocoon. He stuck out his tongue at Gene Owles and focused his mind on the warm soft steady rhythms of Mary behind his back. He longed to turn and snuggle into her but she must have her sleep. He dared to release his grip on the edge of the bed and allow himself to relax. Gene Owles attempted to intrude with a big smirk on his face, but Lyson thrust out his tongue and Gene Owles slunk away in mock horror. A sigh of satisfaction, and Lyson dug deeper under the blanket.

His nose itched and he rubbed it. It itched again and the thought upset him that he'd forgotten to ask the barber to snip off the hairs in his nostrils. They tickled and he rubbed his nose and sought with his finger to determine if the hairs had grown long enough to be offensive to his image. His finger smelt funny. He sniffed at it. The smell was disturbing and he cupped both his hands over his nose and recoiled. Urine and milk! The baby he had to kiss!

He wiped his hands on the sheets but they felt clammy and crawling with microbes. His mother, and Mary, had preached to him all these years about the importance of first stopping by the bathroom before bed, to empty the containers, brush the teeth, wash the hands, and all the other hygienics necessary for a good healthful night's sleep. He was upset with himself. Mary tossed and turned, pulling the blanket from him. Lyson slipped off the bed carefully to the floor. It was completely dark. He dared not stand up and lose his balance. He crawled over the carpet, his hands probing ahead like antenna to the door.

The mezzanine was less dark: a faint glow of grayish light came up from the Great Ballroom below on the right. Lyson gripped the railing and pulled himself up. He was surprised how heavy his body was, how leaden it felt as he struggled to his feet. All down the left of the hallway marched several doorways, blurry in the dark without his eyeglasses. He panicked. Mortima and Evangeline lurked behind two of those doors. Maybe even now they were watching, watching for the opportunity to catch him alone. He hurried down the mezzanine and found to his relief that the bathroom was open. He locked himself in and tested the knob several times. It was good and locked and Lyson hastened to wash his hands in the dark. He washed three or four times, drying and sniffing each time so that the hand towel soon became too damp to adequately dry them. He wiped them dry on his pajamas and then remembered his nose. He washed it too. He scolded himself for having gotten the hand towel so damp that his hands and nose remained moist and cold. He felt around in the dark for a fresh towel. One was hanging over the shower curtain but it smelt of Mortima and he ended up using toilet paper.

Surveying his ghostly image faintly visible in the mirror in the dark, Lyson wondered at the heaviness of his body, his bones, and began some serious thinking. Can't go back now to bed, not until Mary is good and asleep. Besides, Gene Owles won't let me—Lyson thumbed his nose and wiggled his fingers. Only one solution to this problem, he said to himself and went downstairs, feeling his way to the kitchen.

There a soft light glowed on the clock face, and he found under the sink a portly bottle of Benedictine. He hehe'd to himself that two swigs were all that was needed to set him alright. He held himself still, the better to feel it coursing deliciously, oily, liquidly through his body, relaxing his muscles as it trinkled down. Already the dead weight of his body was becoming less dead. Very good. He found a glass and filled it. Patting the bottle affectionately he put it away and conducted the glass like a honored guest to the cushiony armchair in the living room. Ah! he said to the glass and took a lingering sip. The room glowed soft and friendly from street lights buried in trees so that the light came through the windows gently and diffused. A quiet night. No traffic to jar his vision with slashing beams. Lyson pondered over the heaviness and its meaning. I must be very sad, he thought, and do not know it. Yes, I must be very sad. Could be, sadness is heavy whereas happiness is light and buoyant. He frowned and sipped his Benedictine. It was a fine drink and he did not hurry it. Well, it has been a happy dream, he sighed to himself. Yes, very happy. That's the nice thing about dreams: they're so happy . . . so happy.

The Benedictine and the manner by which he handled it was eminently successful: he became sleepy and found himself nodding. He yawned and emptied the glass. There remained more than he thought but all the better. He held up the glass a long time to allow each and every precious drop to work its way down to his waiting mouth wide open, eager, a baby bird in its nest. So great was the Benedictine that even the tiniest drop carried with it the full potency his tongue sought, and he licked the inside of the glass.

Lyson hurried back to the kitchen and saluted the bottle with mock apology. Excuse me! I know I just said good night but—but— He giggled and refilled and drained the glass and licked the inside and his lips. He did not feel so heavy, so sad now. But sleepy, he said to himself nodding with accomplishment.

Up the stairs serenely he went and down the mezzanine, scratching his stomach luxuriantly. Gene Owles attempted to catch his attention but Lyson thumbed his nose. *You're an a—a— hemorrhoid!* Gene Owles recoiled in horror and ran away, whining over his shoulder: *Tell King Deaf! Tell King Deaf!* Lyson thrust an Up Yours and ducked behind the door.

He went around the bed to the far side, careful not to bump it. But something was not quite right about the room. He halted and attempted to bring his eyes into focus, but it wasn't easy, it being too dark to help the focusing mechanism. He stared down at the bed and its occupant barely visible in the dark. The bed looked too small and the woman too large. She was on her back and her mouth wide open. Mystified, Lyson bent down for a closer look. He'd never known Mary to sleep on her back, not with the mouth so open. The eyes opened and blinked and turned to him. Mortima! Lyson spooked and fled the room, down the stairs flapping his wings, across the Great Ballroom and spiralled up the turret to his office.

Lyson was upset. He performed each and every ritual necessary to demonstrate he was really upset. He bit his knuckles. Slapped the forehead. Hopped about. Bit the desk edge and chair back. Pulled open a drawer and took out the big matchbox. All ten thumbs fumbling against each other, he attempted to free his Knight on his Pegasus from its shelter. It gotta get out! It gotta! But he could not free it.

Good thing he did not know that the real, the actual, Pegasus was right up there in the sky, even now soaring above the earth. If he had he would have opened the door and gone out on the roof and really alarmed Mary. He could've caught, at the very least, a bad chill. Instead he bit his thumbs. Again he could not open the matchbox and was about to dash the box against the wall when Mary turned on the lights and seized his sideburn just in time and brought him tumbling to his knees.

That hurts! he cried, trying to unlock her grip on his hair.

Cross your heart! she demanded. Lyson crossed his heart twice. She released him and dropped to her knees beside him and demanded, *Truth!*

The truth appeared in the doorway in the form of Mortima modestly clutching around herself a voluminous bathrobe. *He entered my room! Almost in bed with me! Woke-up on time!*

Deny! Deny! Lyson cried with his hands and buried himself into Mary's chest. Mary closed her eyes and patted Lyson on the head, allowing him refuge in her softness. She firmly patted his cheek, demanding an answer. But he began suckling, his eyes sinking rapidly into his skull. She relented and looked wearily up at Mortima. She caught the gleam shining in Mortima's eye and saw it all.

Call Doctor Fletcher. Quick!

Reverend Dowie? Mortima began in a too transparent pretense at righteousness.

Doctor! snapped Mary. *And Beatrice and the Captain.*

Lyson suckled happily through the nightgown. She looked down at him and saw his peace. She closed her eyes and sighed with the tenderness of a mother toward a child with perfectly legitimate needs. Good Strong Mother Earth.

CHAPTER 29

Tenderly they took Lyson down the island to Port Ellen, through rolling hills bright with the great final outburst of summer before its total surrender to the heavy hand of winter. Lyson sat all bundled up in blankets and comforters in the backseat, his head serenely bowed, doubling up his chin as he revelled in the passing oranges, reds, yellows, browns, greens. Beatrice and Sandy warmed his flanks and held his hands in the cups of theirs. "They're so cold!" Sandy would cry and warm them with her breath.

Lyson smiled like a pampered old man in a nursing home and chuckled, "This isn't so bad, after all—"

"I think this is wonderful!" trilled Beatrice.

"I wouldn't say wonderful," Lyson demurred politely with raised eyebrows. "But it's not so bad, really."

Sandy squeezed his hand with a sharp shake. "The colors are so fantastic! And the day so divine—"

"Of course! I'm sorry!" Lyson wrinkled his nose apologetically. "I meant my condition, I mean my circumstance—"

"It's not everyday a man gets to ride with two pretty women," Beatrice teased.

Lyson laughed. "I mean, my new status. I'm a has-been, a ruined man—"

"No! No!" scolded Beatrice and Sandy. "You're not!"

"Well, that's kind of you. Anyway, better a has-been than a never-been—"

"Silly of you! Giving up so easily."

Lyson rolled his head sidewise and took a deep breath. "Easier said than—"

"It's nothing, really." Sandy said, pinching him on the dimple. "Not important. Nobody knows. Those who do, understand perfectly."

"Who knows?" Lyson said sadly.

"Come on, Lyson," Beatrice patted his hand. "Mary will take care of the damage containment just fine. Besides, we all love you."

"I know, I mean, thank you, I love you too," Lyson said softly. Then: "Well, it ain't so bad being a deaf and dumb mute—"

"You are not!"

Baring his teeth with mock testiness he retorted, "What's wrong with being a deaf and dumb mute?"

The Captain turned from the steering wheel long enough to declare, "Labels, labels, that's what's—"

"Watch your driving!" Lyson yelped.

"Atta boy! That's the spirit!" The Captain jerked up both thumbs. Wally grabbed the steering wheel and rescued the car.

"At least I'm in exalted company: Spiro Agnew, Richard Nixon, Wilbur Mills, Teddy Kennedy—"

"Posh!"

"Besides who wants to live with his old maid sister—"

"Wally!" scolded Beatrice.

"It's not that bad, really—"

"You're right, Lyson—"

"John!"

"It's not that bad. You'll pull through just fine."

"Watch the road!"

"Remember Kennedy! He never gave in. Now he's my fav—"

"John, stop immediately! Let Wally drive!"

"Yes dear." The Captain stopped the car and changed places with Wally. "Lyson, let me tell you something. This morning Doctor Fletcher said to me, John you be sure Lyson gets plenty of rest and those tranquilizers. But Jewell, she interrupted him and demanded, Be sure he's loved." Captain Quayle smiled and thumped Lyson on the knee and continued, "Funny thing, Jewell, she turned on her husband and declared, I'm surprised you didn't prescribe love!"

Lyson giggled and the Captain laughed.

"Doctor Fletcher said I know, I know! You must understand I have to think in terms of medical terms—Jewell, she jumped and said, You know better! You know that my love cured you!"

Lyson laughed with all of them. Beatrice tickled his palm and he wiggled. Sandy kissed his hand and held it against her cheek.

It was a happy drive all the way down, and as they crested the last hill, Port Ellen lay white in the sun below them, the harbor filled with fishing boats, the sea sparkling beyond. Lyson always liked Grandma Moses and exclaimed, "How did you know this is what I need?"

"It's lovely, isn't it?" The Captain swept his hand. "Remember I told you I was born here. It's always good."

"You're lucky you were born in a real house, a home," Lyson said. "I was born in a hos-pi-tal! No wonder I'm so—"

"There, there," laughed Beatrice.

"And I was bottle-fed, can't help it."

"No wonder, no wonder," teased the Captain. Turning to Wally he directed, "The bandstand is on the left a couple blocks down."

A festival flowed around the little bandstand exulting in the gold sun by the harbor. Townsmen young and old, baker, butcher, chemist, grocer, cop, postman played in the band, plucking guitars, tooting horns and harmonicas, striking drums, clashing cymbals. Mothers and children and grandparents on spreads on the grass all around, clapping to the rhythm, munching on sandwiches and chips, hopping, skipping, jumping. On the beach on and under blankets lay the teens. Out on the quay the watermen worked on their watercraft, scrapping, sanding, painting in the good sun. Houses around the little harbor had their windows thrown open to the sweet sun and music; the old, the infirm, the bashful hanging out on folded arms, heads rocking to the beat resounding everywhere. Seagulls flapping insanely over the little bandstand. Dogs lay in the sun, tails limp, ears jerking at insects.

Even before being carried out of the car, Lyson could feel on his chest and the back of his head the booming of drums and the screeching of guitars. For the first time in a long time his soul felt glad.

"That is music!" he cried to Beatrice.

"Yes, Lyson," she said gently. Aside to the Captain she whispered, "Poor Lyson."

Tenderly, the Captain and Wally carried him out to the canvas chaise lounge already being set up by Sandy on a bare patch of lawn among the townsfolk. Eyes widened and mouths dropped at this spectacle; and solicitude gathered about but Beatrice reassured them, "He's just been a little ill. He'll be all right, just needs a bit of sun and to be among you folks."

"So glad to see you Lyson!"

Lyson smiled meekly.

"So good of you to join us."

Sandy tucked a scotch-plaid blanket about him up to his chin. "See, they love you!"

"Lyson," gushed Beatrice, "They're playing Hail to the Chief."

"Maybe you've given up, but they haven't," the Captain said sagely.

Lyson was so happy he was bashful. Captain Quayle opened and held out a bottle. "John!" scolded Beatrice. "Not here!"

"Them're whiskey people," the Captain assured her.

"If you say so," said Beatrice in the dubious way of good women when confronted with the truth as represented in a bottle of whiskey.

Lyson slipped out a hand from under the blanket at his chin and held it up for the bottle. "Just one!" remonstrated Beatrice. She lifted her chin as he lifted the bottle and she watched closely as he partook of the drink.

The whiskey inside, the sun on his face, the band reverberating in his cells, the blanket secure about him, the crowd friendly to his eyes brought a nice warmth to his soul. *Your smile, so beautiful,* shivered Sandy, hugging herself.

Off to the side, Susan suddenly appeared out of the crowd, obviously glad to see him. She hugged and implanted a big kiss on his forehead. She studied his forehead a moment and frowned, dissatisfied. Out of her purse came fresh lipstick, and she tried again. This time on his forehead was firmly imprinted bright red lips. Laughter all around; Lyson tried to wipe the lipstick off but she grabbed his hand and made another imprint on it. Lyson attempted to wipe it on the blanket but she held on.

Your hand, cute, soft, she remarked affectionately.

Lyson blushed. Wally pointed a smirking accusation at him. Gaiety, good humor, throbbing music, friendly sun rays flowed all around. Lyson was tickled happy. He giggled.

The band played on loudly, even more energetically, Lyson thought. People rocked and clapped and swayed. Even the watermen worked in rhythm so that Lyson saw that they were men happy in their work. The seagulls flapped wildly all over them. It was so good he prayed it would continue forever, never end. God, I beg it will always be thus, if you see fit to make me Governor, he prayed and wept.

But before God had a chance to reply the Devil came and struck a mighty blow. People fell down all at once, as if by a giant scythe. A terrible screeching hit Lyson's body, sending a chill throughout. It was an awful irritation like the scratching of a blackboard. Everywhere people rolled writhing in agony, hands over ears, mouths screaming in pain. The bandsmen in the little bandstand, the watermen on the quay, the mothers and children on the lawn, the teens on the beach all rolled and writhed. Dogs ran their ears along the ground. The seagulls fled. Lyson and Susan looked at each other bewildered. They were the only ones not affected by the awful screeching. Even Wally fell, hard of hearing as he was, clawing out his hearing aid and shutting his eyes in pain. John and Beatrice rolled together, covering each other's ears. Sandy arched her back and pounded on her ears. No rhythm, no tempo, no pulse; just an escalating crescendo in the terrible screeching. Lyson and Susan gaped at each other in horror.

Men grinning ear to ear descended upon the gory scene from trucks and began picking up the helpless people of Port Ellen and stacking them in the trucks like so much cordwood, the way a battlefield is cleared, the horrors of warfare obliterated. The awful screeching seemed to intensify as Lyson lay helpless in his cocoon of blankets. Susan spotted a man picking up her children, one under each arm, and making off for a truck. Furious, she ran toward them, knocking over the chaise lounge with Lyson in it to the ground, and sank her nails in the man's eyes. She grabbed her children and fled home.

Susan! Susan! Lyson pleaded as he crawled to his feet alone and forsaken in the debacle of Port Ellen; his friends, nurturers, supporters, and others felled and immobilized and in the process of being loaded on trucks to be carted ignominiously away to God knows where by a grinning enemy. The screeching threatened to collapse his skull and he hopped about for help.

A blue sheen, beautiful and stunning in the sun, caught his eye. Gene Owles! Should've known! Tall and magnificent, Gene Owles strode up and down, a victorious general beaming over his well-trained troops that knew their jobs well and did not require further commands, proddings, or exhortations, so that their commander was free to exult over corpses scattered about the battlefield. In the background shook and vibrated a flatbed truck on which screamed huge megaspeakers. Lyson almost could see the waves emitting from the terrible noise and noticed that all the windows in the little town were shattered to pieces. He bit his knuckles and hopped about.

Gene Owles stared at Lyson, seeing him for the first time. He saw the hopping and biting of knuckles, and exploded in laughter. He flitted about to all his men, calling their attention to Lyson. They saw and laughed uproariously. They clapped hands and thighs and pointed and mocked. Lyson froze, terrified and still as a mouse caught out in the open. His fist seemed glued to his mouth under huge eyes magnified all the huger by his glasses.

Slowly, ominously, menacingly, the men gathered around Lyson, laughing, clapping, pointing, and jostling. Their eyes said they knew they had all the time they cared to have, and were going to play with Lyson for all he was worth, not that he was much but still worth a bit of fun, as a happy cat toys with a terrified mouse, taking care not to kill it and cut short the fun and games. Gene Owles smirked and rubbed his hands at the great good time they were going to have. The circle closed in on Lyson.

Lyson crossed himself and beseeched the bare blue sky for an immediate Rapture.

But before the sky could grab him, the circle of men suddenly threw up their arms and retreated behind Gene Owles. Jaws tight and eyes wide they all stared behind Lyson. He turned and there was Susan with a shotgun pointed fiercely at Gene Owles. Lyson ducked behind her. For a long moment they faced each other, Lyson peeking over Susan's shoulder at Gene Owles, the confrontation a Mexican standoff except that Lyson was blinking all along and Gene Owles looked softly, dreamily at Susan. But she was not impressed; she motioned savagely with the gun toward the quay. Step by measured step she backed them over the quay to the very end, stepping over fallen watermen writhing on the concrete, hands over ears. One was her husband Randy.

Susan shoved the gun into Lyson's hands and fell on her husband. She hugged and kissed and petted but he cried out in agony. Blazing mad, she commanded Lyson to keep Gene Owles and his men in their trap at the end of the quay and she sped down the quay toward the truck with the magespeakers.

The terrible screeching died down so suddenly the silence nearly bowled over Lyson. It felt heavy, abnormal, unnatural, almost frightening.

Lyson stared in horror at Gene Owles. The man in the lovely blue smiled sweetly and took a step forward, his hand out. The men behind took courage and began menacing grimaces. Lyson looked down and noticed with fright the gun in his hands. Aghast, he held it away from himself, pointed down at the quay. Still smiling, Gene Owles moved another step closer, his hand now motioning ever so slightly for the gun. Lyson was about to step back and drop the gun when a sudden shadow spooked him and the gun went off with a roar and buck.

All the Owles men dove off the quay and swam frantically away, leaving Gene Owles alone to face Lyson whose quaking threatened to set off the gun again. Out of the sky descending in a spiral came a helicopter. Channel 8 painted on its sides. Monte! His camera pointed straight at the scene as the helicopter settled into a hover right beside the two men, recording the climatic standoff.

The entire town lifted itself up. The watermen staggered to their feet, rubbing their ears. The bandsmen, the mothers and their children, the teens on the beach, the bodies in the trucks, the elderly in their homes with shattered windows. Beatrice, the Captain, Wally and Sandy all helped themselves and each other to their feet, rubbed their ears, hugged and comforted each other. Seagulls returned in full joy of flight. Dogs scratched their ears.

The watermen were the first to see Lyson and Gene Owles at the end of the quay. They saw the gun and hailed Lyson and seized Gene Owles. The rest of the townsfolk saw too and rushed upon the quay. They lifted Lyson up on their shoulders and bore him amid cheers to the bandstand. Men shook his hand and thumped his back and drank to him. Women kissed him and held up children for him to kiss. The old, the infirm, and the bashful waved back from shattered windows. Dogs licked his hand. Seagulls swooped and looped.

They roared and cheered as the watermen tarred and feathered Gene Owles and put him in an old skiff and raised its tattered sail. The breeze caught and spirited him out of the harbor into the bay where the wind carried him further out to sea.

Once again the band started up. The people whirled Lyson, dancing round and round the bandstand. Beatrice and John danced along. Wally and Sandy whirled round and round. Susan and Randy fell into each other's arms. Everyone danced and leapt for joy. Fires were started on the beach and chickens set roasting and crabs boiling. Bottles popped and frothed and spilled. Glasses and cymbals clashed. The band boomed and played long into the night under stars, under the great wings of Pegasus. The Captain might have pointed it out except Lyson lost his glasses. No matter; he danced and drank and rejoiced with the best of them.

"Lyson, we're so proud of you!" chorused the Captain and Beatrice and Sandy and Wally.

Lyson tried to explain but Susan grabbed his hands and declared, *Lyson, I'm proud you!* And kissed him silent.

Before the party ended, though, a good soul remembered her civic duty and called the Coast Guard to report a lost boat. She also was conscientious enough to remind the Coast Guard of Section 504 of the Vocational Rehabilitation Act of 1973 and to make sure they had a Sign Language interpreter aboard the rescue vessel.

CHAPTER 30

Considerable effort was required to get Lyson out of bed. First, he had crawled in head first so that only his feet showed. Not for long. Tickling only got them deeper under the blanket which finally had to be removed entirely. Then his claws and teeth had to be pried loose from their hold on the mattress. It was not easy but they at last got him dressed and his shoes on.

Lyson, you won! did not get him to his feet. So Wally and Trent carried him on their shoulders down the stairs to the Great Ballroom packed with cheering and waving handkerchiefs. *Lyson! Lyson!*

"Isn't this something?" cried Beatrice.

Wally and Trent set Lyson down on his feet but his legs were too stiff to stand on without help. So they steadied him by the armpits. Lester Lieske observed this phenomenon and promptly thrust a glass of champagne in Lyson's hand and helped pour it down his mouth. It was good and already Lyson could feel his stomach relaxing its grip on his torso.

Hurrah! Fists thrust high in the room. Congrads! clapped hands. *I'm so proud you,* said Mary. *Never dreamt,* gushed Undresa. Behind a television camera Monte and Exota waved. Wally tickled Lyson in the armpit and his hand flew up. Jayne and Jewell smooched him. Crystal nearly felled him with an astonishing kiss. Every kiss turned one ear or the other red. Another kiss and both ears would shine red. Lyson blushed. It was just the way his ears behaved when he received a kiss. He couldn't help it.

Professor Stumpt began inquiring about the directorship of Commerce but Mary interceded, *Tomorrow, tomorrow*. Dottie came up and hugged him. Darcy shook hands like a man. Doctor Fletcher grinned foolishly and Lyson giggled. Andy whooped. Lester raised his eyebrows at Mary and held up the bottle of champagne. Mary examined Lyson, particularly his eyes and legs. She gave a small nod and Lester refilled the glass. It helped relax Lyson's stomach muscles down to the bladder, which in turn triggered the knee rubbing against knee mechanism.

This gave Mary the opportunity for a good heart-to-heart talk alone with Lyson. But first his bladder had to be emptied, she insisted. Otherwise his attention would not be complete and his heart not in it.

"There, feel better?" Mary said, brushing his shoulders. She washed his hands, combed his hair, straightened his tie and jacket and smoothed his eyebrows, checked his ears and nostrils. She noticed his shoes were on the wrong feet. *Never noticed!* he began defensively, but she said never mind and swapped the shoes. *Lyson!* she remonstrated, shaking him by the lapels. *Relax! You won! Your dream came true, finally—*

But impossible!

Impossible what?

Impossible, impossible—Lyson made the signs weakly in disbelief.

There, there. She patted him, dusted his shoulders free of dandruff, double-checked his buttons and zipper and shoe laces, restraightened his tie and lapels, rearranged the handkerchief in his breast pocket and, licking her finger, smoothed his cowlick.

I love you.

Lyson widened his eyes in surprise. *Silly you!* she scoffed and ushered him back to the Great Ballroom where applause erupted again and he had to resume the necessary protocol of modestly acknowledging congratulations, promising jobs, shaking hands and blushing at kisses and a blessing by the Reverend Dowie.

To his and everyone's surprise Gene Owles showed up with Sandy clinging to his arm. Although haggard and reeking of dry-cleaning, he held himself resplendent in his lovely blue and managed a wan smile as he offered his hand as a good sport. Lyson's mouth and hand hung limp. Sandy smiled apologetically, begging forgiveness with her sad eyes. Mary had to pinch Lyson to shake hands like a good winner.

Sit down! Sit down! pleaded Lyson to Mary. *Must sit!*

So they seated him on a soft chair—to allow him to do some heavy thinking. He thought about the strange and wondrous ways of women, so deep, so bottomless, so fathomless. He tried to think about the Tree in Obeke but it was too overwhelming, too grand a tree to take it all in one sitting. He thought some more. After a while he found that sitting does not help find the answer so he gave up and stood up.

The crowd had by now grown so large in the Great Ballroom and up and down Central Promenade that Lyson decreed that the celebration be moved to the Bandstand.

* * *

Governor Wenchell saw the Bandstand lit up like a Christmas tree, strings of little lights winking up and down and around its outlines, and he was furious.

"I never dreamt—" pleaded Doctor Masserbatt.

"You told me—" seethed the Governor.

"I know, I know—"

"You said you would handle things."

"God knows I tried my best—"

"The devil!"

"Who could've known the deaf could pull such a—"

"Dummy!"

"Oh yes, I mean deaf dummy—"

"You! It's you I'm talking about! Dummy!"

"Oh yes, that's right!"

"You said the deaf were dummies and that you could control them!"

"I never did!"

"Yes you did!"

"Let me explain, I never use the term deaf dummy but hearing impaired—"

"Shattup! It's all moot anyway! You made me lose!"

"There, there," Doctor Masserbatt reached over to give the Governor a pat on the head but B-52 seized his wrist and twisted him to his knees so that now the superintendent was in a better position for a proper genuflection.

"I lost, alright," hissed the Governor through clenched teeth, "but you're fired! Fired!" With his cane he whacked Doctor Masserbatt on the shoulder with more force than necessary to knight him. A swift boot from B-52 sent the ex-superintendent tumbling down the stairs into the night outside the Mansion.

Horrified Horace saw Doctor Masserbatt staggering down the walkway from the Governor's mansion. He ran up and cried with clasped hands, "Doctor! Are you all right?"

"Fine, fine. I'm okay, thank you," Doctor Masserbatt reassured Horace with a pat on the head.

"Did they kick you down—"

"No, no!"

"Wait! My sentence is not finished! You always told me to use proper English. Did they kick you down the stairs?"

"No, no," sighed the ex-superintendent. "I fell."

"Are you—let me finish!—Are you hurt?"

"No, I am not."

"What are you not?"

Doctor Masserbatt stretched his back wearily. "I am not fired, no! I mean hurt."

"Good! I am glad you are not hurt," Horace beamed. But then his face fell as they faced the lights at the Bandstand. "What are we going to do? Sign Language is going to win! How are we going to stop it?"

A glimmer came to his eye as Doctor Masserbatt stared at the Bandstand and realized that Governor Wenchell, being adverse to paperwork, would probably forget the firing and never tell the new Governor. Horace saw the thin smile growing into a wide grin. "Tell me! Tell me! What are we going to do?"

Still smiling, the superintendent looked down at Horace with sad eyes and patted his head. "Easy. We'll just have to get on his side and render him every assistance for the sake of the service to the deaf."

"Oh?" Horace frowned. Doctor Masserbatt had spoken too rapidly for him to lipread every word. "Ass—"

"Shh! Not so loud! They can hear!" The superintendent jerked his head toward the Mansion.

"What can they hear?"

"Shh! I have to go. Be seeing you soon." Doctor Masserbatt patted Horace on the head and hurried away toward the Bandstand all bright and merry in its lights.

Horace stared in horror at the departing superintendent. "Assesat, assissen," he mumbled to himself in shock. "Impossible! Assassinate! He could not have said it!" He pressed a fist on his forehead. "Calm yourself, Horace. You know he said it! He said it, he said it because he trusts you. He trusts you because you are the only one who would fight sign language. He trusts you because, because you are brave . . . you are brave . . ."

He pulled himself straight and facing the Bandstand, saluted. "Yes, sir! I will do my duty. You can trust me!"

* * *

The November air had a chill to it but Lyson felt warm under his collar. Not that it was new to him but he could see the blessing was swaying the crowd with restlessness. The people that he could see were resting their chilled bodies on one foot and then the other. The Reverend Dowie was a good man, a good soul, Lyson had to admit to himself, but it is November! And the wind is from the Arctic, not the drowsy Caribbean.

Were it from the south the people could dream, or even take a quick nap on their feet, while the Reverend indulged himself in what Lyson had to admit to himself was a grand communion with—uh, fate! Everybody, Lyson could see with one eye open from a head earnest in its bow, the other closed for propriety's sake, knew the score but he saw that all heads were bowed, if not entirely out of respect but in good sportsmanship, everyone willing to allow—however farfetched—the Good and Humble Reverend his illusion of who is responsible for the good fortune that befell Lyson, uh all the deaf. He crinkled his brow, the better to sort out the many confusing thoughts racing in his head: these deaf who had dared—dared to defy fate—uh, the fate prophesized for them by all the world's great teachings—uh, and who decided instead to work out their own fate through whoever—uh, whoever was lucky enough to have their affection for the moment—Lyson chuckled to his bowed self even while keeping an eye wide open to the reality of his situation—right there in the Bandstand—not only was he in the Bandstand—he was right there in the middle—can any objectivity be possible in the middle of—uh, in the middle of a momentous event, or is it subjectivity . . .

The confusion was still confusing so Lyson attempted a new tack. You won, Lyson! Your dream has come true because, because it was a good dream and—uh, and because many people believed and shared in that dream. Good job, Lyson, he said to himself when the eye he kept open saw the Reverend Dowie bring his hands finally together in an Amen that was really an Amen. Lyson chuckled to himself: an Amen to end all Amens.

The eye Lyson kept open saw the feet of the Reverend Dowie coming toward him, but the eye failed to discern what was coming next until it happened. Suddenly, the Reverend Dowie implanted on Lyson's cheek a kiss, a kiss all the more remarkable because it was wet and startled Lyson into opening his other eye and raising his head.

Now that he had both his eyes open, Lyson saw that he was right in the center of—of uh, the world! He saw eyes upon eyes, one or two being the eyes of television, upon him, Lyson C. Sulla, future, No! now Governor of the Deaf of Islay.

Governor, he said to himself. Governor, he said to himself again. Impossible! His eyes overflowed and Monte zoomed in to catch the tears trinkling down his cheeks. Even though he hadn't yet seen the tape, Lyson knew, just knew, that the tears were twinkling on screens all over Islay. Funny, though, he wasn't ashamed. He let the tears flow all they might. Anybody that doesn't like tears can—can, he hesitated to himself a bit shamefacedly—can, let's go ahead and say shove it.

The crowd roared, applauded, waved handkerchiefs at his tears. The crowd shed tears too. Even Horace shed tears as he clutched the gun, the terrible gun, the gun that must stop, STOP Sign Language. Every eye was wet, too filled to see the gun. Even Horace did not quite see it, although a cell or two in his brain knew it was in his hand, and that it was pointing right at Lyson, right between two globs of squirming water where eyes ought to be, so flowing wet with pangs of the heart that reality melted and dissolved. Yes, things do look differently underwater, particularly if that water is quivering with sentiment.

The only dry eyes in all the crowd were in the Bandstand directing a hand over Lyson. Doctor Masserbatt knew exactly what he was doing. A pat on the head, he knew, and the tail will wag. By Oralification, it will wag! Eyes everywhere were too quivering wet to notice, except the two entirely dry ones that lowered the hand over Lyson, in the beginnings of a pat on the head.

Beatrice, the Captain, Wally, Trent, Mary, the Doctor, the professor, Heather, Dottie and Darcy, Crystal, and all the other loved ones, including Sandy, never saw what was happening. Not even Horace who pulled the trigger. Nor Lyson who would have sooner bit the hand than allowed it to pat him, had he seen it descending over his head.

As it happened, the hand touched Lyson on the top of his head and Lyson ducked. The bullet passed over and struck Doctor Masserbatt in the throat, right where it hurt the most.

EPILOGUE

If you wish to reform a man, you'd have to begin with his grandmother.

—Victor Hugo

Lyson was still dazed even while reality stared him in the face daily; everyday many people sought to kiss his hand, the one with the wedding band, as Mary insisted. Even the most beautiful of them upon grasping his hand and bringing it up to the pucker for the obligatory kiss would notice the wedding band and search his eyes and sigh and kiss the finger shielded by the ring.

There was no getting around it. It would always be there. Even Lyson hid behind it. It was there, and provided quite a comfort. For one thing, it fit perfectly. And always would as long as Mary saw to his diet. Lyson paused and shook his head the way a dog does to rid itself of an itch, a vague discomfort, to obtain a clearer perspective. That is, to clear his head.

Central Promenade stretched down from beneath his feet clear as day. The trees overhead were just beginning to bud out, so that the sun came through sharp and crisp. As he promenaded down Central Promenade, Wally and Trent on either side, Beatrice, the Captain, Andy, Mary and Geraldine, Evangeline and Mortima, and others behind, the Reverend Dowie in front, everything seemed sparkling clear.

Doctor Fletcher was also in the promenade with Jewel and Jayne on either side, both holding his hands tightly for lately he had gotten into the disconcerting habit of spelling out to himself his lament for all the world to see. Doctor Fletcher was sad. He wanted deaf patients but most of his patients were hearing. To the hearing, medical diplomas on a deaf doctor's walls could only mean that he possessed a superior mind, considering how difficult medical school must be for the deaf, let alone the hearing.

The deaf, on the other hand, remained skeptical. They would point at the diplomas and ask, *True, real, honest those diplomas?* Some even had the gall to insinuate, *College itself hearing, right? See yourself deaf; their hearts soften, pity you; give you simple test, help you easy pass?*

So Doctor Fletcher was morose. Lyson took heart and saw to it that the good doctor was included in his daily promenade.

Security men checked garbage cans and behind hedges for Lybians and Iranians and then signalled all clear. Monte flew overhead in the helicopter, filming it all for posterity. Trent, with his clear eyes, said he could see clear to the Bandstand.

The promenade progressed smoothly down the broad street and around the Bandstand and up the stairs to the platform. Everyone stood around the perimeter, leaving Lyson strictly alone in the very middle, right below the lantern. You know, even the Governor himself needs a bit of breathing space.

Feet apart, hands on hip, Lyson surveyed his domain all around. Where his eyes gazed, people ducked so his vision would not be impeded. A Governor needs all the vision he can get. As soon as his gaze passed, people would stand erect and look after where he'd just gazed and wonder what he had seen and its significance.

Of course what could be seen from the Bandstand were trees and more trees. More specifically, the trunks and lower branches of trees. But that is not the way a Governor sees. This takes some understanding, true, but that's how leaders view the world around themselves. That's what separates them from the rest of us. They just can see things invisible to us mortals.

Lyson had nearly completed the daily circuit of seeing things that others don't see when among the trees appeared a form that disrupted his perception of reality long enough to stop that circuit and gain the attention of everyone else.

Doctor Masserbatt! The same dark-blue sharkskin suit and broadly striped tie except for a bib over the throat. And something on his chest hanging by a strap over his neck. It looked suspiciously like a modern portable teletypewriter. So suspicious that Trent and Wally seized him.

They had him by the hands so that he was quite helpless, hopping between them with a desperate plight on his face. Lyson saw and had compassion. *Let him go. It's alright.*

Wally and Trent let go reluctantly, though not entirely, for they stood close by, ready to pounce should he make any false motion with that strange machine on his chest. Doctor Masserbatt gratefully typed on the machine and a digital board lit up: "Thank you so much, Guv! Say, isn't this neat?"

Lyson stared at the machine, which consisted of two portable teletypewriters mounted back to back on a piece of plywood with a speaker erected directly over.

"Come on, type your reply, Guv" urged Doctor Masserbatt. "Your friend Monte had this made up so I could communicate in English. Nice, eh?"

Lyson stared at the machine and up at Doctor Masserbatt, the little bib on his throat puffing and huffing in his excitement. He relented and typed, "Nice. Good of Monte to help you."

"Yes it is!" Doctor Masserbatt typed happily. "It even speaks perfect English for me exactly the way I type it. See the speaker, Guv?"

"Yes, I see." Lyson typed politely.

"It even speaks clearly what you just typed. Marvelous, isn't it, Guv?" went the machine.

"Marvelous," typed Lyson kindly.

"Yes! It makes a normal life possible for me!" happily typed Doctor Masserbatt with two jubilant fingers. "Won't wonders never cease!"

"Wonderful," Lyson typed, careful with his spelling.

They shook hands and Doctor Masserbatt typed and the machine spoke, "Good Day, Guv. I better get going and leave you to your work. You must be awfully busy, Guv. Bye, bye."

"Bye, bye," Lyson typed and Doctor Masserbatt went away with a happy spring to his step.

Lyson stared agape after him and shook his head. Tears brimmed and it required another full circuit of his domain, a repeat, before things cleared enough for him to see things as they are. That is, the way they are meant to be seen. Of course, by a Governor, no less.

And on a bench nearby the old man was still stubbornly feeding his squirrels and pigeons. Of course he's not saying. Could be, he doesn't want to let on he was only dreaming.